Pattern Recognition and Machine Learning

Pattern Recognition *and* Machine Learning

Yuichiro Anzai

Department of Electrical Engineering
Keio University
Yokohama, Japan

ACADEMIC PRESS, INC.
Harcourt Brace Jovanovich, Publishers
Boston San Diego New York
London Sydney Tokyo Toronto

This book is printed on acid-free paper. ♾

ACADEMIC PRESS, INC.
1250 Sixth Avenue, San Diego, CA 92101

United Kingdom edition published by
ACADEMIC PRESS LIMITED
24-28 Oval Road, London NW1 7DX

Library of Congress Cataloging-in-Publication Data

Anzai, Yuichiro, 1946—
[Ninshiki to gakushu. English]
Pattern recognition and machine learning / Yuichiro Anzai.
p. cm.
Translation of: Ninshiki to gakushu.
Includes bibliographical references and index.
ISBN 0-12-058830-7
1. Pattern perception. 2. Machine learning. I. Title.
Q327.A5813 1992
006.3'7—dc20 92-7073
CIP

Printed in the United States of America
92 93 94 95 BB 9 8 7 6 5 4 3 2 1

Contents

Preface

Both pattern recognition and machine learning belong to the most advanced areas of software science. Numeric methods combined with artificial intelligence techniques have been especially successful for pattern recognition. Research in the area of learning is now recognized as a basic part of software science as well as having application to knowledge acquisition in artificial intelligence systems and contributing to understanding human cognition. We wrote this book to provide a basic knowledge of pattern recognition, learning notions, and the models and learning of neural networks.

This book has the following three properties:

(1) It explains both recognition using a computer and the basic methods of learning in one book.
(2) The first half of the book describes various methods of representing information and ways of transforming these representations that are necessary to recognize patterns and learn.
(3) Each chapter is self-contained so that a reader can start reading the book anywhere.

Let us explain these characteristics in more detail.

Traditionally, pattern recognition and machine learning have been studied as individual fields. For this reason Chapters 4 and 5 of this book are primarily about recognition, whereas Chapters 6–10 explain learning. However, if we are interested in the representation of knowledge in a computer, we can think of both recognition and learning as a transformation of representation. Chapters 1–3 discuss various forms of representing information and their transformations in preparation for such a unified view.

The idea of looking at recognition and learning as the transformation of one representation into another has not been developed enough to unify individual algorithms; however, this idea suggests one way of looking at these ideas.

We have stated that each chapter is an independent unit, and in each chapter we have not described how it is related to the others or to another field of study. For example, generalization in the study notions and learning using a discrimination tree are related, and generalization based on explanation is related to partial evaluation in programming language processing. Also, learning in neural networks relates to the relaxation method in pattern recognition. Since more advanced texts talk about such relationships, this book does not include them. We also think that it is better not to systematize the basic ideas of recognition and learning since such knowledge has not yet been established. Of course, there are other methods of arranging the content of this book. We would be glad to hear your opinions.

Both recognition and learning have been studied in philosophy, psychology, and other fields. This book looks at recognition and learning in the traditional sense as related to the computer. In the future, we believe the meaning of recognition and learning in the field of computers will change as software science develops and we would like to contribute to such a change.

Many people have helped us create this book. We first would like to thank Professor M. Nagao (Kyoto University) and the editorial boards, who gave us the opportunity to create a book on recognition and learning. Professor T. Matsuyama (Tohoku University) and Professor Y. Ota (Tsukuba University) let us use the original photographs in Figure 5.14 and Figure 5.7, respectively. We also would like to thank Mr. S. Sato (Kyoto University), who reviewed the manuscript of this book and made many valuable suggestions.

We would also like to thank students in the Anzai Group at the Engineering Department of Keio University. Y. Akiyama, H. Ozawa, T. Maruichi, A. Yamashita, and K. Shinozawa read parts of the manuscript and made useful comments. The output of the sample exercise in Chapter 4 has been done by Shinozawa and the exercise in Chapter 10 was done by M. Wakamatsu, Y. Yamamoto, and M. Kajiura. The programs and the examples in the Appendix have been generated by Wakamatsu, Yamamoto, and Kajiura and summarized by Nakauchi. Y. Ajioka, Yamashita, T. Nishizawa, and H. Yasui also helped me in programming the exercises. The photographs in Chapters 2–5 have been done by Wakamatsu.

Yokohama, Japan

Study Guide

• What we can do and what we want to do on a computer?

The high speed and memory capacity of computers have been changing our lives. Computers can now do many things that were once possible only in dreams. We want people who study software science to have even bigger dreams. We want people to dream about what new things we could do on a computer if we understood the technology better.

One of these dreams is to improve our information processing ability by building a system that can recognize objects in the world and learn new information about them. In fact, many researchers and engineers have already started working on this dream and part of the dream has already been implemented. The effort of these researchers and progress in computer science and computer technology mean that even college students are now in a position to study the problems of recognition and learning by computer.

We hope people will learn the basics of pattern recognition and learning by computer and go on to challenge the capabilities of future computers in these areas. This book is intended to help such students.

• Pattern recognition

In order to recognize an apple in front of us, we need to be able to determine the edge of the apple and its background. We also need to be able to tell an apple from an orange using our knowledge of fruit. It was a dream of engineers to make a computer recognize things that we recognize unconsciously. What made this dream come true has been the data processing capability and speed of modern computers. These capabilities, which include both basic computer operations and symbolic processing, like high-speed inference, have made it possible for us to build sophisticated pattern recognition systems.

Today, in visual pattern recognition, a computer can interpret properties of an image by using knowledge to understand what objects appear in a pattern. This technology and other basic methods are currently applied in various everyday information processing tasks like reading characters, numbers, and illustrations automatically, analyzing photographs, recognizing three-dimensional patterns, understanding moving objects, etc. The fields requiring sophisticated pattern understanding technology have been expanding and they now include medical diagnosis, library information, knowledgeable robots, space technology, and support for working in extreme environments.

This book explains methods of pattern recognition that are the bases of such technology for visual patterns.

- **Learning new information**

If we could arrange data in a new way and adjust a system so it could handle input of unknown form, the value of the computer as an information processing tool would improve substantially. The study of making a computer have the ability to incorporate new information is motivated not only by the simple desire to reduce the complexity of computer programs but also by the possibility of usefulness in actual applications.

For systems that use artificial intelligence technology, i.e., the technology of doing inference using large amounts of structured knowledge, one problem is how to input and manage large amounts of knowledge. Some people have been studying tools for making computers acquire knowledge semi-automatically. The basic methods of learning are important in improving knowledge acquisition technology.

There are several methods a computer can use to learn; it can remember the input information as it is received, remember input information in an internal machine representation, learn using examples, learn using analogy by creating new information similar to already known information, etc. There are also methods of learning using different forms of representation for the learned information and using different methods to display the input information.

This book describes representative methods of learning by computer.

• Generation and transformation of representation

There are many representation methods. For example, at the lowest level machine language programs are represented as bit arrays of 0's and 1's. Information in high-level computer programs is expressed using numbers and letters. A computer can be thought of as a machine for generating and transforming these information representations.

This interpretation of a computer is especially applicable in the area of pattern recognition and learning. Pattern recognition can be thought of as the representation of properties of the input data using a representation that is different from the input data. Learning can be thought of as the creation of a new representation of the data using the input and some information already stored in the computer. Using this interpretation, we can think of both pattern recognition and learning on a computer as highly sophisticated examples of creating and manipulating the representation of information.

This book is based on the idea that the generation and transformation of information representations can be used to explain both pattern recognition and learning, problems that have traditionally been studied as different subjects.

• The structure of this book

This book describes the details of the basic methods of pattern recognition and learning. You will be able to understand the main points by careful reading. It can be used as a textbook for a half-year or one-year undergraduate course or a beginning graduate course.

Chapter 1 defines recognition and learning on a computer from the point of view of the generation and transformation of information. Chapters 2 and 3 describe different methods of representing information that will be used in pattern recognition and learning and also gives methods for creating and manipulating such representations. Chapters 1, 2, and 3 are preparation for the rest of the book and are also useful as basic information for learning about artificial intelligence as a whole. We recommend reading these chapters first even if you are only interested in pattern recognition or in learning.

Since pattern recognition and learning use different algorithms, you can learn the individual algorithms independently. Chapters 4 and 5 explain pattern recognition and Chapters 6–9 explain learning. Chapter 10 explains methods of a type different from those in Chapters 4–9. Readers can turn to either Chapters 4 and 5, 6–9, or 10 after reading Chapters 1–3.

Chapter 4 describes methods for extracting the properties of patterns and Chapter 5 discusses methods for understanding what objects are included in a pattern once these properties have been extracted. These two chapters are the main chapters on learning to recognize patterns.

Chapters 6–9 describe methods of learning using symbols for representing information. Chapter 6 covers the basics of learning on a computer. Chapters 7, 8, and 9 describe different learning methods. Readers can turn to any of these chapters after reading Chapter 6.

Chapter 10 describes a method of learning using a distributed pattern representation. It goes on to describe a method that unifies pattern recognition and learning, which is different from the methods explained in Chapters 4–9. This chapter can be read independently of Chapters 4–9.

This book is structured so that readers can choose whichever chapters interest them. For your reference, Figure G.1 shows the relation among chapters.

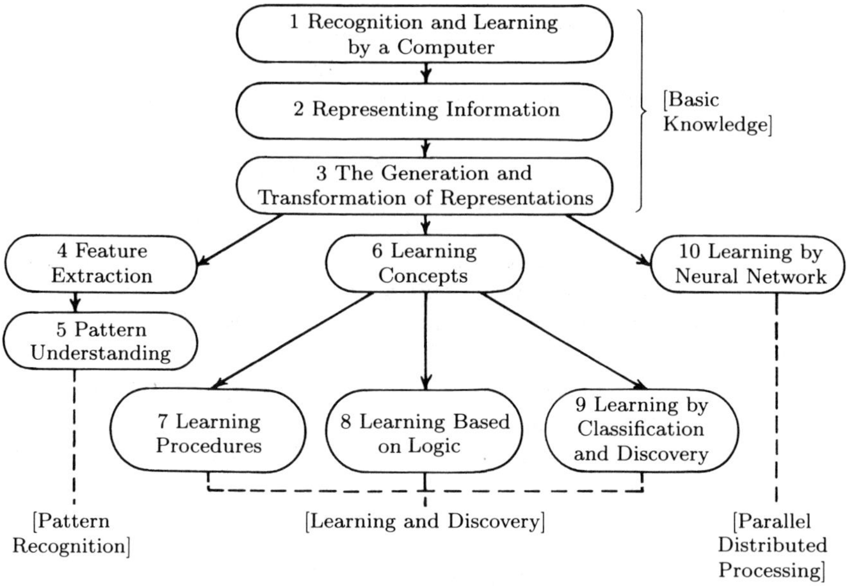

Figure G.1 The structure of the book.

• Exercises

At the end of each chapter there are exercises to help readers understand the main ideas and algorithms better. Some exercises contain important representation methods and algorithms that this book could not cover.

Answers for all the exercises are available. We hope you make good use of these problems.

• Knowledge necessary to read this book

We have designed this book so that readers with the mathematical knowledge of a sophomore in engineering or science can understand it well. It does not require any higher mathematics. Although the representation of information in this book includes diverse subjects like infinitesimal calculus and formal logic, one of the nice things about pattern recognition and learning is that we can treat representations that look totally different in a uniform way. In this sense, we think the study of recognition and learning on a computer can provide knowledge and tools that are applicable in many areas.

• What this book does not cover

Since the problems of pattern recognition and learning stretch over wide areas of knowledge, it is impossible to gather them together in one book. This book describes the things that we think are basic. Specialists in this field may find that this book lacks some important research problems. For example, this book covers recognition only for image patterns. It does not describe voice pattern recognition, which is also an important topic. It also does not cover three-dimensional image patterns, which are a popular research topic. In learning, we do not talk about solving logical problems using inductive inference, learning grammars, or the problem of bias due to differences in expression. Each of these is an important topic. We have also omitted descriptions of genetic algorithms.

The reason for not including these subjects is that the book's purpose is to supply basic and useful knowledge for students who are going to study software science. This book minimizes the number of topics in order to include as many concrete examples as possible. Subjects that this book does not cover belong in an advanced textbook, although they are all important. To learn about the things that are not included here, please refer to the list of references at the end of this book. These include other books in the Iwanami Software Science Series, especially *Knowledge and Inference* (volume 14), *Natural Language Processing* (volume 15), and *Models and Representation* (volume 17). I also recommend writing computer programs.

This book does not pay much attention to which programming language is used. (It includes examples in C, Lisp, Pascal, and Prolog, but you can understand them without knowing about such languages.) This is because we have limited our explanation of the algorithms to the conceptual level so that the reader can understand the point of the method more clearly. However, it is important to learn programming languages. You should study recognition and learning while you acquire a basic understanding of software science as a whole. This includes knowledge of computer architecture, operating systems, programming languages, algorithms, knowledge models and their representation, etc. Otherwise, you will understand only the surface of software science. We recommend that you read other books of this series along with this book.

1 Recognition and Learning by a Computer

In the past computers have been used mainly as tools for data processing. As the processing speed and the amount of data that can be processed by a computer have increased, we have discovered that we can use computers as more intelligent information processing tools. With this idea in mind, we can look at how a computer could be used for recognizing patterns and learning new information. This book is based on the idea that recognition and learning by a computer can be looked at as the process of generating an appropriate representation for information and transforming it into another representation using both the high speed of modern computers and their ability to process a large amount of data. In this chapter, we describe what we mean by the representation, generation, and transformation of information on a computer.

1.1 What Is Recognition by a Computer?

Many academic fields, like philosophy and psychology, use the word "recognition." In each field it has a slightly different meaning. The literal meaning of recognition is to know again what has been known before. In computer science we use the word "recognition" to mean that a computer can recognize that the patterns of objects are ones that it has seen before. By the *pattern* of an object we mean any chronological or spatial data received from the object by an input device and entered into the recognition system. Although it is important to study the meaning of "recognition" in fields other than computer science, in this book we will use the computer science meaning of this word.

Suppose we have a pattern consisting of an object A and a background B as shown in Figure 1.1. In order to distinguish A from the background B in this pattern, we need to find the boundary that separates A from B. Usually, patterns such as Figure 1.1 include not only the object A and the background B but also *noise* (input information other than the data that are directly obtained from the object). Furthermore, the boundary may not be a continuous line. So, in order to find the boundary of A, we not only need to check the light and shading of each point on the boundary but also need to estimate the shape of the whole boundary.

Figure 1.1 A pattern consisting of an object A and a background B.

If we can estimate where to find the boundary line between A and B, we can determine the region encompassed by the boundary, and, as a result, we will be able to distinguish A from B. However, we still do not know what the object A is. In order to know whether A is a glass, a vase, or a coffee cup, that is, in order to know A conceptually, we need to have some knowledge about the shape and function of a glass, a vase, and a coffee cup. Only after we look at the pattern using such knowledge will we be able to figure out that Figure 1.1 consists of a coffee cup and a wall.

This means that we need at least two kinds of algorithms in order to do recognition by computer. They are

(1) algorithms for extracting the boundary and region of a pattern, and
(2) algorithms for recognizing the original object conceptually based on knowledge of the object, its patterns, and how it is used.

In the above description of Figure 1.1, we used (1) and then (2). In other cases (2) can come before (1) or (1) and (2) can be executed alternately.

In addition to visual patterns, like that in Figure 1.1, there are many other types of patterns, such auditory or tactile, that can be recognized by a computer. This book, however, will discuss only visual patterns.

1.2 Representation and Transformation in Recognition

Frequently, a pattern is represented as a function. For example, the pattern of the coffee cup in Figure 1.1 could be represented using a *pattern function* whose input is coordinates of a point and whose value is the image density at each point. For visual patterns, we also call this a *(visual) image function.* A pattern function usually contains noise and often does not contain complete data.

Once we have estimated the boundary and region of a pattern and we have used general knowledge to recognize it conceptually, the information about this pattern will have a different structure than the original pattern function. For example, once a pattern has been recognized conceptually, it might include symbolic information describing the object such as "coffee cup" and "table" or symbols representing a relation between objects such as "the coffee cup A is on the table." Figure 1.2 shows sample representations for a coffee cup.

As you can see, the process of *pattern recognition* can use many different representations including pattern functions, sets of regions divided by boundary lines, symbols describing an object, and relations among objects. These representations can be represented in a computer using many different data structures. For example, symbols and relations among symbols can be represented using graph theory (see Section 2.3). We call the data structures used to describe these representations in a computer the *representation* of the information.

Now we can say that the process of pattern recognition is either to create a new representation or to change one representation into another, starting from an object's representation as a pattern function. We can also say that the purpose of pattern recognition by a computer is to *generate* and *transform* useful representations of information using the high speed and the massive data processing capability of the computer.

Based on the above, the study of pattern recognition needs to consider the following two problems:

(A) What methods of representation are available for patterns?
(B) What methods are available for transforming one representation into another?

(a) The pattern represented using eight grades of density

(b) The pattern represented using two grades of density

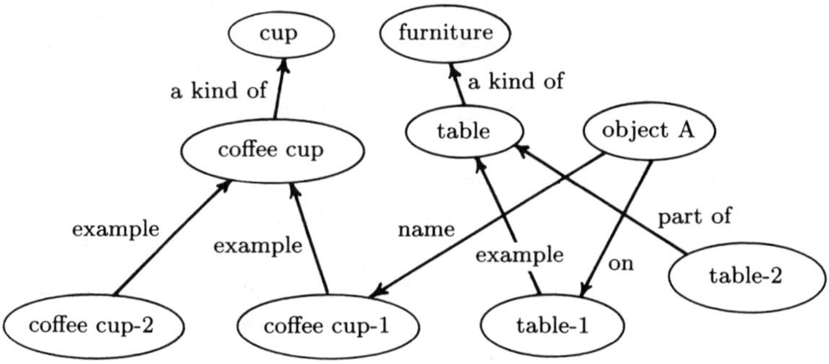

(c) A symbolic expression for the relation between objects

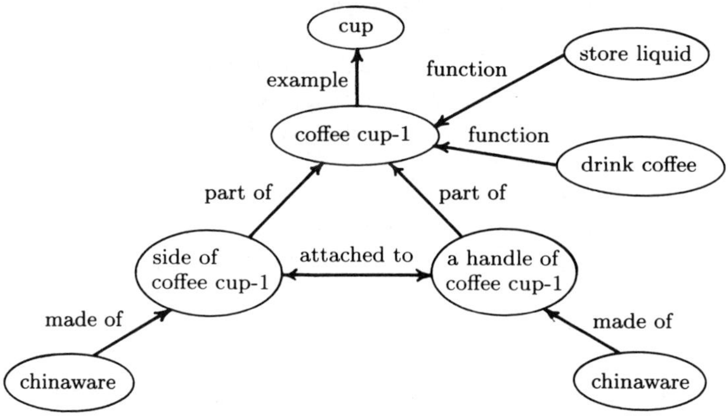

(d) A symbolic expression including functions and characteristics

Figure 1.2 Various representations for the coffee cup shown in Figure 1.1.

Since the algorithms (1) and (2) mentioned earlier are for transforming representations, they belong to (B). We will describe this kind of algorithm in Chapter 3 and in more detail in Chapters 4 and 5. We will provide popular methods for representing patterns in Chapter 2.

Many possible representations can be obtained by creating and transforming the original pattern. There is often more than one transformation method possible at one time, and different orders of making these transformations may produce different results. Therefore, pattern recognition is a kind of *underconstrained problem* since in general we do not have enough information to decide if we have a unique solution. In order to decide on the correctness of a solution to a problem, we need to specify either the representation to be used or the method of transformation, or we need to supply some *evaluation function* for the solution. When we read Chapters 4 and 5, we will see that both types of specifications can be used together.

When we look at the problem of pattern recognition as the generation and transformation of representations, recognition algorithms can be divided into two parts. One part of the algorithm is the low-level information processing necessary for extracting features of a given pattern and for estimating the boundaries and regions of a pattern. The other part is the high-level algorithm for estimating, based on symbolic knowledge, what the given pattern is. (See Section 2.13 for more exact meanings of "pattern" and "symbol.")

1.3 What Is Learning by a Computer?

Like recognition, the word "learning" is used in many fields such as psychology and education. In computer science, when a system automatically generates a new data structure or program out of an old one and thus irreversibly changes itself with some purpose for a certain amount of time, we call it *machine learning.* As with recognition, although it is important to study the meaning of the word "learning" as used in fields other than computer science, in this book we will use the above meaning specific to computer science.

Suppose we have objects C, D, E as in Figure 1.3 and we have the following data about C, D, E:

C: Top diameter 10 cm	Bottom diameter 8 cm
D: Top diameter 6 cm	Bottom diameter 4 cm
E: Top diameter 5 cm	Bottom diameter 3 cm

Now we suppose C, D, E are all examples of an object U. What should we imagine that the object U is? There are many ways to decide what

Figure 1.3 Various objects.

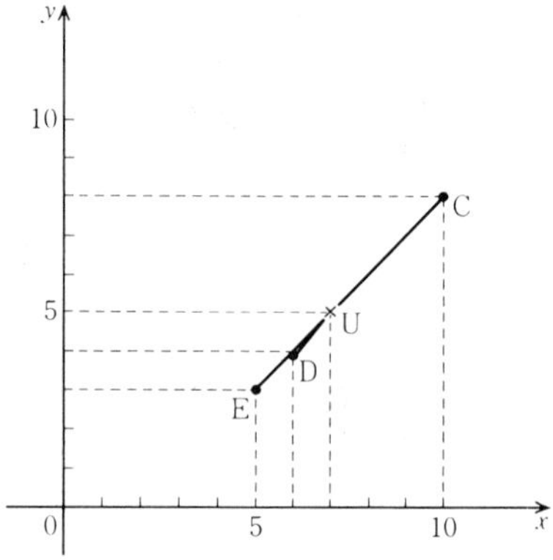

Figure 1.4 The point U where the sum of the distances from points C, D, and E is smallest.

U is. For example, since the top diameter of C, D, E is larger than the bottom diameter, we can use the notion of "the thing whose top diameter is bigger than its bottom diameter" for U. Or, we can imagine that C, D, and E are points whose top diameter and bottom diameter are their x and y coordinates (in two-dimensional Euclidean space) and consider the point where the sum of the distances from these points is smallest to be U. With this method, we can decide that the object whose top diameter is 7 cm and whose bottom diameter is 5 cm is U (see Figure 1.4). When U is determined like this, we call it a prototype of the sample group C, D, E and the samples C, D, and E are considered to be objects "similar to" U. (Generally, a prototype does not just depend on the average values.)

The above example illustrates the problem of creating some data that generalize some other set of data. Like pattern recognition, this is also an underconstrained problem since we are not generally given enough information to determine only one answer. In order to solve problems like this, as in pattern recognition problems, we need to specify a method for determining an answer or we need to supply some criteria for evaluating how to select methods of determining an answer. Both of these strategies are in actual use. Chapter 6 and later chapters will have many examples of using these methods.

Suppose that when we input the data C, D, and E into a computer, we get an example object U with the following characteristics:

U: Top diameter 7 cm   Bottom diameter 5 cm

This U is "new" data generated from the given data. Once the computer creates this prototypical U, the information it will output about U will be different from the output produced before. It can use this characteristic version of U when it needs a general representation of the samples C, D, and E. In this way we can consider the generation of U as a form of machine learning as described above.

Some readers might think that, since the procedure for determining U has been given from the outside and the computation of U is a fixed procedure, U is not new data. This is true if you mean that every step in a computation on a computer is not doing anything new. In that sense, a computer does not produce any new information.

We will call a process *a machine learning process* if

(1) the process is complicated and the data resulting from this process are quite different from the original data and
(2) as a result of this process, the future output of the system will be changed.

If a process satisfies only (1), we do not call it learning. For example, the process of solving a complex differential equation will not be called learning unless the computer changes the output of the system using its solution for some purpose.

This idea of learning is based on the assumption that knowing and making use of the results of a computation and learning become almost identical as the amount of the computation increases. Note that this idea assumes that the computers we are using are large enough to carry out the computations we are considering.

1.4 Representation and Transformation in Learning

In computer systems that learn, the data or programs that are part of the original system, or are added from the outside, are used to transform existing data or programs into something new. During this process, both the original data and programs and the newly created data and programs are represented in the computer by some kind of data structures.

For example, in Figure 1.3, the given data C, D, and E and the synthesized U can be thought of as pairs containing the values (top diameter, bottom diameter). In some circumstances these pairs may be represented symbolically. If the only information that a system is told about U is that "the top diameter is bigger than the bottom diameter", then the system would use a very different abstract representation of U than it would use for the representation of the original data C, D, and E.

It is important to understand that the characteristic of allowing multiple representations is the essence of the learning process rather than simply one aspect of learning. It is this characteristic that fits the above definition of learning. In other words, we say that learning by a computer is a process of generalizing and transforming representations.

Based on the definition above, the opposite of this is not always true; that is, the process of generalization and transformation of a representation is not always "machine learning." Remember that pattern recognition by a computer as described in Section 1.1 is also a process of generalizing and transforming representations. We see that recognition and learning by a computer, which are the main subjects of this book, are both processes of generalization and transformation of representations.

As in the case of pattern recognition, we need to consider the following two problems in the study of learning:

(A) What methods for representing information are appropriate for learning?

(B) What methods are available for transforming one representation into another?

Methods of representing information for both learning and recognition, (A), will be described in Chapter 2. Transformation algorithms, (B), will be described in Chapter 3. Algorithms for learning will be described in detail in Chapters 6–10.

1.5 Example of Recognition/Learning System

In order to have a clear picture of the problems mentioned in the previous sections, let us consider a simple example of a computer system that includes pattern recognition and learning. The content of such systems will be explained in Chapters 4, 5, and 8.

Suppose we have a pattern for a "hammer." We input this pattern bit by bit into the pattern recognition system. This system will first extract characteristics of this pattern and will then obtain the outline shown in Figure 1.5. The system then represents the structure of the pattern, using the network as shown in Figure 1.6, by matching extracted characteristics with knowledge it has gathered on the structure of the "hammer." We can think of this as the process of a sequence of transformations starting with the representation of the input pattern and ending with a symbolic representation using a relational network of concepts.

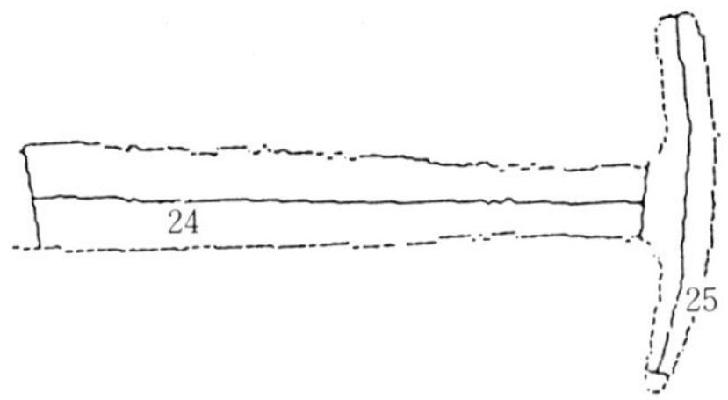

Figure 1.5 An outline of a "hammer" (Connell and Brady, 1987).

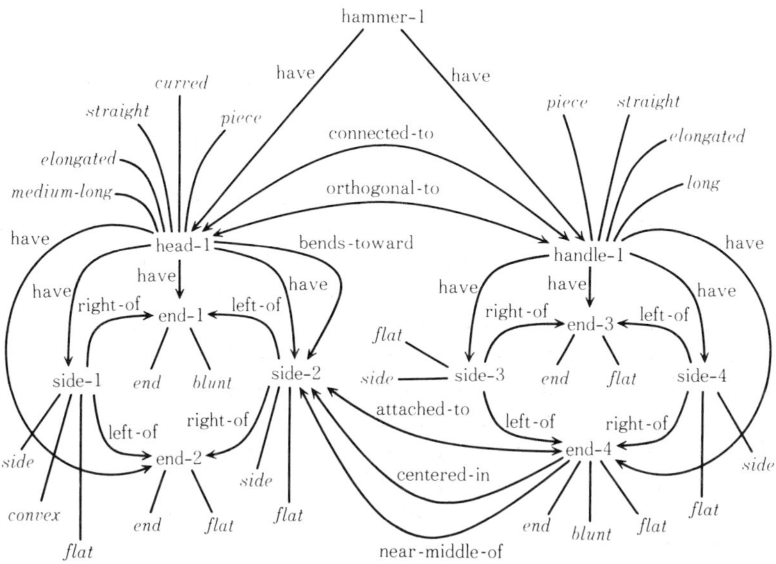

Figure 1.6 A network representation of a "hammer" (Connell and Brady, 1987).

After the system represents some "hammer" patterns using the network, it compares the similarities between patterns. By extracting structurally identical parts of several networks, we can interpret the common parts as a representation of the "general hammer." An example of such a representation is shown in Figure 1.7.

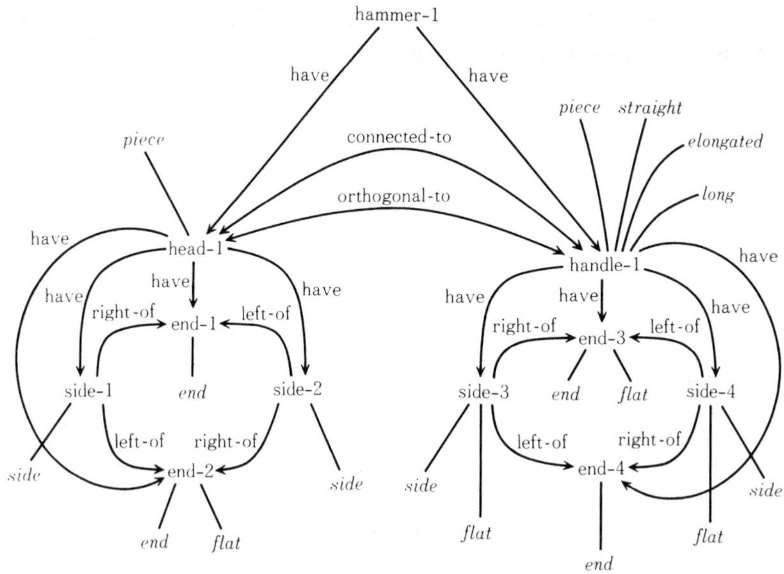

Figure 1.7 A network representation for the "general hammer" (Connell and Brady, 1987).

We might actually construct the system so that it outputs the representation for the "general hammer" after being given several network representations of some "hammers" as inputs. This system could use the "general hammer" representation to check whether some newly input network representation actually represents a "hammer" or not. In addition, the system could update the representation of the "general hammer" every time it checks for similarity. This system could be called a learning system according to the definition of learning given in Section 1.3.

By combining a pattern recognition system and a learning system, we could design a system for judging whether a given object is a "hammer" or not. Such a system would be interesting as an existence proof for a system that combines pattern recognition and learning and as an example showing directly that recognition and learning are the process of the generalization and transformation of representations.

Summary

Chapter 1 described the nature of pattern recognition and learning by a computer.

1.1 Pattern recognition and learning are areas of software science for intelligent information processing by making use of the high speed and massive data processing capability of a computer.

1.2 Pattern recognition by a computer is the process of transforming a pattern function to a more structured representation of information.

1.3 Learning by a computer is the process of generating a representation of information that is suitable for accomplishing some goal.

1.4 It is possible to construct a computer system that combines pattern recognition and learning.

Keywords

pattern recognition, learning, representation, underconstrained problem, generalization, transformation, recognition/learning system

Exercises

1.1 Give the definition of recognition by a computer and explain the difference in meaning between recognition by a computer and "recognition" as we usually use it informally.

1.2 Give the definition of learning by a computer and explain the difference in meaning between learning by a computer and "learning" as we usually use it informally.

1.3 Explain the similarities and the differences between recognition and learning by a computer.

1.4 Suppose we have the following first-order simultaneous inequalities as an example of an underconstrained problem. In order to make the point satisfying this inequality unique, how would you change the value of the right side of (a)? Find the coordinate of such a point.

$$-x - y \leq -3 \qquad (a)$$

$$-x + 4y \leq 12 \qquad (b)$$

$$3x - 2y \leq 4 \qquad (c)$$

2 Representing Information

This chapter provides basic methods for representing information in a computer. In particular, we will describe the important techniques for representing patterns, data structures, characteristics of objects, and procedures. As we described in Chapter 1, the process of generating a new representation or transformation into another representation is the basic process of recognition and learning on a computer. This chapter forms the basis of the whole book. There are, however, many methods of representing information. This chapter describes only some representative ones.

2.1 Pattern Function and Bit Pattern

In order to study various methods of representation, let us first look at the pattern of an object that is distributed in space. The coffee cup on the table shown in Figure 1.1 and the pattern of a human face shown in Figure 2.1(a) are such examples. A typical method of representing such a pattern in a computer is to use some distribution of values like the intensity of the reflected light at each point of the object. We can distinguish a coffee cup from its background by determining which values represent whether a point in the picture is light or dark. An example is shown in Figure 1.2(a).

As one method of representing such a pattern, let us consider a function $f(x, y)$ that has a value for each point (x, y) of the space containing the object (here, we consider only two-dimensional Euclidean space). We generally call such a function, f, a *pattern function* and its value the *intensity* at a point. Using this pattern function, we can distinguish an object

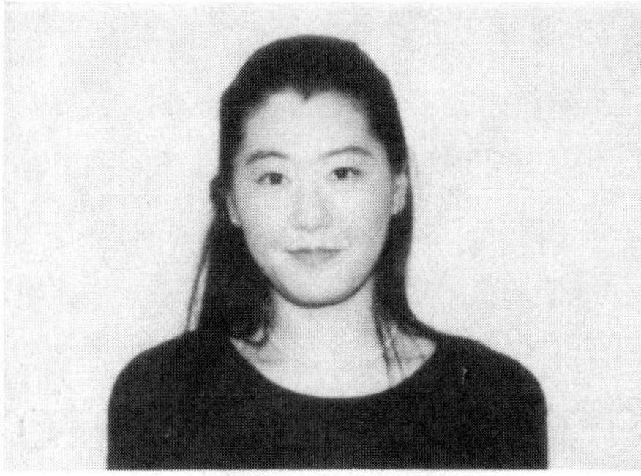

(a) A photograph of a human face

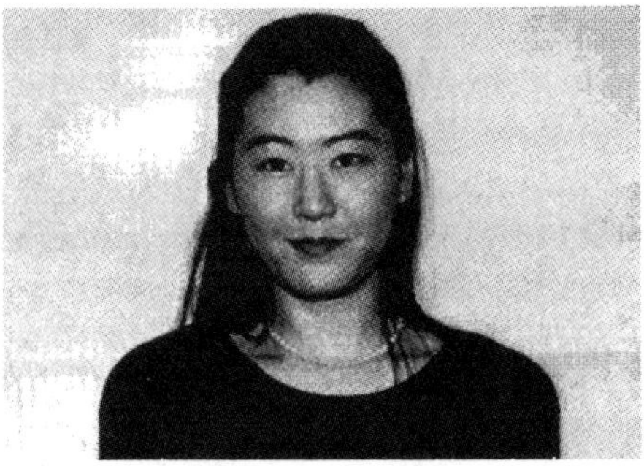

(b) A picture obtained by dispersing each point of the photograph and giving intensity to each point.

Figure 2.1 A photograph of a human face and an example of its pattern function.

from its background by looking at differences in the intensity values of the pattern function.

We can use many different forms and measures of intensity for a pattern function. For example, we can use a function that takes the density of each point in a photograph as a value, or if the picture is a screen image seen through a lens we can use a function that takes the distribution of brightness as its values. The above pattern function is a scalar function, but it could also be a vector function. For example, if we express the brightness of each point as $f(x, y)$ and its color as $g(x, y)$, then we can use the vector function $h(x, y) = (f(x, y), g(x, y))$ as the pattern function of the object in a color picture.

This kind of spatial distribution of density and brightness can be defined as a function with a continuous range. However, since a digital computer is best at processing discrete values, such as binary processing using only 0 and 1, it is often more convenient to represent the domain or the range of a function discretely. So, let us consider a method for representing patterns discretely.

The basic unit for representing discrete information in a computer is a *bit.* One bit can be considered as the information necessary for selecting one out of two possibilities. The bit is useful as the minimum unit for representing information. Let us consider building a pattern function out of information that contains only one bit of information as its *pattern element.* In other words, let us define a two-valued function $h(v, y)$ that takes the value 0 or 1 at each point (x, y) of two-dimensional Euclidean space E^2 (and that can easily be generalized to the case of n-dimensional Euclidean space). Here we consider only the points (x, y), where $x = x_0 + m\Delta x$, $y = y_0 + n\Delta y$ $(m, n = 0, \pm 1, \pm 2, \ldots)$. This divides E^2 into a grid. Now, when we look at the set $S = \{(x, y) | 0 \le x \le 63, 0 \le y \le 25\}$ on this grid shown in Figure 2.2, we can represent the pattern function $v(x, y)$ using the (two-dimensional) *bit pattern* $d(x, y)$ on the 64×26 points in S.

```
0000000000000000000000011111000000000000000000000000000000000000
0000000000000000001111111111111101100000000000000000000000000000
0000000000000101111111111111111111111100000000000000000000000000
0000000000000010111111111111111010101111000000000000000000000000
0000000000000111110111010111101011111111110000000000000000000000
0000000000001110101111110111111101011111111100000000000000000000
0000000000000111010111011101111010101011110100000000000000000000
0000000000001000001011111101111111011111111100000000000000000000
0000000000111000000000001001111011111111011100000000000000000000
0000000000011010000000000000000000000110010110000000000000000000
0000000000010000110110000100000110110011010110000000000000000000
0000000001111010000000000000000000000100111000000000000000000000
0000000001111000111110000000000111110000111100000000000000000000
0000000001111000000100000010000000000001011110000000000000000000
0000000011110000000000000100000000000001101100000000000000000000
0000000011011000000000000000000000000001101010000000000000000000
0000000011111000000000001001000000000011111110000000000000000000
0000000100010100000000000000000000000001110111000000000000000000
0000000010100110000000000100000000000011110111100000000000000000
0000000001101001000000001111100000000011110101000000000000000000
0000001010101010100000000000000000001111011101000000000000000000
0000101010101011010000000000000000110111111100111100000000000000
0000000101010000101010000000000011001111111111100011000000000000
0000000011111100000000001010101000000011010101010101010000000000
0000000001111000000100000000000000011111111111111111100000000000
0000000000000000000000000000000001111111111111111111111111110000
```

Figure 2.2 A bit pattern representation of a human face.

In this example, the value of $d(x, y)$ at each point (x, y), i.e, the pattern element, is either one of two values 0 or 1. More general pattern functions may be represented by functions whose pattern elements can take three or more different values. Limiting the range of the pattern function f to the discrete points $(x_0 + m\Delta x, y_0 + n\Delta y)$ $(m, n = \pm 1, \pm 2, \ldots)$ is generally called a *sampling* of f. Limiting the values of f to several discrete values is called a *quantization* of f, and each value is called a quantization level. A quantization using 2^k quantization levels is generally called the k-bit quantization. Based on these ideas, we say that a bit pattern is a pattern with one-bit quantization that takes only the values 0 and 1 as quantization levels. The value of a pattern element in a sampling pattern function and in a quantized pattern function is also called its intensity.

When a pattern function is a two-dimensional visual image function, we call the above-defined pattern element a *pixel*; we call it a *boxel* if the image function is three-dimensional.

2.2 The Representation of Spatial Structure

The pattern function representation described in Section 2.1 is a simple example of representing spatial structures. There are many other methods for representing objects in a space. For example, geometry is an important method of spatial representation.

An $n-1$-dimensional hyperplane in n-dimensional Euclidean space E^n can be represented as $a^T x = b$, where a is a fixed n-dimensional real number vector and b is a fixed real number. In particular, a straight line in E^2 can be represented by $a_1 x_1 + a_2 x_2 = b$. If a hyperspace in which some objects are included is already known, then some set of fixed real numbers (for example, a_1, a_2, b in the case of a straight line in E^2) is sufficient to determine the hyperspace.

A polyhedron in E^n can be represented using the spatial relation among its vertices. For example, a square in E^2 can be represented as a sequence of end points, $((x_k, y_k), (x_{k+1}, y_{k+1}), (x_{k+2}, y_{k+2}), (x_{k+3}, y_{k+3}))$. Further, if we let (x_k, y_k) be a variable and express the x, y coordinates of the other vertices as a difference from x_k and y_k, then we can represent any square in E^2. Generally, we call this type of representation a *wire-frame representation*. The square shown in Figure 2.3(a) can be represented using the wire-frame representation shown in Figure 2.3(b).

Even a complicated structure such as one containing overlapping polyhedra or one including a curve can be represented to some degree by using the positions of the points of intersection, the distance between points or lines, the rate of curvature or symmetry, and the position of unusual points or inflection points.

Not only rectangular coordinates but also spherical coordinates can be used for representing a spatial structure. For example, Figure 2.4 shows a camera placed at the origin of three-dimensional Euclidean space, E^3. When the camera takes a picture of the points (x, y, z) that are spread out

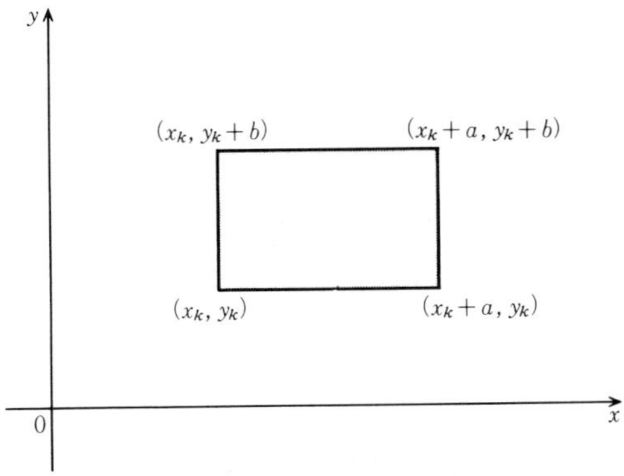

(a) A quadrangle on a two-dimensional Euclidean space

$$((x_k, y_k), (x_k + a, y_k), (x_k + a, y_k + b), (x_k, y_k + b))$$

(b) A wire-frame representation of a quadrangle

Figure 2.3 Examples of representations of spatial structure.

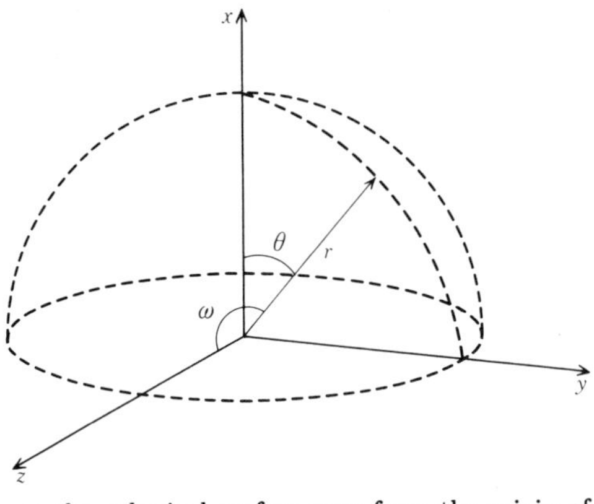

Figure 2.4 Points on the spherical surface seen from the origin of three-dimensional Euclidean space.

on the spherical surface whose radius is r from the origin of E^3, these points can be generally represented as $(r\cos\theta, r\sin\theta, r\cos\omega)$ with parameters θ and ω as illustrated in Figure 2.4.

The above methods are used for representing objects in Euclidean space. Euclidean space is a special case of a metric space where a distance is defined, and the above method of representation can be considered as a special case of representing an object in space by specifying its position.

A representation in which position can be determined using some metric such as distance is generally called a *metric representation.*

2.3 Graph Representation

Not all representations of an object are metric. We often cannot use a metric characteristic (such as distance) to represent the structure or a property of an object. In this section we discuss the popular nonmetric method of *graph representation.* Graph representation is an example of *topological representation* that makes use of simple topological relations among symbols rather than distance represented by numbers.

First, let us consider the intuitive way of thinking about this. We call a representation determined by some *nodes* and the links between some nodes a graph representation or a *network representation.* For example, the picture of train routes shown in Figure 2.5(a) can be modeled as the graph representation shown in Figure 2.5(b) if we consider each station to be a node and each line between stations as a link.

A graph representation can be defined more exactly using the terms of graph theory as follows, where N is a set of natural numbers, R is a set of real numbers, and A is a finite set of symbols:

Definition 1 (undirected graph) For two given sets $U = \{u_1, \ldots, u_n\}$ ($u_i \in N$) and $L \subseteq \{\{u_i, u_j\} | u_i, u_j \in U\}$, we call $G = (U, L)$ an *undirected graph.* For an undirected graph $G = (U, L)$, we call each element of U a node of G and each element of L an *undirected edge* or simply an *edge* of G.

Intuitively, we can consider an edge of an undirected graph, $\{u_i, u_j\}$, to be a link connecting the two nodes u_i and u_j. As you can see from the fact that an edge is defined as the "set" of two nodes, the direction of the link is arbitrary, either from u_i to u_j or from u_j to u_i. The name "undirected" comes from this fact. For example, in the picture of the routes in Figure 2.5(a), if we think of each station as a node and agree that an edge between nodes exists only when two stations are neighbors of each other, we can obtain the undirected graph shown in Figure 2.5(b).

Definition 2 (directed graph) For two given sets $U = \{u_1, \ldots, u_n\}(u_i \in N)$ and $L \subseteq \{(u_i, u_j) | u_i, u_j \in U\} \subseteq U \times U$, we call $G = (U, L)$ a *directed graph.* In a directed graph $G = (U, L)$, we call each element of U a node of G and each element of L a *directed edge* or simply an *edge* of G.

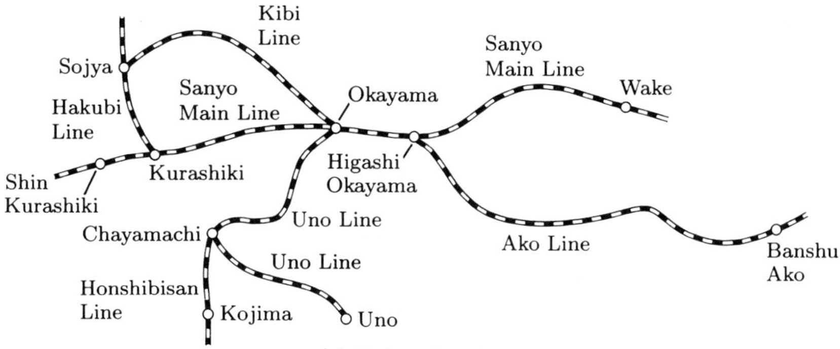

(a) Railroad routes

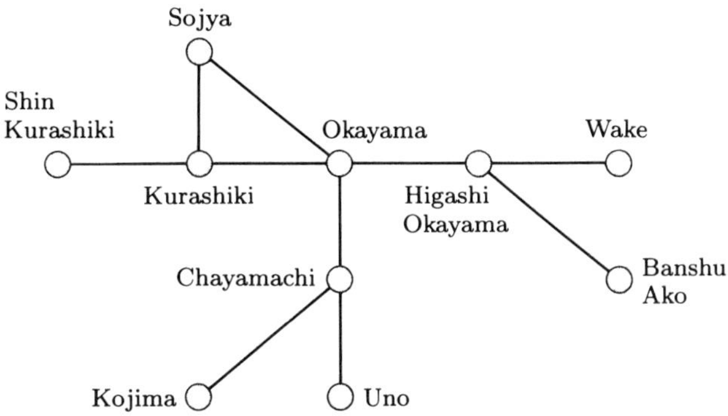

(b) The undirected graph representation

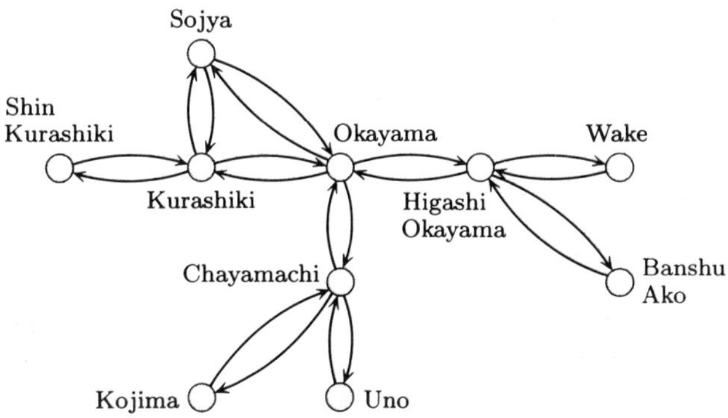

(c) The directed graph representation

Figure 2.5 Examples of graph representations.

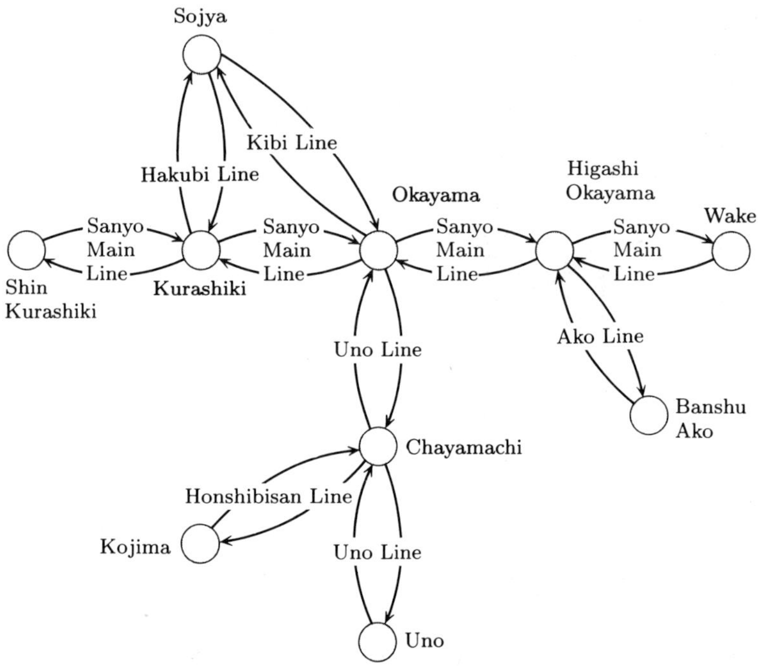

(d) The labeled direct graph representation

Figure 2.5 *Continued.*

A directed graph is different from an undirected graph only in that an edge is defined by an ordered pair, (u_i, u_j), of two nodes. This definition distinguishes the edge (u_i, u_j) that goes from the node u_i to the node u_j from the edge (u_j, u_i) that goes from u_j to u_i. For example, in the graph shown in Figure 2.5(a), if we think of each station as a node and define the direction of an edge to be determined by the direction of a route that would be traveled by a train, we obtain the directed graph shown in Figure 2.5(c).

Definition 3 (labeled directed graph) In a directed graph $G = (U, L)$, suppose a *label* $a_{ij} \in A$ corresponds to each edge $(u_i, u_j) \in L$. We expand the definition of an edge to include this label using $L^* = \{(u_i, u_j, a_{ij}) | (u_i, u_j) \in L\}$. We call the graph $G^* = (U, L^*)$ defined using this definition of edge a *labeled directed graph* generated from G, or simply a labeled directed graph. Similarly, we can define a labeled undirected graph.

We can think of a labeled directed (undirected) graph as a graph with a "name" for each edge. For example, if we take the set of railroad routes, Sanyo Honsen, Akaho Sen, and so on, as a set of labels, A, and imagine that each route name in the original picture (Figure 2.5(a)) corresponds to an edge in the directed graph shown in Figure 2.5(c), we can define the labeled directed graph shown in Figure 2.5(d). In this case we are assuming that each route corresponds to only one route name.

Definition 4 (weighted directed graph) Suppose, in a given directed graph $G = (U, L)$, a real number $r_{ij} \in R$ corresponds to each edge $(u_i, u_j) \in L$. We can expand the definition of edge using these numbers to $L' = \{(u_i, u_j, r_{ij}) | (u_i, u_j) \in L\}$. We call the graph $G' = (U, L')$ defined using such a set of edges a *weighted directed graph* generated from G or simply a weighted directed graph. We call r_{ij} the *weight* of (u_i, u_j). Similarly, we can define a weighted undirected graph.

A weighted directed (undirected) graph is a graph where each edge has a weight parameter. The distance between two nodes (the length of an edge) and the communications capacity (thickness of an edge) are often represented as a weight parameter. For example, if we attach the distance between neighboring stations in the original route picture (Figure 2.5(a)) to each edge of the undirected graph in Figure 2.5(b) as a weight, we get a weighted undirected graph.

When we use graphs as defined above to represent some object (e.g., we used a graph as the representation of the route picture above), we call such an representation a graph representation. A graph representation is suitable for representing objects and relations among objects. For example, the photograph of the scenery in Figure 2.6(a) contains a plain, a mountain, a path, and so on. There are also spatial relations among such objects, like the plain being in front of the mountain. We represent objects such as the plain and the mountain as a node and connect two objects that are in some spatial relation by an edge. We then attach the name of the relation as a label to each edge. In this way, we can represent the objects in the photograph and the relations among them as the labeled directed graph as shown in Figure 2.6(b).

We now describe some properties of graphs that we use later in this book and give some more definitions.

When two graphs become identical by simply changing the names of the nodes or the labels of the edges, we say that the two graphs are *isomorphic*. (See Exercise 5.2 in Chapter 5 for a more precise definition.) The graphs shown in Figure 2.7 are isomorphic.

In the directed graph shown in Figure 2.8, we can travel from node 0 to node 3 by following the edges (0,1), (1,2), (2,3). A list of such edges (or sometimes a corresponding list of nodes) is generally called a path from one node to another or simply a *path*. We can define a path in the same way for an undirected graph by imagining that we can go along either (u_i, u_j)

(a) A photograph of scenery and a mountain

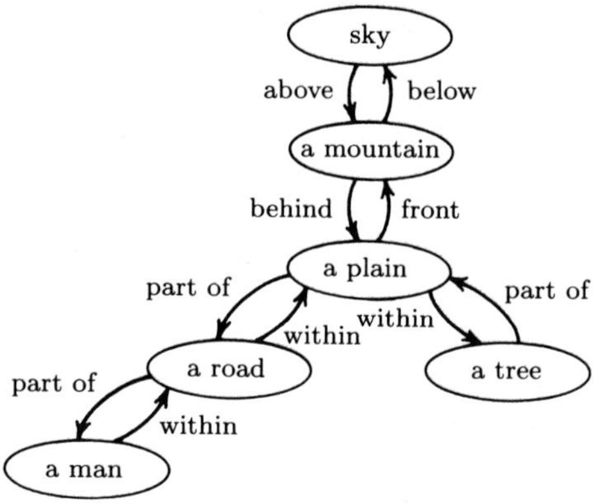

(b) A labeled directed graph representation of the scenery (a)

Figure 2.6 A pattern and its graph representation.

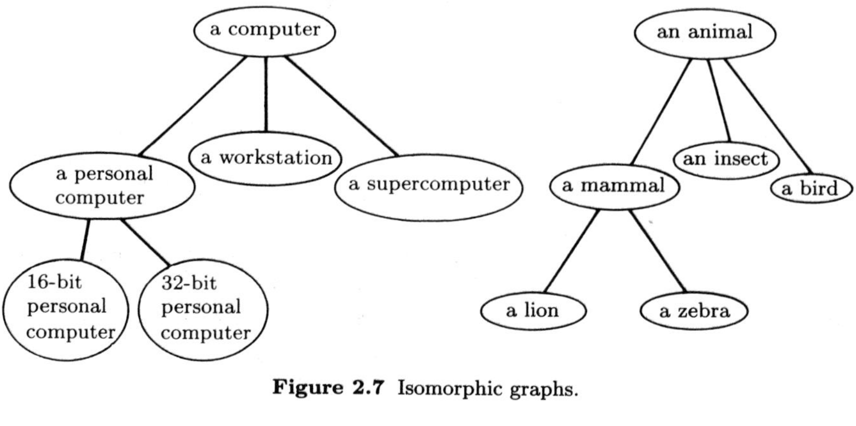

Figure 2.7 Isomorphic graphs.

or (u_j, u_i) for the edge $\{u_i, u_j\}$. A path that returns to a node that it has already visited is called a closed path, a cycle, or a *loop*. In a weighted directed graph, a path that goes from node n_i to n_j and for which the sum of the weights of the edges included in this path is the minimum over all possible paths from n_i to n_j is called the *shortest path* from n_i to n_j. Even in an unweighted graph, if we consider the weight of each edge to be 1, we can also define a shortest path. We call the number of edges included in a path the *length* of the path.

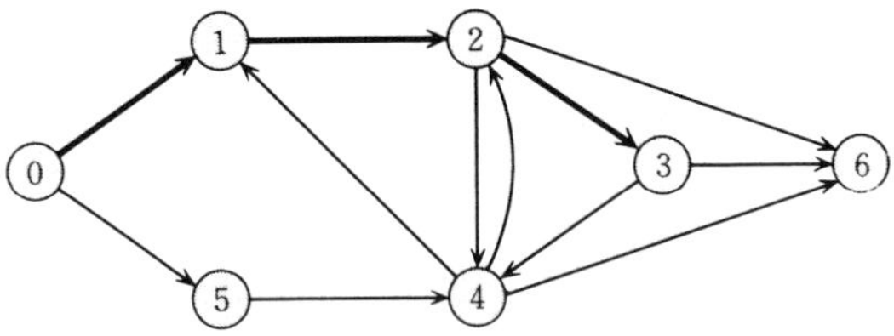

Figure 2.8 A path in a graph.

When the nodes u_i and u_j of a graph G are on the same path, we write $u_i \sim u_j$. Suppose we start from u_i and exhaust all the nodes that can be related to it by $\sim$. If, for any node u_i in G, the set of such nodes is the entire set of the nodes of G, we call G a *connected graph.* In this book, a graph means a connected graph. A connected graph where any node has an edge connecting it directly to any of the other nodes is called a *perfect graph.* An object may be represented as a perfect graph if any two of its components are related.

For a graph $G = (U, L)$, $G' = (U', L')$ (where $U' \subset U, L' \subset L$) is called a *subgraph* of G. A subgraph where the number of elements in its set of nodes U' is k ($0 \leq k \leq n$; n is the number of nodes in G) is called a *kth-order subgraph* of G. When subgraphs of two graphs are isomorphic, we say that those graphs are *subgraph isomorphic.* When a kth-order subgraph $G' = (U', L')$ is a perfect graph, we call G' (or U') a *kth-order clique* of G. Generally, for any k ($0 \leq k \leq n$), we call such a subgraph a *clique.* If for some clique C in G, no subgraph of G properly including C is a clique, we call C a *maximal clique.* Generally, there is more than one maximal clique for a graph. Among the maximal cliques of G, a clique with the largest number of nodes is called a *maximum clique* of G. Generally there is more than one maximum clique for a graph.

In a directed graph $G = (U, L)$, when we can divide U into mutually disjoint subgroups $U_1, \ldots, U_m$, and $u_i \in U_{k_1}$, $u_j \in U_{k_2}$ ($k_1, k_2 \in \{1, \ldots, m\}$, $k_1 < k_2$) hold for any edge $(u_i, u_j) \in L$, we say G is a *feedforward graph.* For example, the graph shown in Figure 2.9 is a feedforward graph. A feed-

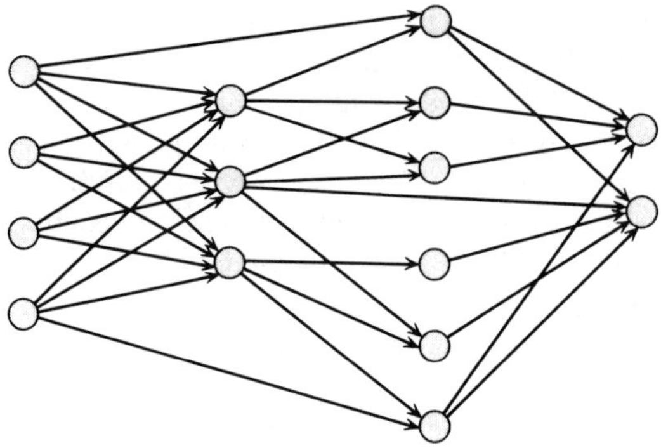

Figure 2.9 A feedforward graph.

forward graph can be used for the graph representation of a hierarchical or a cascade structure.

The difference between a feedforward graph and a general directed graph is that a general directed graph may include edges that go back to a node whose index is smaller in $U_1, \ldots, U_m$. Such an edge is called a *feedback edge* or a *feedback connection.*

2.4 Tree Representation

In this section we describe the popular representation technique of using trees. We will consider trees to be a special case of graph representation. Intuitively, a tree representation is a representation using a tree-structured graph. For example, as illustrated in Figure 2.10, a family tree and the structure of the relations between different kinds of polygons are examples of tree representations.

We now look at the definition of a tree more carefully.

Definition 5 (tree) A graph that does not include a loop is called a *tree.* If there exists a node u_0 in a tree G and there is a path from u_0 to each node in the tree, we call G a *directed tree.*

From Definition 5, we know a tree $G = (U, L)$ has the following features:

(1) There is only one node $u_o \in U$ where an edge of the form (u_k, u_0) does not exist. This node is called the *root node* or the *root* of G.

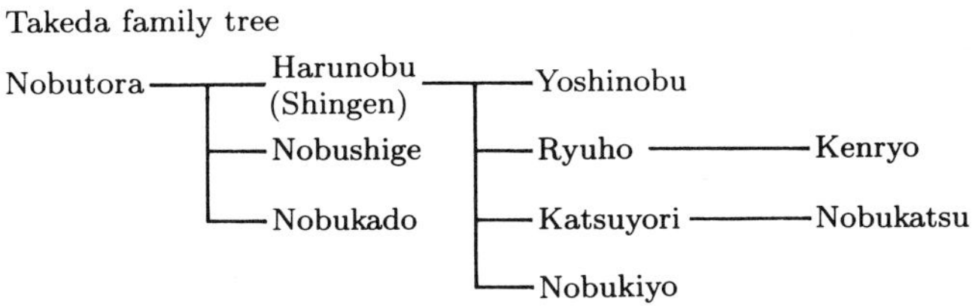

(a) A family tree

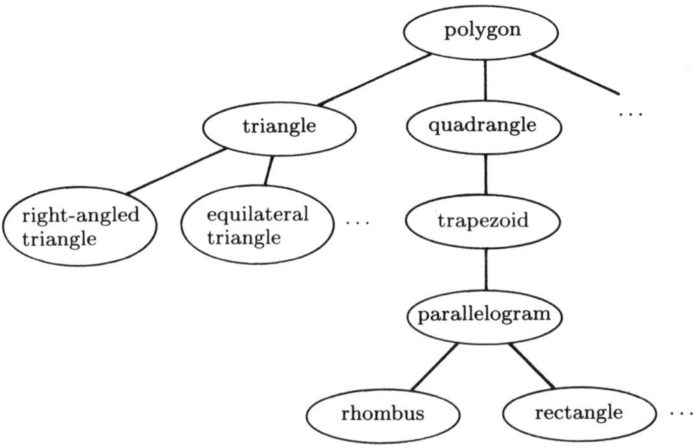

(b) A structure of the relations among polygons

Figure 2.10 Examples of tree representation.

(2) For $u_j \in U - \{u_0\}$, there is only one edge that has the form (u_i, u_j) (where $u_i \neq u_j$). We call u_i the *parent node* of u_j and u_j a *child node* of u_i. Using these terms, we can say that each node that is not the root node has only one parent node. (From (1), we can see that the root node does not have a parent node.)

(3) Edges of a form other than (2) do not exist. A node u_j that is not connected to an edge of the form (u_j, u_i) is called a *leaf*, and a node that is not a root node or a leaf is called an *intermediate node.*

Generally, in this book we will not distinguish a general tree from a directed tree and we assume that an edge goes along each path from a root to a leaf.

We can use a tree to represent many different types of objects. If each node of a tree, except its leaf nodes, has 2, 4, 8, or n child nodes, it is called a *binary tree*, *quad-tree*, *octa-tree*, or *n-tree*, respectively.

2.5 List Representation

In this section we describe *list representation*, which is also a special case of graph representation.

An ordered sequence of elements of a set A of given symbols is called a *list* (of A). We write a list by writing its elements in order separated by empty space and enclosed within "(" and ")." For instance, we can represent a group of prefecture names, a = (Aomori Akita Yamagata Iwate Miyagi Fukushima), as a list. One characteristic of a list is that the elements of the list are ordered from left to right. The list a is different from the list a' = (Aomori Akita Fukushima Iwate Miyagi Yamagata): a is a list of six prefecture names in the Tohoku area that are listed from the northmost prefecture, a' is a list of the six prefecture names in alphabetic order.

Consider the eight objects in Figure 2.11. To distinguish these objects, we need only know the *values* of three *attributes*: shape, size, and color (whether the shape is a circle or an ellipse, whether the size is big or small, whether the color is red or blue). This suggests that we can represent these eight objects using a list of pairs (lists of length 2) showing the following attribute-values:

Object 1: ((*shape circle*) (*size large*) (*color red*))
Object 2: ((*shape ellipse*)(*size small*) (*color red*))
Object 3: ((*shape ellipse*)(*size small*) (*color blue*))
Object 4: ((*shape circle*) (*size large*) (*color blue*))
Object 5: ((*shape ellipse*) (*size large*) (*color red*))
Object 6: ((*shape circle*) (*size small*) (*color blue*))
Object 7: ((*shape circle*) (*size small*) (*color red*))
Object 8: ((*shape ellipse*) (*size large*) (*color blue*))

Please note that each element in this list is itself a list. For example, Object 1 is represented by the list of three lists (*shape circle*), (*size large*), (*color red*) in that order. A list can be nested so that it has another list as an element. If we list the above eight lists for Objects 1 to 8, we will have the following list with three nestings:

((*object1* ((*shape circle*) (*size large*) (*color red*))
(*object2* ((*shape ellipse*)(*size small*) (*color red*))
(*object3* ((*shape ellipse*)(*size small*) (*color blue*))
...)

A string as the smallest unit that can appear as an element of a list is called an *atom*. For example, in the above, *object1*, *shape*, *circle*, and *large* are atoms, but (*shape circle*) is not an atom.

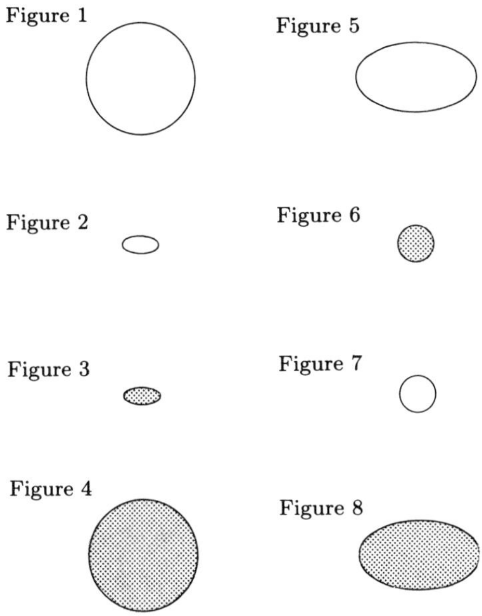

Figure 2.11 The world of objects

Now let us consider representing a tree as a list as another example. If we think of a list as a pair containing the name of a node and the list of its subnodes, a tree can be represented as a nested list of such lists. For example, let us look at the simple tree shown in Figure 2.12(a). The list of subnodes of the root 0 is (1 3 4), so we let the list $s_0 = (0\ (1\ 3\ 4))$. Similarly, we let the list $s_1 = (1\ (2))$ and $s_4 = (4\ (5\ 6))$ for the nodes 1 and 4, respectively. Since the nodes 2, 3, 5, 6 are leaves that do not have subnodes, we do not make a list for these nodes. Now, if we replace 1 and 4 in s_0 by s_1 and s_4, respectively, we will have the list $s = (0\ ((1\ (2))\ 3\ (4\ (5\ 6))))$. In this way, s is a list representation of the tree shown in Figure 2.12(a).

A group of symbols also can be represented as a set. For example, the names of the six prefectures in the Tohoku area can be represented as the set $B = \{$Aomori Akita Yamagata Iwate Miyagi Fukushima$\}$. According to the definition of a set, the set B is considered to be the same as another set such as $B' = \{$Aomori Akita Fukushima Iwate Miyagi Yamagata$\}$. As opposed to this, the lists of six prefectures in the Tohoku area, a and a' given earlier, are considered to be different. This is because a list is defined with the order of its elements and is thus a more structured object than a set.

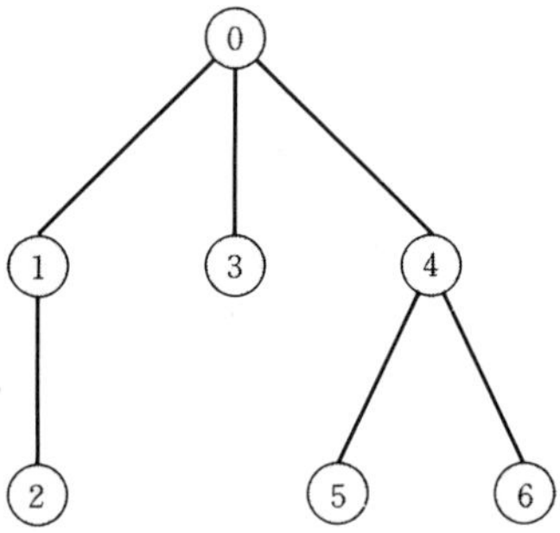

(0 ((1 (2)) 3 (4 (5 6))))

(a) A simple tree (b) A list representation of the tree

Figure 2.12 A tree and its list representation.

As we can see from the above, a tree can be represented simply using a list. Information we want to represent usually has some structure. List representation is used especially for symbolic information that can be placed in order or can be represented as a tree structure.

2.6 Predicate Logic Representation

(a) First-order predicate logic

The method of using *predicate logic* to represent information is even more structured than using lists. There are various forms of predicate logic. We will begin by looking at first-order predicate logic.

Consider the eight objects shown in Figure 2.11. In Section 2.5 we represented these objects using a list. We can also represent these using the three *predicates*, $shape(W, X)$, $size(W, Y)$, $color(W, Z)$. Here *shape*, *size*, and *color* are the names of the predicates and W, X, Y, Z are variables.

Intuitively, a predicate is a function from the domain of n variables $X_1 \times X_2 \times \cdots \times X_n$ to the set $\{T, F\}$ containing the two elements T and F. T and F represent whether the predicate is semantically *true* or *false* for the domain. (A more exact definition will be given later.) Whether the value of the function is T or F depends on the world we are considering. For example, in the world of Figure 2.8, $shape(W, X)$ can be thought of as a function from $X_1 \times X_2$ to the set $\{T, F\}$ where the set $X_1 = \{object1, object2, \ldots, object8\}$ and the set $X_2 = \{circle, ellipse\}$.

In this world, if we think of Object 1 as an object, then we will have $shape(object1,\ circle) = T$, $shape(object1, ellipse) = F$. In other words, for Object 1 we can read $shape(object1, circle) = T$ as "it is true that the shape of Object 1 is a circle" and $shape(object1, ellipse) = F$ as "it is false that the shape of Object 1 is an ellipse."

Now, we can represent Object 1 in Figure 2.11 as

$$shape(object1, circle) \wedge size(object1, large) \wedge color(object1, red)$$

$\wedge$ is the symbol for conjunction, and the above representation is a logical conjunction (this will be defined later). The representation means that "it is true that the shape of Object 1 is a circle, Object 1 is big, and Object 1 is red." This representation is an example of a *first-order predicate* representation. A first-order predicate can only bind an object to a variable. A predicate that can use another predicate as the value of a variable is called a second-order predicate. Further, it is possible to define nth-order predicate logic. Among those predicate logics, only first-order predicate logic has been proved to be effectively used on a computer. So, when we say predicate logic in this book, we will mean first-order predicate logic using first-order predicates, unless we specifically say something else.

We can interpret first-order predicate logic as a method for representing an object in a given world and describing relations among such objects using a group of predicates that take the value of true or false. In order to further understand this method of representation, let us give a formal definition of the rule for using first-order predicate logic as a form of representation.

(b) Symbols

We can define predicate logic by specifying the *symbols* we will use for description, the *syntax* that defines the possible expressions in the logic, and a *semantics* that gives meanings to the expressions allowed by syntax. First, we define the symbols used in building predicate logic expressions.

(1) Delimiters: ( ) { }

(2) Function symbols: f_i^n $(i \geq 1, n \geq 0)$
We call f_i^0 $(i \geq 1)$ a constant symbol. Below, we will write constant symbols as $a, b, c, \ldots$. Sometimes a constant symbol simply is called a constant. Function symbols where $n \geq 1$ are sometimes written $f, g, h, \ldots$.

(3) Predicate symbols: p_i^n $(i \geq 1, n \geq 0)$
We call p_i^0 $(i \geq 1)$ a propositional symbol. Below, we will write proposition symbols as $A, B, C, \ldots$. Predicate symbols where $n \geq 1$ are sometimes written $P, Q, \ldots$.

(4) Logical operators: $\sim \quad \rightarrow \quad \wedge \quad \vee \quad \forall \quad \exists$
They are called the negation symbol, the implication symbol, the conjunction symbol, the disjunction symbol, the universal quantifier, and the existential quantifier, respectively.

(c) Syntax

Expressions that can be formed using the symbols mentioned above are constructed using the following syntax:

(1) Term
- A constant symbol is a term.
- If s_i $(i = 1, \ldots, n)$ is a term, the expression f_j^n $(s_1, \ldots, s_n)$ is also a term.
- Only the expressions defined above are terms.

(2) Atomic formula
- A proposition symbol is an atomic formula.
- If s_i $(i = 1, \ldots, n)$ is a term, the expression p_j^n $(s_1, \ldots, s_n)$ is an atomic formula.
- Only the expressions defined above are atomic formulas.

(3) Well-formed formula
- An atomic formula is a well-formed formula.
- If X is a well-formed formula, $\sim X$ is also a well-formed formula.
- If X and Y are well-formed formulas, $X \rightarrow Y$ is also a well-formed formula.
- If X and Y are well-formed formulas, $\sim(X \rightarrow (\sim Y))$ is also a well-formed formula using the above definition. This well-formed formula can be written as $X \wedge Y$. $X \wedge Y$ is a well-formed formula. $X \wedge Y$ is the *logical conjunction* of X and Y.
- If X and Y are well-formed formulas, $(\sim X) \rightarrow Y$ is also a well-formed formula using the above definition. This well-formed formula can be written as $X \vee Y$. $X \vee Y$ is a well-formed formula. $X \vee Y$ is called the *logical disjunction* of X and Y.
- A *variable symbol* can be part of a well-formed formula X in the following way: First, we let $Z = \{z_1, \ldots, z_n\}$ be a set of constant symbols and V another symbol. We assume that V appears in X and write $X(V)$ instead of X to emphasize this fact. We write $X(z)$ for the expression formed by replacing $z \in Z$ for all occurrences of V in X. If each of $X(z_1), \ldots, X(z_k)$ is a well-formed formula, we call the symbol V a variable symbol with A as its domain. A variable symbol is written using a capital letter as in V. A variable symbol can also simply be called a variable. Variable symbols and constant symbols are both sometimes called *atoms*.
- Using the above definition of a variable symbol, the well-formed formula $X(z_1) \wedge X(z_2) \wedge \ldots \wedge X(z_k)$ can be written as $(\forall V)X(V)$. $(\forall V)X(V)$ is a well-formed formula.
- Although the above definition describes X as a function of one variable V, we generally can define $X(V_1, \ldots, V_m)$ as a function of m

variables $V_1, \ldots, V_m$. When $X(V_1, \ldots, V_m)$ is a term of the form $f_i^m(V_1, \ldots, V_m)$, we call X an *m-variable function (symbol)*. When it is an atomic formula whose form is $p_i^m(V_1, \ldots, V_m)$, we call X an *m-place predicate (symbol)*.

- The well-formed formula $\sim(\forall V)(\forall X(V))$ can be written as $(\exists V)X(V)$. $(\exists V)X(V)$ is a well-formed formula.
- Only the expressions defined above are well-formed formulas.

Based on the definition of syntax above, we can decide whether some expression is a well-formed formula or not. For example, $\sim P(a, f(b)) \wedge Q(f(a,b), g(a,b,d), d)$ is a well-formed formula, but $P(A(a))$ and $\sim g(a,b)$ are not.

Consider the following simple example: Suppose we have four sets of constant symbols, $W_0 = \{object1, object2, \ldots, object8\}$, $V_0 = \{circle, ellipse\}$, $Y_0 = \{large, small\}$, $Z_0 = \{red, blue\}$. Let W, V, Y, and Z be variable symbols whose domains are W_0, V_0, Y_0, and Z_0, respectively. Let *shape*, *size*, and *color* be predicate symbols. We then define the two-place predicates $shape(W, V)$, $size(W, Y)$, $color(W, Z)$ using these predicate symbols. $shape(object1, circle)$, $shape(object2, ellipse)$, $size(object1, small)$, and $color(object8, blue)$ are all atomic formulas. We can also see that

$$\sim shape(object3, circle)$$
$$shape(object1, circle) \rightarrow color(object1, red)$$
$$size(W, large) \wedge color(W, blue)$$
$$shape(W, circle) \wedge size(W, large) \vee shape(V, ellipse) \wedge color(W, blue)$$
$$(\forall W) shape(W, circle)$$
$$(\exists Y)(\exists Z) size(object2, Y) \wedge color(object2, Z)$$

are all well-formed formulas.

(d) Semantics

Suppose we have a set S that is not empty. We associate the elements of S to the symbols in a well-formed formula using the following operations:

(1) Let each element of S correspond to a constant symbol.
(2) Let each n-variable function symbol f_j^n $(n \geq 0)$ correspond to a function from S^n into S.
(3) Let each n-place predicate symbol p_i^n $(n \geq 0)$ correspond to an n-place relation on S^n.

Here, an n-place relation on S^n is a subset of $S \times S \times \cdots \times S$.

For example, let us write S for the union of the set of prefecture names and the set of real numbers, {Hokkaido, Aomori, Yamagata, Iwate, ...,

Kyoto, Osaka, ..., Okinawa$\} \cup R$. Here R is the set of real numbers. Let us apply the above operations (1)–(3) to the following well-formed formula:

$$more\_than(population(hokkaido), population(kyoto))$$

The constant symbols included in the above well-formed formula are *hokkaido* and *kyoto*. We associate the elements "Hokkaido" and "Kyoto" of S to these two constant symbols. Then, we must associate a function of one variable, $f(x)$, from S^1 into S with the one-variable function symbol *population*. We define f to be the function that, given a prefecture, returns the population (a real number) as its value and, given a real number, simply returns the same number. We also associate the two-place relation, $>$, on S^2, with the two-place predicate symbol *more_than*. Here $>$ has the following definition as a subset of $S \times S$:

$$\begin{aligned} \text{if } x \in R, y \in R, \text{and } x > y \ \ &\text{then } (x, y) \in > \\ &\text{otherwise } (x, y) \notin > \end{aligned}$$

As you can see, the symbols of a well-formed formula are meaningless in themselves. They become meaningful only when they are associated with elements of a world S, functions on such elements and relations between elements of S, and so on. For example, the predicate symbol *more_than* acquires meaning as the size relation between two real numbers only when we associate it with the relation $>$, which determines the size relation between two real numbers in the domain of real numbers.

Using (1)–(3) to associate a nonempty set with the symbols of a well-formed formula (or formulas) is called giving the well-formed formula (or formulas) an *interpretation*, and the underlying set S is called the *universe.* A well-formed formula becomes meaningful only when we specify an interpretation of that well-formed formula in some universe. Now, let us define "meaning" more clearly.

Suppose that given a well-formed formula and an interpretation of that formula in some universe, the value T (true) or F (false) is given to each atomic formula that is part of the well-formed formula. The values T and F are called *truth values.* If we start from the truth value of each atomic formula and repeatedly use the rules shown in Figure 2.13, we can determine the truth value of the whole well-formed formula. Here, we take the truth value of $(\forall V)X(V)$ to be the same as the truth value of $X(z_i) \wedge X(z_2) \wedge \ldots \wedge X(z_k)$ if the domain of the variable symbol V is the set of constant symbols $\{z_1, \ldots, z_k\}$. In other words, the truth value of $(\forall V)X(V)$ is T only when the truth values of $X(z_1)$ $(i = 1, \ldots, k)$ are all T. Similarly, the truth value of $(\exists V)X(V)$ is the same as the truth value of $X(z_1) \vee X(z_2) \vee \ldots \vee X(z_k)$. In other words, $(\exists V)X(V)$ takes the value T only when at least one of the truth values of $X(z_i)$ $(i = 1, \ldots, k)$ is T. We

X	Y	$\sim X$	$X \wedge Y$	$X \vee Y$	$X \rightarrow Y$
T	T	F	T	T	T
T	F	F	F	T	F
F	T	T	F	T	T
F	F	T	F	F	T

Figure 2.13 Truth values of a well-formed formula.

also agree that $\sim$, $\wedge$, $\vee$, $\rightarrow$ is the order for processing the logical operators when we obtain the truth value of a given well-formed formula.

For a given universe and interpretation, the "meaning" of a well-formed formula is the truth value of such a formula. Making a well-formed formula meaningful using this method is called the *model semantics* (of two-valued predicate logic). (The predicate logic is "two-valued" because it allows the use of only two truth values, T or F. Some people have studied logics that can take more than two truth values; however, we will not talk about these in this book.)

(e) Summary

Using the definitions of symbols, syntax, and semantics given above, we can determine the meaning of a well-formed formula. Predicate logic is a pair consisting of a set of well-formed formulas with the truth value of T (called axioms) and a set of operational rules (called inference rules, to be explained in Section 3.7).

Predicates in predicate logic and lists described in Section 2.5 look similar if we only consider what they look like when we write them down. For example, we represent the information "the shape of Object 1 is a circle" as *shape*(*object1*, *circle*) using the predicate *shape* in predicate logic. The same information is represented as (*object1 shape circle*) using a list representation. They look similar. However, there is a big difference between using predicates as a representation and the use of lists. Predicates implicitly have more structure because of their formally defined syntax and the way in which this can be used to assign them meaning. The only structure implicit in using a list is that the order of the elements is fixed and nesting is allowed. We need to keep this difference in mind and consider the structure of objects and the purpose of a system when we need to decide whether it is better to represent things in lists or predicate logic (or even to use some other kind of representation).

2.7 Horn Clause Logic Representation

Full predicate logic expressions have a rich structure, but they are sometimes too inefficient in processing on a computer. In this section, we will describe *Horn clause logic*, whose representation is more structured but generally more efficient in processing.

First we make some definitions. In predicate logic, an atomic formula or the negation of an atomic formula (a well-defined formula defined by an atomic formula with the negation operator, $\sim$, at its head) is called a *literal.* A literal not including $\sim$ is called a positive literal, and a literal including $\sim$ is called a negative literal. A literal not including a variable is called a *ground literal.* A well-formed formula combining literals using the disjunction operator $\vee$ is called a *clause form* or simply a *clause.*

It is known that any well-defined formula in the first-order predicate logic can be transformed into a clause form or a formula combining more than one clause form using the conjunction operator $\wedge$ (equivalently, a set of clause forms) without changing its meaning, in other words, without changing its truth value: T or F. There is an algorithm for changing a well-formed formula into a set of clause forms.

Since representing an idea using a clause form is simple and clear, it is important to think about using clause form representation when using first-order predicate logic. Let us write a clause form that includes only one positive literal as

$$\sim P_1 \vee \sim P_2 \vee \ldots \vee \sim P_m \vee Q$$

and a clause form not including any positive literal as

$$\sim P_1 \vee \sim P_2 \vee \ldots \vee \sim P_m$$

where $m \geq 0$.

A clause form written in this way is generally called a *Horn clause.* A Horn clause is, by definition, a clause form with at most one positive literal. By using the fact that the truth values of $\sim X \vee Y$ and $X \rightarrow Y$ are the same and by using the implication operator $\rightarrow$ (we use $\leftarrow$ for the implication operator and "," for the conjunction operator), a Horn clause can be rewritten as follows:

(1) $Q \leftarrow P_1, P_2, \ldots, P_m$
(2) $\leftarrow P_1, P_2, \ldots, P_m$
(3) Q
(4) $\leftarrow$

(3) and (4) are for $m = 0$. (2) and (4) are for a clause form that does not include a positive literal.

In a Horn clause, the left side of $\leftarrow$ is called the *head* and the right side is called the *body*. In (1)–(4) above, a Horn clause in format (2) is called a *goal*. In other words, a goal is a Horn clause without the head. A Horn clause in format (4) is called the *empty clause*.

We can think of a clause of format (3) as representing factual data if it contains only positive literals. On the other hand, (2) is equivalent to the disjunction of negative literals. We will explain why this is called a goal in Chapter 3.

Horn clauses are suitable for logic representation of factual data or of simple inference using factual data. For example, from the set of Horn clauses

$$\begin{array}{l} female(hanako) \\ male(taro) \\ mutual\_love(hanako, taro) \\ can\_marry(V_1, V_2) \leftarrow mutual\_love(V_1, V_2), female(V_1), male(V_2) \end{array}$$

we can easily infer that $can\_marry(hanako, taro)$ is true. We will explain the method of inference in Section 3.7.

2.8 Declarative Representation

Representations using bit patterns, graphs, trees, predicates, and so on are suitable for representing factual data such as visual patterns or the structure and characteristics of an object. These are called *declarative representations*, similar to the word "declaration" from programming languages. We can represent the fact "the small red box is on the big black box" using list representation as follows:

$$\begin{array}{l} ((on\ box1\ box2)(box1\ (class\ box)\ (size\ small)\ (color\ red)) \\ \ (box2\ (class\ box)\ (size\ large)\ (color\ black))) \end{array}$$

The same data can be represented as follows in predicate logic using a conjunction of well-formed formulas that take the value T:

$$\begin{array}{l} on(box1,\ box2) \wedge class(box1,\ box) \wedge size(box1,\ small) \\ \quad \wedge\ color(box1,\ red) \wedge class(box2,\ box) \wedge size(box2,\ large) \\ \quad \wedge\ color(box2,\ black) \end{array}$$

2.9 Procedural Representation

As opposed to declarative representation, it is possible to represent information in the form of a procedure for interpreting data. For example, the fact "the small red box is on the big black box" can be represented procedurally using the following three "imperative" statements:

(1) Remove all the objects on the small red box.
(2) Remove all the objects on the big black box.
(3) Put the small red box on the big black box.

Each imperative can be written as a procedure. Below we use *store* for the procedure for storing a property of an object x with its value, *cleartop* for the procedure for removing all the objects on the object x, and *puton* for the procedure for putting the object y on the object x. We call the whole procedure (1)–(3) *make_on*. The statements above can then be written as the following procedure:

```
Procedure  make_on
 argument  x y
   procedure store
     argument x
      : Store the list ((class box) (size small) (color red))
        as a pair of the property of x and its value.
   procedure  store
     argument y
      : Store the list ((class box) (size large) (color black))
        as a pair of the property of y and its value.
   procedure cleartop
     argument x
      : remove all the objects on x.
   procedure cleartop
     argument y
      : remove all the objects on y.
   procedure puton
     argument x y
      : put x on y.
```

Using this version of *make_on*, if we replace the arguments x and y with *box*1 (the small red box) and *box*2 (the big black box), respectively, and execute *make_on*, we will obtain "the small red box is on the big black box."

To represent facts by procedures is generally called *procedural representation*. The above example shows one kind of procedural representation using a function as the procedure. Procedural representation is suitable for knowledge about doing something. For example, in order to represent knowledge of how to solve a simple equation, we usually describe the solution as an algorithm, which is a form of procedural representation.

Although it is more difficult to represent factual data using a procedural representation than a declarative representation, the procedural representation has the following two advantages:

(1) Since it describes data as a collection of subprocedures, it is possible to have a flexible representation system by replacing some subprocedures with other procedures or reordering them.

(2) As you can see in the above example of *make_on*, some factual data are better interpreted procedurally. It is sometimes better to represent such facts using a procedural representation.

For example, we can obtain the procedure for getting "two objects are stuck together" by simply changing the subprocedure *puton* inside of *make_on* to a procedure for gluing two objects together. Using this procedure, we can represent the fact "the small red box and the big black box are stuck together." This is an example of using advantage (1). However, the structure and the content of a procedural representation tend to be complicated and individual. It is easy to lose the direct perspective of declarative representation. In order to prevent this, we often restrict the definition of a procedural representation by allowing only predefined forms of representation. Section 2.10 shows an example of this kind.

2.10 Representation Using Rules

One kind of procedural representation is of the form "if ... is satisfied, then do ...." The procedure *cleartop* in the procedure *make_on* shown in Section 2.9 can be represented as "if 'the object x exists' is satisfied, then remove all the objects on x."

Generally, the form of this representation is a pair consisting of a set of *conditions* and a sequence of *actions*. This is called a *production rule*, or simply a *rule*. A rule is usually written

$$\text{(condition\_1)(condition\_2)} \ldots \text{(condition\_}m\text{)}$$
$$\Rightarrow \text{(action\_1)(action\_2)} \ldots \text{(action\_}n\text{)}$$

Sometimes the left side of the symbol $\Rightarrow$, the condition side, is called the *left-hand side* and the right side, the action side, is called the *right-hand side*. In order to describe a rule, we need to determine how to represent conditions and actions. The most popular method is to use a list for a condition and a procedural representation for an action. For example, the following rule, which can be used by Ichiro while in Osaka, is described using this method of representation:

$$\begin{array}{l}(osaka\ temperature\ hot)(osaka\ weather\ fine)\\ (ichiro\ health\_state\ healthy)\\ \qquad \Rightarrow (*open\ osaka\ windows)(*takeoff\ ichiro\ shirt)\end{array}$$

**open* and **takeoff* are procedures for "opening" windows and "taking off" shirts, respectively. Using this method of representation, the symbol $\Rightarrow$ is meant to join the left-hand side and the right-hand side procedually. In order to define this combination correctly, we need to define the execution procedure for this rule. There are many possible execution procedures that could be used for a rule, and in Section 3.8 we will give some examples of such procedures.

The above method is not the only method for representing a rule. Another one is to use predicate logic expressions for both the conditions and the actions. The following rule is an example:

$$\begin{array}{l}size(object1,\ large),\ color(object1,\ red)\\ \qquad \Rightarrow shape(object1,\ circle)\end{array}$$

This rule can be interpreted as "If Object1 is big and red, then the shape of this object is a circle." In other words, the left-hand side of the rule is a conjunction, $\wedge$, and $\Rightarrow$ acts as an implication operator $\rightarrow$. With such an understanding, the above rule is simply a well-formed formula and is a declarative representation rather than a procedural one. In order to interpret this rule procedurally, we need to define a procedure for executing the rule. Section 3.7 will explain such a procedure.

Since the examples of rules mentioned above do not include variables, their descriptive capability is limited. Usually, a rule is set up so that it can contain variables. Let us look at the following rule that introduces variables into the two rules above:

$$\begin{array}{l}(\$y\ temperature\ hot)(\$y\ weather\ fine)(\$x\ health\_state\ healthy)\\ \qquad \Rightarrow (*open\ \$y\ windows)(*takeoff\ \$x\ shirt)\\ size(Z, large), color(Z, red) \Rightarrow shape(Z, circle)\end{array}$$

In these rules, $\$x$, $\$y$, and Z are variables. By using variables in this way, we are able to obtain a rule that works not only for specific objects such as Ichiro, Osaka, and object1 but also for many other objects.

2.11 Semantic Networks and Frames

(a) Semantic networks

The representation methods we have described so far are popular methods for representing information in a computer. However, they are not perfect. One of their defects is that the declarative representations used in these methods by themselves are not always effective in representing complex relations among many objects. Let us look at the following structure:

$$\{(day\ isa\text{: } time\_instant)$$
$$(day\ year\text{: } \langle integer\rangle)$$
$$(day\ month\text{: } \langle month\_name\rangle)$$
$$(day\ day\_number\text{ : } \langle integer\rangle)$$
$$(day\ day\_of\_week\text{ : } \langle weekday\_name\rangle)\}$$

This provides a symbolic representation of the notion "day." Variables are written using $\langle \ldots \rangle$. Each element in this set is represented as a list, but if we consider the first element and the third element as nodes and the second element as the label of the edge from the first element to the third element, the whole set can be thought of as a graph (Figure 2.14 shows what this graph looks like.) This representation method is generally called a *semantic network.* Although the graph in Figure 2.14 consists only of edges that are going outward from the node *day* as the center, a semantic network generally can have a more complicated graph structure.

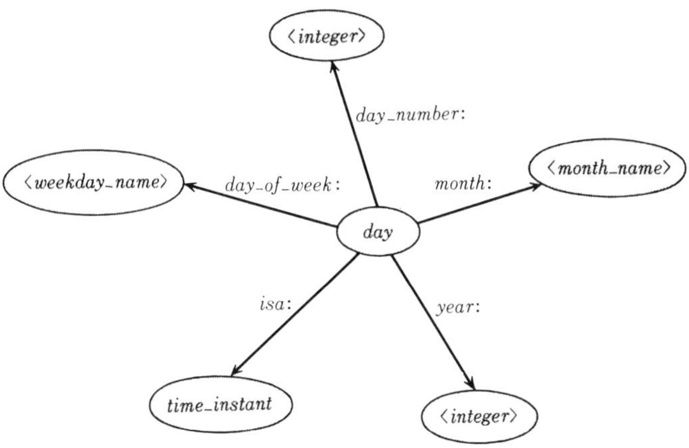

Figure 2.14 A semantic network representation of "day."

(b) Frames

A semantic network can represent an attribute-value pair by placing the attribute at the label of an edge and the value at the destination node. However, when we try to use attribute-value pairs to do inference, it is frequently the case that the value of an attribute is unknown or the value may need to be replaced. In such cases, we can represent the structure of an object using a set of pairs consisting of a *slot* for naming the attribute and a *filler* for containing the value. This form of representation is called a *frame*.

Frame representations can describe various objects simply by describing the representations used in some of their slots and fillers. For example, we can give a typical value to the filler for some particular slot. This typical value is called the *default value* for the slot.

Generally, a frame is thought of as a declarative representation, but frames may also include procedural information.

Frames and semantic networks can relatively easily represent the structure of classes of objects. Suppose we want to represent the types and properties of birds. For example, let us suppose we have two facts: "a swallow is a bird" and "a bird flies." We need to make sure that "a swallow flies" can be inferred by showing that "a swallow" is one type of "a bird," without having to represent the fact "a swallow flies" explicitly.

Generally, when we have

$$(\$x \ \textit{isa}\colon \$y)$$
$$(\$y \ \textit{attribute}\colon \$z)$$

we can automatically infer $(\$x \ \textit{attribute}\colon \$z)$. In the case of a swallow, where we have

$$(\textit{swallow isa}\colon \textit{bird})$$
$$(\textit{bird attribute}\colon \textit{canfly})$$

we can infer $(\textit{swallow attribute}\colon \textit{canfly})$. In this representation method, we say that the property of being a "bird" is inherited by a "swallow." Or, based on the class structure, we can say that a "swallow" is a type of a "bird."

Generally, for frames and semantic networks, the fact that a low-level node automatically has the features of a higher-level node is called property *inheritance.* A node can have more than one node above it. For example, the nodes above "a swallow" may not only be "a bird" but could also be "a thing that has a tail." This form of inheritance is called *multiple inheritance.*

In order to represent the structure of classes, we can use other attributes than the attribute *isa*: that represents the relation "is a type of ...." For example, we can infer the fact that "a point a is a part of the tetrahedron $abcd$" from the two facts "the point a is a part of the triangle abc" and "the triangle abc is a part of the tetrahedron $abcd$." In order to make this inference, we can represent the point a, the triangle abc, and the tetrahedron $abcd$ in a hierarchical structure using the attribute *partof*: to represent the relation "is a part of ...."

(c) Procedural attachment

Another reason why the representation methods we have described up to Section 2.10 are not perfect is that the declarative and the procedural parts of the representation are separated. Let us look at the semantic network shown in Figure 2.14. Some constants have replaced variables in this representation. In order to check whether it was correct to replace a variable with a constant, we describe a procedure for checking the variable that corresponds to the constant that is being replaced.

In Figure 2.14, the value of x to be substituted for ⟨*integer*⟩ under the attribute *day_number* : should be $1 \leq x \leq 30$ if the value of *month*:, ⟨*month_name*⟩, is April, June, September, or November; $1 \leq x \leq 31$ if the value is January, March, May, July, August, October, or December; $1 \leq x \leq 29$ if the value is February and it is a leap year; $1 \leq x \leq 28$ if the value is February and it is not a leap year. Any value other than these would be an error. (We are excluding the exception that happens only once every 400 years.) For this procedure we can write a function that checks the relation between ⟨*integer*⟩ and ⟨*month_name*⟩ given the value ⟨*integer*⟩ of the *day_number* :. This function, which we call *when_filled*, will be evaluated automatically whenever a value is placed at ⟨*integer*⟩.

Attaching a procedure to the declarative representation is called *procedural attachment*. It is possible to attach many kinds of procedures besides *when_filled*. A bottom-up procedure that is automatically executed is called a *demon*. In general, procedures used for procedural attachment are demons. Not only functions but also other procedural representations such as production rules can be used for procedural attachment.

In addition to what we have described here, there are many other methods for representation. Object-oriented representation is a method of representing related objects. Representation treating not only space but also time is also important. We will describe some other methods when they appear later in this book.

2.12 Representation Using Fourier Series

What we described in Section 2.1 can be thought of as a method for approximately representing a pattern function using a function with a discrete domain. There are other methods that represent a pattern function with a more continuous function.

We will describe Fourier series expansion as one such method. Below we will use a real-valued function on the real numbers; however, our explanation can be extended to more general pattern functions.

If a function $f(x)$ satisfies some appropriate conditions, it can be evaluated using a series of the following form:

$$f(x) = \frac{a_0}{2} \sum_n \left(a_n \cos \frac{n\pi}{L} x + b_n \sin \frac{n\pi}{L} x \right) \quad (n = 1, 2, \ldots) \tag{2.1}$$

where L is a constant. In this case, $2L$ represents the period of the trigonometric functions. The coefficient of each term is

$$a_0 = \frac{1}{L} \int_{-L}^{L} f(x)\, dx \tag{2.2}$$

$$a_n = \frac{1}{L} \int_{-L}^{L} f(x) \cos \frac{n\pi}{L} x\, dx \tag{2.3}$$

$$b_n = \frac{1}{L} \int_{-L}^{L} f(x) \sin \frac{n\pi}{L} x\, dx \tag{2.4}$$

This series expansion is called a *Fourier series expansion* or simply a Fourier series.

Let us look at the Fourier series of the following function:

$$f(x) = \cos x \quad \left(-\frac{\pi}{2} \leq x \leq \frac{\pi}{2} \right) \tag{2.5}$$

A function $f(x)$ is a function of period $2L = \pi$ (see Figure 2.15(a)). From the formulas (2.2), (2.3), and (2.4), we obtain

$$a_0 = \frac{1}{\frac{\pi}{2}} \int_{-\frac{\pi}{2}}^{\frac{\pi}{2}} \cos x\, dx = \frac{4}{\pi}$$

$$a_n = \frac{1}{\frac{\pi}{2}} \int_{-\frac{\pi}{2}}^{\frac{\pi}{2}} \cos x \cos \frac{n\pi}{\frac{\pi}{2}} x\, dx = \frac{2}{\pi} \frac{(-1)^n(-2)}{4n^2 - 1} \cos n\pi$$

$$b_n = \frac{1}{\frac{\pi}{2}} \int_{-\frac{\pi}{2}}^{\frac{\pi}{2}} \cos x \sin \frac{n\pi}{\frac{\pi}{2}} x\, dx = 0$$

In this way we can represent the Fourier series of the function $f(x)$ as follows:

$$f(x) = \frac{4}{\pi}\left(\frac{1}{2} + \frac{1}{3}\cos 2x - \frac{1}{15}\cos 4x + \frac{1}{35}\cos 6x - \frac{1}{63}\cos 8x + \cdots\right) \quad (2.6)$$

If we write the function as $f_k(x)$, the sum of the right-hand side of formula (2.6) up to the kth term, then $f_k(x)$ can be thought of as the kth approximate representation of $f(x)$. Figure 2.15(b) shows $f_2(x)$ and $f_3(x)$. $f_2(x)$ and $f_3(x)$ give an (approximate) representation of $f(x)$.

When a set of real-valued functions, $\{g_i(x)\}$, is given and the following is true for the integrals of $g_i(x)$ on the interval $[a, b]$:

$$\int_a^b g_k(x)g_l(x)dx \begin{cases} = 0 & (k \neq l) \\ \neq 0 & (k = l) \end{cases}$$

then $\{g_i(x)\}$ is called a *system of orthogonal functions.* If a function $f(x)$ can be represented in the following form using a system of orthogonal functions $\{g_i(x)\}$:

$$f(x) = c_1g_1(x) + c_2g_2(x) + \cdots + c_ig_i(x) + \cdots \quad (2.7)$$

this formula is called an *orthogonal expansion* of $f(x)$.

If a function has an orthogonal expansion, we can represent it using just an array of coefficients such as c_i $(i = 1, 2, \ldots)$ in (2.7). The Fourier series expansion above is one of the representation methods that provide orthogonal expansions.

2.13 Classification of Representation Methods

Let us organize the various representation methods we have described. We classify them into three aspects:

(1) Pattern representation and symbolic representation
(2) Declarative representation and procedural representation
(3) Distributed representation and local representation

We will describe (1) first. So far, "pattern" and "symbol" do not have any unified definition. In this book, "pattern" means "information in that one element itself does not mean anything and the relation between elements as a whole means something." "Symbol" means "information in that each element means something." Using these definitions, we will call representations using patterns and representations using symbols *pattern*

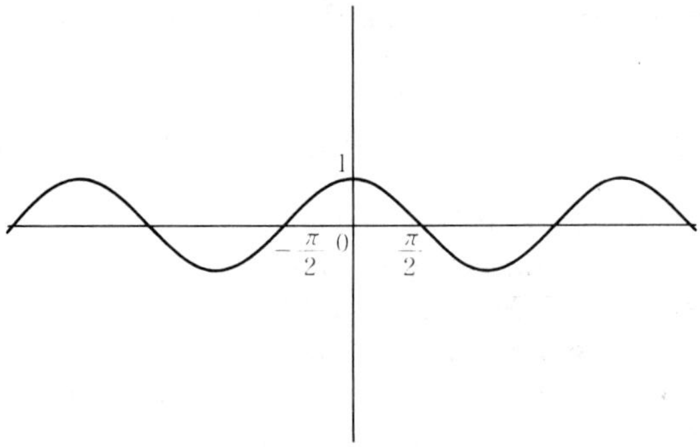

(a) $f(x) = \cos x$

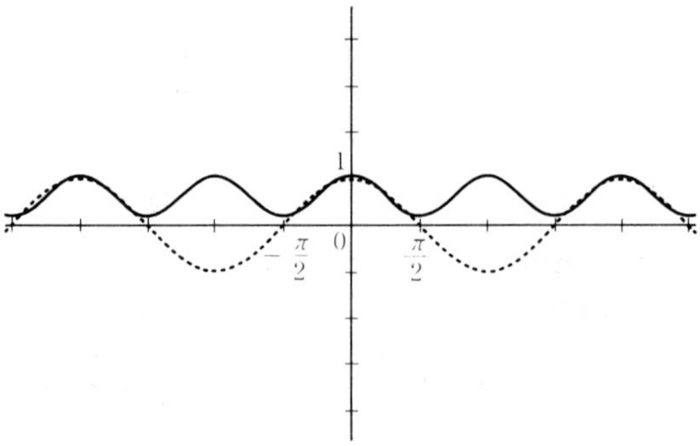

(b) $f_2(x) = \dfrac{2}{\pi} + \dfrac{4}{3\pi}\cos 2x$

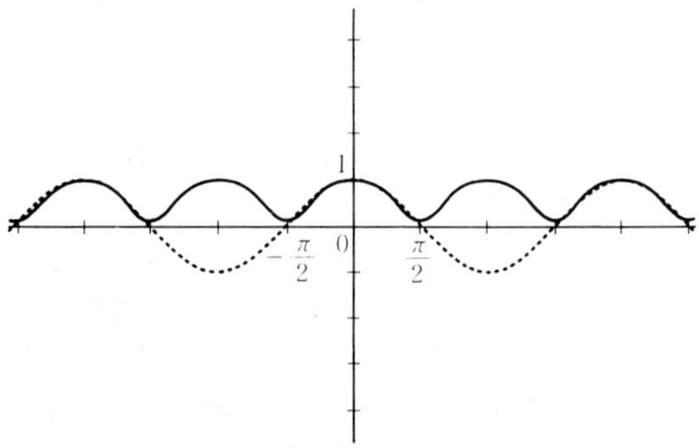

(c) $f_3(x) = \dfrac{2}{\pi} + \dfrac{4}{3\pi}\cos 2x - \dfrac{4}{15\pi}\cos 4x$

Figure 2.15 Fourier series for a periodic function.

representations and *symbolic representations*, respectively. We now know that the pattern functions or the bit patterns described in Section 2.1 are examples of pattern representations. Representations using graphs, lists, predicate logic, semantic networks, frames, and so on are examples of symbolic representations since each element of the representation has a meaning. Basically, this view of the definition of pattern and symbol comes from the idea of model semantics described in Section 2.6, but there are many other methods for defining information.

Now let us look at (2). From Sections 2.8 and 2.9, we know that representation can be divided into declarative and procedural representation. It is handy to represent concepts and facts using a declarative representation. On the other hand, it is helpful to represent our knowledge of how to do things using a procedural representation. Both representation methods are more for symbolic representation than for pattern representation.

Finally, let us consider (3). In a *distributed representation* information is distributed throughout the pattern. A *local representation* is one in which each constituent of the information is localized. Distributed and localized representations can be identified mostly with pattern and symbolic representations, respectively, though the former pays attention to whether the representation is distributed throughout the structure or is localized, while the latter pays attention to the difference in the (model semantic) meaning of the information.

From the viewpoint of the information being represented, the classifications (1)–(3) are overlapping and the representation of any information can be classified by any of (1)–(3). For example, Figure 1.2 shows how a coffee cup on a table can be represented using several different methods.

Any information can be represented using many different methods. Which method is the most appropriate depends on the problem and the context in which the problem is to be solved. In this chapter we have shown the most popular methods.

Summary

In this chapter we explained some basic methods for representing information in a computer in order to do pattern recognition and learning by a computer.

2.1 Methods of representing information in a computer can be classified by the dichotomies of pattern and symbolic representation, declarative and procedural representation, distributed and local representation, and so on.

2.2 Pattern representations include those with pattern functions using sampled and quantized data, orthogonal expansions of functions, spatial structures, graphs, and trees.

2.3 There are many methods of symbolic representation such as using graphs, trees, lists, predicates, and so on.

2.4 The symbolic representation of information with a complicated structure includes representations using rules, semantic networks, and frames.

Keywords

pattern function, pattern element, bit pattern, Fourier series expansion, system of orthogonal functions, orthogonal expansion, spatial representation, wire-frame representation, metric representation, topological representation, graph, path, connected graph, subgraph, clique, feedforward graph, network, label, weight, tree, n-tree, list, predicate logic, first-order predicate logic, Horn clause logic, declarative representation, procedural representation, rule representation, production rule, semantic network, frame, inheritance, multiple inheritance, procedural attachment, object-oriented representation, pattern representation, symbolic representation, distributed representation, local representation

Exercises

2.1 Write a program that is given as input a bit pattern representing a polyhedron in which the value of each pattern element on the edges of the polyhedron is 1 and the rest of the values are 0, as shown in Figure 2.16, and that outputs the list of the coordinates of all the vertices. You can assume that there is only one polyhedron and there is no loss of data or noise. Use any programming language.

2.2 For a tree $G = (N, E)$, suppose that the numbers of nodes and edges are $|N|$ and $|E|$, respectively. Prove $|E| = |N| - 1$.

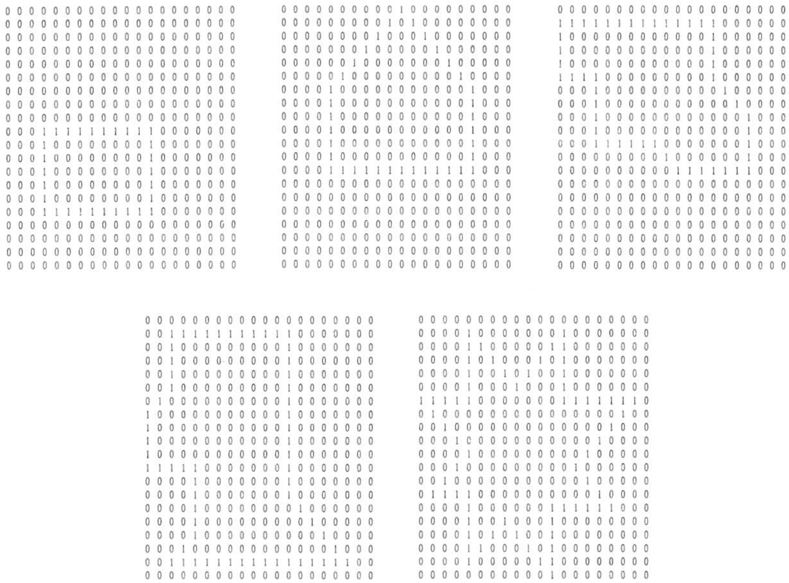

Figure 2.16 A bit pattern representing a polyhedron.

2.3 Suppose we have two nodes $n_o, n_d \in N$ in a weighted directed graph $G = (N, E, W)$. Describe an algorithm for finding a shortest route from n_o to n_d.

2.4 Write a program that receives a list as input and outputs the list of its elements in reverse order. For example, if (*red green yellow blue*) is the input, the program should output (*blue yellow green red*).

2.5 Of the following expressions, which are well-formed formulas of the first-order predicate logic? Let P, Q and R be predicate symbols; f and g function symbols; a, b, and c constant symbols; and W, X, Y, and Z variable symbols.

(a) $P(a(a, b, c))$
(b) $P(f(X, Y)) \wedge Q(g(X), Y, Z) \vee F(f(a, b), G(c))$
(c) $F(p(X), Q(Y, Z, W))$
(d) $(\forall X)(P(X) \rightarrow Q(X, f(X, Y), c)$
(e) $(\exists X)(\forall Y)(\sim R(X, Y) \wedge P(X) \wedge Q(a, Y, X))$
(f) $(\forall X)(\exists Y)(\sim R(X, Y) \wedge P(X) \wedge Q(a, P(Y), X))$

2.6 Represent the following sentences using production rules:

(a) "If it is raining, wear a raincoat and use an umbrella."

(b) "If the light is out but the switch is on, check whether the filament is broken."
(c) "If the light is out, the switch is on, and the filament is not broken, check whether the fuse is out."

2.7 Give a semantic network for the following objects:

(a) an animal, a thing that can fly, a machine, a calculable thing, a human being, an ostrich, a computer, a thing that can run, a robot, a lion, a snake, a television, an airplane.
(b) a face, a right eyeball, a left eyeball, a right eye, a left eye, a nose, a mouth, a left cheek, a right cheek, a forehead, a chin, an eye, an elbow, a cheek, the upper part of a face, the middle part of a face, the lower part of a face.

3 Generation and Transformation of Representations

This chapter gives some basic methods for generating new representations and for transforming a given representation into another representation. The generation and transformation of representations can be regarded as procedures for creating output that is represented differently from the one used as input. Each method depends on the type of representation used. We will describe the linear transformation of patterns, the generation of spatial structure representations, the generation of trees, problem solving by heuristic search, inference in predicate logic, inference using rules, and inference using frames. These methods, along with those in Chapter 2, are the fundamental techniques needed to understand Chapter 4 and later chapters. There are many methods for the generation and transformation of representations. What we describe in this chapter are examples of these methods.

3.1 Methods of Generating and Transforming Representations

The generation and transformation of different representations can be thought of as procedures for creating output information whose form of representation is different from that of the input information. "Generation" and "transformation" are not very different. We call the process "generation" when we direct our attention to a newly created form of representation and "transformation" when we are interested in the process of making one representation from another.

Let us look at an example:

[Example Problem] Suppose we have the two-dimensional bit pattern shown in Figure 3.1. Transform this so that it is represented by a spatial structure. Also transform it into a graph.

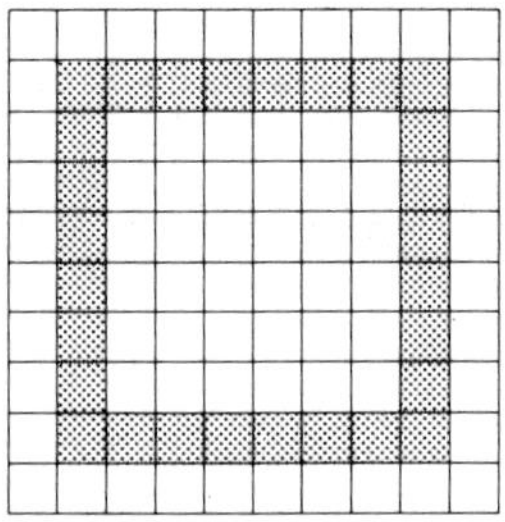

Figure 3.1 A bit pattern representation of a square.

We represent the two-dimensional bit pattern in Figure 3.1 using the set $A = \{f(x,y) | 0 \leq x \leq 9, 0 \leq y \leq 9,\ x,\ y \text{ integer}\}$. In A, when a point (x,y) corresponds to ▩ , we let $f(x,y) = 1$, and when it corresponds to □ , we let $f(x,y) = 0$. The only set of four points such that $f(x,y) = f(x \cdot 1, y) = f(x, y \cdot 1) = 1$ (where $\cdot$ is $+$ or $-$) is $(1,1), (1,8), (8,1), (8,8)$. We can see that by simply checking each point, (x,y), where $f(x,y) = 1$. A little thought will show that this criterion uniquely determines a square. Another way of looking at this is to consider the points that can be reached by changing only either one of the x and y coordinates. For example, the four points (1,1), (8,1), (8,8), (1,8) are in this order. We can write this as $B = ((1,1), (8,1), (8,8), (1,8))$. Here B is the spatial structure representation described in Section 2.2 that results from transforming the original representation A.

Let us now transform the representation B into a graph representation. Suppose we write B in the form (b_1, b_2, b_3, b_4) and represent the relation that a point in B is "next to" another point by the label "neighbor." When each of b_i $(i = 1, \ldots, 4)$ is a node and b_{i+1} is next to b_i, and if we define the directed edge from b_i to b_{i+1} and give it the label "neighbor," we obtain the graph shown in Figure 3.2. If we call this graph C, C is a graph representation obtained by transforming B.

The example above shows a particular transformation method that is closely tied only to this example. In the following sections, we will look at more general methods for transforming various representations.

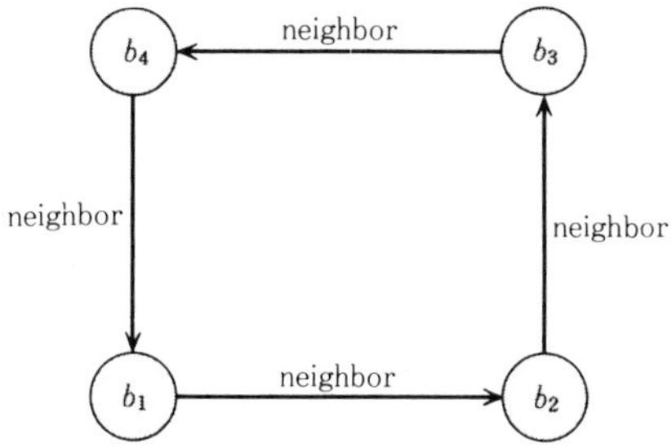

Figure 3.2 A graph representation of Figure 3.1.

3.2 Linear Transformations of Pattern Functions

A pattern function defined on a continuous domain usually includes noise and is based on incomplete data. In such a case, it may be more convenient to transform it into some other function in order to find some additional information or structure in a form of the new function. Among the methods for transforming a pattern function on a continuous domain to another function, we first describe the use of linear transformations.

Throughout this book, we will omit detailed descriptions of assumptions that need to be made about the functions we are looking at. These include the continuity, differentiability, and boundedness of functions as well as the cardinality of the set of local maxima and minima of the functions. Basically, we assume that what we describe in this book will be true for functions that are bounded, second-order differentiable, and satisfy appropriate boundary conditions.

(a) Convolution integral

First, we describe the following simple method of transforming a pattern function. Let us consider the situation where a pattern function $f(x, y)$ is transformed into another pattern function $g(x, y)$ using the transformation h shown in Figure 3.3. In other words, $g(x, y) = h(f(x, y))$.

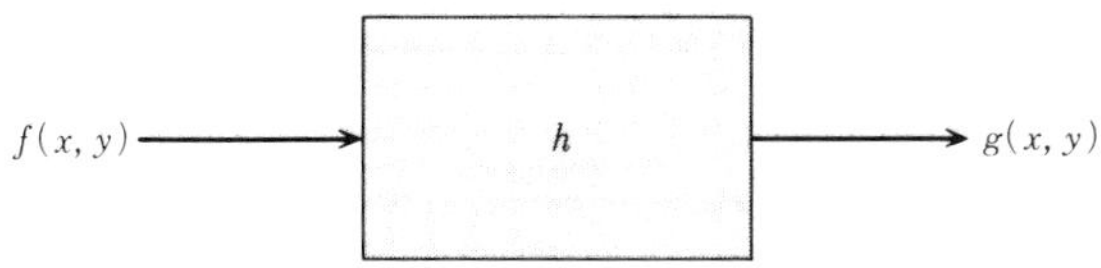

Figure 3.3 A linear transformation of a pattern function.

Let us also assume that the following property is true for x and y in the two pattern functions, $f_1(x, y)$ and $f_2(x, y)$, for some real constants r and s:

$$h(rf_1(x, y) + sf_2(x, y)) = rh(f_1(x, y)) + sh(f_2(x, y))$$

A transformation h with this property is called a *linear transformation.* We now look at the function $\delta(x, y)$ with the following property:

$$\delta(x, y) = \begin{cases} \infty & \text{if } x = y = 0 \\ 0 & \text{otherwise} \end{cases}$$

$$\int_{-\infty}^{\infty} \int_{-\infty}^{\infty} \delta(x, y)\ dx\ dy = 1$$

The function with such characteristics is generally called the (two-dimensional) *delta function* (δ function). The intuitive form of the delta function is illustrated in Figure 3.4.

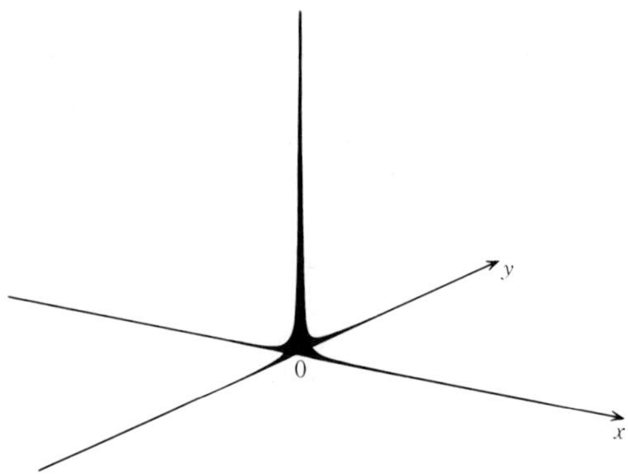

Figure 3.4 A picture of the (two-dimensional) delta function.

Using the definition above, we can represent the transformation h using the delta function. First, we can obtain the value of $f(x, y)$ at the point (a, b) by evaluating

$$f(a, b) = \int_{-\infty}^{\infty} \int_{-\infty}^{\infty} f(x, y)\delta(x - a, y - b)\ dx\ dy$$

In this equation, a, b and x, y can be exchanged. Namely,

$$f(x, y) = \int_{-\infty}^{\infty} \int_{-\infty}^{\infty} f(a, b)\delta(a - x, b - y)\ da\ db \tag{3.1}$$

Also, we let

$$\phi(x, y, a, b) = h(\delta(x - a, y - b))$$

This ϕ is called the *point spread function* or the *impulse response* of the transformation h. It is called a point spread function because a function with a value only at one point like the delta function in Figure 3.4 can "spread" its value through the transformation h. The point spread function ϕ is obtained by using the function h to transform the delta function that takes the value ∞ only at the point $(x, y) = (a, b)$. We are assuming here that ϕ has the same form independent of the location of (a, b). In other words, we assume that $\phi(x, y, a, b)$ can always be expressed as $\phi(x-a, y-b)$. Such a ϕ is called a *shift-invariant* point spread function.

When ϕ is a shift-invariant point spread function, we have

$$\begin{aligned}
g(x,y) &= h(f(x,y)) \\
&= h\left(\int_{-\infty}^{\infty}\int_{-\infty}^{\infty} f(a,b)\delta(a-x,b-y)\ da\ db\right) \\
&\qquad \text{from (3.1)} \\
&= \int_{-\infty}^{\infty}\int_{-\infty}^{\infty} f(a,b)h(\delta(a-x,b-y))\ da\ db \\
&\qquad h \text{ is a linear transformation} \qquad\qquad (3.2) \\
&= \int_{-\infty}^{\infty}\int_{-\infty}^{\infty} f(a,b)\phi(x-a,y-b)\ da\ db \\
&\qquad \phi \text{ is shift-invariant} \\
&= \int_{-\infty}^{\infty}\int_{-\infty}^{\infty} f(a,b)f(x-a,y-b)\phi(a,b)\ da\ db \\
&\qquad \text{a variable transformation of the integral}
\end{aligned}$$

In equation (3.2), intuitively, the function $g(x, y)$, which is the result of transforming the function $f(x, y)$ using h, represents the sum of the product of the original function $f(x, y)$ and the point spread function $\phi(a, b)$ while keeping x and y fixed and varying a and b. Generally, an integral of the form

$$\int_{-\infty}^{\infty} p(x-\tau)q(\tau)\ d\tau$$

or, in two-dimensional form, a double integral

$$\int_{-\infty}^{\infty}\int_{-\infty}^{\infty} p(x-\tau_1, y-\tau_2)q(\tau_1,\tau_2)\ d\tau_1\ d\tau_2$$

is called a *convolution integral* and is written $p(x) * q(x)$ or $p(x, y) * q(x, y)$. Using this convolution integral, equation (3.2) can be written

$$g(x,y) = f(x,y) * \phi(x,y)$$

Thus the new pattern g that can be obtained by applying the linear transformation h to f will be a convolution integral of f and a point spread function ϕ.

(b) Fourier transform

Although the convolution integral is an important method of performing a linear transformation on a pattern function, it is sometimes difficult to calculate the integral. Instead we can transform the convolution integral over a spatial domain (x, y) to a representation in another domain, do the calculation in that space, and retransform the result to the original (x, y) space. The frequency domain is often used for the alternative domain. We will now explain the Fourier transform as such a transformation.

If we rewrite equation (2.1) for the Fourier transform described in Section 2.12 into the complex function form using the Euler formula

$$\cos x = (e^{jx} + e^{-jx})/2, \quad \sin x = (e^{jx} - e^{-jx})/2j$$

where $j^2 = -1$, we get

$$f(x) = \sum_{k=-\infty}^{\infty} d_k e^{kj\pi x/L} \tag{3.3}$$

$$d_0 = \frac{a_0}{2}, \quad d_k = \frac{a_k - jb_k}{2}, \quad d_{-k} = \frac{a_k + jb_k}{2}$$

Therefore, we generally obtain the following:

$$d_k = \frac{1}{2L} \int_{-L}^{L} f(x) e^{-kj\pi x/L} \, dx \tag{3.4}$$

If

$$\omega_k = \frac{k\pi}{L}, \quad \Delta\omega = \omega_k - \omega_{k-1} = \frac{\pi}{L} \tag{3.5}$$

$$G(\omega) = \frac{1}{2\pi} e^{j\omega x} \int_{-L}^{L} f(s) e^{-j\omega s} \, ds \tag{3.6}$$

we will get the following from expressions (3.3)–(3.6):

$$f(x) = \sum_{k=-\infty}^{\infty} G(\omega_k) \Delta\omega$$

If we make $L \to \infty$ and thus $\Delta\omega \to 0$, under appropriate conditions, we will get

$$f(x) = \int_{-\infty}^{\infty} \left[\frac{1}{2\pi} e^{j\omega x} \int_{-\infty}^{\infty} f(s) e^{-j\omega s} \, ds \right] d\omega \tag{3.7}$$

Expression (3.7) is called the *Fourier integral.* If we make

$$F(\omega) = \mathcal{F}(f(x)) = \frac{1}{2\pi}\int_{-\infty}^{\infty} f(s)e^{-j\omega s}\,ds \tag{3.8}$$

(3.7) can be rewritten as

$$f(x) = \mathcal{F}^{-1}(F(\omega)) = \int_{-\infty}^{\infty} F(\omega)e^{j\omega x}\,d\omega \tag{3.9}$$

Equation (3.8) is called a *Fourier transform* and equation (3.9) is called an *inverse Fourier transform.* Figure 3.5 shows an example of a Fourier transform.

So far we have used functions of one variable. Let us extend our representation to include functions of two variables and, at the same time, make the appropriate variable transformation. Using the function $\exp(-2\pi j(ux + vy))$ on the two-dimensional frequency domain (u, v), the function $f(x, y)$ on the spatial domain (x, y) can be transformed to the following function in the frequency domain:

$$F(u,v) = \int_{-\infty}^{\infty}\int_{-\infty}^{\infty} f(x,y)\exp(-2\pi j(ux+vy))\,dx\,dy \tag{3.10}$$

This transformation is one of the forms for the (two-dimensional) Fourier transform. u and v are called the *spatial frequencies.* The Fourier transform $F(u, v)$ for $f(x, y)$ is written $\mathcal{F}(f(x, y))$.

The transform from the frequency domain to the spatial domain can be defined as

$$f(x,y) = \int_{-\infty}^{\infty}\int_{-\infty}^{\infty} F(u,v)\exp(2\pi j(ux+vy))\,du\,dv \tag{3.11}$$

This transform is the (two-dimensional) inverse Fourier transform. The inverse Fourier transform of $F(u, v)$ is written $\mathcal{F}^{-1}(F(u, v))$.

There are many relations between the Fourier transform or the inverse Fourier transform and the convolution integral. One of them is the following *convolution theorem.*

Theorem 1 (convolution theorem). The Fourier transform of the product of two functions, $f(x, y)$ and $g(x, y)$, is equal to the product of the Fourier transforms $F(u, v)$ and $G(u, v)$. In other words,

$$\mathcal{F}[f(x,y) * g(x,y)] = F(u,v)G(u,v) \tag{3.12}$$

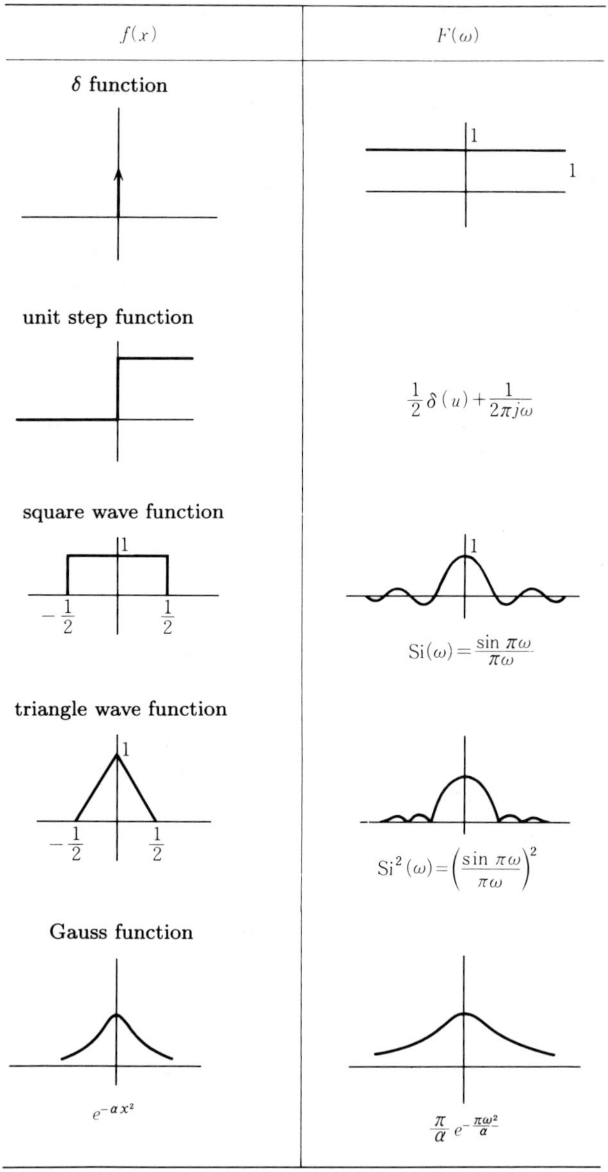

Figure 3.5 An example of a (one-dimensional) Fourier transform.

Proof.

$$
\begin{aligned}
&\mathcal{F}[f(x,y) * g(x,y)] \\
&= \int_{-\infty}^{\infty}\int_{-\infty}^{\infty}\left[\int_{-\infty}^{\infty}\int_{-\infty}^{\infty} f(x-a,y-b)g(a,b)\ da\ db\right]\exp(-2\pi j(ux+vy))\ dx\ dy \\
&= \int_{-\infty}^{\infty}\int_{-\infty}^{\infty}\left[\int_{-\infty}^{\infty}\int_{-\infty}^{\infty} f(a,b)g(x-a,y-b)\ da\ db\right]\exp(-2\pi j(ux+vy))\ dx\ dy \\
&= \int_{-\infty}^{\infty}\int_{-\infty}^{\infty} f(a,b)\left[\int_{-\infty}^{\infty}\int_{-\infty}^{\infty} g(x-a,y-b)\exp(-2\pi j(ux+vy))\ dx\ dy\right] da\ db \\
&= \int_{-\infty}^{\infty}\int_{-\infty}^{\infty} f(a,b)G(u,v)\exp(-2\pi j(ua+vb))\ da\ db \\
&= F(u,v)G(u,v)
\end{aligned}
$$

If we take the inverse Fourier transform of both sides of expression (3.12), then, by Theorem 1, we get the following:

$$\mathcal{F}^{-1}\mathcal{F}[f(x,y) * g(x,y)] = \mathcal{F}^{-1}[F(u,v)G(u,v)]$$

In other words,

$$f(x,y) * g(x,y) = \mathcal{F}^{-1}[F(u,v)G(u,v)]$$

So, if we take the Fourier transforms for two functions in the spatial domain, take the product of them, and take the inverse Fourier transform of the result, we will obtain the convolution integral of the original functions.

Fourier transforms also have the following properties: If we perform a linear transformation of the function $\exp(2\pi j(ux+vy))$ by the convolution using the transformation h, we will get the following:

$$
\begin{aligned}
&h[\exp(2\pi j(ux+vy))] \\
&= \int_{-\infty}^{\infty}\int_{-\infty}^{\infty} \phi(a,b)\exp(2\pi j(u(x-a)+v(y-b)))\ da\ db \\
&= \exp(2\pi j(ux+vy))\int_{-\infty}^{\infty}\int_{-\infty}^{\infty} \phi(a,b)\exp(-2\pi j(ua+vb))\ da\ db \\
&= \Phi(u,v)\exp(2\pi j(ux+vy))
\end{aligned}
$$

where

$$\Phi(u,v) = \int_{-\infty}^{\infty}\int_{-\infty}^{\infty} \phi(a,b)\exp(-2\pi j(ua+vb))\ da\ db$$

The above result shows that a linear transformation of $\exp(2\pi j(ux+vy))$ is the product of the Fourier transforms of the point spread function ϕ, $\Phi(u,v)$, and the original function, $\exp(2\pi j(ux+vy))$. Generally, $\exp(2\pi j(uv+vy))$ is called an *eigenfunction* of the linear transformation h, and $\Phi(u,v)$ is called its *eigenvalue*.

3.3 Sampling and Quantization of Pattern Functions

(a) Sampling

As we observed in Section 2.1, a pattern function can be represented on a continuous domain or can be a discrete representation such as a bit array. In this section we explore how to approximate a pattern function on a continuous domain by a discrete function on a quantized domain.

To simplify, we will consider only functions $f(x)$ on the real line as the pattern functions on a continuous domain. Further, we assume that $f(x)$ can be represented approximately by a comb-shaped function with interval Δx, as shown in Figure 3.6.

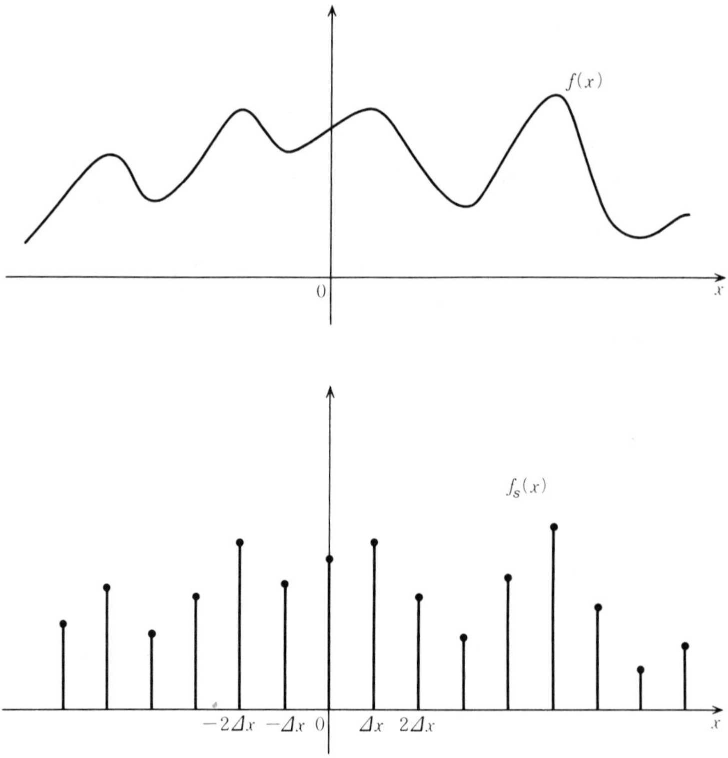

Figure 3.6 Comb-shaped function approximation for a pattern function.

Taking the value of a function defined on a continuous domain only at discrete points, as described in Section 2.1, is called *sampling* the function. If we let $f_s(x)$ be the function that takes those sampling points as its domain, then for integer n we have

$$f_s(x) = f(x) \sum_n \delta(x - n\Delta x)$$

If we take the Fourier transform of both sides, we get

$$\begin{aligned} F_s(u) &= F(u) * (1/\Delta x) \sum_n \delta(u - (n/\Delta x)) \\ &= (1/\Delta x) \sum_n F(u - (n/\Delta x)) \end{aligned} \quad (3.13)$$

by using $F(u) * \delta(u - (n/\Delta x)) = F(u - (n/\Delta x))$. Expression (3.13) shows that the sampling of $f(x)$ takes the sum in the interval $1/\Delta x$ for the Fourier transform of $f(x)$.

When $|u| > 1/(2\Delta x)$, we assume that the value of $F(u)$ is always 0. (We say that such an $F(u)$ is *bandlimited.*) In this case, the inverse Fourier transform

$$G(u) = \begin{cases} 1 & |u| < 1/(2\Delta x) \\ 0 & \text{otherwise} \end{cases}$$

multiplied by $f_s(u)$ is equal to the original function $f(x)$. In other words,

$$f(x) = \mathcal{F}^{-1}[F_s(u)G(u)]$$

All of these results can be collected in a theorem called the *sampling theorem.*

Theorem 2 (sampling theorem). If the Fourier transform of a pattern function does not include more than half of the spatial frequency component of the sampled frequency, we can reconstruct the original function on the spatial domain from the sampling values in the frequency domain.

According to the sampling theorem, if the Fourier transform $F(u)$ of the original function $f(x)$ does not include high-frequency components, the transformation by sampling is sufficiently effective. Although this condition seems to be too strict, it is possible to make it work in the real world if we preprocess the high-frequency components of $F(u)$ using a low-pass filter.

(b) Quantization

The purpose of sampling as described in (a) is to discretize the domain of a pattern function. On the other hand, segmenting the values of a function, as we described in Section 2.1, is called *quantization.* Quantization is done by limiting the value of a function to only a few quantization levels. For example, Figure 3.7(b) shows quantization into three-bit levels for the pattern shown in Figure 3.7(a).

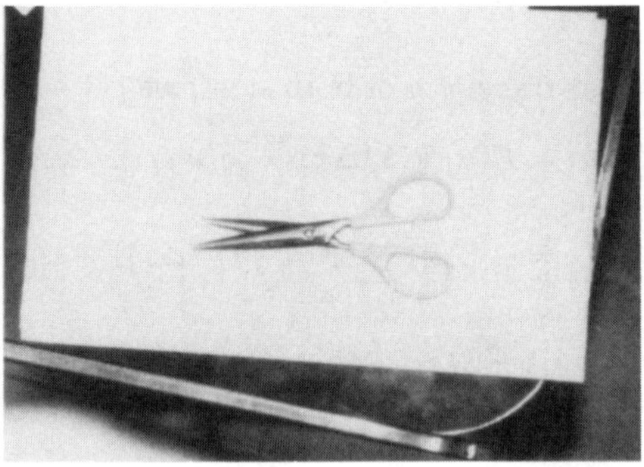

(a) A pattern example of a pair of scissors

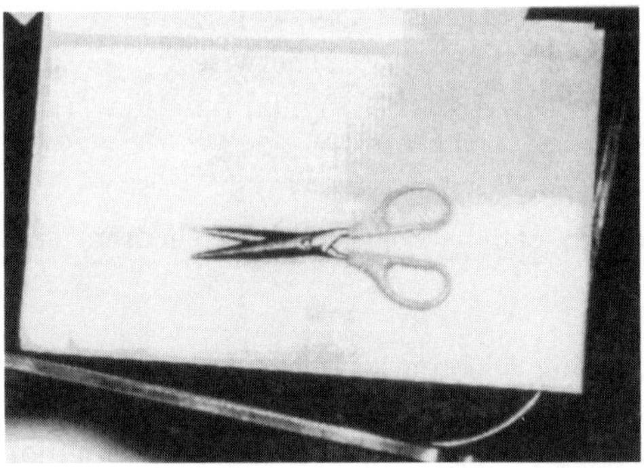

(b) Quantization of the pattern (a)

Figure 3.7 An example of quantizing a pattern.

In order to generate a one-bit quantization pattern, $\hat{f}(x)$, for a pattern function $f(x)$, we first obtain the frequency distribution of the intensity values of the pattern elements of $f(x)$. We then let α be the minimum intensity in the distribution and make

$$\text{If } f(x) > \alpha, \text{then } \hat{f}(x) = 1$$
$$\text{If } f(x) \leq \alpha, \text{then } \hat{f}(x) = 0$$

3.4 Transformation to Spatial Representations

There are many methods for generating spatial representations from a pattern function. Chapter 4 will provide several popular methods. In this section, we will describe one example, a method for creating a curve by interpolating points, which are given as a set of sampled points. This problem occurs when we try to infer the boundary line or the region of an incomplete pattern. Let us consider the set of sample points shown in Figure 3.8(a). How could we approximate a path through these points that is as smooth as possible? As a method for the approximation, here we will describe *spline function approximation*, in particular the *B-spline* function method.

(a) A set of sample points

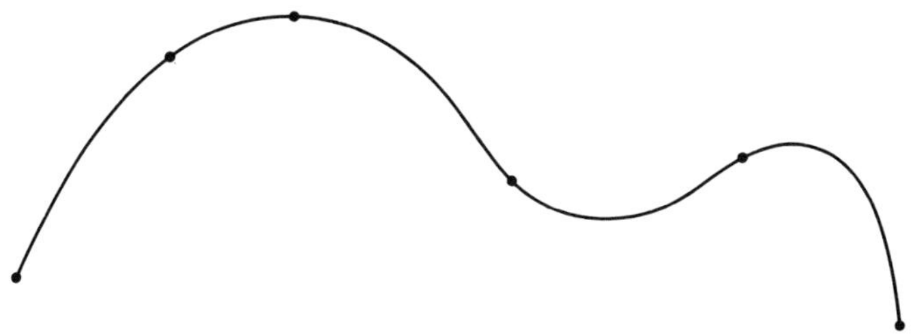

(b) Interpolation by using a cubic B-spline curve

Figure 3.8 Example of spline function approximation.

We define the curve going through n sample points, $a_1, \ldots, a_n$, as follows using the parameter s:

$$a(s) = \sum_{k=0}^{n+1} b_k B_k(s) \tag{3.14}$$

To simplify, we assume $a_i = a(i)$ $(i = 1, \ldots, n)$. We also assume that each interval $(i, i+1)$ $(i = 1, \ldots, n-1)$ has the same length along s. Furthermore, we assume

$$\begin{aligned} b_1 &= (b_0 + b_2)/2 \\ b_n &= (b_{n-1} + b_{n+1})/2 \end{aligned}$$

for the coefficient b_k $(k = 0, 1, \ldots, n+1)$. These are boundary conditions that the curvatures at the end points a_1 and a_n are 0.

Our purpose is to find a curve, $a_i(s)$ $(i = 1, \ldots, n-1)$, for connecting two neighboring points a_i and a_{i+1} in the form of expression (3.14). Suppose each $a_i(s)$ is represented as a cubic polynomial function. (The method of using a cubic polynomial function is called the *cubic B-spline* method.) This can be done in the following way:

We assume that the function $B_k(s)$ $(k = 0, 1, \ldots, n+1)$ on the right side of (3.14) takes only nonnegative values, and it may not be 0 only on the four curved parts between (a_{k-2}, a_{k+2}). In other words, for the curve $a_k(s)$, only $B_{k-1}(s)$, $B_k(s)$, $B_{k+1}(s)$, $B_{k+2}(s)$ have nonnegative values. We can determine the coordinates $a_k(s^*)$ of the point s^* within the kth interval (a_k, a_{k+1}) as follows:

$$a_k(s^*) = b_{k-1}C_3(s^* - k) + b_kC_2(s^* - k) + b_{k+1}C_1(s^* - k) + b_{k+2}C_0(s^* - k)$$

where

$$C_m(s - k) = D_{k-m+2,m}(s) \quad (m = 0, 1, 2, 3)$$

($D_{k,m}(s)$ is the $m+1$th part among the four nonnegative parts of $B_k(s)$.)

$$\begin{aligned} C_0(\xi) &= \xi^3/6 \\ C_1(\xi) &= (-\xi^3 + 3\xi^2 + 3\xi + 1)/6 \\ C_2(\xi) &= (3\xi^3 - 6\xi^2 + 4)/6 \\ C_3(\xi) &= (-\xi^3 + 3\xi^2 - 3\xi + 1)/6 \end{aligned}$$

It is known that, using this method, we can obtain a curve that has a continuous second-order derivative at the original sample points a_i $(i = 1, \ldots, n)$. We can obtain the curve shown in Figure 3.8(b) at the sample points of Figure 3.8(a). A cubic B-spline is often used as a method of approximating curves, but from the viewpoint of a method of transforming representations, we can consider it a method for creating a curve, which is a spatial structure representation, from the coordinate representation of discrete points. The method we described in this section is just one of many possible methods. We will give some more of them in Chapter 4.

3.5 Generation of Tree Representation

So far we have explained methods for transforming a pattern function to other representations. In this section we will describe a simple method for generating a tree representation as one example of a method for creating a symbolic representation.

Let us consider the problem of discriminating between two lists. In the lists $(a\ b\ c)$ and $(a\ c\ d)$, the first element of both lists is a, but the second elements, or the third, of these lists are different. In order to discriminate between these two lists, we need only check whether the second element is b or not. This can be represented as the tree shown in Figure 3.9(a). In this tree, node 0 has the procedure "if the second element is b, then output T. Otherwise, output F." Notice that nodes 1 and 2, which are leaves, correspond to the lists. For a given list, if we start from the root of the tree, execute the procedure at any node we pass, go along the edge labeled with the output, and look at the leaf we reach, we can discriminate between lists. For example, if the given list is $(a\ b\ c)$, the output of the procedure at node 0 is T and, as a result, when we reach node 1 we can decide that the list is $(a\ b\ c)$.

Now, suppose we have the list $(e\ b\ f)$. If we execute the procedure above for this list and the tree shown in Figure 3.9(a), we will also reach node 1. As a result, $(e\ b\ f)$ will be decided to be the list at node 1, that is $(a\ b\ c)$. Since this decision is wrong, we need to delete the list $(a\ b\ c)$ from node 1 and add a new procedure for discriminating between $(a\ b\ c)$ and $(e\ b\ f)$. Let us make the new procedure "if the first element is a, then output T. Otherwise, output F." Also, we need to generate new nodes 3 and 4 as subnodes of node 2 and let the new nodes have the lists $(a\ b\ c)$ and $(e\ b\ f)$, respectively. Further, we need to label the edge from node 1 to node 3 with T and the edge from 1 to 4 with F. What we get is the tree shown in Figure 3.9(b). Now let us give the list $(e\ b\ g)$ to the tree shown in Figure 3.9(b). As before, we assign the new procedure "if the third element is f, output T. Otherwise output F" to node 4. As a result, we generate a new tree with two new nodes 5 and 6 as subnodes of 4. We show the result in Figure 3.9(c).

Such a tree is called a (binary) *discrimination tree* for lists. We can summarize the algorithm for generating a discrimination tree for lists as follows, where the lists will be presented in the order $L_1, L_2, \ldots$:

Algorithm 3.1 (generation of a discrimination tree for lists)

[1] Generate the root node n_0.

[2] If the first element of L_1 is l_1, let n_0 be assigned the procedure "If the first element is l_1, output T. Otherwise, output F."

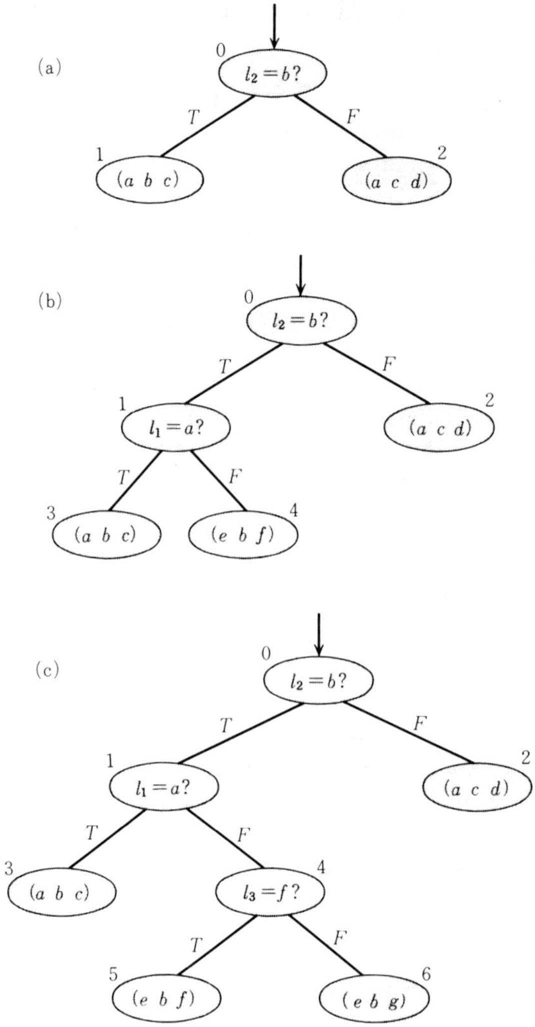

Figure 3.9 Generation of a discrimination tree.

[3] Generate n_1, n_2 as subnodes of n_0 and let L_1 be assigned to n_1. Also, let the symbol "fail" be assigned to node n_2.

[4] Call the tree obtained in [3] G. Let $i = 2$. When a node n_j has an associated list, call the list $L(n_j)$.

[5] Assign L_i to the root node n_0 of G, execute the procedure assigned to this node, determine the edge to follow from the output obtained, and go to the appropriate subnode. Repeat this operation. Call the

leaf we reach n_{i^*}. If L_i is already known and we are in the middle of generating the rest of the tree, go to [6]. If L_i is unknown and we are discriminating L_i, go to [7].

[6] If L_i does not match $L(n_{i^*})$, do the following substeps (to generate the discrimination tree). When the substeps are done, go to [8].

[6.1] Generate a procedure for discriminating L_i and $L(n_{i^*})$. The procedure should receive L_i and $L(n_{i^*})$ as inputs and output T when the test isolates L_i. Otherwise, it should output F.

[6.2] Generate n_{m+1} and n_{m+2}, the subnodes of n_{i^*}. (We assume that the number for the node created most recently was n_m.) Let $L(n_{m+1}) = L_i$, $L(n_{m+2}) = L(n_{i^*})$ and remove $L(n_{i^*})$ from n_{i^*}.

[6.3] Generate an edge from n_{i^*} to n_{m+1} and label it T. Also, generate an edge from n_{i^*} to n_{m+2} and label it F.

[6.4] Let G be the whole tree to be obtained.

[7] Assume that L_i is the list to be assigned to n_{i^*} and go to [8] (make use of the discrimination tree.)

[8] If there are no lists left, stop. If there is a list remaining, let $i = i+1$ and go to [5].

This method of generating a discrimination tree for lists can be thought of as a method for transforming a representation of a set of lists into a representation using a tree. In this section, we described how to discriminate lists. By improving the way we decide what procedure to use at each node, we can use a discrimination tree for many different kinds of objects. We will describe some more examples in Chapter 9.

3.6 Search and Problem Solving

(a) Search

So far we have explained several examples of the methods used for transforming one representation into another. We should note that a procedure used for generating a new representation is itself described using a procedural representation. In this section we will explain *search*, a popular method for finding procedures to attain a goal.

Suppose we have some arrangements of three blocks on a table as shown in Figure 3.10(a). Each possible arrangement can be regarded as a spatial structure representation of a thing we could call "three blocks and a table." Let us generate a procedure for generating a new arrangement from a given

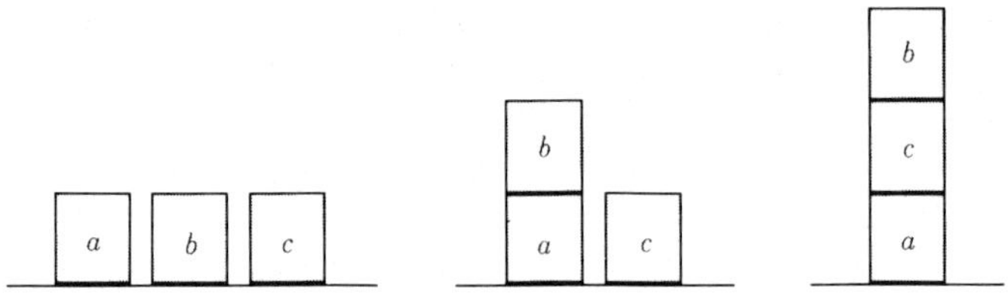

(a) Various arrangements of blocks

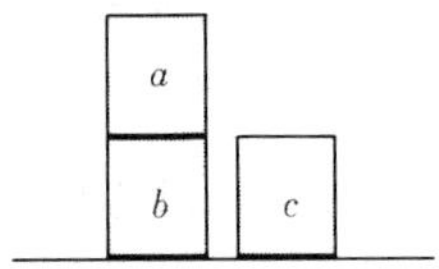

(b) The initial state of the problem

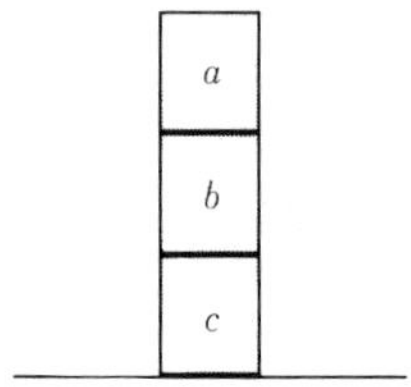

(c) The goal state of the problem

Figure 3.10 Examples of arrangements of the blocks.

arrangement. We assume that we can ignore the relative left/right positions of the blocks.

We assume the following:

(1) One arrangement is given. We call this the initial state.
(2) The arrangement to reach in the end is given. We call this the goal state.
(3) There is a procedure for transforming one state into another.
(4) There is a way to calculate the appropriateness of each state.

Suppose the list

$$((cleartop\ a)(on\ a\ b)(ontable\ b)(cleartop\ c)(ontable\ c))$$

that represents the arrangement shown in Figure 3.10(b) is given as the initial state. Let us call the initial state s_o. Also, the list

$$((cleartop\ a)(on\ a\ b)(on\ b\ c)(ontable\ c))$$

that represents the arrangement shown in Figure 3.10(c) is given as the goal state. Let us call it s_d.

Let the following three production rules represent the procedure for transforming one state into another:

(*cleartop* $x)(*on* $x $y)
⇒ (**delete* (*on* $x $y))(**add* (*cleartop* $y))
(**add* (*ontable* $x))
(*cleartop* $x)(*cleartop* $y)(*ontable* $x)
⇒ (**delete* (*cleartop* $y))(**delete* (*ontable* $x))
(**add* (*on* $x $y))
(*cleartop* $x)(*cleartop* $z)(*on* $x $y)
⇒ (**delete* (*cleartop* $z))(**delete* (*on* $x $y))
(**add* (*cleartop* $y))(**add* (*on* $x $z))

where $x, $y, and $z are variables that can be replaced by the names of specific blocks. Also, **delete* is the procedure for deleting an element of the currently considered list, and **add* is the procedure for adding an element to this list as its last element. For example, we can interpret the first rule as

> "If the currently considered list includes both (*cleartop* $x) and (*on* $x $y), delete (*on* $x $y), and add (*cleartop* $y) and (*ontable* $x) in this order."

In other words, this rule represents the procedure for

> "If there is nothing on the block $x, and $x is on $y, remove $x from $y and put it on the table."

This procedure will be executed only when the currently considered list includes both elements (*cleartop* $x) and (*on* $x $y). The other two rules can be interpreted similarly.

Using the rules above, we can directly transform one arrangement of blocks into another.

Furthermore, let us define the appropriateness of an arrangement, s, for blocks x and y by the following, where s_o and s_d are the initial and goal states, respectively:

(1) Let $f(s)$ be the number of lists that are included both in s and in s_d.
(2) Let $g(s)$ be the number of lists that are of the form (*on* x y) and are included in s but not in s_d.
(3) Let $h(s)$ be the number of lists that are of the form (*cleartop* x) or (*ontable* x) and are included in s but not in s_d.
(4) Let $k(s)$ be the number of lists that are included in s_d but not in s.
(5) Define the appropriateness of s, $A(s)$, as

$$A(s) = f(s) - (3g(s) + h(s) + k(s))$$

For example, the appropriateness of the initial arrangement, s_o, is

$$A(s_o) = 3 - (3 \times 0 + 2 + 1) = 0$$

Now, we start from the initial state, s_o, execute each of the three production rules whose condition side matches the currently considered list to generate a new state, and repeat the execution until we reach the goal state.

Usually, more than one rule can be executed to produce a new state. For example, if we search all the states that can be generated from the initial state, we will generate the tree shown in Figure 3.11. In Figure 3.11, the number attached to each state represents its appropriateness computed using the above definition.

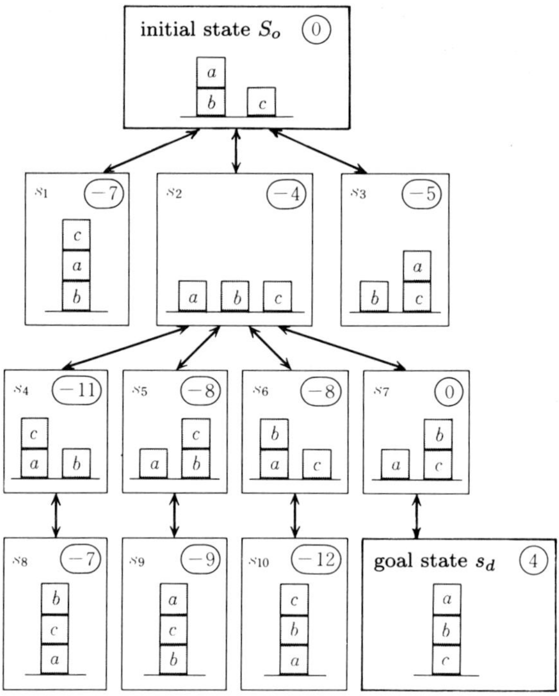

Figure 3.11 Tree for the state search.

We call a tree like the one in Figure 3.11 a *search tree* and the method of search that generates a search tree a *tree search*. In Figure 3.11, the path from s_o to s_d is the path passing through the states s_o, s_2, s_7, s_d. If we list the rules that were executed in generating this path, such a list would be a representation of the procedures for generating the goal state, s_d, from the initial state, s_o.

There are many methods for generating a tree like the one shown in Figure 3.11. We will give some more later. Before we do that, we need to formalize what we have explained so far. In particular, the search described above is actually a kind of representation transformation called problem solving. Now we briefly describe problem solving.

(b) Problem solving

We view each arrangement of the blocks shown in (a) as a *state* and call the collection of possible arrangements the *state space.* Searching for a path from the initial state s_o to the goal state s_d is equivalent to searching for a sequence of states starting from the *initial state* and reaching the *goal state* in a given state space. Moving from one state to another is called *state transition*, and the procedure for making a state transition is applying a state transition *operator* to the present state. A state transition can be defined as a rule for taking the pair of a state and an operator and making it correspond to the state that is moved to. Such a rule is called a *state transition rule.*

Suppose we have a state space S, a set of operators A, a set of state transition rules M, the initial state s_o, and the goal state s_d, both in S. We call the tuple of these five elements $P = \langle S, A, M, s_o, s_d \rangle$ a *problem.* Sometimes an operator and a state transition rule can be identified. In such a case this definition is redundant.

For a problem P, to find a sequence of operators that will move s_o to s_d is called *problem solving*, and an obtained sequence of operators is called a *solution* to P. For example, the arrangement of the blocks shown in (a) can be considered to be a problem if we make the following definitions:

(1) Let a possible arrangement of the blocks be a state and the set of all such arrangements the state space S.
(2) Let $A = \{r_1, r_2, r_3\}$ be the set of operators, where r_1, r_2, and r_3 are the three rules shown in (3), respectively.
(3) Suppose we have a state $s \in S$ and a rule r_i that can be applied to that state. If we apply r_i to s, we obtain another state s'. This state transition can be defined as the rule $r_i : s \Rightarrow s'$. We regard such a rule as a state transition rule and call the set of all possible such rules the set M of state transition rules.
(4) Let the initial arrangement s_o given in (a) be the initial state s_o.
(5) Let the goal arrangement s_d in (a) be the goal state s_d.
(6) Based on (1)–(5), we define the problem $P = \langle S, A, M, s_o, s_d \rangle$.

Generating a procedural representation that corresponds to a path from

s_o to s_d shown in the example (a) is the same as obtaining a sequence of operators for generating a path from s_o to s_d in the problem P.

In this example, we used lists to represent information. There are many other methods for representing S, A, M, s_o, s_d, and P.

(c) Depth-first search

As we noted, in general there may be more than one state that can be reached from a state s in the state space. Thus, the following algorithm can be used as a search method: First, pick a state that can be reached from s but has not been visited before, and move to such a state s'. Then, pick and move to another such possible state. Repeat this operation until we reach the goal state s_d. If there is no state that can be reached from s and has never been visited before, go one step backward from s and search down another possible state that can be reached from s. This backward-step procedure in the search is called *backtracking.*

Using this algorithm, the direction of the search usually goes in a deeper direction from the initial state, so this kind of algorithm is called *depth-first search.* This search method is well-adapted to finding a deeper path, or a long route, but it can take a long time to reach the goal when you go deep into one direction but the goal state lies in a different direction.

We now show the most basic algorithm for depth-first search.

Algorithm 3.2 (depth-first search)

[1] Let $s = s_o$, $Z = \{s_o\}$, $Q = (\ )$, $s_b = (\ )$.

[2] If $s = s_d$, then stop. The sequence of operators given in Q is a solution. Otherwise, go to [3].

[3] Find a state that can be directly reached from s but is not included in Z, and call it s'. Let $Z = Z \cup \{s'\}$. For $a(s, s')$, an operator for moving s to s', add the new element $a(s, s')$ to the front of the list Q. Let the new list be Q and go to [4]. If such an s' does not exist, go to [5].

[4] Let $s = s'$. Add the new element s to the front of the list s_b, and let the new list be s_b. Go to [2].

[5] If $s_b = (\ )$, then stop. There is no solution. Otherwise, let s be the first element (s^1) of the list s_b. Delete s^1 from s_b and let s_b be the list s_b without s^1. Furthermore, delete the first element of Q, $a(s^1, s)$, from Q and let the new list be Q. Go to [3].

If we use Algorithm 3.2 on the example shown in (a), we will obtain the following state transitions in Figure 3.11 starting from s_o:

$$s_o \Rightarrow s_1 \Rightarrow s_o \Rightarrow s_2 \Rightarrow s_4 \Rightarrow s_8 \Rightarrow s_4 \Rightarrow s_2 \Rightarrow s_5 \Rightarrow s_9 \Rightarrow s_5 \Rightarrow s_2 \Rightarrow s_6$$
$$\Rightarrow s_{10} \Rightarrow s_6 \Rightarrow s_2 \Rightarrow s_7 \Rightarrow s_d$$

(d) Breadth-first search

The method of depth-first search repeats the process of searching only one state that is directly accessible and has not been searched before. Thus, the search goes deeper and deeper. On the other hand, *breadth-first search* is a method that tries to search all states that are directly accessible and have not been searched, before going down deeper. Unlike depth-first search, an algorithm for breadth-first search does not include a procedure for back-tracking. Instead, it may take longer to solve a problem that requires a deeper search. The following is the basic algorithm for breadth-first search. In order to make it more understandable, some of the descriptions are redundant.

Algorithm 3.3 (breadth-first search)

[1] Let $Y = \{s_o\}$, $Z = \emptyset$.

[2] If $s_d = Y$, then stop. The sequence of operators that created the path from s_o to s_d, $a(s_o, s_1), a(s_1, s_2), \ldots, a(s_{k-1}, s_k), a(s_k, s_d)$, is a solution. (The length of the sequence could be 0.) Otherwise, go to [3].

[3] If $Y = Z$, then stop. There is no solution. Otherwise, go to [4].

[4] Do the following substeps for all $s \in Y$ and then go to [2].

[4.1] Find all states that can be directly reached from s and that are not included in Z and call the set of these states Y'. (Y' could be $\emptyset$.) For each element of Y', s', remember an operator, $a(s, s')$, that transfers s to s'.

[4.2] Let $Y = Y \cup Y' - \{s\}$.

[4.3] Let $Z = Z \cup \{s\}$.

If we apply the above algorithm to the example shown in (a), we obtain the following state transitions in Figure 3.11 starting from s_o:

$$s_o \Rightarrow s_1 \Rightarrow s_2 \Rightarrow s_3 \Rightarrow s_1 \Rightarrow s_2 \Rightarrow s_4 \Rightarrow s_5 \Rightarrow s_6 \Rightarrow s_7 \Rightarrow s_3 \Rightarrow s_4$$
$$\Rightarrow s_8 \Rightarrow s_5 \Rightarrow s_9 \Rightarrow s_6 \Rightarrow s_{10} \Rightarrow s_7 \Rightarrow s_d$$

(e) Best-first search

One characteristic of both depth-first and breadth-first search is that the algorithms are independent of the content of states. In other words, they do search without using the "appropriateness" of the state in problem solving. For example, search is done without using the idea of "closeness" to the goal state. The algorithms usually take time for the search and are not very efficient. For instance, in the example in (a), we see that both these search methods need to visit almost every state in Figure 3.11 in order to find s_d.

This suggests that we should use an *evaluation function* to assign a value that gets larger as we approach the goal state. When depth-first search picks one state to move to, it could choose, from all the states that can be reached directly and have not been searched before, a state whose evaluation value is the biggest. Depth-first search with this evaluation heuristic is called *best-first search.* Best-first search can be thought of as a kind of depth-first search, but it needs to check the value of the evaluation function for all the states that can be reached directly and have not been searched before in order to determine the state to move to. The following is the basic algorithm for best-first search. This algorithm is the same as the algorithm for depth-first search shown in subsection (c) except for the way to choose s' in step [3].

Algorithm 3.4 (best-first search)

[1] Let $s = s_o$, $Z = \{s_o\}$, $Q = (\ )$, $s_b = (\ )$.

[2] If $s = s_d$, then stop. The sequence of operators given in Q is a solution. Otherwise, go to [3].

[3] Generate all states that can be reached directly from s and are not included in Z, and calculate the evaluation function values of such states. Pick one state that gives the largest evaluation function value and call it s'. Let $Z = Z \cup \{s'\}$. When an operator for moving s to s' is $a(s, s')$, add the new element $a(s, s')$ to the front of the list Q. Let the new list be Q and go to [4]. If such an s' does not exist, go to [5].

[4] Let $s = s'$. Add the new element s to the front of the list s_b and let the new list be s_b. Go to [2].

[5] If $s_b = (\ )$, then stop. There is no solution. Otherwise, let s be the first element (s^1) of the list s_b. Delete s^1 from s_b and let s_b be the list s_b without s^1. Furthermore, delete the first element of Q, $a(s^1, s)$, from Q and let the new list be Q. Go to [3].

Let us apply this algorithm to the example shown in (a). We regard the appropriateness of a state as the value of the evaluation function for the state. Then the value of the evaluation function on a state will be the numbers shown in Figure 3.11. We search the state space in the direction of a state with the largest evaluation function value by calculating these numbers during the search. In this way we reach s_d after visiting only two states on the way.

$$s_o \Rightarrow s_2 \Rightarrow s_7 \Rightarrow s_d$$

We could find this goal state by generating only a small number of states in the above example. However, that is not always the case. As in depth-first search, we usually need to do backtracking. Depending on the form of the evaluation function, the number of states generated in best-first search will be different. For example, in example (a), if we define appropriateness to be

$$A(s) = f(s) - (g(s) + h(s) + k(s))$$

the number of states to be generated in the search will be greater than the number above.

(f) Heuristic search

Best-first search uses only an evaluation function value for choosing a possible state to move to and thus it uses only local information in choosing that state. Therefore, it cannot always do the best search. In problem solving using search, the bigger the state space is, the more likely that the search needs to be determined by local information. In this case we try to decide the direction in which to continue the search by making use of information specific to each problem. Such a method is generally called *heuristic search.* Best-first search can be considered to be a simple form of heuristic search.

In this section, we started with the problem of searching for new states, but we usually cannot know or analyze beforehand the whole space of possible states. This means that a global evaluation for deciding the search direction cannot be found, so, for such a problem, we need to use the method of heuristic search.

3.7 Logical Inference

The framework of representation transformation using heuristic search often uses lists, because the search procedure is more applicable to a weaker representation such as a list than to a more structured representation such as predicate logic. This actually means that the transformation of representations using heuristic search often depends on the individual problem. By using predicate logic as a representation, we can look at the problem of representation transformation from a more logical, problem-independent framework. In this section we will explain the method of logical inference using first-order predicate logic and its application to generating representations.

(a) Theorem proving

In Section 2.6 we explained that well-formed formulas are the basic elements of representation in the framework of predicate logic. Here we will describe an algorithm for theorem proving as a representative example of using logical inference to transform one well-formed formula into another.

As we noted in Section 2.6, there are many ways to interpret a well-formed formula depending on what domain we use to interpret its symbols. A well-formed formula that always has the value T for any interpretation is called a *valid well-formed formula.*

We say that an interpretation I *satisfies* a set of well-formed formulas W when the value of each of the formulas in W is T for I. We say that an interpretation I satisfies a well-formed formula w if the value of w is T for I. When no interpretation satisfies W (or w), we say that W (or w) is *unsatisfiable.* If all the interpretations that satisfy a set of well-formed formulas W also satisfy a well-formed formula w, we say that w is a *logical consequence* of W. When w is a logical consequence of W, we also say that w is *proved* from W, and we call each element of W an *axiom* and w a *theorem.* Generally, when Γ is a well-formed formula or a set of well-formed formulas and γ is a well-formed formula, we write $\Gamma \vdash \gamma$ to mean that γ is proved from Γ and $\Gamma \not\vdash \gamma$ meaning that γ is not proved from Γ.

Let us consider an *inference rule* as a transformation rule for well-formed formulas. For any interpretation that makes all the formulas in some set of well-formed formulas take the value T, an inference rule guarantees that the value of some other well-formed formula under that interpretation is also T.

For example, for predicates P and Q,

$$\frac{P, P \to Q}{Q}$$

is an inference rule. In other words, it promises that "for all the interpretations in which the well-formed formulas P and $P \to Q$ take the value T, the value of the well-formed formula Q is T." An inference rule in this form is usually called *modus ponens.* Another example

$$\frac{(\forall X)P(X)}{P(a)}$$

is also an inference rule. This rule guarantees that "for all the interpretations in which, for any X, the value of $P(X)$ is T, the value of $P(a)$ is T (where the constant symbol a is included in the domain of X)." A logical inference using an inference rule is called a *deductive inference*, and the transformation of well-formed formulas using deductive inference is called deductive transformation.

The fact that w is a logical consequence of W means that the value of w becomes T when the value of all the well-formed formulas included in W is T, no matter what kind of world we use to interpret w and W. For example, if we take $P(a)$ as the formula w and $\{(\forall X)Q(X), Q(a) \to$

$(\forall X)(P(X) \vee R(a)), \sim R(a)\}$ as the set of formulas W, we have that w is a logical consequence of W no matter how we interpret these symbols.

In this sense, in order to verify that w is a logical consequence of W, we need only reach w by repeatedly applying inference rules to the formulas included in W. For instance, in the above example, we can conclude that the value of $P(a)$ is T using the following reasoning:

$$\frac{(\forall X)Q(X)}{Q(a)}$$

$$\frac{Q(a), Q(a) \rightarrow (\forall X)(P(X) \vee R(a))}{(\forall X)P(X) \vee R(a)}$$

$$\frac{(\forall X)(P(X) \vee R(a)), \sim R(a)}{(\forall X)P(X)}$$

$$\frac{(\forall X)P(X)}{P(a)}$$

As we said, the fact that w is a logical consequence of W is another way of saying that w can be proved from W. So, by using some inference rules, the fact that w can be proved from W means that w can be proved from any set of formulas including W given any interpretation. This process is called *theorem proving.*

For first-order predicate logic, it is known that an algorithm that can find out whether a well-formed formula is provable from a set of well-formed formulas in a finite number of steps does not exist. In this sense, first-order predicate logic is *undecidable.* However, if we know beforehand that the formula we want to prove is a valid well-formed formula, then there is a procedure that proves this formula in a finite number of steps. In this sense, first-order predicate logic is *semidecidable.*

As you can imagine from what we said so far, theorem proving can be thought of as a process for generating a new well-formed formula (whose value is T) from some set of well-formed formulas.

(b) Resolution principle

We will now describe an algorithm for actually proving theorems. Of all such algorithms, we will describe here the method using the resolution principle.

First, the fact that a well-formed formula w can be proved from a set of well-formed formulas W is equivalent to the fact that $\{\sim w\} \cup W$ is unsatisfiable. (The proof is omitted.) Using this, we need only show the unsatisfiability of $\{w\} \cup W$ in order to prove w from W. To do that, we execute the following two steps:

(1) Transform $\{w\} \cup W$ to a set of clauses.
An algorithm for transforming a well-formed formula into a set of clauses is known, although we are not going to describe it here. We use this algorithm on each formula in $\{w\} \cup W$ and gather all the clauses in the set.

(2) If two clauses $P \vee \sim Q$ and Q exist in the set of clauses obtained in (1), we can infer P from these clauses using the inference rule

$$\frac{P \vee \sim Q, Q}{P}$$

We add P to the original set of clauses and repeat the same operations.

To perform (2) is called *resolution*, and a clause that is a consequence of a resolution is called the resolution clause or *resolvent*. We are not going to prove it here, but it is known that, if w can be proved from W, we can derive the empty clause by doing a finite number of resolutions. This fact is called the *resolution principle*.

(c) Unification

In this section we describe a method for doing resolution for two given clauses. In order to do resolution, we need to verify that constant and variable symbols included in each clause can be matched.

Transforming literals into the same literal by substituting appropriate terms into some terms is called *unification*. The operation of substituting a value for the same variable in several clauses can be done by unification if we consider the set of all the literals that appear in those clauses. Thus we can extend the use of unification to a set of clauses. In unification, the set of pairs of a term to be substituted and an original term is called a *substitution* for the unification, or a *unifier*. Generally, we write the unifier θ for substituting each term $t_1, \ldots, t_n$ into each term $v_1, \ldots, v_n$ respectively as

$$\theta = \{t_1/v_1, \ldots, t_n/v_n\}$$

For example, if we use the unifier $\theta = \{(a, x), (a, w), (b, z)\}$ on the set of literals $\{P(x, y, g(z)),\ P(a, y, g(b)),\ P(w, y, g(z))\}$, we obtain the literal $P(a, y, g(b))$.

Actually, there is generally more than one unifier for a set of literals. It is known that it is sufficient to use the "weakest" unifier (called the most general unifier, or *mgu*) in the algorithm for theorem proving based on the resolution principle. Here "weakest" means that, if we take one of the mgu's, ξ, then for any unifier θ there exists a substitution λ that makes $\theta = \xi\lambda$. An mgu always exists for any set of literals. Furthermore, for a set of literals, an algorithm is known for finding an mgu if a unification is possible and for detecting the impossibility if unification is not possible. Such an algorithm is called a *unification algorithm.*

(d) The refutation process

An algorithm for theorem proving based on the resolution principle can be obtained by combining step (2) of the resolution described in subsection (b) with some unification algorithm. Below we describe such an algorithm only in conceptual terms.

Algorithm 3.5 (theorem proving based on the resolution principle)

[1] For a set of axioms W and a theorem w, let $L = \{\sim w\} \cup W$ and transform L into a set of clauses.

[2] Take two clauses from L and obtain their mgu using the unification algorithm.

[3] Apply this mgu to the two clauses.

[4] After applying the mgu, find the resolvent by applying the inference rule of resolution to two clauses.

[5] If the resolvent obtained is the empty clause, then stop. The theorem was proved. Otherwise, add the resolvent to the original set L and go to [2].

For example, suppose we want to prove the theorem, $P(a)$, from the set of axioms $W = \{P(X) \vee \sim Q(X), Q(Y) \vee R(Z), P(a) \vee \sim R(W)\}$. First we consider

$$\begin{aligned} L &= \{\sim w\} \cup W \\ &= \{\sim P(a), P(X) \vee \sim Q(X), Q(Y) \vee R(Z), P(a) \vee \sim R(W)\} \end{aligned}$$

which is already a set of clauses. From this L, we take two clauses, for example, $P(X) \vee \sim Q(X)$ and $\sim P(a)$. If we unify these two clauses using the unification algorithm, we obtain $\xi\{a/X\}$ as the mgu. If we then apply ξ to $P(X) \vee \sim Q(X)$ and $\sim P(a)$, we obtain

$$\{P(a) \vee \sim Q(a), \sim P(a)\}$$

Now, applying the inference rule of resolution to this, we obtain $\sim Q(a)$ as a resolvent. We then add $\sim Q(a)$ to L.

Next, if we select $\sim Q(a)$ and $Q(Y) \vee R(Z)$, we obtain $\xi = \{a/Y\}$ as the mgu using unification. Applying ξ to the two clauses generates

$$\{\sim Q(a), Q(a) \vee R(Z)\}$$

as the set of unified clauses. If we apply the inference rule of resolution to this, we obtain the resolvent $R(Z)$. So, we add $R(Z)$ to L. Similarly, we obtain, for example, the resolvent $\sim R(W)$ from $\sim P(A)$ and $P(a) \vee \sim R(W)$. We also add $\sim R(W)$ to L. Finally, if we take $R(Z)$ and $\sim R(W)$ from L and apply the unification algorithm, we obtain $\xi = \{Z/W\}$ as the mgu. Applying ξ and then the resolution to these two clauses, we obtain the empty clause.

In this way we can show the unsatisfiability of a given set of clauses if they are actually unsatisfiable and thus show that w can be proved from W. The process of deleting unsatisfiable clauses using resolution is called a *refutation process.* The refutation process described in the above example is illustrated in Figure 3.12.

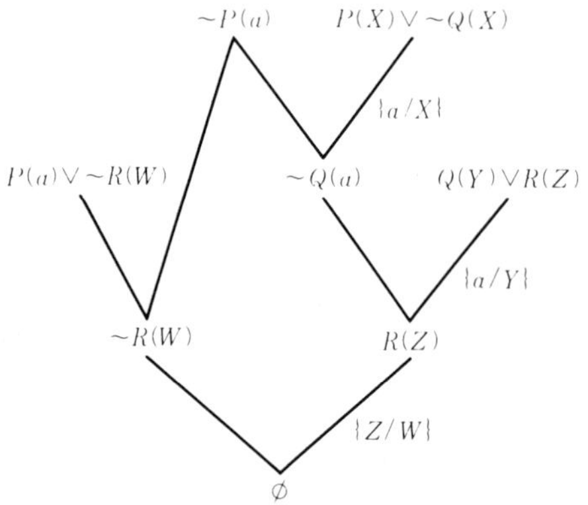

Figure 3.12 Unification and the refutation process.

(e) Logical inference and generating representations

The algorithm for theorem proving based on the resolution principle described above can be applied generally to first-order predicate logic, although it usually takes a long time to compute. When a set of clauses is large, the efficiency of computation depends on which clauses we pick for the refutation. On the other hand, by applying this method to the Horn clause logic rather than first-order predicate logic, we can execute efficient theorem proving on a computer. Actually, the basic part of Prolog can be regarded as a language for processing a unification algorithm applied only to Horn clause logic.

We now show how the algorithm for theorem proving based on resolution can be applied to generation and transformation of representations.

First, notice that this algorithm not only determines whether a theorem can be proved or not but also constructs a proof. In other words, the refutation process described above is itself a proof process. So, just as in the case of search described in Section 3.6, we can regard the algorithm as generating a procedure for deriving a formula (theorem) from a set of formulas (an axiom set).

Second, although the proof process is for proving a given theorem, we can generate a new representation by generalizing the process itself, for example, by substituting new variable symbols for some constant symbols. Actually, such a method of generation has been applied to learning by a computer and is called "explanation-based learning." We will describe this in detail in Chapter 8.

Third, it is known that we can use the unification algorithm for judging the similarity between two sets of well-formed formulas in Horn clause logic. A judgment of similarity is the basis for learning by analogy, which will also be described in Chapter 8.

Thus, theorem proving as logical inference using predicate logic representation is a powerful method for generating representations.

3.8 Production Systems

Production rules as described in Section 2.10 are not usable if we simply describe rules. We need a system for interpreting and executing rules. Such a system is generally called a *production system*. Like search and logical inference, a production system can be a powerful tool for generating and transforming representations. In this section we explain production systems.

(a) Production systems using ordered rules

First, let us consider the following collection of rules:

r_1 (*windows state* \$$x$)(*temperature state* \$$y$)
(\$$x$ *related* \$$y$)(\$$x$ *opposite* \$$z$)
⇒ (∗*delete* (*windows state* \$$x$))
(∗*add* (*windows state* \$$z$))

r_2 (*windows state* \$$x$)(*temperature state* \$$y$)
(\$$y$ *opposite* \$$z$)
⇒ (∗*delete* (*temperature state* \$$y$))
(∗*add* (*temperature state* \$$z$))

$$r_3 \quad (\textit{windows state } \$x)(\$x \textit{ related } \$y)$$
$$\Rightarrow (*\textit{add } (\textit{temperature state } \$y))$$

$$r_4 \quad \Rightarrow (*\textit{add } (\textit{windows state closed}))$$

where $\$x$, $\$y$, $\$z$ are variables.

We now define *working memory* for rules r_1–r_4. Working memory is represented by a list of lists. Suppose its initial state is

((*closed related hot*)(*open related cold*)
(*closed opposite open*)(*open opposite closed*)
(*hot opposite cold*)(*cold opposite hot*))

We also suppose that $*add$ and $*delete$ in the action side of the rules are procedures for deleting its argument from working memory and for adding its argument to the top of working memory, respectively.

We examine r_1–r_4 from the top and execute the action side of a rule whose condition side matches working memory when some constant is substituted for a variable in the rule. By repeating this *recognition-action cycle* (or recognize-act cycle), working memory changes as shown in Table 3.1 every time a rule is executed.

Table 3.1 Recognition-action cycle

Executed rule	Working memory after the execution of the rule
r_4	((*windows state closed*) (*closed related hot*)...)
r_3	((*temperature state hot*) (*windows state closed*) (*closed related hot*)...)
r_1	((*windows state open*) (*temperature state hot*)...)
r_2	((*temperature state cold*) (*windows state open*)...)
r_1	((*windows state closed*) (*temperature state cold*)...)
r_2	((*temperature state hot*) (*windows state closed*)...)
r_1	...

If we define a rule with an appropriate termination procedure on its action side, we can terminate the execution of the recognition-action cycle, although this is not included in the above example.

The mechanism of a production system can be summarized as illustrated in the diagram in Figure 3.13. That is, it checks the rules in order from the first one, matching working memory against the condition side of the rule and executing the procedures given in the action side of the rule. If working memory changes because of this, another rule may match. By giving a set of rules and an initial state of working memory to such a system, we can do the inference as exemplified in Table 3.1.

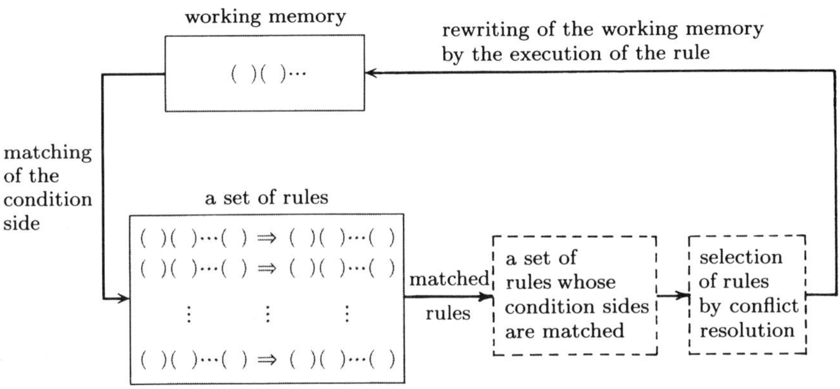

Figure 3.13 The structure of a production system.

(b) Production systems using a discrimination tree

The above example assigns an order to rules and checks them in order. However, as the number of rules increases, matching takes too long to be practical for computation. To avoid it, we can put the condition sides of rules together and compile them into the form of a discrimination tree.

For example, for the following two rules, p_1, p_2, we can generate the discrimination tree shown in Figure 3.14 before we apply the rules:

p_1 (*context take_banana $x banana*)
(*relation location $x banana can_touch*)
⇒ (**delete* (*relation location $x banana can_touch*))
(**add* (*relation location $x banana grasp*))

p_2 (*context take_banana $y banana*)
(*relation location $y banana too_far*)
⇒ (**delete* (*context take_banana $y banana*))
(**delete* (*relation location $y banana too_far*))
(**add* (*context walk_to $y banana*))

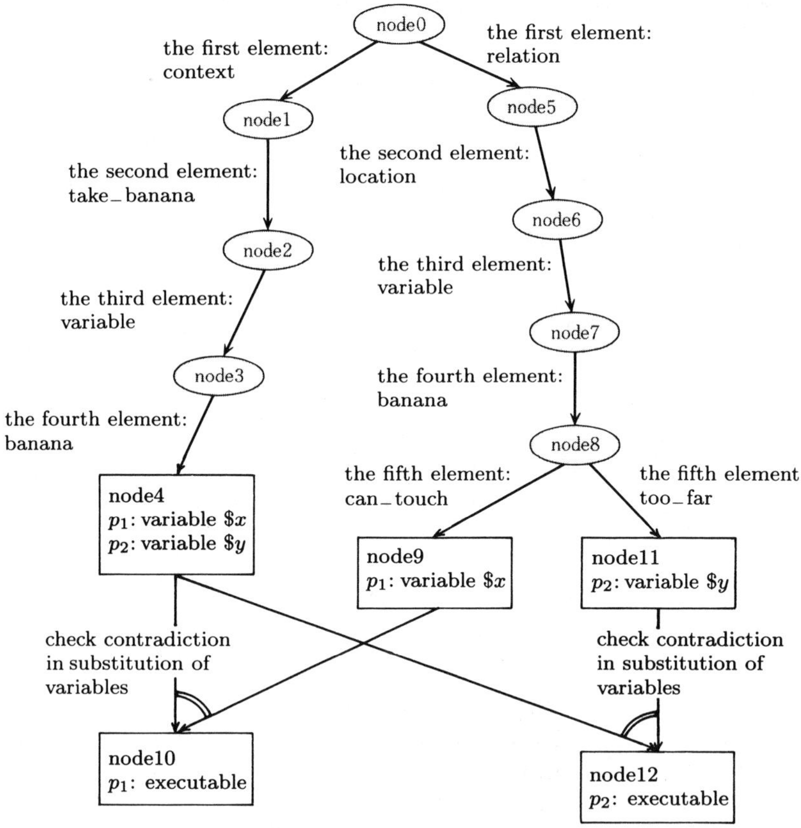

Figure 3.14 A discrimination tree for the example production system.

We can easily check whether a rule matches the working memory by putting the list in the working memory through the discrimination tree and then checking for a contradiction due to binding variables to constants. Moreover, by remembering states of variable bindings that occurred in the discrimination tree, we can find the set of matched rules by discriminating only lists added or deleted in the previous recognition-action cycle.

However, a system using a discrimination tree may get more than one rule that matches working memory. In such a case, we need to decide which rule to execute. Such a decision is called *conflict resolution.* The mechanism of a production system that includes conflict resolution will contain the part with broken lines in Figure 3.13.

(c) Production system and generating representations

In a production system, many methods besides those described above can be used. Currently, when we say a production system, we often mean a general framework of an inference system using production rules as a representation. Here we would like to point out that the production systems described in (a) and (b) are suitable for generating rule representation.

Suppose we add the following rule to the top of the set of rules, r_1–r_4:

r_0 (*windows state closed*)(*temperature state cold*)
⇒ (∗*build rs*
((*windows state closed*)
(*temperature state cold*)
⇒
(∗*add* (*windows state with_curtain*))
(∗*delete* (*windows state closed*))))

∗*build* is a procedure for adding to the top of the set of rules a rule that has a name as its first argument and the body of a rule as its second argument.

If we repeat the recognition-action cycle for rules r_0–r_4 using the method described in (a), r_0 will be executed after r_1 is executed twice. As a result, by the procedure in its action side, it will ∗*build* the new rule

r_s (*windows state closed*)(*temperature state cold*)
⇒ (∗*add* (*windows state with_curtain*))
(∗*delete* (*windows state closed*))

and add it to the top of the set of rules. When that happens, the new rule r_s will be executed next and the inference will proceed differently. This simple example is only for explanation, but we can create complicated changes in the inference process by including variables in the argument of ∗*build*, or not writing a whole rule within ∗*build* but making it possible to generate parts of the rule by recognition-action cycles. However, in the case of a system using discrimination trees as described in (b), we need to create a new discrimination tree every time a new rule is generated, and as a result the computation will take extra time.

A production system that can generate a new rule by itself during the inference process is called an *adaptive production system*. We will say more about this kind of system in Chapter 7. In a production system, we do inference by changing working memory. So, if working memory or a part of it represents some object, we can consider it to be a system for generating new representations even if it is not an adaptive production system.

3.9 Inference Using Frames

Like production rules, a system for doing inference is important for semantic networks and frames. We can do such inference by making use of the search techniques described in Section 3.6. In this section, we will consider inference using frames.

In a representation using frames (or semantic networks), nodes are classified as either a *class* or an *instance*. A class is used to represent a general object or a class of individual objects, and an instance is used in representing an individual object in a class. For example, when a class called "computer" represents computers as a whole, one particular computer is represented as an instance. On the other hand, as we said in Section 2.11, we can make a set of classes represent a hierarchical structure by adding edges having the slot *isa* : as a label. In such a structure, if a subclass inherits properties of the superclass, we call it property inheritance. When there is more than one superclass to inherit properties from, we call it multiple inheritance.

In a class hierarchy with inheritance, a complicated problem can arise when properties to be inherited are contradictory. For example, a penguin is a bird but cannot fly. Thus it should not inherit the property "can fly" of a bird. This is because the class called penguin does not satisfy one of the properties, "mobility," of the class bird. The simplest way to allow exceptions is to describe the property "cannot fly" explicitly as the filler of the slot "mobility" of a penguin, and, if the filler of the slot of a superclass (bird, in this example) is different from the filler of the same slot of the subclass (penguin, in this example), not to inherit the property and give priority to the filler of the subclass. This method is called *blocking* inheritance.

There have been attempts to represent a frame in first-order predicate logic. For example, "a human being is a mammal" can be represented in a frame: "human being" is a subclass of "mammal" and the filler of the slot *isa* : of "human being" is "mammal." This can be expressed by a well-formed formula as

$$(\forall X)(person(X) \rightarrow mammal(X))$$

where *person* and *mammal* are predicate symbols representing a human being and a mammal, respectively.

We will not explain further the relation between frames and predicate logic in this book. It is important to study the properties of first-order predicates that represent exceptions in frame systems. For example, *non-monotonic logic*, which will be described in Chapter 8, is useful for formulating the logical meaning of exceptions.

Implementing inheritance on a computer, without multiple inheritance, is easy. However, it may be slow if we compute inheritance dynamically as part of the inference process. Therefore, it may be more effective for the overall performance of an inference system to compute all properties to be inherited by each class and instance before execution. Such a precompiler will decrease the amount of computation necessary during execution, although it will increase the amount of information we need to store. This suggests that, in practical situations, inheritance is not a basic function of inference, but rather it makes programs easier to code and understand.

3.10 Constraint Representation and Relaxation

Some methods of representing an object use the idea of *constraint*.

For example, consider the spatial relation *on*. Suppose there are two rectangles, 1 and 2, in two-dimensional Euclidean space as shown in Figure 3.15. The relation *on* meaning that 1 "is on" 2 can be represented by the following set of linear simultaneous inequalities:

$$x_{1c} < x_{2b}$$
$$x_{2a} < x_{1d}$$
$$y_{1c} = y_{1d} = y_{2a} = y_{2b}$$

where x_{in} and y_{in} are the x and y coordinates of vertex n of rectangle i, respectively.

We can use this kind of representation not only for metric representations such as coordinate representations but also for symbolic representations such as predicate logic. Generally, the representation of objects by a set of constraints that those objects need to satisfy is called *constraint*

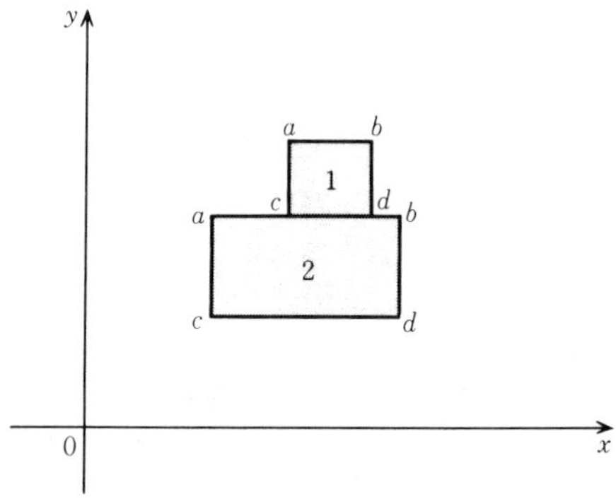

Figure 3.15 Constraint representation of the relation "is on."

representation. The *relaxation method*, an algorithm for finding a point that satisfies all the given constraints, is well known as a popular inference method for constraint representation. We will describe the relaxation method in Chapters 5 and 10.

3.11 Summary

In this chapter we explained basic methods for transforming information in a computer from one representation to another and methods for generating new information from old.

3.1 The generalization and transformation of representations are defined as procedures for transforming input information in some representation to output information in another representation.

3.2 Methods of generalization/transformation for pattern functions include convolution integrals, Fourier transforms, sampling, quantization, and transformation to some form of spatial structure representation such as spline function approximation.

3.3 Methods of generalization/transformation for symbolic representations include generation of trees and problem solving based on tree search and state transition.

3.4 Methods of generalization/transformation for more complicated symbolic representations include inference techniques using production systems, frames, and so on, and the relaxation method for constraints.

Keywords

linear transformation, point spread function, shift-invariant function, convolution integral, Fourier transform, convolution theorem, sampling, sampling theorem, quantization, interpolation of curves, spline function, problem solving, tree search, search tree, depth-first search, breadth-first search, best-first search, heuristic search, theorem proving, substitution, unification, resolution principle, refutation process, production system, working memory, recognition-action cycle, discrimination tree, conflict resolution, adaptive production system, semantic network, frame, inheritance, multiple inheritance, constraint representation, relaxation method

Exercises

3.1 In (3.8) and (3.9) in Section 3.2(b), show that we can obtain (3.10) and (3.11) if we do the appropriate variable transformation and extend it to two dimensions.

3.2 The following expression is called the *Laplacian* of the function $f(x, y)$:

$$\nabla^2 f(x,y) = \frac{\partial^2 f(x,y)}{\partial x^2} + \frac{\partial^2 f(x,y)}{\partial y^2}$$

Prove that

$$\mathcal{F}(\nabla^2 f(x,y)) = -4\pi^2(u^2+v^2)\mathcal{F}(f(x,y))$$

3.3 Suppose a function $f(x)$ is defined as

$$f(x) = (x-2)^2/4 + (y-1)^2$$

Find the values of x and y that make $f(x)$ the smallest. (Hint: use the Lagrange multiplier method given in Section 4.5.)

3.4 A weighted directed tree is a directed tree with a weight on every edge. Given a weighted directed graph, $G = (V, E, W)$, write an algorithm for finding a subtree of G such that the sum of its weights is the smallest. (Such a tree is called a *minimum spanning tree* of the original graph G.) For simplicity, we assume that G is a connected graph and does not include an edge of the form (v, v) (i.e., a *self-loop*).

3.5

"VLSI chips are LSI chips."
"If something is an LSI chip, then it can be used in the computer called bonyson."
"A VLSI chip that can be used in a computer can be used in the CPU of that computer."
"m68386 is a VLSI chip."

Given the above information, determine which computer can use m68386 for CPUs. Use a theorem-proving algorithm based on the resolution principle.

3.6 Suppose the discrimination tree shown in Figure 3.14 is generated for the production rules p_1 and p_2 shown in Section 3.8(b) and its working memory looks like the following:

$$((context\ take\_banana\ monkey\ banana)$$
$$(relation\ location\ monkey\ banana\ can\_touch))$$

Explain how the recognition-action cycle will be executed.

3.7 Suppose the slot "walking method" and its filler "walks on two legs" are given in the frame for a "human being." Represent the relation between these three using predicate logic. Also, explain, using examples, the difference between inference using frames and inference in predicate logic.

4 Pattern Feature Extraction

In Chapter 1 we said that the basis of pattern recognition is the ability to transform a pattern function into another representation. In particular, extracting features from a pattern function can be regarded as generating different representations of the pattern.

In this chapter we will discuss various methods for extracting features from a pattern function and various methods for representing the extracted features. The patterns we consider here are visual patterns. The features of a visual pattern provide the macro information that enables us to distinguish one pattern from another. For example, edges for distinguishing light and shadow, boundary lines or surfaces of an object included in the pattern or the region surrounded by such lines or surfaces, the texture of a surface, and the direction of movement are typical features in a visual pattern. There are many methods of representing these features. In this chapter we will describe algorithms for extracting some of these features and methods of representing the extracted features.

4.1 Detecting an Edge

First we describe a method for detecting an *edge* in a visual pattern. The edge of an object is a local boundary that distinguishes the surface of the object from other objects or surfaces. The reason we say local is that we use the word edge to mean a part of the boundary rather than the whole boundary line or surface. The edge of an object generally corresponds to a part of the pattern where the value of the pattern function changes drastically. Therefore, in order to detect an edge, we first need to compute the spatial change in the value of a pattern function.

Below we describe the zero-crossing method using second-order differentials and the difference operator method using first-order differences. Both are popular methods for finding spatial change in the intensity values of pattern functions.

(a) The zero-crossing method

In the visual recognition systems of some organisms, there is a mechanism called the *Mach band.* This mechanism, as shown in Figure 4.1, makes contrast more pronounced by automatically computing the differential of the intensity of light across the edge of an object that abruptly changes brightness when projected on the retina. By formalizing this mechanism, we obtain a method where, in a pattern function that represents the intensity of light, we find the points that make the second-order differential of the function equal to 0, generate a line combining these points, and use this line as an edge of an object. This is called the *zero-crossing method.* We explain the zero-crossing method in detail below.

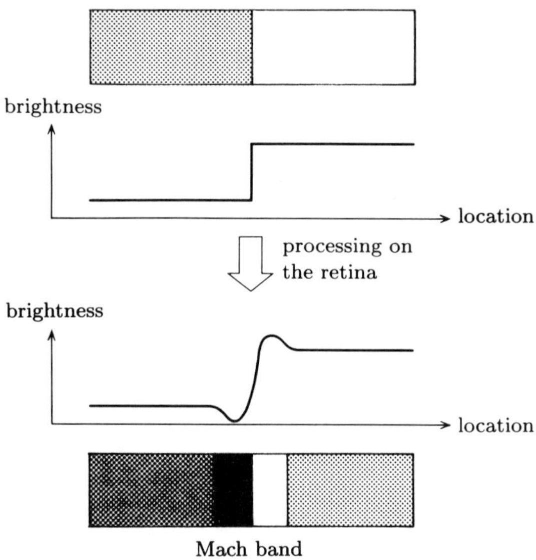

Figure 4.1 The Mach band in the visual recognition system of an organism.

Let $f(x, y)$ be a pattern function in two-dimensional Euclidean space. Since a pattern function like $f(x, y)$ usually includes noise, we first remove the noise by applying some method of *smoothing*. For example, by taking a local weighted average of the original values of a pattern function as the value at some pattern element, the values of a pattern function at neighboring pattern elements change smoothly. In this way we can hope to remove noise in a pattern function and recreate the original data. By using the Gaussian operator

$$H(x, y) = \frac{1}{2\pi\sigma^2} e^{-\frac{x^2+y^2}{2\pi\sigma^2}}$$

as a smoothing function, the value of the pattern function after smoothing, $g(x, y)$, is

$$\begin{aligned} g(x, y) &= \int_{-\infty}^{\infty} \int_{-\infty}^{\infty} H(x - a, y - b) f(a, b) \, da \, db \\ &= H(x, y) * f(x, y) \end{aligned}$$

The second-order differential of $g(x, y)$ is found by applying $g(x, y)$ to the two-dimensional Laplacian operator

$$\nabla^2 = \frac{\delta^2}{\delta x^2} + \frac{\delta^2}{\delta y^2}$$

Thus, the second-order differential of $g(x, y)$ is

$$\begin{aligned} k(x, y) &= \nabla^2 g(x, y) \\ &= \nabla^2 [H(x, y) * f(x, y)] \\ &= (\nabla^2 H(x, y)) * f(x, y) \\ &= \nabla^2 H(r) * f(x, y) \end{aligned}$$

where

$$\begin{aligned} \nabla^2 H(r) &= \frac{r^2 - 2\sigma^2}{2\pi\sigma^6} e^{-\frac{r^2}{2\sigma^2}} \\ r^2 &= x^2 + y^2 \end{aligned}$$

A point where $k(x, y) = 0$ is called a *zero crossing*. By connecting zero crossings, we can obtain an edge. Figure 4.2 shows a section of $\nabla^2 H(r)$. Figure 4.3 shows an example of edges extracted using the method of zero crossings.

(b) The difference operator method

We now describe the use of the method of first-order differences as applied to pattern functions. It is possible to formalize this using first-order differ-

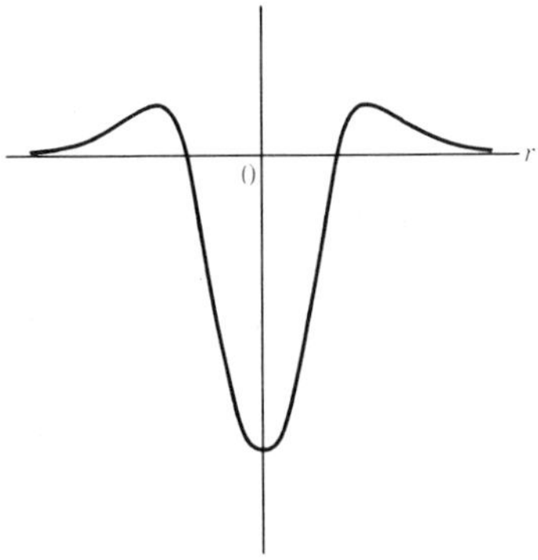

Figure 4.2 A section of $\nabla^2 H(r)$.

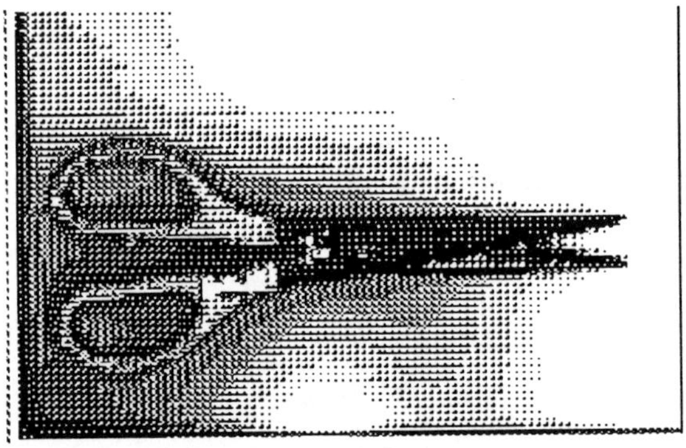

(a) Quantization pattern of an original screen

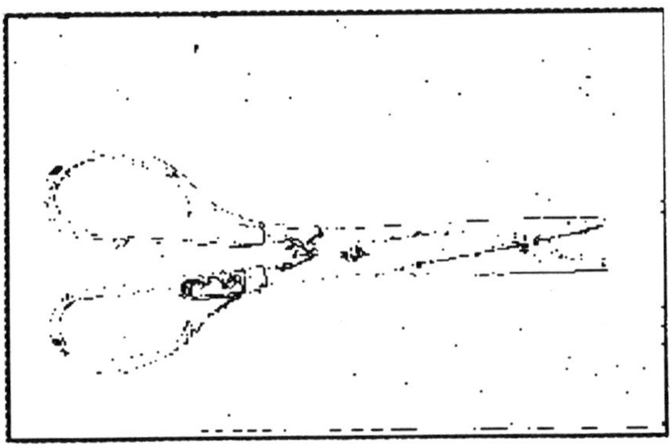

(b) Edges extracted using the method of zero crossing

Figure 4.3 Extraction of edges using zero crossings.

entials, but, since our goal is to find an edge using a computer, we think it is more practical to formulate it using differences.

First, we assume that a given pattern function represents the intensity distribution of the image. In order to make it simple, we also assume that we know the direction of the change in intensity. If we let the x axis be the direction of the change of intensity and let the intensity at the point x be $f(x)$, the difference of the intensity at x is

$$\Delta_k(x) = f(x+k) - f(x-k)$$

where k is the length of the difference interval. Now, in order to remove noise, we can do smoothing by averaging over k. For example,

$$\Delta_{k_1,k_2}(x) = \frac{1}{k_2 - k_1 + 1} \sum_{i=k_1}^{k_2} \{f(x+i) - f(x-i)\}$$

For usual applications, values around $k_1 = 1$, $k_2 = 2$–5 are used. The advantage of the above formula is that $f(x+i)$ and $f(x-i)$ can be computed directly using data from the pattern function.

We compute $\Delta_{k_1,k_2}(x)$ in some interval, $[x_1, x_2]$, and then estimate the location of an edge. Although the location of an edge should be at a point $\hat{x}$ where the difference, $\Delta_{k_1,k_2}(x)$, takes a maximum in $[x_1, x_2]$, we usually use the following algorithm, which takes the interference of noise into account.

Algorithm 4.1 (estimating the location of an edge)

[1] Estimate the existence of an edge using the following substeps. If the system succeeds in estimating the existence of an edge, go to [2]. Otherwise, stop.

[1.1] Find the maximum value of $\Delta_{k_1,k_2}(x)$ on the interval $[x_1, x_2]$. Call this value $\Delta_{\max}$ and let $\hat{x}$ be one of the points that take $\Delta_{\max}$ $\hat{x}$.

[1.2] Let Δ_{left} and Δ_{right} be the minimum values of $\Delta_{k_1,k_2}(x)$ on the intervals $[x_1, \hat{x}]$ and $[\hat{x}, x_2]$, respectively.

[1.3] If the following is true for some given threshold values α_1 and α_2, assume that an edge exists near $\hat{x}$:

$$\Delta_{\max} - \Delta_{\text{left}} \geq \alpha_1$$
$$\Delta_{\max} - \Delta_{\text{right}} \geq \alpha_1$$
$$\Delta_{\max} \geq \alpha_2$$

[2] Estimate the location of an edge using the following substeps:

[2.1] For given parameters β_1 and β_2 ($\beta_1 > 0$), set

$$\gamma = \beta_1 \Delta_{k_1,k_2}(\hat{x}) + \beta_2$$

[2.2] Among points to the left of $\hat{x}$ on the x axis, let x_{left} be the leftmost point such that $\Delta_{k_1,k_2}(x) \geq \gamma$ is true for each point between such a point and $\hat{x}$. In other words,

$$x_{\text{left}} = \min_x \{x | x \in [x_1, \hat{x}], \Delta_{k_1,k_2}(x') \geq \gamma \quad \text{for all } x' \in [x, \hat{x}]\}$$

[2.3] Among points to the right of $\hat{x}$ on the x axis, let x_{right} be the rightmost point such that $\Delta_{k_1,k_2}(x) \geq \gamma$ is true for each point between such a point and $\hat{x}$. In other words,

$$x_{\text{right}} = \max_x \{x | x \in [\hat{x}, x_2], \Delta_{k_1,k_2}(x') \geq \gamma \quad \text{for all } x' \in [\hat{x}, x]\}$$

[2.4] Estimate the location of the edge, x_0, as the midpoint between x_{left} and x_{right}. In other words,

$$x_0 = \frac{x_{\text{left}} + x_{\text{right}}}{2}$$

Figure 4.4 shows an example of estimating the location of an edge using the above algorithm.

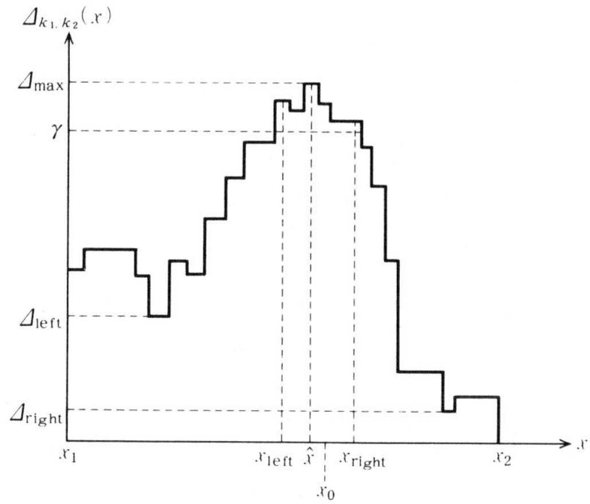

Figure 4.4 Estimating the location of an edge (in one dimension).

(c) Estimating the direction of intensity change

In method (b) we assumed that the direction of the edge was orthogonal to the x axis. If the direction of the edge is unknown, this method is useless. In this case, we need to find the direction of the intensity change, in other words, the direction that meets the edge at a right angle. We now describe a method for finding this direction. Consider the 3×3 window with some point (x, y), in two-dimensional Euclidean space E^2, as its center, as shown in Figure 4.5. The (difference) gradient of light at (x, y)

$$\nabla f(x, y) = (\nabla_x f(x, y), \nabla_y f(x, y))$$

is obtained using the following formulas:

$$\begin{aligned}\nabla_x f(x, y) &= \{f(x_1, y_1) + 2f(x_1, y) + f(x_1, y_{-1})\} \\ &\quad - \{f(x_1, y_{-1}) + 2f(x_{-1}, y) + f(x_{-1}, y_{-1})\} \\ \nabla_y f(x, y) &= \{f(x_1, y_{-1}) + 2f(x, y_1) + f(x_1, y_1)\} \\ &\quad - \{f(x_{-1}, y_{-1}) + 2f(x, y_{-1}) + f(x_1, y_{-1})\}\end{aligned}$$

(x_1, y_{-1})	(x, y_1)	(x_1, y_1)
(x_{-1}, y)	(x, y)	(x_1, y)
(x_{-1}, y_{-1})	(x, y_{-1})	(x_1, y_{-1})

Figure 4.5 A 3×3 window.

Furthermore, the direction of the gradient vector at (x, y), ν, can be obtained from

$$\nu(x, y) = \tan^{-1}(\nabla_y f(x, y) / \nabla_x f(x, y))$$

We can use $\nu(x, y)$ as the direction of the x axis in (b). In that case, the direction of the edge is $\nu + \pi/2$ at the point (x, y). Also, the magnitude of the gradient, in other words, the change of intensity at (x, y), is

$$\mu(x, y) = \sqrt{\{\nabla_x f(x, y)\}^2 + \{\nabla_y f(x, y)\}^2}$$

In the above example, we used a 3×3 window; however, we can use a bigger window, for example, 5×5. In this case, the formulas for the gradient will be slightly different.

4.2 Detection of a Boundary Line

In the recognition of visual patterns, it is important to detect boundary lines that distinguish an object from its background, or two surfaces of an object. Detection of a boundary is usually done by somehow grouping many small edges discovered using the methods described in Section 4.1. Constructing a line segment or curve by grouping local edges is called *segmentation.* In this section we explain the edge tracing method, the edge prediction method, and the Hough transformation method, all of which are popular methods for detecting boundary lines.

(a) Edge tracing

Once we have found the direction of the gradient of each edge from a visual pattern function, we can detect a boundary line by tracing the edge in the direction orthogonal to the gradient. This method is called the *edge tracing method.* The edge tracing method traces an edge using heuristic search on a graph that is constructed using the directions of gradients. What to use as an evaluation function for the heuristic search depends on what kind of boundary lines we are looking for. For example, by using shortest-path search, a boundary line is determined by a group of the shortest lines. Evaluation functions including the magnitude of the gradient or curvature (which can be obtained from the difference in the direction of neighboring gradients) can also be used.

As an example, let us suppose that we have found the direction orthogonal to the gradient at each point as shown in Figure 4.6(a). Let us imagine the graph G shown in Figure 4.6(b), which takes each point with the direction of the gradient at that point as its nodes and has a directed edge in that direction. We assume that, of the three neighboring nodes that are within $\pm$ 90 degrees of the orthogonal direction, ρ, of the gradient at a node, u_i, of G, only the nodes that are closer than ± 90 degrees from ρ are direct destinations of edges from u_i. For example, in G, the node u_1 has an edge to u_2, u_3, and u_4, respectively. Also, the node u_2 has an edge to u_5 and u_6. However, there is no edge from the node u_5 to u_6.

Next, let us assume that the end points u_i and u_j of the boundary line are already known. Now, if we search for the shortest path from the end point u_i to u_j on the graph, we will be able to construct the boundary line we are looking for as a set of segments. For example, in the graph G in Figure 4.6(b), one of the shortest routes from u_1 to u_{10} is the path passing through u_1, u_2, u_5, u_7, u_8, u_9, and u_{10}. We can use edges on this path as a representation of the boundary line.

Below, we will show the basic algorithm for the edge tracing method.

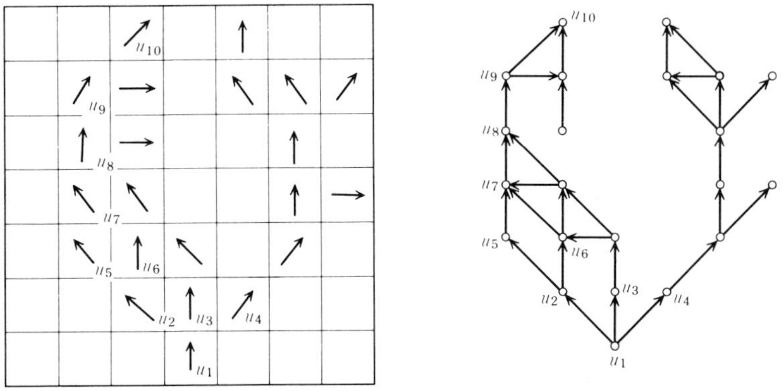

(a) Directions which are orthogonal to the gradient

(b) The graph G that corresponds to (a)

Figure 4.6 Generating a graph for the edge tracing method.

Algorithm 4.2 (edge tracing)

[1] Using the method described in Section 4.1, compute the direction of the gradient

$$\nu(x, y) = \tan^{-1}(\nabla_y f(x, y)/\nabla_x f(x, y))$$

and the magnitude of the gradient

$$\mu(x, y) = \sqrt{\{\nabla_x f(x, y)\}^2 + \{\nabla_y f(x, y)\}^2}$$

for each point (x, y) in the domain of the pattern function. Assume $\rho(x, y) = \nu(x, y) + \pi/2$.

[2] Define the graph $G = (U, L)$ as follows:

(i) Make each point (x, y) for which we have computed $\rho(x, y)$ correspond to a node of G.

(ii) Let u_i and u_j be the nodes that correspond to two neighboring points, (x_i, y_i) and (x_j, y_j). Assume that a directed edge from u_i to u_j exists if and only if (x_j, y_j) is one of the three neighboring points in the $\rho(x_i, y_i)$ direction from (x_i, y_i) and when all of the following inequalities hold:

$$|\rho(x_i, y_i) - \rho(x_j, y_j)|_{\text{mod } 2\pi} < \pi/2 \quad (1)$$

$$\mu(x_i, y_i) > k \quad (2)$$

$$\mu(x_j, y_j) > k \quad (3)$$

where k is a given positive constant.

[3] Pick two nodes of G, u_o and u_d, and let u_o be the initial state s_o and u_d be the goal state s_d. Do the shortest-path search from s_o

to s_d using the best-first search described in Section 3.6. For the shortest-path search, we use an evaluation function whose value at a node is the length of the path followed so far.

Formula (1) in condition (ii) of [2] above is a heuristic rule to make the orthogonal direction of the gradient closer to u_d. Formulas (2) and (3) are heuristic rules for recognizing only gradients of a certain magnitude as contributing to the boundary line, in order to prevent confusion between an edge and noise.

(b) Edge prediction

In this section we describe the *edge prediction method*, a boundary detection method similar to the edge tracing method. Intuitively the edge prediction method starts from an edge, predicts the direction of a neighboring edge, and combines edges based on that prediction. The basic algorithm is shown below. The algorithm for this method is simple, and it is possible to use it along with other edge detection methods. Also, it is, in principle, possible to generate not only line segments but also curves. However, since this method computes serially using local data from the pattern function, it may find different boundaries depending on what we take as the initial edge. It is also easily affected by noise.

Since the following algorithm is conceptual, to turn it into a program, we would need to supply programs for edge detection or extrapolation of line (or curve) segments.

Algorithm 4.3 (edge prediction)

[1] Pick one edge and assume that it is the currently considered edge. Assume no boundary lines have been obtained so far. Let the current edge be the initial boundary line. (Selection of the initial edge)

[2] Extend the boundary obtained so far along the current edge and predict the location of the end of the extension and its direction. The direction of the extension is generally not unique but is usually distributed over some area. (Prediction of the neighboring edge)

[3] Find a neighboring edge within the area predicted in [2] using some edge detection method. If a neighboring edge was found as predicted, add it to the boundary and go to [2]. If an edge was detected outside the predicted area, go to [4]. If an edge could not be found, go to [5]. (Detection of a neighboring edge)

[4] Assume that one boundary line ends at the current edge and stop the algorithm. (Termination of prediction)

[5] If an edge could not be found persistently for several trials, decide that the boundary ends at the current edge and stop the prediction.

Otherwise, decide that the reason for not being able to find the edge is the effect of noise, go to [2], and predict another direction. (Decision to continue prediction)

(c) Hough transformations

Fitting a curve to many local edges can be done by finding a formula for a curve that passes through as many points as possible that make the magnitude of the gradient larger than a certain value. One method for detecting a boundary line by making use of this idea is called the *Hough transformation method.* The Hough transformation works particularly well when many edges have been obtained. Compared with the edge tracing method and the edge prediction method, it is less likely to be affected by noise. Let us consider the Hough transformation method here.

As an example, suppose we fit a straight line to a set of edges generated from a pattern function in two-dimensional Euclidean space. Let $\{p_1, \ldots, p_n\}(p_j = (x_j, y_j), j = 1, \ldots, n)$ be points where the magnitude of the gradient goes over a given threshold. If the straight line $y = \hat{a}x + \hat{b}$ passes through the points $p_1, \ldots, p_k$ $(1 \le k \le n)$, then $y_j = \hat{a}x_j + \hat{b}$ $(j = 1, \ldots, k)$ holds. This means that, if we map these functions into the space of the parameters (a, b), there are k straight lines $b = -x_j a + y_j$ $(j = 1, \ldots, k)$ that intersect at one point, $(\hat{a}, \hat{b})$. That is, grouping the original n points, $p_1, \ldots, p_n$, and putting the points of each group on a straight line is equivalent to finding the intersection point of straight lines in the space of the parameters, (a, b).

Suppose, as shown in Figure 4.7(a), we have the points, $\{p_1, \ldots, p_5\} = \{(2,2), (2,3), (4,4), (5,5), (6,5)\}$. In this case, the straight lines that correspond to $p_1, \ldots, p_5$ in the parameter space will be the following:

$$b = -2a + 2$$
$$b = -2a + 3$$
$$b = -4a + 4$$
$$b = -5a + 5$$
$$b = -6a + 5$$

(see Figure 4.7(b)). The number of points of intersection of these five straight lines is five, $A, \ldots, E$, as shown in Figure 4.7(b). Each point corresponds to the straight line that combines the points in Figure 4.7(a). We assume here that the points p_1 and p_2 have the same x coordinate and that the straight lines corresponding to p_1 and p_2 are parallel in the parameter space, since the slope of the straight line a, which combines p_1 and p_2, is infinite.

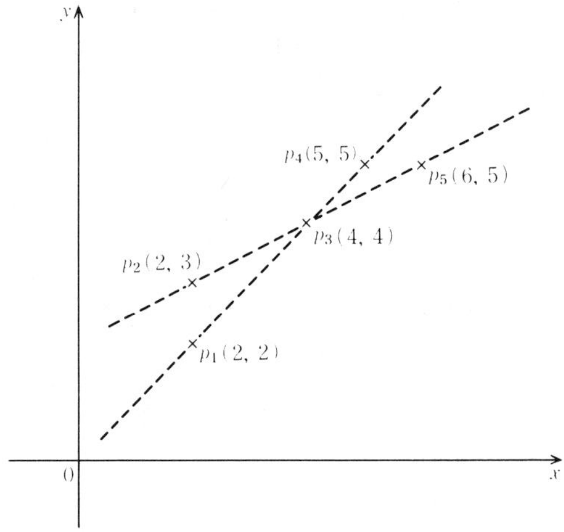

(a) A point with a big gradient

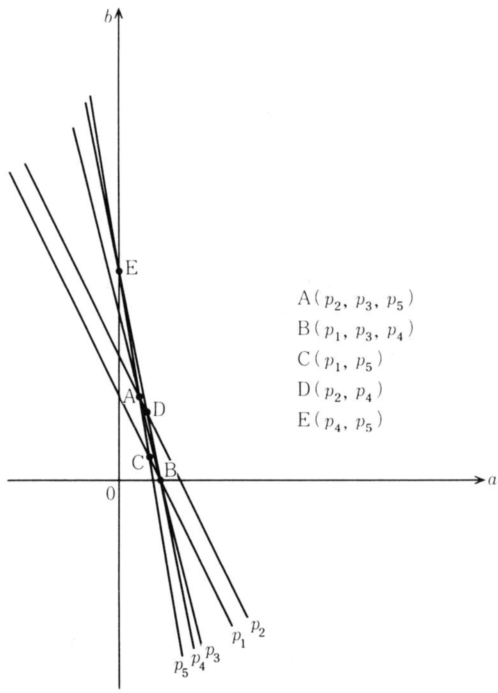

(b) Straight lines and points of intersection in the parameter space

Figure 4.7 The Hough transformation of straight lines.

As you can see from this example, in general, the number of straight lines that intersect at a point is different for each point of the intersection in the parameter space. Usually, when you use this method for detecting a boundary, it is desirable to choose, as a boundary line, a straight line that passes through as many points as possible in the original space, or equivalently a point of intersection where as many lines as possible intersect in the parameter space (called the maximal intersection). In the above example, points A and B in Figure 4.7(b) are the points with maximumal intersection. The straight lines that correspond to A and B in the original space are the two broken straight lines shown in Figure 4.7(a). These two straight lines segment the edges.

The method above can be used not only for straight lines but also for simple curves. The method of detecting a boundary line by transforming the original problem to one of computing points of intersection in a parameter space is called the Hough transformation method. An algorithm for the Hough transformation for finding a straight line that passes through as many as points as possible can be summarized as follows:

Algorithm 4.4 (Hough transformation for fitting a straight line)

[1] Quantize the parameter space between the maximum values and the minimum values that a and b can take. Call the quantized parameters $a_1, \ldots, a_r$, $b_1, \ldots, b_s$. (Quantization of the parameter space)

[2] Make $a_j = 0$ $(j = 1, \ldots, r)$, $b_k = 0$ $(k = 1, \ldots, s)$. (Initialization of parameters)

[3] For each point $p_i = (x_i, y_i)$ whose gradient magnitude exceeds a certain threshold value, let

$$\begin{aligned} a_{j_i} &= a_{j_i} + 1 \\ b_{k_i} &= b_{k_i} + 1 \end{aligned}$$

for a_j, b_k such that $y_i = a_{j_i} x_i + b_{k_i}$. (Detection of an intersection point in the parameter space)

[4] Find a point (a, b) that takes a maximal value in the quantized parameter space. This (a, b) corresponds to a set of points that have large gradients and are all on one straight line. (Detection of a straight line)

However, as we noted in the previous example, this algorithm cannot find a straight line passing through two points whose x coordinates are the same in the original space, in other words, a straight line passing through two points arranged vertically. Thus we often use the above method with a polar coordinate space as the parameter space and transform a point (x, y)

to a sine wave in the space of parameters (r, θ) by using $x\cos\theta + y\sin\theta = r$. The Hough transformation method is often used as a boundary detection method for cases with many local edges or with noise.

4.3 Extracting a Region

Once boundary lines have been detected, we can use this line to extract the region surrounded by the boundary lines. In this section we will describe two popular algorithms for extracting a region, the splitting method and the merging method. Before we do that, we need to define the word "region." A region is a set of pattern elements defined as follows:

Definition 1 (partition and region) Let D be a finite set of pattern elements from a given pattern function and let 2^D be the set of subsets of D. Let $Q(D)$ be a predicate on 2^D that, for any subset of pattern elements, $D \in 2^D$, returns T if the elements in the subset have uniform values and returns T returns F otherwise. A set of pattern element sets $D_1, \ldots, D_n$ is called a *partition* of I for a predicate Q if

$$I = \bigcup_{i=1}^{n} D_i$$

$$D_j \bigcap D_k = \emptyset \quad (j \neq k)$$

and

$$Q(D_i) = T \quad \text{for all } i$$
$$Q(D_j \cup D_k) = F \quad \text{for all } j \neq k$$

Each pattern element set, D_i $(i = 1, \ldots, n)$, of the partition is called a *region*.

(a) Splitting method

As noted in Definition 1, in order to determine a region, we need a predicate for judging whether the pattern elements included in that region have uniform values or not. Let us consider the following predicate Q as an example:

$$Q(D) = \begin{cases} T & \text{for all } x \in D, f(x) > c \\ F & \text{for all } \ x \in D, f(x) \leq c \end{cases}$$

where $f(x)$ is a pattern function and c is a given constant.

For this predicate Q, we are only considering a pattern element set D where either all $x \in D$ make $f(x) > c$ or all $x \in D$ make $f(x) \leq c$. Therefore, Q is a predicate applicable only when the value of a pattern function distinguishes an object from its background. In other words, if we let D_1 and D_2 be the sets of pattern elements for an object and its background, respectively, then Q is a predicate for extracting D_1 and D_2 so that $Q(D_1) = T$ and $Q(D_2) = F$.

Region extraction of this kind can be done approximately by setting an appropriate threshold value c. For example, if we make a histogram for the values of a pattern element, $f(x)$, and remove small variations of values by smoothing it, then we can use the minimal value as the value of c. We can smooth a histogram, for example, using the method of fitting the histogram to the sum of two normal distributions and determining the threshold value from the estimated parameter values.

The above method of region extraction is generally called the *splitting method.* This method can extract smaller regions by using the same method of splitting recursively. An algorithm for such a recursive splitting method is as follows:

Algorithm 4.5 (region extraction using the recursive splitting method)

[1] Let the domain, D, of a given pattern function, $f(x)$, be the initial region. Set $\mathcal{D} = \{D\}$. (Definition of the initial region)

[2] Construct the histogram of the values of $f(x)$ on the pattern elements. (Construction of the histogram)

[3] Smooth the histogram and determine the threshold value as the minimal value in the histogram. (Finding the threshold value)

[4] If there is no minimal value in the histogram, stop. D is the extracted region. Otherwise, go to [5] using c as the threshold value. (Termination condition)

[5] Let $D_1 = \{x|f(x) > c\}$ and $D_2 = \{x|f(x) \leq c\}$. Let $\mathcal{D} = \mathcal{D} \cup \{D_1, D_2\} - \{D\}$. (Extracting a region)

[6] Do [2]–[5] for all $D \in \mathcal{D}$. (Recursion)

The splitting method is a global method for extracting regions based on the whole distribution of intensity values of a pattern function and is robust against noise. We can also search for threshold values by constructing a multidimensional histogram using, for example, intensity and some other attributes like color. It is sometimes even easier to find threshold values if we use a multidimensional histogram.

(b) Merging

While the splitting method uses global data, the *merging method* uses local data. The merging method first considers a small set of pattern elements as one region. As the smallest set, it can take each pattern element. It then merges neighboring regions when the difference between the average values of the pattern function in those regions is smaller than some given threshold value. By repeating this operation, we can extract a larger region with uniform values of the pattern function. Depending on how we define the average value of a region, many methods are possible. We will provide one of them below.

Algorithm 4.6 (region extraction by merging using the difference in values of the pattern function on two sides of a boundary line)

[1] Detect boundary lines by applying some boundary detection algorithm to a given pattern function.

[2] Do the following substeps for all boundary lines, k:

  [2.1] Assume that the sets of pattern elements found on the two sides of the boundary line k are regions a_k and b_k, respectively.

  [2.2] Let L_k be the length of k. Let M_k be the sum of the lengths of the parts of k for which differences in values of the pattern elements in a_k and b_k are smaller than a given value.

  [2.3] For a given threshold value, c, merge a_k and b_k, and delete k only when $M_k/L_k < c$.

[3] If the merge does not happen for any of the current boundary lines in [2], then stop. Otherwise, go to [2].

There is also a method, called the split-and-merge method, that combines the splitting method and the merging method.

4.4 Texture Analysis

There are visual patterns that can be considered as single patterns at the level of a region, though local features such as directions of edges and differences of intensity are similar in each of those patterns. For example, Figure 4.8, part of a tatami mat, produces a pattern by repeating similar elements. A pattern like this, which is created by repeating elements with some invariant feature, is called a texture. An element constituting texture is called a *texture primitive* or a *texel.*

To consider texture as one feature of the surface of an object and extract such a feature from the pattern function corresponding to the object is called *texture analysis.* In this section, we will explain some methods of texture analysis.

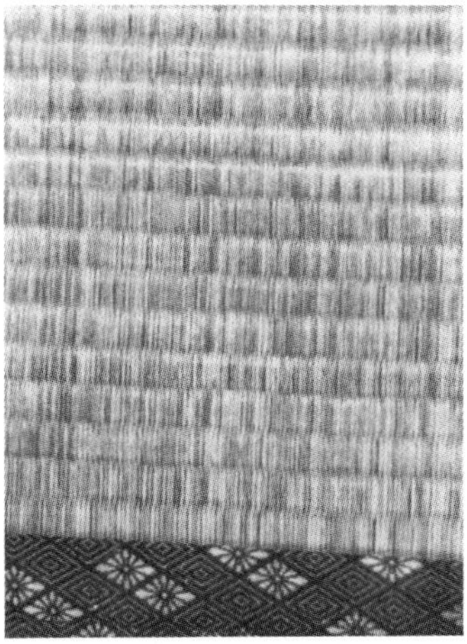

Figure 4.8 The texture of a tatami mat.

(a) Structure analysis

Considering the fact that a texture usually is generated by repeating elements that are similar in shape but are placed slightly differently, we can do texture analysis based on a kind of grammar whose elements are shapes. For example, let us consider the texture shown in Figure 4.9(a). This texture is generated by iterating ○ and ✣. In order to generate such a texture, we can use the grammar, $\{S, C, R, S_0\}$, shown in Figure 4.9(b), where S, C, R, and S_0 represent the set of terminal symbols, the set of nonterminal symbols, the set of grammar rules, and the initial symbol, respectively. (S_0 is equivalent to a sentence in a linguistic grammar.)

By starting from the initial symbol, S_0, and applying one of the grammar rules, r_1–r_6, we can generate the texture shown in Figure 4.9(c). (In the rules, ○, ○̇, ○̣, and ˙○ and ✣, ✣̇, ✣̣, and ˙✣ are identified, respectively.) A grammar like the one shown in Figure 4.9(b) is called a *shape grammar*. In order to apply a shape grammar to a given pattern function, we apply the following algorithm to the data after we have finished region extraction:

Algorithm 4.7 (texture analysis using a shape grammar)

[1] Find a region whose shape is similar to the initial symbol, where regions generated by geometrical operations such as rotation, inversion, expansion, and contraction on the region are identified. If such a region cannot be found, then stop. Otherwise, consider the initial

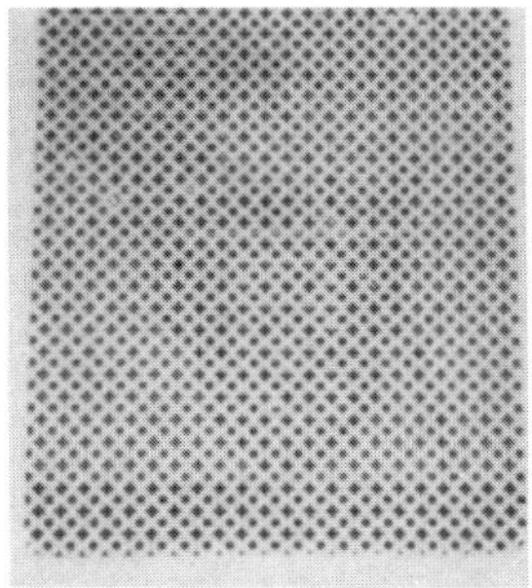

(a) The original screen pattern

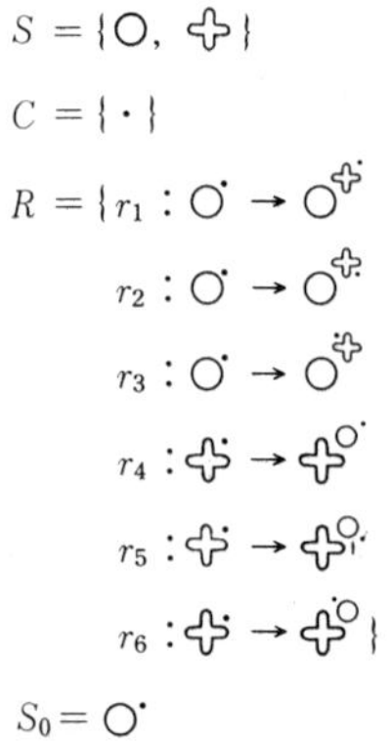

(b) The shape grammar

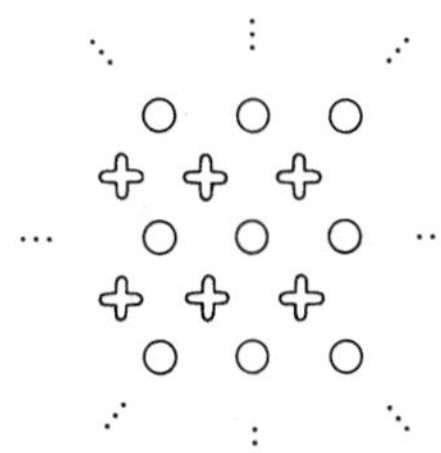

(c) The texture expression

Figure 4.9 Structure analysis of a texture.

symbol as the currently matching symbol, and find a grammar rule whose left side is the currently matching symbol. (Detection of the initial symbol)

[2] If such a rule cannot be found, then stop. If it is found, apply the same geometrical operations as [1] or [3] to the pattern that corresponds to the symbol in the right side of the rule. (Application of a grammar rule).

[3] Generate a new pattern by replacing the pattern in the left side of the rule used in [2] by the right side of the same rule. Find a grammar rule whose left side matches part of the new pattern, considering geometrical operations such as those used in [1]. (Generation of a new pattern)

[4] Repeat [2] and [3]. (Repetition)

Generally, more than one grammar rule can be obtained in [1] or [3]. So it may actually be necessary to use a tree search method in searching for matching rules, although Algorithm 4.7 omits that part. The method of using a shape grammar is a kind of texture analysis called *structure analysis*. There are many other methods known as structure analysis.

(b) Statistical analysis

Structure analysis is useful when the texture has distinctive regularity; however, in reality, this is not always the case. This is especially true for patterns that include noise or data deficiencies, and statistical analysis is often more appropriate for such patterns. Examples of statistical analysis include cluster analysis using characteristics of pattern elements or regions and methods for extracting features in the spatial frequency domain that are obtained by Fourier analysis of the data.

(c) Texture gradients

Texture often appears because surfaces have a slope. In these cases, the direction of the slope of a surface can be considered to be the direction of the maximum change of the size of the texel. So, if texels making up the texture have already been extracted, we can estimate the direction of the slope of a surface by computing the direction that gives the maximum rate of change in the size of texels.

4.5 Detection of Movement

In previous sections, we described pattern recognition of a static object. In this section, we will consider an object that moves as time goes by. With the human visual system, we are unable to see the outside world if the movement of our eyeballs is synchronized perfectly with the movement of the outside world. Our ability to see the outside world depends on the small but constant movement of our eyeballs. Note that this is equivalent to the view that there are stationary eyeballs that are seeing the slightly moving outside world. So, recognition of a moving object rather than a static one is basic to human vision.

On the other hand, pattern recognition by computer has emphasized the study of static objects until recently. Also, recent studies of feature extraction from moving visual images often involve extending the methods used for static images. For example, in detecting a moving boundary line, we can extend boundary detection methods for static images by considering boundary lines with both time and location as parameters.

However, a new approach for feature extraction has appeared that puts fundamental emphasis on detection of movements as in human vision. As an example of a pattern recognition method that is different from the methods we have explained so far, we will describe a method for detecting movement based on optical flow.

(a) Optical flow and its computation

The fact that an object "moves" smoothly at some speed means that each point on the object generates a velocity field that is continuous in space-time. We call this velocity field *optical flow.* For example, we can represent the location of a point at time t in two-dimensional Euclidean space E^2 as $(x(t), y(t))$ and its velocity vector as $(dx/dt, dy/dt)$ if $x(t)$ and $y(t)$ are differentiable. The velocity field can be considered to be the set of such velocity vectors in some region of E^2. We can detect the movement of an object by computing its optical flow. Note that optical flow is also observed if an object stays still and the observer is moving. Now, let us consider how to compute optical flow.

First, we define a pattern function $f(x, y, t)$ as a function of the location of a pattern element (x, y) and the time t. $f(x, y, t)$ can be approximated by the following Taylor expansion:

$$f(x + dx, y + dy, t + dt) \approx f(x, y, t) + \frac{\partial f}{\partial x}dx + \frac{\partial f}{\partial y}dy + \frac{\partial f}{\partial t}dt \qquad (4.1)$$

If we assume that the intensity value of a pattern element does not change while it is moving,

$$f(x + dx, y + dy, t + dt) = f(x, y, t) \qquad (4.2)$$

Therefore, from formulas (4.1) and (4.2), we have

$$\frac{\partial f}{\partial x}\frac{dx}{dt} + \frac{\partial f}{\partial y}\frac{dy}{dt} + \frac{\partial f}{\partial t} = 0 \qquad (4.3)$$

Formula (4.3) shows that the time rate of change $\partial f/\partial t$ of f at the point (x, y) can be expressed (as a linear approximation) by the inner product of the spatial rate of change for f, $(\partial f/\partial x, \partial f/\partial y)$, and the velocity vector, $(dx/dt, dy/dt)$, at the point (x, y).

All that is left is to find the optical flow, i.e., $(dx/dt, dy/dt)$ the velocity vector at each point (x, y). Although formula (4.3) is one of the constraints to be satisfied by the velocity vector, there are infinitely many velocity vectors that satisfy (4.3). So, let us look for a velocity vector that makes the following error function E a minimum:

$$E(x,y,t) = (f_x u + f_y v + f_t)^2 + \lambda(u_x^2 + u_y^2 + v_x^2 + v_y^2) \tag{4.4}$$

where

$$\begin{aligned} f_x &= \partial f/\partial x, & f_y &= \partial f/\partial y \quad f_t = \partial f/\partial t \\ u &= dx/dt, & v &= dy/dt \\ u_x &= \partial u/\partial x, & u_y &= \partial u/\partial y \\ v_x &= \partial v/\partial x, & v_y &= \partial v/\partial y \end{aligned}$$

The first term of the right side in formula (4.4) is the square of the left side of formula (4.3), and the second term is the sum of the squares of the rate of change in the velocity components. Formula (4.4) is a Lagrangian function corresponding to the minimization problem for making the first term minimum under the condition of making the latter term smaller (a condition for choosing a locally smooth vector as the velocity vector), and λ corresponds to the Langrange multiplier.*

To find the optical flow, we need only compute the u and v that make formula (4.4) minimum. First, we differentiate (4.4) using u and v and make the results equal to 0:

$$(f_x^2 + \lambda^2)u + f_x f_y v = \lambda^2 u^* - f_x f_t \tag{4.5}$$

$$f_x f_y u + (f_y^2 + \lambda^2)v = \lambda^2 v^* - f_y f_t \tag{4.6}$$

where $u^* = u - \nabla^2 u$, $v^* = v - \nabla^2 v$.

*For real-valued functions $h(x)$, $g_i(x)$ $(i = 1, \ldots, m)$ with a space D as their domain, the problem of finding an $x \in D$ that satisfies the constraints $g_i(x) = 0$ $(i = 1 \ldots, m)$ and that makes $h(x)$ minimum is called a *constrained minimization problem*. A necessary condition for some $x^* \in D$ to be a solution to the constrained minimization problem is as follows: When defining the function

$$L(x, \lambda_1, \ldots, \lambda_m) = h(x) + \sum_{i=1}^{m} \lambda_i g_i(x)$$

some $\lambda_1^*, \ldots, \lambda_m^*$ should exist where $x^*, \lambda_1^*, \ldots, \lambda_m^*$ satisfy the simultaneous equations

$$\frac{\partial L}{\partial x} = 0, \quad \frac{\partial L}{\partial \lambda_i} = 0 \quad (i = 1, \ldots, m)$$

$L(x, \lambda_1, \ldots, \lambda_m)$ is called the *Lagrangian* for this problem, and λ_i $(i = 1, \ldots, m)$ are called the *Lagrange multipliers*. The method of solving a constrained minimization problem by finding solutions to those simultaneous equations is called the *Lagrange multiplier method*. The Lagrange multiplier method is useful not only for problems involving equality constraints but also for problems that include constraints involving inequalities. However, in a problem including inequality constraints, the above simultaneous equations should be simultaneous inequalities and the signs of the Lagrange multipliers should be limited. The Lagrange multiplier method can also be used for solving minimization problems with constraints on unknown *functions* (called *problems of variations*).

If we make

$$A = f_x^2 + f_y^2 + \lambda^2$$
$$B = f_x u^* + f_y v^* + f_t$$

then by formulas (4.5) and (4.6) we have

$$u = u^* - (B/A) f_x \tag{4.7}$$
$$v = v^* - (B/A) f_y \tag{4.8}$$

To obtain u and v satisfying formulas (4.7) and (4.8) approximately on a computer, we can use the following algorithm applying the Gauss-Seidel method:

Algorithm 4.8 (computation of optical flow using the Gauss-Seidel method)

[1] Let $u(x, y, 0) = 0$, $v(x, y, 0) = 0$, $t = 1$. (Initialization)

[2] At each point (x, y), compute

$$u(x, y, t) = u^*(x, y, t-1) - (B/A) f_x$$
$$v(x, y, t) = v^*(x, y, t-1) - (B/A) f_y$$

(Iterative computation)

[3] If $t = \hat{t}$ (the final time of the data), stop. Otherwise, make $t = t + 1$ and go to [2]. (Termination condition)

Figure 4.10 shows a time-varying image of a square moving across a screen (at six points of time) in two-dimensional Euclidean space and the optical flow obtained at $t = 6$. Note that there are many other methods for computing optical flow.

(b) Detecting the direction of movement using optical flow

Let us consider a method for determining the direction of movement of a surface as an example of feature extraction applying optical flow. Suppose, as in Figure 4.11, an observer with a single eye stands at the origin of three-dimensional Euclidean space and is looking at the pattern of a static surface S at distance r from the origin that is being projected onto the surface of the unit sphere (sphere with radius 1) around the origin. As you can see from Figure 4.11,

$$y = x \tan\theta$$

So,

$$\theta' = (v - u\tan\theta)/(x\sec^2\theta) \tag{4.9}$$

holds, where $\theta' = d\theta/dt$, $u = dx/dt$, $v = dy/dt$.

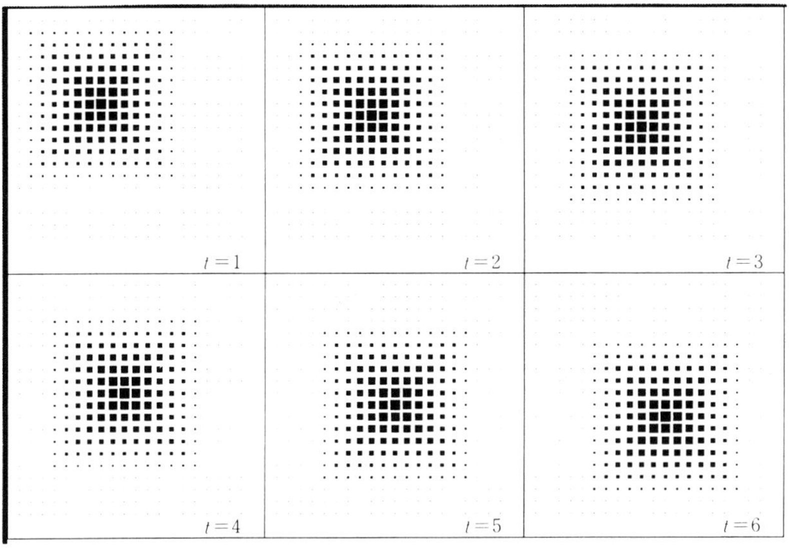

(a) A time-varying image pattern of a moving square

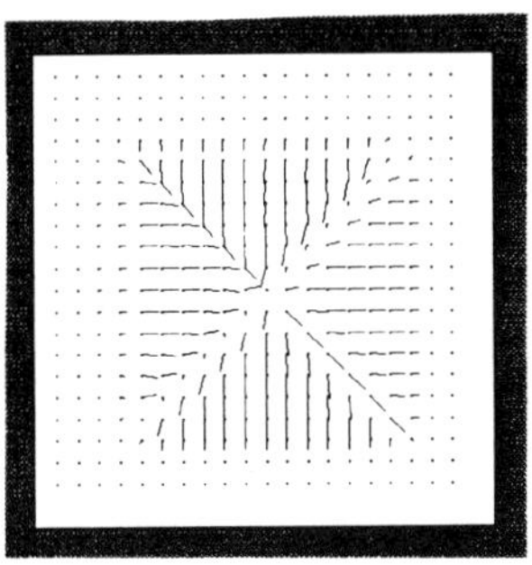

(b) A computation example of optical flow

Figure 4.10 Result of computing optical flow.

If we substitute $x = r\sin\phi\cos\theta$ into (4.9), we have

$$\theta' = (v\cos\theta - u\sin\theta)/r\sin\phi \tag{4.10}$$

On the other hand, by using $z = r\cos\phi$,

$$\phi' = (r'\cos\phi - w)/r\sin\phi \tag{4.11}$$

where $\phi' = d\phi/dt$, $\gamma' = dr/dt$, $w = dz/dt$.

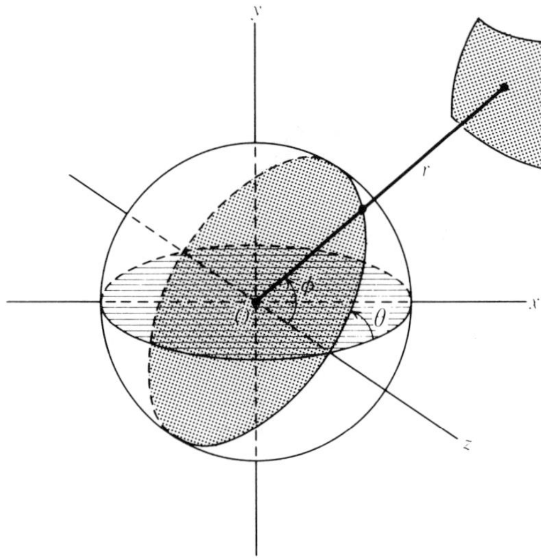

Figure 4.11 A surface seen from the origin of the spherical coordinates.

Now if we substitute $r'(xu + yv + zw)/r$ into (4.11),

$$\phi' = \{(xu + yv + zw)\cos\phi - rw\}/r^2 \sin\phi \tag{4.12}$$

(4.10) and (4.12) are the angular velocity in the θ and ϕ directions, respectively. Therefore, they are the equations that need to be satisfied by the optical flow in spherical coordinates.

Now, suppose the observer at the origin moves at the speed $-V$ in the z direction, facing the static surface S (see Figure 4.12). (Relatively, this is the same as the situation where the object is moving at a certain speed, facing the observer.) Since

$$u = 0, \quad v = 0, \quad w = -V$$

we substitute them into (4.10) and (4.12) and obtain

$$\theta' = 0 \tag{4.13}$$

$$\phi' = (V \sin\phi)/r \tag{4.14}$$

Now let us compute the normal n of the surface S at a point a on S using the optical flow given in (4.13) and (4.14). First, let us consider the angles σ and τ on the planes aoz and boa that satisfy

$$\tan\sigma = \frac{1}{r}\frac{\partial r}{\partial \phi} \tag{4.15}$$

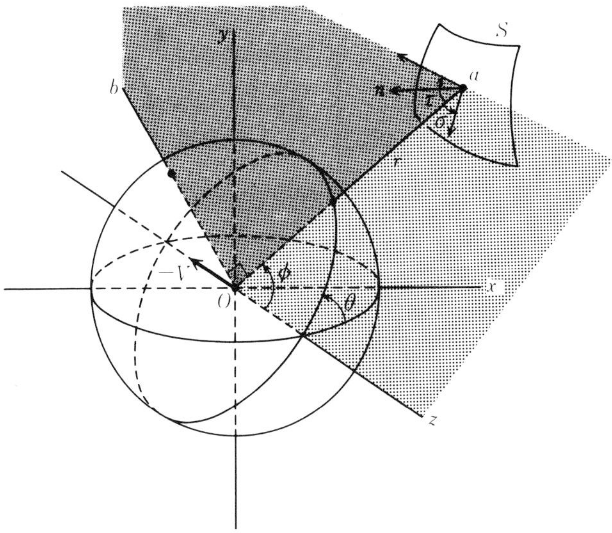

Figure 4.12 The direction of the surface based on the optical flow that is generated by going farther on the z axis.

$$\tan \tau = \frac{1}{r} \frac{\partial r}{\partial \phi} \tag{4.16}$$

σ and τ each represent the rate of change of the distance to the point a of the object with respect to ϕ and θ when the observer moves. The normal n of S can be computed using σ and τ. Now we differentiate (4.14) using ϕ and θ, respectively,

$$\frac{\partial r}{\partial \phi} = \left\{ V \left(\phi' \cos \phi - \frac{\partial \phi'}{\partial \phi} \sin \phi \right) \right\} / \phi'^2$$

$$\frac{\partial r}{\partial \theta} = -\left\{ V \frac{\partial \phi'}{\partial \theta} \sin \phi \right\} / \phi'^2$$

If we substitute these into (4.15) and (4.16), we get

$$\tan \sigma = \cot \phi - \frac{\partial \ln \phi'}{\partial \phi} \tag{4.17}$$

$$\tan \tau = -\frac{\partial \ln \phi'}{\partial \theta} \tag{4.18}$$

(4.17) and (4.18) show that it is easy to obtain σ and τ from the optical flow in the ϕ direction. In particular, note that (4.17) and (4.18) can be computed independently of the speed of the observer V, the distance r between the observer and the object, and the rate of change of r, that is, $\partial r / \partial \theta$ and $\partial r / \partial \phi$.

(c) Ill-posed problems and their regularization

As noted in (a) and (b), we cannot generally find a unique solution to a feature extraction problem based on optical flow. For example, in extracting the direction of a surface as in (b), we gave general equations for the flow using spherical coordinates in (4.10) and (4.12); however, by using only these equations, it is generally difficult to extract a feature such as the direction of the movement of a surface. To compute a specific flow, we need to introduce an external constraint, for example, an observer moving at a fixed speed along a coordinate axis (as we did in (b)). Also, in the method of computing flow explained in (a), (4.3) is an equation to be satisfied by the flow; however, there are infinitely many flows that satisfy (4.3). Therefore, in (a) we used the external constraint that makes the flow locally smooth.

In this subsection, we will have a more general discussion of the problem of not being able to determine a feature uniquely based only on optical flow. The reason why we cannot compute flow determining a feature uniquely using only data provided by the pattern function is that a visual system is a special information processing system that transforms three-dimensional information into two-dimensional information and then reconstructs the three-dimensional information. We can assume that the visual system determines the three-dimensional information uniquely by constraining the information from outside by the structure of the system itself. The methods explained in (a) and (b) are special cases of formalizing the idea that the visual system solves an insufficiently constrained problems. Below we will give a general description of feature extraction as an insufficiently constrained problem and methods for solving such a problem.

(1) *Ill-posed problems*

When a unique solution to a problem P exists and is continuous in the initial conditions, we call P a *well-posed problem.* Otherwise, we call P an *ill-posed problem.* For example, ordinary linear differential equations satisfying appropriate conditions on continuity are well-posed problems, while simultaneous algebraic equations with more variables than the number of equations are generally ill-posed problems. Feature extraction by the visual system can be regarded as a kind of ill-posed problem.

(2) *Calculus of variations and regularization*

Let us consider the calculus of variations as a basic method for solving ill-posed problems. First, consider the problem P of obtaining a vector y that satisfies the simultaneous linear equation

$$Ay = x \tag{4.19}$$

for a given data vector x, where A is a linear operator.* When y is not determined uniquely for x (for example, when the inverse of the coefficient matrix A does not exist for the simultaneous linear equations in (4.19)), we can introduce another constraint for y and determine y uniquely "as much as possible." For example, for an arbitrary linear transformation B, we can choose y to minimize the norm $\|By\|^2$. In this case, the original problem P can be formulated as the following problem.**

$$\text{Find a } y \text{ such that } \min_{y} \|Ay - x\|^2 + \lambda \|By\|^2.$$

This is a problem in the calculus of variations using a quadratic functional, and λ is the undetermined Lagrange multiplier. As we assumed above, if A and B are linear operators and $\|\cdot\|$ is the square norm, a unique solution exists and it is continuous in the initial conditions. In other words, this problem is a well-posed problem. To transform a problem that is originally ill-posed into one that is well-posed is called *regularization* of the ill-posed problem, and λ is called the *regularization parameter.*

(3) *Applying regularization to pattern recognition*

Regularization can be applied to many pattern recognition problems including feature extraction. Some applications are shown in Table 4.1.

Let us consider the detection of an edge. Let $i(x)$ be the quantized value of a pattern element, $f(x)$ be the original pattern function, and Q be the sampling operator for $f(x)$. Regularization, in this case, can be stated as the problem of reconstructing $f(x)$ from the given quantized data $i(x)$ under the condition that $f(x)$ be as smooth as possible. In other words, if we represent this regularization problem in the form of a variation problem, it becomes the problem of finding an $f(x)$ that gives the following minimum value:

$$\min_{f(x)} \int \{(Q(f(x) - i(x))^2 + \lambda f_{xx}(x)^2\} \, dx$$

where $f_{xx}(x)$ is the second-order differential of $f(x)$.

The problem of reconstructing the original visual pattern from moving image data can be formulated similarly, provided we use, as a constraint, the condition that makes the inner product of the gradient ∇f of the pattern function and the velocity vector V as close as possible to f_t, the change of the intensity over time. This condition corresponds to (4.3).

*The simplest example of a linear operator is the coefficient matrix of simultaneous linear equations. The arguments here encompass more general instances and apply to a wide range of linear operations.

**It can also be defined as the problem of finding a y that minimizes $\|By\|^2$ and satisfies $\|Ay - x\| < \epsilon$ for some $\epsilon > 0$.

Table 4.1 Regularization in visual recognition (Poggio et al., 1985)

Problem	Regularization problem
Edge detection	$\min_f \int [(Qf - i)^2 + \lambda(f_{xx})^2]\, dx$
Restoring patterns in a moving image	$\min_f \int\int\int [(Qf - i)^2 + \lambda(\nabla f \cdot V + f_t)^2]\, dx\, dy\, dt$
Optical flow (extraction from a region)	$\min_{u,v} \int\int [(i_x u + i_y v + i_t)^2 + \lambda(ux^2 + u_y^2 + v_x^2 + v_y^2)]\, dx\, dy$
Reconstruction of the surface	$\min_f \int\int [(Qf - d)^2 + \lambda(f_{xx}^2 + sf_{xy}^2 + f_{yy}^2)]\, dx\, dy$
Color	$\min_z \|I^\nu - Az\|^2 + \lambda\|Pz\|^2$
Optical flow (extraction from contours)	$\min_\nu \int [(V \cdot N - V^N)^2 + \lambda(\frac{\partial V}{\partial s})^2]\, ds$

(For symbols, refer to the text.)

Also, the regularization problem for optical flow in a region in Table 4.1 corresponds to the result described in (a). Furthermore, the problem of reconstructing the location of the surface of an object can be formalized as the regularization problem of obtaining the smoothest $f(x, y)$ that makes the quantized sample $Q(f(x, y))$ of the surface coordinate $f(x, y)$ have a value as close as possible to the depth $d(x, y)$. For color, the problem of obtaining the intensity distribution that represents the distribution of the intensity data I^ν well and makes the change in intensity minimum can also be obtained. The regularization problem of computing optical flow from contours of a pattern function can be formulated as the problem of obtaining, under the condition that the velocity vector V changes as smoothly as possible on the contours, the V for which there is the smallest difference between its projection toward the normal $V \cdot N$ (N is the unit vector to the normal direction) and $V^N(s)$, the normal direction component of V, when $V^N(s)$ (s is the length of a contour) is given as data.

Many other problems of visual pattern recognition are known to be formalizable as regularization problems.

(4) *The characteristics of pattern recognition using regularization*

The problems summarized in Table 4.1 have the following two characteristics:

(1) The regularization problem can sometimes give a good explanation of the visual information processing of an organism.
(2) Some neural network algorithms, similar to those explained in Chapter 10, can be used to solve regularization problems using quadratic functionals. Also, those problems can be solved using linear analog circuits.

Optical illusion is an example of (1). For example, there are cases in which a horizontal optical flow appears as a vertical flow in the solution to a regularization problem. This is a phenomenon similar to the one that occurs when we see a rotating barber's sign. (2) suggests that the method of using regularization may give a fast algorithm. This is an important characteristic that may lead to the application of highly parallel computers to these problems.

4.6 Representing a Boundary Line

So far we have described methods for feature extraction in pattern recognition. These methods can be regarded as algorithms that generate and transform representations of features. However, we have not systematically explained how to represent the extracted features. From this section through Section 4.8 we will describe methods for representing features, especially boundaries, regions, and solid bodies. First, we will provide a method for representing a boundary line in two-dimensional Euclidean space.

(a) Representation using polygonal line approximation

When we can assume that the boundary of an object is a continuous, smooth curve, we can represent this boundary approximately by using a linear polygonal line. For example, Figure 4.13 shows the use of a polygonal line approximation for a curve.

An algorithm for obtaining a polygonal line approximation for a given curve is as follows:

Algorithm 4.9 (obtaining a polygonal line approximation of a curve)

[1] Make a segment by joining both ends of the curve, and let the segment be the initial state of a polygonal line approximation. (Generation of an initial segment)
[2] Do the following substeps for each segment of the polygonal line. (Improvement of the representation)

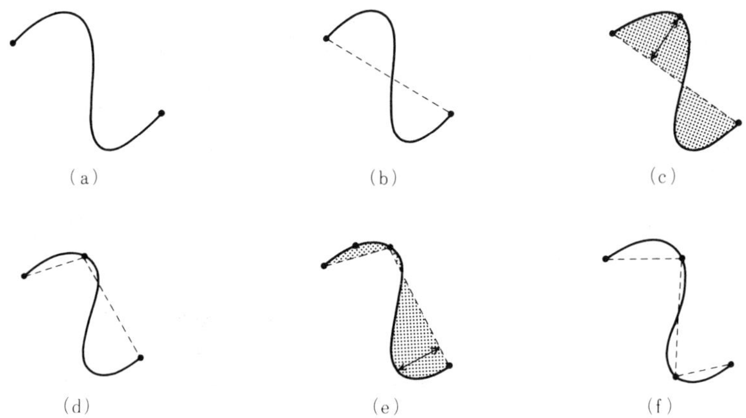

Figure 4.13 Polygonal line approximation for a curve.

[2.1] Draw a perpendicular line from each point of the curve to the segment.

[2.2] If the length of the longest perpendicular line is smaller than a given threshold value, then stop. Otherwise, replace the original segment with the polygonal line approximation in two segments with an end point on the curve that makes the longest perpendicular line at end points.

[3] If [2.2] stops for all the segments in [2], stop the algorithm. Otherwise, go to [2]. (Recursive application)

(b) Chain code representation

Let us consider a boundary made of segments such that the direction of neighboring pattern elements along the boundary that are attached to each other can be represented using a parameter for expressing some particular direction. For example, suppose we have the boundary shown in Figure 4.14(a). If we define the direction parameter to have eight values as in Figure 4.14(b), we obtain the series of direction parameter values shown in Figure 4.14(c) from point p_1 to point p_2. Such a series is generally called a *chain code*, and representing a boundary using a chain code is called *chain coding*.

A chain code representation has the following characteristics:

(1) It can compress information as compared to the original boundary data.

(2) The chain code can be used easily to restore the original boundary data.

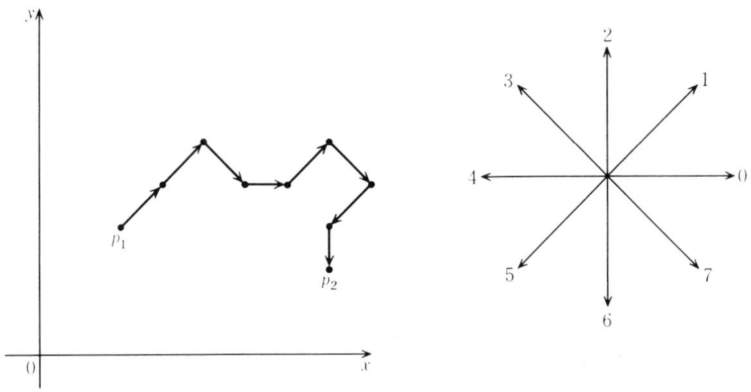

(a) A sample boundary line (b) A direction parameter

1 1 7 0 1 7 5 6

(c)

Figure 4.14 Representing a boundary using a chain code.

(3) If we take the first-order differences of the chain code (differences of neighboring pairs of parameter values in the code modulo the number of direction parameters), the obtained representation becomes invariant under rotation of the boundary. Using this characteristic, we can judge the similarity of two boundaries that do not change under rotation.

(4) If the boundary is closed (that is, two end points coincide), it is easy to compute the area of the surrounded region.

(5) We can easily find a segment of certain length (and a segment of shorter length than that) whose end is an end point of the boundary. This characteristic can be used in eliminating noise.

(6) We can easily find the common part of two boundaries. This characteristic can be used in merging regions with a common boundary.

For example, with regard to (4), an algorithm for obtaining the area from the chain code representation of a closed boundary is the following when there are four direction parameters, up, down, right, and left:

Algorithm 4.10 (computing the area of a closed region using a chain code)

[1] Let the initial area $|D| = 0$ and let y be the y coordinate of the initial point. (Initialization)

[2] For each parameter value included in the chain code, do the following. (Computation of area)

$$\begin{array}{rl} \text{When the direction parameter is } \rightarrow: & D = D - y \\ \uparrow: & y = y + 1 \\ \leftarrow: & D = D + y \\ \downarrow: & y = y - 1 \end{array}$$

[3] Output the value of $|D|$.

(c) Fourier series expansion

We will explain the method for representing a boundary that is a continuous curve using a Fourier series expansion for the amplitude of the tangential line. Suppose the boundary l is a continuous closed curve. We write $\theta(s)$ for the amplitude of the tangential line at a point whose distance is s along l from the initial point on l as shown in Figure 4.15. Furthermore, if we let L be the whole length of l and let

$$\overline{\theta}(s) = \theta(s) - (2\pi s)/L$$

then $\overline{\theta}(s)$ becomes a periodic function of period L. If we do a Fourier series expansion of $\overline{\theta}(s)$, we obtain

$$\overline{\theta}(s) = \sum_k \{a_k \cos(2\pi ks)/L + b_k \sin(2\pi ks)/L\}$$

Therefore, we have represented the original boundary using the amplitude of the tangential line at the initial point and the Fourier coefficients a_k and b_k $(k = 0, 1, \ldots)$.

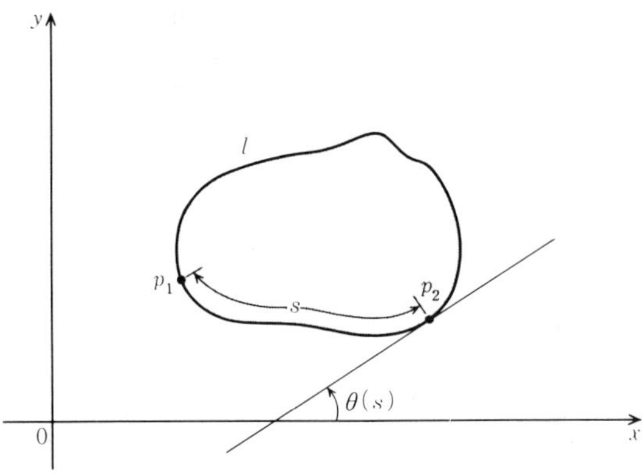

Figure 4.15 Representing a boundary using a Fourier series expansion.

As you can see from this example, we have obtained not only the boundary but also a representation for the figure surrounded by the boundary itself. So, if we use the values of the Fourier coefficients, we can relatively easily judge the similarity of two figures or distinguish the shape of a figure. Also, we can restore the original function from the values of the Fourier coefficients. Therefore, in the above method, we can restore the original boundary just by remembering the values of the Fourier coefficients (and the value of the amplitude of the tangential line at the initial point). In this sense, we sometimes call the Fourier coefficients in the Fourier series expansion the *Fourier descriptor*.

(d) Other methods

There are many other methods for representing a boundary. The cubic spline function approximation explained in Section 3.4 is often used as a method for approximating a boundary given a set of sample points of a curve. Other methods include using conic sections and representing the boundary using a binary tree with rectangles of various sizes and directions as nodes.

4.7 Representing a Region

We will explain some methods for representing a region in two-dimensional Euclidean space.

(a) x-coordinate and y-coordinate representations

First, we will describe the x-coordinate and y-coordinate representations. We start by quantizing a rectangle in the (x, y) plane that includes the given region. For the (quantized) interval of the x-axis $[x_0 \pm n\Delta x, x_0 \pm (n+1)\Delta x](n = 0, 1, \ldots, N_x)$, we enumerate quantized sections that include a pattern element whose value is not 0. For example, let us look at the region shown in Figure 4.16(a). This region, using the above method, can be represented as the list of names of sections shown in Figure 4.16(b). Each element of this list consists of a list whose first element is the the name of a section on the x-axis and whose second and later elements consist of lists of two elements, the name of a quantized section on the y-axis where the region begins and the name of a section on the y-axis where the region ends.

A list representation indexed by the names of the quantized sections that contain the region along the x-axis is called the *x-coordinate representation* of the original region. Similarly, a list representation indexed by the

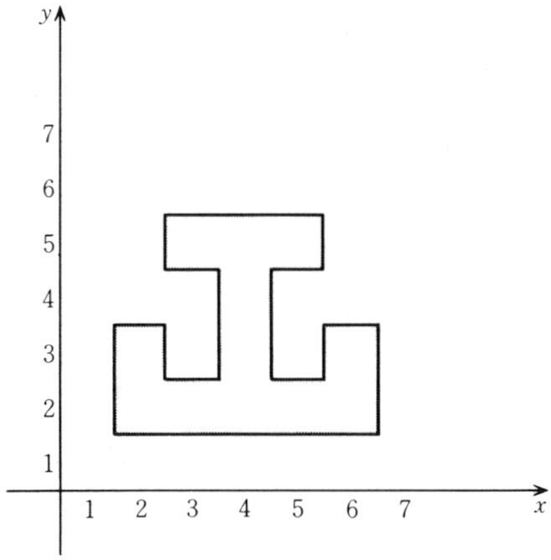

(a) The quantized domain

(2 (2 3)) (3 (2 2) (5 5))

(4 (2 5)) (5 (2 2) (5 5))

(6 (2 3))

(b) The list representation of each interval

Figure 4.16 The x-coordinate representation of a domain.

names of the quantized sections along the y-axis is called the *y-coordinate representation* of the original region. Since the x-coordinate representation and y-coordinate representation are simple enough to be easily generated from data of the region, they are often used to represent a region.

(b) Quad-tree representation

The x-coordinate and y-coordinate representations are methods for representing a region at the level of each pattern element composing the region and, thus, are one-level representations. On the other hand, there are methods for representing regions using a hierarchical structure of partial regions. As a popular method of this kind, we will describe the *quad-tree representation.*

Suppose a region in the (x, y) plane is quantized along the coordinates as in (a). Let us consider the following multilevel structure whose nodes are given a value. First, we define the lowest level that corresponds to the level of each pattern element. Next, for each set of four neighboring pattern elements at this level, we provide a new pattern element at one level higher. When the values of the four original pattern elements are all 1 (that is, all included in the region to be represented), we set the value of the new pattern element to 1. Also, when the values of the original four pattern elements are all 0 (that is, they are not included in the region to be represented), we set the value of the new pattern element to 0. Furthermore, if they do not belong to either case, in other words, when the four neighboring pattern elements have both values, 0 and 1, we set the value of the newly provided pattern element to 0.5. By repeating this operation to create superordinate levels, pattern elements in higher levels are generated; as a result, we obtain the pattern represented using a multilevel structure in that the whole pattern is represented by one pattern element in the highest level.

Let us consider the pattern shown in Figure 4.17(a). Suppose that the pattern elements represented as ▩ have the value 1 and other elements have the value 0, and the set of pattern elements whose value is 1 is the region. The multilevel structure for this pattern is illustrated in Figure 4.17(b), where ■, ▩, □ represent the values 1, 0.5, 0, respectively.

The representation of a pattern using a multilevel structure as above is called a *pattern pyramid*. In the case of a visual image pattern, it is called a (visual) image pyramid.

Considering the hierarchical structure that corresponds to a pattern pyramid, we can define a tree where the highest level of the pyramid corresponds to the root node. When the pattern element is □ or ■, the pattern element corresponds to a leaf of the tree. When the pattern element is ▩, it corresponds to an intermediate node that has edges connected only to neighboring levels. For example, for the pyramid shown in Figure 4.17(b), we can obtain the tree structure shown in Figure 4.17(c). A tree generated in this way has the structure of a quad-tree, where every node except a leaf has four child nodes. This tree structure can easily be represented on a computer as a list. Also, by counting the number of ■, we can compute the area of the original region. Furthermore, we can choose a representation with cruder levels rather than using the level for the original pattern elements. We can also easily pick nodes of appropriate depth in the tree structure. However, it is not easy to do geometric operations such as rotation, expansion, and contraction of the region.

(c) Skeletal representation

Extracting a long thin region, or a set of connected line or curve segments, that is a subset of the original region and that in some ways maintains the same distance from the boundary is called *skeletonization* of the original region. A representation obtained by skeletonization is called a *skeletal representation*. To generate line segments going through the center of the region and preserving the connectivity of the region is called *linear skeletonization*, and a representation obtained by linear skeletonization is called a *linear skeletal representation*. This method of representation is appropriate for representing a region composed by stick-shaped subregions such as a human body.

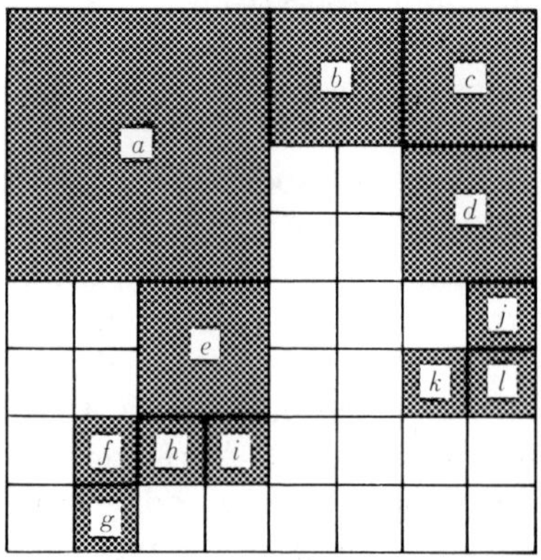

(a) The quantized domain

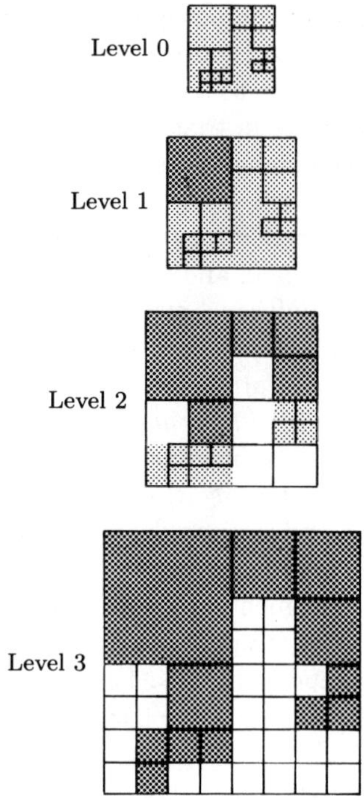

(b) The pattern pyramid

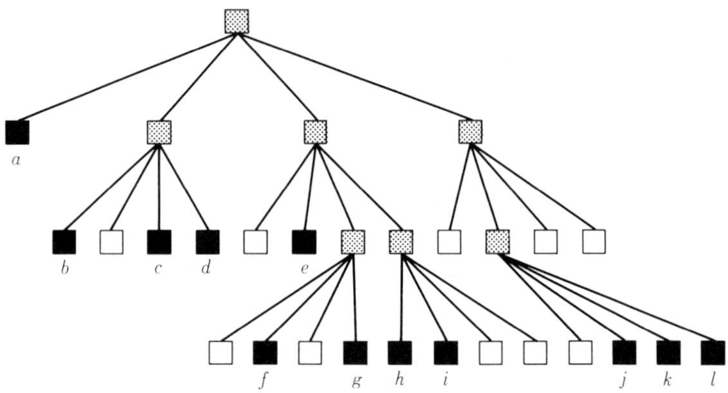

(c) The quad-tree representation of the domain

Figure 4.17 The quad-tree representation of a region using a pattern pyramid.

4.8 Representation of a Solid

Let us consider the representation of a pattern obtained from a solid object in three-dimensional Euclidean space (we will call this just the representation of a solid). Methods of representing solids are roughly divided into the following three groups:

(1) Representation using boundary lines
(2) Representation using boundary surfaces
(3) Representation using volume

We will explain each group below.

(a) Representation using boundary lines

A well-known method of representation using boundary lines is the wire-frame representation described in Section 2.2. For example, the rectangular parallelepiped shown in Figure 4.18(a) can be represented using the coordinates of each vertex and the neighbor relation of vertices determined by the sides. Such a representation is shown in Figure 4.18(b). If we consider x, y, z as variables, we can look at Figure 4.18(b) as representing a general rectangular parallelepiped that is parallel to the coordinate axes and with one vertex at the origin.

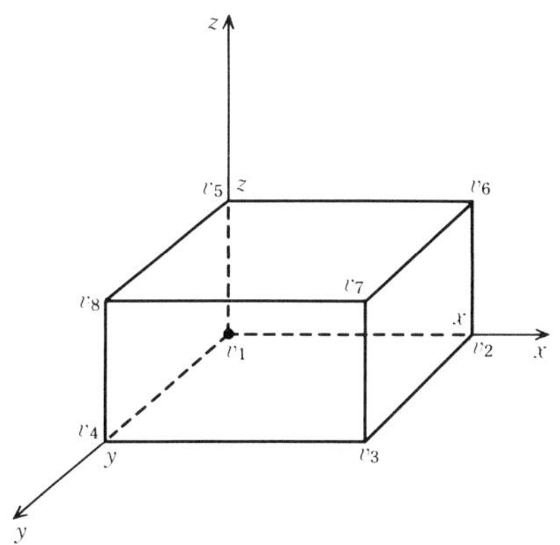

(a) A rectangular parallelepiped

$$v_1 : (0,0,0) \quad v_2 : (x,0,0)$$
$$v_3 : (x,y,0) \quad v_4 : (0,y,0)$$
$$v_5 : (0,0,z) \quad v_6 : (x,0,z)$$
$$v_7 : (x,y,z) \quad v_8 : (0,y,z)$$

$$(v_1,v_2),(v_2,v_3),(v_3,v_4),(v_4,v_1),$$
$$(v_5,v_6),(v_6,v_7),(v_7,v_8),(v_8,v_5),$$
$$(v_1,v_5),(v_2,v_6),(v_3,v_7),(v_4,v_8)$$

(b) Wire-frame representation of a rectangular parallelepiped

Figure 4.18 Representation using boundary lines.

(b) Representation using boundary surfaces

The winged-edge model method, the surface patch method, and the spherical function method are methods of representation using boundary surfaces.

(1) *The winged-edge model method*

The method of representing a solid by a graph that assigns its surfaces, angles, and vertices as the nodes and takes the neighbor relations as edges is called the *winged-edge model method.* (Sometimes this method does not use the surfaces of a solid, but just some parts of the solid and their neighbor relations.) For example, the triangular conic shown in Figure 4.19(a) can be represented as the graph in Figure 4.19(b).

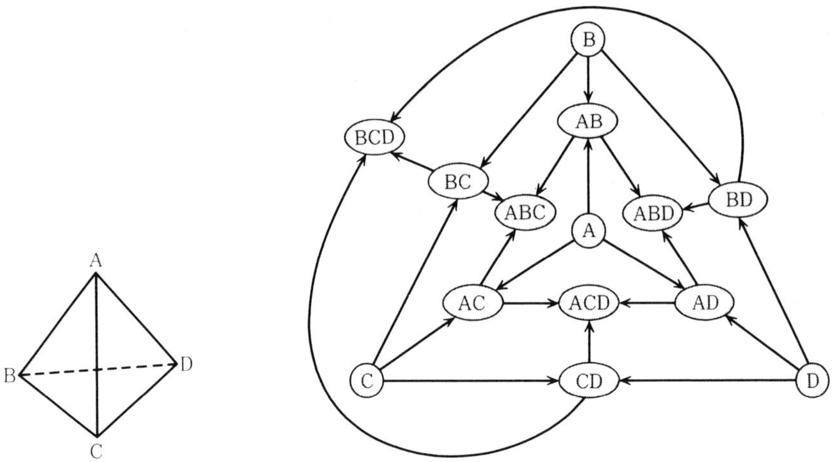

(a) A trigonometric cone

(b) A graph representation of a trigonometric cone

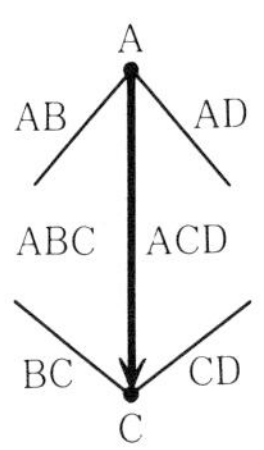

(c) A relation among vertex/side/surface

initial vertex: A
final vertex: C
initial surface: ACD
final surface: ABC
initial side (clockwise side): AD
initial side (counterclockwise side): CD
final side (clockwise side): BC
final side (counterclockwise side): AB

(d) the winged-edge description of the angle AC

Figure 4.19 A winged-edge model representation of a triangular conic.

In the winged-edge model, the attribute-value pair for each node in the graph can be stored separately in the following form:

(i) Vertex: the coordinate location of the vertex in the object-centered system of coordinates and the observer-centered system of coordinates.
(ii) Side: the topological relation of the side with the neighboring vertices, sides, and surfaces.
(iii) Surface: surface features such as the orientation of the surface (can be represented as a normal vector), reflection rate, texture, color, and so on.

For example, for the side AC in the triangular conic shown in Figure 4.19(a), the relation with the vertices, angles, and surfaces shown in Figure 4.19(c) can be stored as the data given in Figure 4.19(d). As in Figure 4.19(d), it is usual to describe an angle as turning in the counterclockwise direction relative to the observer. The winged-edge model method not only gives simple representations but also can easily describe features of the surface and the location of the solid.

(2) *Surface patch method*

When a surface of a solid is a curved surface, we need to construct a representation that takes into consideration the curvature of sides and surfaces. This generally requires a complicated representation. As one of the simplified methods, we can approximate the surface by patching together some parts of planes or of curved surfaces. This method is called the *surface patch method.* This general method includes a method for generating partial curved surfaces from the three-dimensional information about the original solid and a method for imagining a curved surface with four sides as a partial curved surface and approximating those sides using B-spline functions.

(3) *Spherical function method*

The method of representing a surface of a solid as a function on a sphere is called the *spherical function method.* For example, there is a method for using a sphere where the distance between its center and a point on the surface of a solid is a function of its direction vector. Such a sphere is called a *Gaussian sphere.* We can project the normal vector at each point on the surface of a solid to the surface of the Gaussian sphere and let the normal vectors in the same direction take their vector sum. This vector field is generally called the *extended Gaussian image.* The representation method using the extended Gaussian image is one kind of spherical function method.

The extended Gaussian image preserves the congruent relation between convex* solids. Using this property, we can judge the congruency of two convex solids. There are also other spherical function methods, including methods using spherical harmonic functions.

(c) Representation using volume

We can also represent a solid by using features of three-dimensional volumes rather than local features in one- or two-dimensional space such as edges or surfaces. Using volume is more appropriate for representing a complex object since it can create macroscopic, concise representations. We will explain the generalized cylinder method and constructive solid geometry, two popular representation methods using volume.

(1) *The generalized cylinder method*

The solid obtained by generalizing the bottom surface and each cross section of a cylinder from a circle to a general simple closed curve or by changing the central line from a straight line segment to a curve segment is called a *generalized cylinder*. The method of representing a solid by using the position of its parts, assuming that the original solid is made of some pieces, and by representing each piece as a generalized cylinder is called the *generalized cylinder method*. We can construct a generalized cylinder by assigning a curve in three-dimensional Euclidean space, E^3, as a *spine* and specifying a moving surface orthogonal to this spine by allowing the surface to change its shape as it moves from one end point of the spine to the other end point (such a move is called *sweeping*). Thus, a generalized cylinder can be described using the following elements:

(i) A curve in E^3, in other words, the spine, its initial point, and its final point.
(ii) The shape of a sweeping surface at the initial point of the spine.
(iii) A rule for deciding how the shape changes during the sweep.

For example, the generalized cylinder shown in Figure 4.20(b) can be described as in Figure 4.20(c).

One characteristic of the generalized cylinder method is that we can easily compute the volume of a solid. Let p_1, p_2, and s be the initial point of spine, its final point, and the distance along the spine from p_1, respectively. Also, let $S(s)$ be the area of the surface orthogonal to the

*We say a set D in n-dimensional Euclidean space is a *convex set* if, for any $x_1, x_2 \in D$ and real number $\mu \in [0,1]$, $\mu x_1 + (1-\mu)x_2 \in D$. A convex solid is a convex set in three-dimensional Euclidean space.

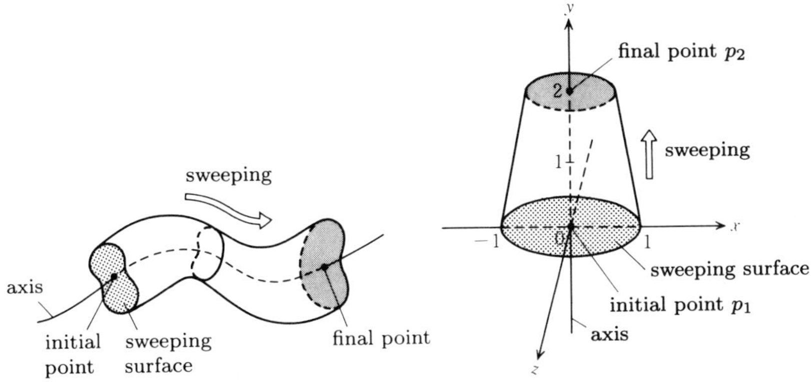

(a) A complicated solid

(b) A generalized cylinder

(i) axis: $x = z = 0$
initial point: $p_1 = (0, 0, 0)$
final point: $p_2 = (0, 2, 0)$

(ii) sweeping surface: shape: circle
center: $c_1 = (0, 0, 0)$
radius: $r_1 = 1$

(iii) sweeping rules: equation of the boundary line of the sweeping surface:
$x^2 + (y - s)^2 + z^2 = r^2$
provided that s is the distance from the initial point on the axis to the center of the sweeping surface (sweeping distance),
r is the radius of the sweeping surface, and
$r = -\frac{1}{4}s + 1 \quad (0 \leq s \leq 2)$

(c) Three elements of the generalized cylinder

Figure 4.20 Representing a solid using a generalized cylinder.

spine, or the section, at distance s from p_1 along the spine, and let $L(s)$ be the length of the boundary of the surface. Furthermore, let τ be the length of the arc on the boundary and represent a point p on the boundary as $p = (x(s, \tau), y(s, \tau), z(s, \tau))$ using s and τ as parameters. The volume V of the generalized cylinder can be obtained by

$$V = \int_{p_1}^{p_2} S(s)\, ds$$

$$S(s) = \frac{1}{2} \int_0^{L(S)} \left(x \frac{\partial y}{\partial \tau} - y \frac{\partial x}{\partial \tau} \right) d\tau$$

For example, for the generalized cylinder in Figure 4.20(b),

$$S(s) = \pi((-1/4)s + 1)^2$$

Therefore

$$V = \int_{(0,0,0)}^{(0,2,0)} \pi((-1/4)s + 1)^2 \, ds = (7/6)\pi$$

Using the generalized cylinder method, it is known that, if we look at the three-dimensional orthogonal coordinate system called the *Frenet frame* as a local coordinate system with each point on the spine as the origin, we can easily obtain much information about a pattern. The generalized cylinder method is suitable for representing a solid whose spine is not very bent. It can also easily transform the slope of a solid by changing values of parameters. However, it is hard, using the generalized cylinder method, to represent a solid that is so bent that sections overlap as in Figure 4.21(a) or a solid branched as in Figure 4.21(b).

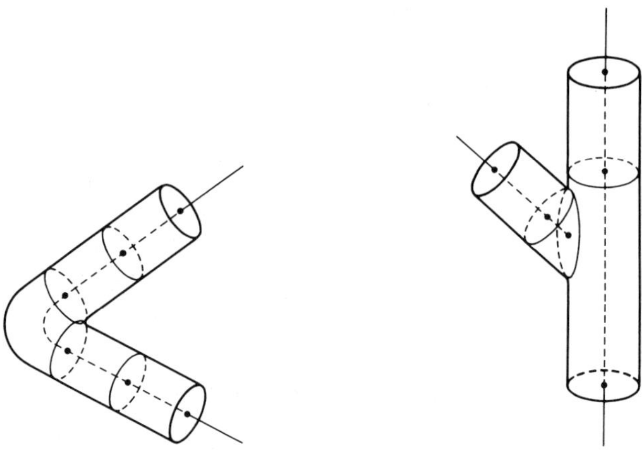

(a) A solid whose sections overlap (b) A branched solid

Figure 4.21 Generalized cylinder representations for bent solids.

It is not easy to generate a generalized cylinder from a pattern function. One method for doing that is to obtain a skeletal representation of the region using some linear skeletonization algorithm and find the shapes of the sections at several points along this skeleton. However, with this method, it is difficult to generate completely a representation like Figure 4.20(c). So the generalized cylinder method is often used as a method for representing a three-dimensional model to be stored in a knowledge base, rather than for representing a visual pattern.

(2) *Constructive solid geometry*

If we assume that a solid is made up of some *solid primitives*, we can reconstruct the original solid from them by defining their transformation operations. As solid primitives, we usually use rectangular parallelepipeds, circular cylinders, spheres, and generalized cylinders as described in (1). As transformation operations for a solid primitive, we use combinatorial operations such as sum and difference and operations on movement. This method of representing solids is called *constructive solid geometry.*

For example, the solid shown in Figure 4.22(a) can be constructed by the

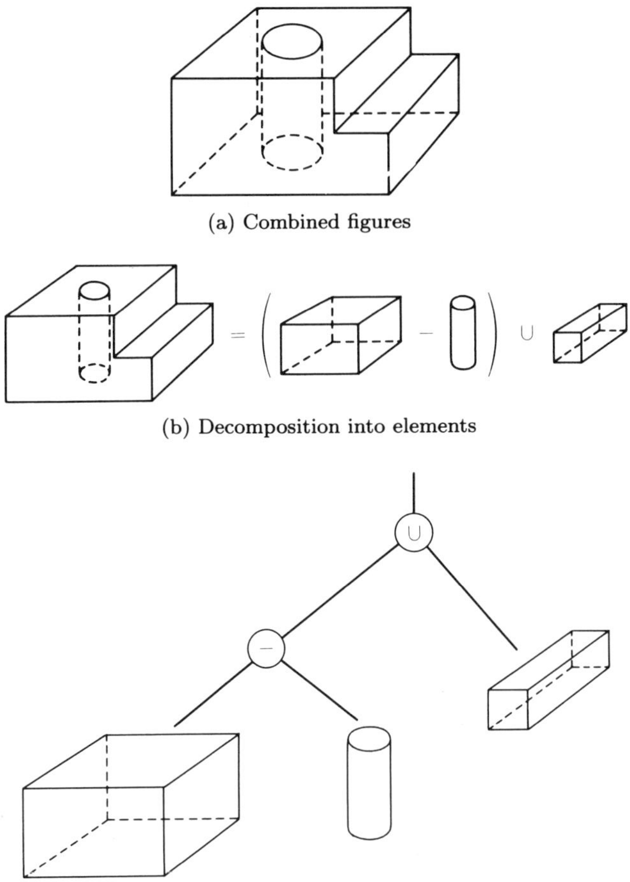

(a) Combined figures

(b) Decomposition into elements

(c) A tree representation of a solid primitive

Figure 4.22 Representing a solid using constructive solid geometry.

combinatorial operations of solid primitives shown in Figure 4.22(b). Or, using a tree structure, we can use the tree shown in Figure 4.22(c), which has solid primitives at its leaves and operators as intermediate nodes.

Using constructive solid geometry, we can represent not only individual solids but also a class of solids by parameterizing the attributes of the solid primitives (such as the length of a side of a rectangular parallelepiped). If we combine this method with the generalized cylinder method described in (1), we can represent many kinds of solids like those in Figure 4.23. However, in order to use constructive solid geometry we need to know the positional relation among the solid primitives that we used, as well as information about their locations, relative angles, and extent.

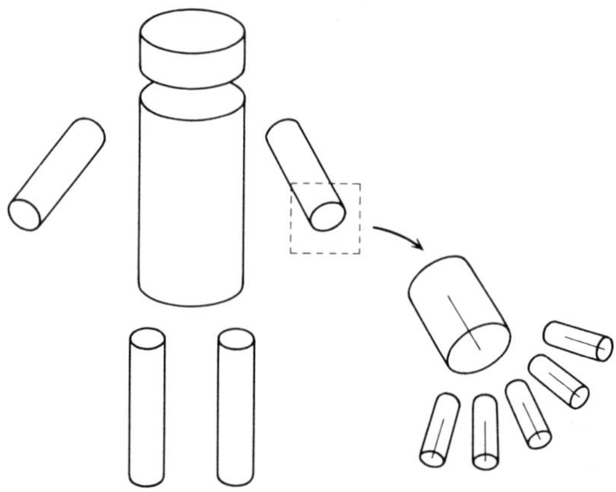

Figure 4.23 Combining constructive solid geometry with the generalized cylinder method (modified from Marr and Nishihara, 1978).

4.9 Interpretation of Line Drawings

In this chapter we have so far explained methods for extracting features and representing them in a computer. In particular, we gave methods for representing solids in Section 4.8. In this section we will explain a method for finding, in a pattern consisting of overlapping solids, what kinds of solids are contained in the pattern and where they are relatively positioned.

A pattern including more than one object is called a *scene*. In particular, a scene including only polyhedra is sometimes called a polyhedral scene. Finding the structure and attributes of objects or positional relations among objects in a scene is called *scene analysis*. Scene analysis is one of the important problems in pattern recognition. Here we will look at the simplest case, where the scene is a *line drawing* as in Figure 4.24. To obtain a line drawing from a given pattern function, we can combine and use the appropriate feature extraction methods described so far. Let us suppose we have already obtained a line drawing and think about a method for finding the objects contained in the line drawing and their relative positions. Scene analysis for a line drawing in this sense is called an *interpretation* of the line drawing.

(a) The Guzman method

A method that is often used for interpreting a line drawing is to classify the shape of each vertex and its neighborhoods, generate a graph based on the connective relations among the classified shape characteristics for vertices (called vertex elements), and interpret the line drawing by matching this graph and a graph that corresponds to a solid primitive. Of such methods, we will first describe one of the classics, the Guzman method.

Let us consider the six kinds of vertex elements shown in Figure 4.25(a). By using these vertex elements, we can represent a line drawing using a graph based on the connection among elements. On the other hand, we represent each solid primitive using a graph whose nodes are vertex elements, so that, if any subgraph of the graph for the original line drawing matches the graph of a primitive solid, we can recognize the solid primitive in the original line drawing. For example, we can represent the line drawing in Figure 4.24 as the graph G_1 in Figure 4.25(b). On the other hand, suppose the graph G_2 for a rectangular parallelepiped shown in Figure 4.25(c) is given as the graph of a solid primitive. If we ignore the nodes of G_1 that correspond to the T-shaped vertices, G_2 matches a subgraph of G_1.

By repeating this sort of matching with the graphs of solid primitives, we can interpret a line drawing as more than one solid primitive. The Guzman method, as illustrated in the above example, is not always perfect in matching two graphs and generally requires rules for ignoring some nodes. Since such rules depend largely on the structure of each graph, there can be many exceptions for matching. Also, since this is a method for directly matching two graphs, a lot of calculation is required to interpret a complicated line drawing.

(b) Huffman–Clowes method

Whereas the Guzman method matchs graphs based on the shapes of vertex elements, there are methods for interpreting line drawings by making use of properties of boundary lines. One of these methods is the Huffman–Clowes

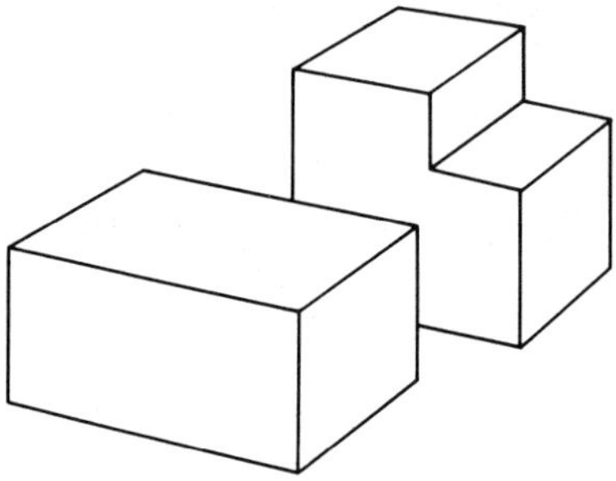

Figure 4.24 A scene using a line drawing.

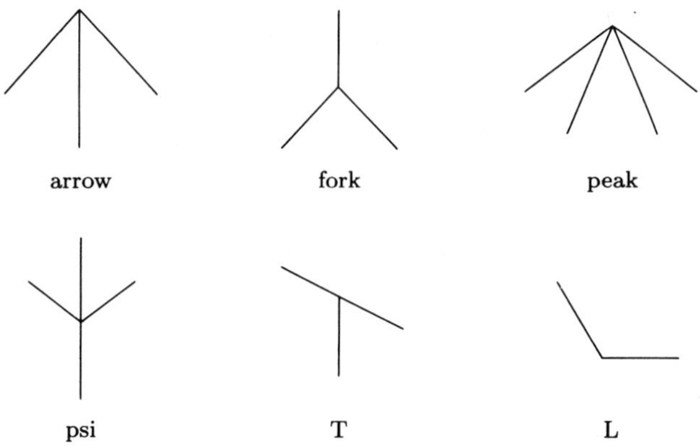

(a) Six kinds of vertex elements (Guzman, 1968)

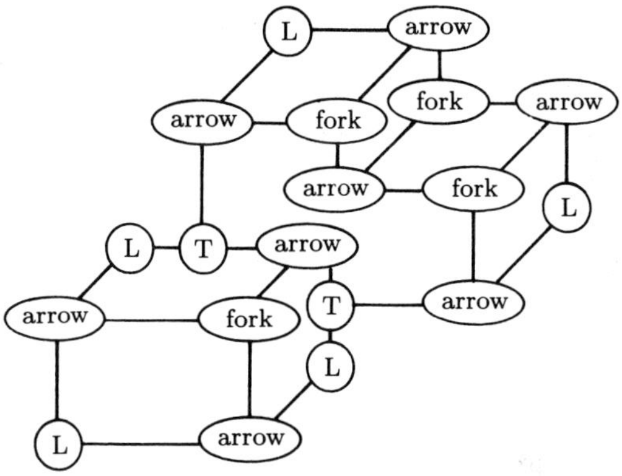

(b) Graph representation G_1 for Figure 4.24

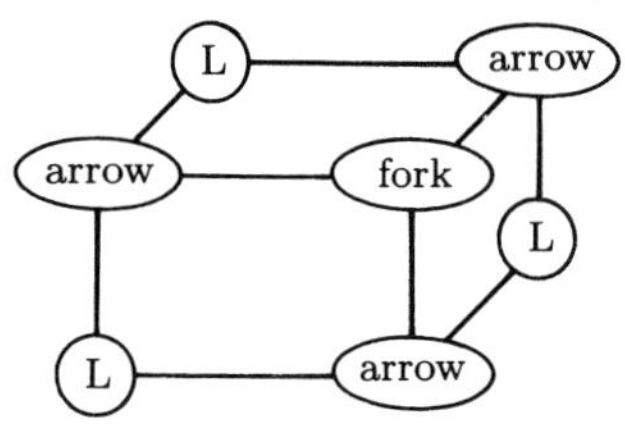

(c) Graph representation G_2 for a rectangular parallelepiped

Figure 4.25 Representing a line drawing using the Guzman method.

method. We start by assigning one of the labels +, −, or > to a boundary line in a line drawing.

(1) If a boundary line is convex from the viewpoint of the observer, assign +.
(2) If a boundary line is concave from the viewpoint of the observer, assign −
(3) If a boundary line has one of its adjacent surfaces* hidden, assign >, provided that the hidden surface should be on the left side of the line and the surface that is visible should be on the right side of the line.

(The Clowes method also uses ↑ as the label for the direction of a shadow line.)

If we use these rules for assigning labels, there will be only 16 possible labelings for a vertex of a polyhedron whose vertex connects only three surfaces (trihedral-vertex polyhedron). Figure 4.26 shows the 16 labelings. In the case of a trihedral-vertex polyhedron, the Huffman–Clowes algorithm assigns one of the vertex elements shown in Figure 4.26 to each vertex of a given line drawing. However, this method uses only local information about the shape of each vertex and its neighborhood, so it may label meaningless line drawings without contradiction or assign an impossible label in a meaningful line drawing.

(c) The Waltz method

One shortcoming of the Huffman–Clowes method is that the algorithm for labeling may not be applied to all possible line drawings. The Waltz method, though like the Huffman–Clowes method it is based on labeling boundary lines, uses a more farsighted global algorithm for labeling a line drawing, which is called *constraint filtering.* Let us look at an outline of the algorithm.

Algorithm 4.11(1) (labeling a line drawing using the Waltz method—outline)

[1] Enumerate all possible labelings for each vertex in a line drawing. (Enumeration of labelings)
[2] For each line segment in the line drawing, remove any labeling from the labelings enumerated in [1] that does not satisfy the following constraint. (Constraint filtering)

*Sometimes the word "face" is used instead of "surface," particularly for polyhedral solids. But we use the word "surface" consistently in this book.

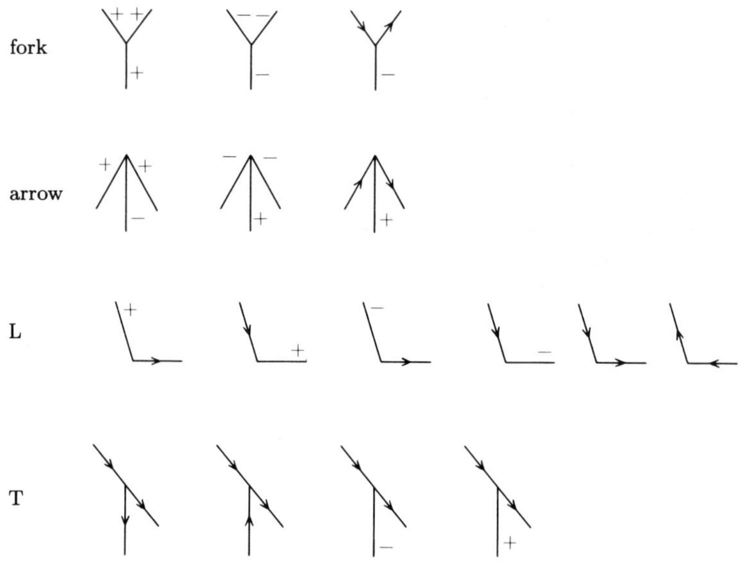

Figure 4.26 Huffman's labeling for a trihedral-vertex polyhedron (Huffman, 1971).

Constraint on labeling: any line segment has to have the same label on both end points.

[3] Repeat [2] until all the line segments satisfy the constraint. (Relaxation)

The algorithm outlined above is an instance of an optimization method called the *relaxation method.* Let us look at this algorithm in more detail from the standpoint of a relaxation method.

Algorithm 4.11(2) (labeling a line drawing using the Waltz method)

[1] Name the vertices of a given line drawing $1, \ldots, n$ and do the following substeps for each pair of vertices i, j:

[1.1] Set $r_{ik} = 1$ when assigning label k to vertex i is possible; otherwise set $r_{ik} = 0$.

[1.2] When the vertices i, j are neighbors and labeling k, l is possible for i, j, respectively, do the following:

[1.2.1] If labeling k, l gives the same label to the segment that joins i, j, set $s(i, j, k, l) = 1$. Otherwise, set $s(i, j, k, l) = 0$.

[2] Enumerate possible labelings $k_{il}, \ldots, k_{in_i}$ for each vertex i. (Enumeration of labelings)

[3] For any vertex i and its neighboring vertex j, if $s(i, j, k, l)r_{jl} = 0$ is

true for all $l = k_{j1}$, change the value of r_{ik} from 1 to 0. (Constraint filtering)

[4] Do [3] for each vertex i and repeat this operation. (Relaxation)

Not only does the Waltz method introduce constraint filtering into the Huffman–Clowes method, it also can interpret a line drawing that includes shadow lines and cracks. The number of locally possible labelings will increase in a line drawing that includes shadow lines and cracks, but by using an algorithm with constraint filtering our experience tells us that only one or at most a few possible interpretations will be obtained that keep consistent labelings for all segments.

Section 5.2 will explain the Waltz method in more detail with examples.

(d) The Kanade method

The methods we described so far can be used on line drawings of scenes built out of convex polyhedrons. The Kanade method is a constraint filtering algorithm that can interpret not only such line drawings but also

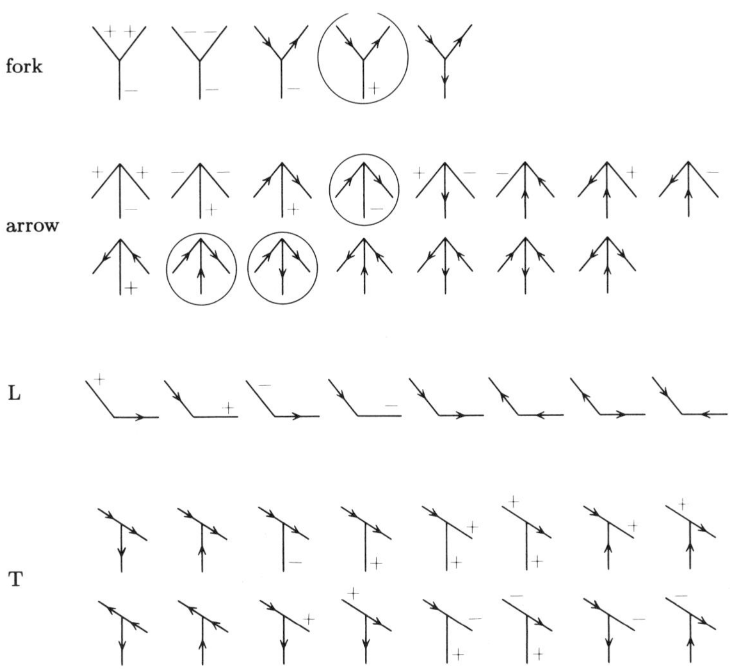

Figure 4.27 Labeling for the origami world by Kanade (see the text for the ones with a circle) (Kanade, 1980).

line drawings including folded-up polyhedrons (the origami world). This method, using labelings with the vertex elements shown in Figure 4.27, performs constraint filtering similar to that in the Waltz method. For example, the result of interpreting the line drawing of a box (shown in Figure 4.28(a)) is shown in Figure 4.28(b).

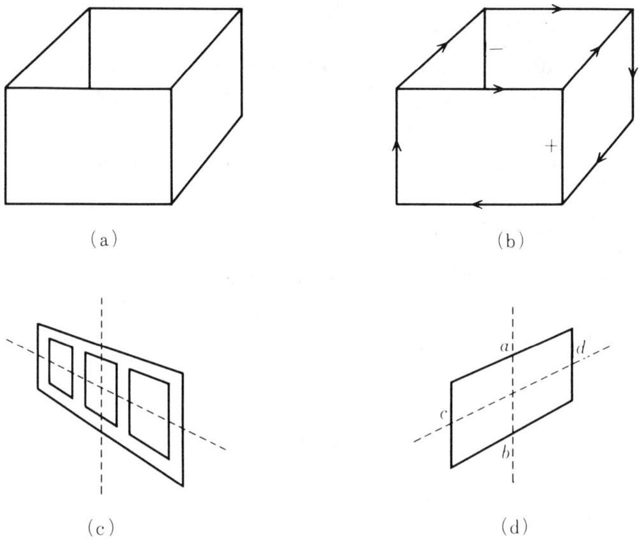

Figure 4.28 Interpretations of line drawings by the Kanade method (Kanade, 1980).

In Figure 4.28(b) there are four vertex elements that are not included in the list of vertex elements for the Huffman–Clowes method. They are circled in Figure 4.27. Those elements are a consequence of allowing folded-up polyhedra.

On the other hand, if we think of a line drawing as the projection of a solid in three-dimensional Euclidean space onto two-dimensional Euclidean space E^2, the resulting constraints can be used to reduce the multiplicity of interpretations. In particular, if we use the following two heuristic constraints, we can reduce the number of interpretations in the origami world.

(1) Skew symmetry: we assume that, in E^2, a figure that is symmetrical in an oblique coordinate system is symmetrical in the original orthogonal coordinate system in E^3.
(2) Preserving parallelism: we assume that two line segments that are parallel in E^2 are also parallel in E^3.

For example, the object in Figure 4.28(c) is symmetrical in an oblique coordinate system, and it is assumed by (1) to be symmetrical in the orthogonal coordinate system in E^3. Also, by (2), the parallel segments in Figure 4.28(d), a and b, or c and d, are assumed to be parallel in E^3.

Summary

This chapter described algorithms for extracting features from a visual pattern.

4.1 The zero-crossing method and the difference operator method can be used to detect an edge.

4.2 The edge tracing method, the edge prediction method, and the Hough transformation method can be used for extracting boundary lines.

4.3 The splitting method, the merging method, and a method that combines both can be used for extracting a region.

4.4 Structure analysis, statistical analysis, and the texture gradient method are used for texture analysis.

4.5 Optical flow is used for detecting movement.

4.6 Many pattern feature extraction problems can be formulated as regularizations of an ill-posed problem. Detection of movement using optical flow is one example.

4.7 A boundary line can be represented by a polygonal line approximation, a chain code, or a Fourier series expansion.

4.8 A region can be represented by an x-coordinate representation, a y-coordinate representation, a quad-tree representation, or a skeletal representation.

4.9 A solid can be represented using boundary lines as in a wire-frame representation; using surfaces as in the winged-edge model method, the surface patch method, or the spherical function method; and using volumes as in the constructive solid geometry and the generalized cylinder method.

4.10 The Guzman method, the Huffman-Clowes method, the Waltz method, and the Kanade method are used for scene analysis of line drawings.

Keywords

pattern recognition, visual image recognition, feature extraction, edge detection, zero-crossing method, detection of a boundary line, Hough transformation, edge tracing method, edge prediction method, extraction of a region, splitting method, merging method, texture analysis, detection of movement, optical flow, ill-posed problem, regularization, representation of a shape, representation of a boundary, polygonal line approximation, chain code, spline function approximation, representation of a region, quad-tree representation, skeleton, skeletal representation, linear skeletonization, linear skeletal representation, representation of a solid, wire-frame representation, winged-edge model method, surface patch method, generalized cylinder method, constructive solid geometry, interpretation of a line drawing, Guzman method, Huffman-Clowes method, Waltz method, relaxation method, constraint filtering, Kanade method

Exercises

4.1 Explain how the formula in Section 4.1(a), $k(x,y) = \nabla^2 H(r) * f(x,y)$, should be transformed to run the zero-crossing method on a computer. How many multiplications and exponentiations are necessary to compute the zero crossing, using the transformed formula?

4.2 Solve the example problem for the Hough transformation described in Section 4.2(c) (see Figure 4.7) using polar coordinates (r, θ) as the parameter space.

4.3 Write an algorithm for finding the skeletal representation of a region represented by a two-dimensional bit pattern.

4.4 Describe the difference between wire-frame representation and representation by the winged-edge model method. Also explain the merits of combining these two kinds of representation.

5 Pattern Understanding Methods

One of the goals of pattern recognition is to find an object included in a pattern as well as its attributes and its relationship to other objects in the pattern. This is generally called pattern understanding. Attributes and relationships of objects can be represented by the methods described in Chapter 3. The job of pattern understanding is to generate representations of these attributes and relationships from a given representation of a pattern or from the representation of extracted features. Pattern understanding requires knowledge about an object. Feature extraction methods can recognize the boundaries and regions included in a pattern, but they cannot understand the pattern: understanding a pattern requires knowledge of the corresponding objects. This chapter will explain methods of pattern understanding based on knowledge of objects. Pattern understanding, in this sense, requires algorithms for matching stored knowledge and extracted features and methods for controlling the process from feature extraction to pattern understanding. This chapter discusses both of these problems in order.

5.1 Pattern Understanding and Knowledge Representation

Before we explain the methods of *pattern understanding*, we need to think about how the knowledge necessary for understanding can be represented in a computer. In this section we discuss knowledge representation methods appropriate for pattern understanding.

(a) What is knowledge representation?

We need knowledge in order to understand what is in a picture. For example, if we have knowledge about roads and buildings, we understand that Figure 5.1(a) is a picture of a building. However, if we do not have enough knowledge, we will not understand what kind of picture it is. For example, some people may not understand what is in Figure 5.1(b).

(a) A photograph of a building

(b) A pattern which is hard to understand what it is

Figure 5.1 Looking at a picture using knowledge.

If we do not have knowledge about the shape of a building or a road, we cannot understand the pattern in Figure 5.1(a). In representing this knowledge, we can use a declarative representation, such as "the shape of a building from above is usually a rectangle" or "a road, from above, has a long and narrow belt shape," or a procedural representation for connecting such knowledge to features such as boundaries and regions. Furthermore, this kind of knowledge becomes useful for pattern understanding only when it can be effectively used in conjunction with an *inference mechanism* that can generate the attributes of an object such as a building or a road or a relation between objects from a pattern and its features. A framework for representing knowledge in a computer, so that the information necessary to carry out intellectual activities such as pattern understanding and an inference mechanism for actually accomplishing this intellectual activity satisfy the following three conditions, is called a *knowledge representation*:

(1) It can represent human knowledge possibly as it is.
(2) The inference system is highly efficient.
(3) It is easy to describe and modify knowledge and to understand the descriptions.

It is convenient to use symbols when representing human knowledge in a computer. Thus the representation methods using symbols, like lists, semantic networks, rules, and frames, are often used for knowledge representation. Knowledge represented using a declarative representation is called *declarative knowledge*, and knowledge represented using a procedural representation is called *procedural knowledge.*

(b) Basic techniques of knowledge representation

Here we provide the basic techniques of knowledge representation for pattern recognition.

(1) *The representation of declarative knowledge using semantic networks*

First let us consider, using an example, a method for representing declarative knowledge. Suppose we have an object "triangle." Our declarative knowledge about the object "triangle" includes the attributes of triangles in general, their values, and their relation with other objects.* Consider the fact that there are three vertices in a triangle. This fact can be represented, if we represent a triangle by the symbol *triangle* and the attribute, the number of vertices, by the symbol *number_of_vertices*, as the following list of three elements:

$$(\textit{triangle number\_of\_vertices } 3)$$

If we represent the attribute that is the number of sides of a triangle using the symbol *number_of_sides*, the fact that a triangle has three sides can be represented as

$$(\textit{triangle number\_of\_sides } 3)$$

In this way, if we represent each characteristic of an object in the form of a list

$$(\langle\text{name of the object}\rangle\langle\text{attribute}\rangle\langle\text{value}\rangle)$$

we can represent the characteristics of an object, or equivalently the object itself, as a set of such lists. This representation is one example of a semantic network.

Next, let us consider relations among objects. For example, an equilateral triangle inherits the general characteristics of a triangle. If we

*A "triangle" is a concept. In order to describe our knowledge of an object declaratively, we need to consider how to describe the concept of the object. However, in this section, rather than discussing concepts in detail, we will assume that a set of characteristics common to instances of an object constitutes a concept. We will define the idea of a concept more clearly in Chapter 6.

represent this inheritance relation using the attribute *isa:*, we can represent the relation between a triangle *triangle* and an equilateral triangle *equilateral_triangle* as the list

(*equilateral_triangle isa*: *triangle*)

Also, the relation between "a triangle" and one of its sides is the relation that the side "is a part of" a triangle. If we represent this relation using the attribute *partof*:, we can represent the relation that the side *ab* is a part of the triangle *abc* using the list

((*side a b*) *partof*: (*triangle a b c*))

Usually, *isa*: is called the superordinate-subordinate relation and *partof*: is called the part/whole relation. Both of these are often used in representing attributes of objects for pattern understanding.

On the other hand, we can think about the inverse relation of *isa*: or *partof*:. As opposed to the inheritance of a characteristic using the attribute *isa*:, we can represent the fact that a triangle is superordinate to an equilateral triangle as follows using the attribute *supers*::

(*triangle supers*: *equilateral_triangle*)

This is the inverse relation to (*equilateral_triangle isa*: *triangle*). Similarly, the relation that a triangle *abc* has the side *ab* as a part can be represented as follows using the attribute *haspart*::

((*triangle a b c*) *haspart*: (*side a b*))

So far, we have used the atom *triangle* and the list (*triangle a b c*) for representing a triangle and the triangle *abc*, respectively. The former is a general term representing the class of triangles; the latter is the particular triangle *abc* and represents one instance. Suppose we attach, to *triangle*, variables $\$x$, $\$y$, $\$z$ representing the three vertices as arguments. Then, we can represent the class of triangles as (*triangle* $\$x$ $\$y$ $\$z$). The fact that (*triangle a b c*) is an instance of the class called (*triangle* $\$x$ $\$y$ $\$z$) can be represented as follows using the attribute *class*::

((*triangle a b c*) *class*: (*triangle* $\$x$ $\$y$ $\$z$))

If we represent the inverse relation of *class*: using the attribute *instance*:, we can represent the fact that the class (*triangle* $\$x$ $\$y$ $\$z$) has the instance (*triangle a b c*) as follows:

((*triangle* $\$x$ $\$y$ $\$z$) *instance*: (*triangle a b c*))

Extending the above arguments, we can describe a general triangle (*triangle* $\$x$ $\$y$ $\$z$), its instance (*triangle a b c*), and the equilateral tri-

(a) Triangle

(*triangle argument*: ($\$x$ $\$y$ $\$z$)
isa: *polygon*
haspart: (*side* $\$x$ $\$y$);
(*side* $\$y$ $\$z$);
(*side* $\$z$ $\$x$);
(*vertex* $\$x$);
(*vertex* $\$y$);
(*vertex* $\$z$))
supers: *equilateral_triangle*
instance: (*triangle a b c*)
number_of_vertices: 3
number_of_sides: 3

(b) Instance of the triangle

(*triangle argument*: ($\$x$ $\$y$ $\$z$)
class: *triangle*)

(c) Equilateral triangle

(*equilateral_triangle argument*: ($\$x$ $\$y$ $\$z$)
isa: *triangle*;
equilateral_polygon
equal: ((*length* (*side* $\$x$ $\$y$))(*length* (*side* $\$y$ $\$z$)));
((*length* (*side* $\$y$ $\$z$))(*length* (*side* $\$z$ $\$x$)));
((*length* (*side* $\$z$ $\$x$))(*length* (*side* $\$x$ $\$y$))))

Figure 5.2 A semantic network representation of a triangle.

angle (*equilateral_triangle* $\$x$ $\$y$ $\$z$) using the semantic network shown in Figure 5.2.

In Figure 5.2, we assume that $\$x$, $\$y$, $\$z$ are local variables defined only inside *triangle* but their scope extends to objects that inherit the properties of *triangle*. For example, since an *equilateral_triangle* is a *triangle* by virtue of the inheritance of the attribute *isa*:, the value of each attribute of *triangle* is inherited, with its variables, to *equilateral_triangle*. Therefore, *equilateral_triangle*, just like *triangle*, has (*vertex* $\$x$), (*vertex* $\$y$), (*vertex* $\$z$) as its parts.

(2) *Inference using a semantic network*

Now, let us consider how we do inference using semantic networks. For example, how would we answer the question "how many sides does an equilateral triangle have?"? Suppose the equilateral triangle *equilateral_triangle* is represented as in Figure 5.2. If we check the value of its *isa*: attribute, we are led to *triangle*, and by looking in *triangle* we find that the number of the sides is three. Here, the attribute *isa*: means that the properties of the superordinate class *triangle* are inherited by the subordinate class *equilateral_triangle*.

As we noted in Chapter 2, the case of multiple inheritance causes problems when trying to do inference by inheritance. For example, the equilateral triangle *equilateral_triangle* could be thought of as having two different superclasses, *equilateral_polygon* and *triangle*. If we are to infer the number of the sides of an equilateral triangle, it must inherit its number of the sides from a triangle, not from an equilateral polygon. In this case, we can represent the number of sides explicitly as the value of an attribute of *equilateral_triangle* using the blocking method.

(3) *Representing procedural knowledge using rules*

Here we explain how to represent procedural knowledge for pattern understanding using rules. First we consider how to infer properties of an object from local features that can be extracted from a pattern. For this purpose, let us define the following production rules:

> **if** there are two ⊐ shaped figures among the extracted features
> **and** they face each other (⊏ ⊐)
> **then** conclude that there is a rectangular object made by
> extending the horizontal sides of ⊏ and ⊐
>
> **if** there are two line segments among the extracted features
> **and** they cross each other obliquely
> **then** conclude that the two line segments intersect
> orthogonally in three-dimensional space

These rules are not always logically correct. They are *heuristic rules* in the sense that they are likely to give correct results. Usually, procedural knowledge tells what to do in particular situations like this example. When representing knowledge for use in pattern understanding, we need to build a knowledge representation system that can understand various different kinds of patterns, and methods that can represent heuristic rules, like production rules, are often effective.

(c) Knowledge representation for pattern understanding

In this section we discuss some problems of knowledge representation as applied to pattern understanding and how we might solve them.

(1) *Superordinate/subordinate relation between classes of objects*

There are many different levels of representation for one pattern function, and there are different methods of representation for each level. The diversity of different representations is one of the most interesting and most difficult problems in knowledge representation for pattern understanding. For example, there are the level of pattern elements, the level of boundaries and regions, the level of an object's attributes and relations among objects, and the level of scenes that may include many objects. Each of these levels requires its own representation methods. There are even different representation methods for the same level, like the chain code representation and spline function representation of a boundary line.

(2) *The whole/part relation between objects*

For pattern understanding, the whole/part relation between objects is a more complicated problem than it is for general knowledge representation. For example, in a usual semantic network the whole/part relation can be completely described by using the attributes *partof*: and *haspart*:. However, in pattern understanding, the relative spatial location and the topological connection of two objects or the number of parts of an object can be factors that determine the whole/part relation.

When representing the shape of an object that is closely tied to the whole/part relation, there may be many levels of representation as explained in (1). So the whole/part relation of knowledge representation when used in pattern understanding, especially the relation of spatial positions, requires a detailed representation method.

Let us look at the pattern of the "hammer" shown in Figure 5.3(a). A hammer as an object can be represented by the class *hammer* as shown in Figure 5.3(b). It has two parts, the class of "head of a hammer," *hammer_head*, and the class of "handle of a hammer," *hammer_hand*.

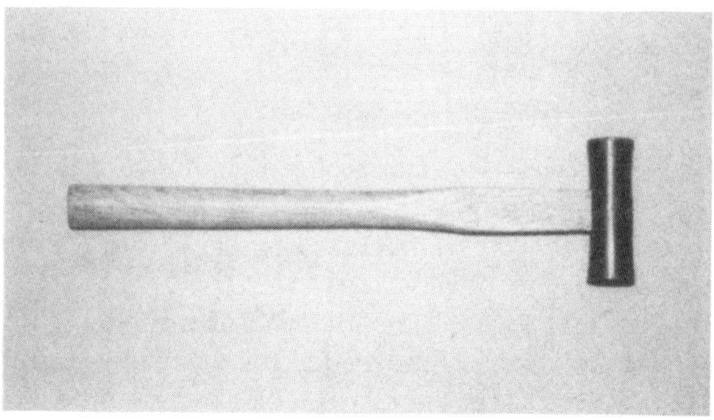

(a) A pattern of a hammer

Figure 5.3 A semantic network representation of a hammer.

```
(hammer          isa:        hardware_tool
                 supers:     (black_hammer nail_hammer)
                 haspart:    (hammer_head hammer_head)
                 shape:      qualitative: T-shaped
                 size:       (10 cm–50 cm)
                 function:   (nail_down))
(hammer_head     isa:        metal_stick
                 partof:     hammer
                 shape:      generalized_cylinder:
                               cross_section:  type circle
                                               radius(1 cm–5 cm)
                               spine:          type straight
                                               length(3 cm–20 cm)
                               sweeping_rule: constant
                 contact:    with:  (end_of hammer_hand)
                             where: (center_of $self)
                             angle: 3π/2)
(hammer_hand     isa:        stick
                 partof:     hammer
                 shape:      generalized_cylinder:
                               cross_section:
                                 type          ellipse
                                 long_radius   (2 cm–5 cm)
                                 short_radius  (1cm–4 cm)
                               spine:   type straight
                                        length(10 cm–30 cm)
                               sweeping_rule:   constant
                 contact:    with:    (center_of hammer_head)
                             where:   (end_of $self)
                             angle:   π/2)
```

(b) Knowledge used for pattern understanding

Figure 5.3 *Continued.*

Figure 5.3(b) represents the shape of a hammer as the value of the attribute *shape*:. In other words, the value *qualitative*: *T-shaped* of *shape*: states that the general shape of a hammer is qualitatively T-shaped, where *qualitative*: is a *subattribute* of the *shape*:.

On the other hand, the class *hammer_head* uses the more quantitative representation of generalized cylinders for its value of *shape*:. We also use *generalized_cylinder*: as the subattribute for representing a generalized cylinder and *cross_section*:, *spine*:, *sweeping_rule*: as the sub-subattributes for representing the shape of a section, the shape of a spine, and a sweeping rule, respectively. The shape of *hammer_hand* is also represented using a generalized cylinder.

In Figure 5.3(b), the topological connection among objects is represented by the attribute *contact*:. The value of *contact*: is what part of two objects are connected and to what degree. We also make *with*:, *where*: and *angle*: subattributes representing "with" what object, "where," and "at what angle" an object is connected, respectively. For example, the value of the attribute *contact*: in *hammer_head* gives that "the handle of a hammer" is connected to the end of "the head of a hammer" at its center with 270 degrees in a two-dimensional plane. $*self* is a variable that binds the name of the class in which it is defined.

The following are examples of spatial relations between two objects X and Y:

(i) When X and Y are connected.
X is in the center of Y; *center_of*:, X is at the end of Y; *end_of*:, X is on the right of Y; *right_of*:, X is on the left of Y; *left_of*:, X is under Y; *under*:, X is overlapping with Y; *overlapped_with*:, etc.

(ii) When X and Y are not connected.
X is to the right of Y; *toward_right_of*:, X is to the left of Y; *toward_left_of*:, X is above Y; *above*:, X is below Y; *below*:, X is far from Y; *far_from*:, X is to the north of Y; *north_of*:, etc.

In general, there are many patterns that correspond to a given symbolic representation of a spatial relation. This is certainly true for two connected objects. For example, think about representing "box $b1$ is on box $b2$." By thinking of $b1$ and $b2$ as instances of the class of boxes, *box*, this can be represented as an attribute-value pair on the instance $b1$, ($b1$ *on*: $b2$).

However, even if we are given this list, patterns corresponding to it will not be unique. For example, in Figure 5.4, ($b1$ *on*: $b2$) is used to represent both the case in which $b1$ is right on $b2$ and the case in which $b1$ is slightly off to the right or left on $b2$.

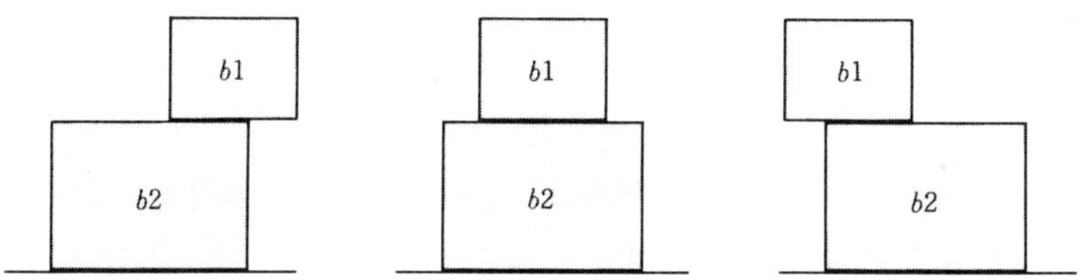

Figure 5.4 Different patterns for "the box $b1$ is on the box $b2$."

For this reason spatial relations like *on*: are more appropriately represented by a set of constraints that determine the position of corners of boxes. For example, if we regard $b1$ and $b2$ as two-dimensional rectangles and let $(x1, y1)$ and $(x2, y2)$ be the coordinates of two vertices on the bottom side of $b1$ from the left and $(a1, b1)$ and $(a2, b2)$ be the coordinates of two vertices on the top side of $b2$ from the left, we have the following feature level representation corresponding to the symbolic representation ($b1$ *on*: $b2$):

$$\{x2 \geq a1, x1 \leq a2, y1 = y2 = b1 = b2\}$$

This is a set of constraints on the coordinates of the corners.

The method of using fuzzy sets is another way of representing spatial relations, though it will not be considered in this book. Knowledge of the correspondence between a symbolic representation and a feature level representation can itself be a powerful tool for finding a symbolic representation of an object and its relation to other objects from features extracted from a pattern.

(3) *Hierarchical representation*

For some purposes in pattern understanding we need only understand the rough structure of a pattern rather than analyze the whole in detail. If we do not know anything about what we are looking at before we try to understand a pattern, we could extract a crude representation first and then try to understand each part in more detail from that information. In order to use this method effectively, it is better to represent knowledge in a hierarchical fashion.

Figure 5.5 illustrates how to represent parts of a human body using generalized cylinders. Using this hierarchical representation based on the

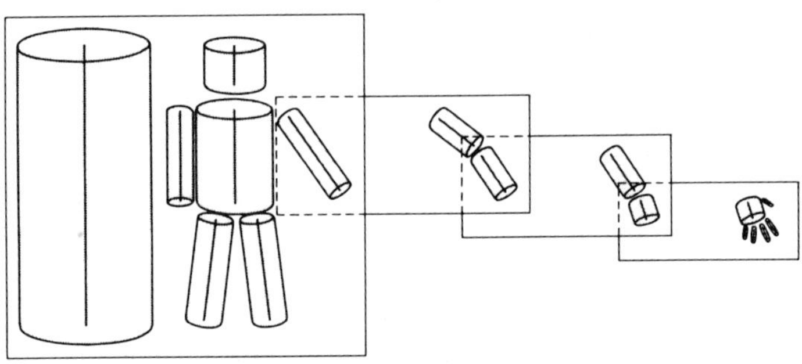

Figure 5.5 Representation of "a person" using generalized cylinders (modified from Marr and Nishihara, 1978).

whole/part relation, we can first try to match classes at a high level in the hierarchy with the pattern at low resolution. If we succeed, then we can try to understand the more detailed parts by matching classes lower in the hierarchy with the pattern at a higher resolution.

(4) *Knowledge representation for pattern understanding 1*

Here we give an example of knowledge representation used in pattern understanding. Suppose that by feature extraction, we have divided the scene shown in Figure 5.6(a) into regions as shown in Figure 5.6(b).

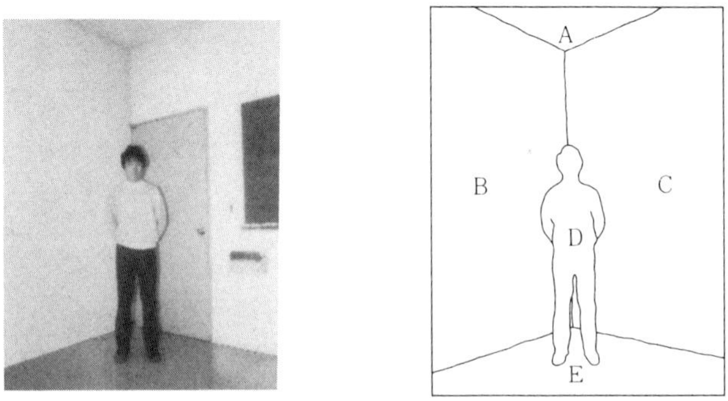

(a) A pattern of a scene (b) Divided regions

Figure 5.6 A pattern of a scene divided into regions by feature extraction.

Also, let us suppose that a pattern understanding system has the following procedural knowledge in its rule base:

(i) **If** the region X is the uppermost region
then conclude that X is a ceiling or the sky.
(ii) **If** the region X is the lowest region
then conclude that X is a floor or the ground.
(iii) **If** the region X is a quadrangle
and X is connected to both the uppermost and lowest regions
then conclude that X is a wall.
(iv) **If** the boundary of a region X includes a curve
and X is connected to both the uppermost and lowest regions
then conclude that X is a forest.
(v) **If** the region X is connected to the lowest region
and X is not connected to the uppermost region
then conclude that X is a human being.

(vi) **If** a human being is included in the scene
then conclude that the uppermost region is a ceiling.

Based on this knowledge, the problem is to infer what object corresponds to each of the regions, A–E, in Figure 5.6(b). Let us call the name of the object corresponding to the region A the label of A. Then the problem is to label the regions. In our example we examine the production rules from the top in order. If we use the inference method using ordered rules, we will obtain the following labeling:

Rule used	Labeled region and its label
(i)	label(A) = *ceiling or sky*
(ii)	label(E) = *floor or ground*
(iii)	label(B) = *wall*
(iii)	label(C) = *wall*
(v)	label(D) = *human*
(vi)	label(A) = *ceiling*

In other words, we can conclude that the regions A, B, C, and D can be regarded as a ceiling, a wall, a wall, and a human being, respectively. Since the region E can be thought of as either a floor or the ground, we have inferred that the scene in Figure 5.6(a) is a room containing a human being.

Of course, this result depends on the reliability of the knowledge used in making the inferences and may not be perfectly reliable. Also, this example is very simple and uses only one kind of knowledge representation. Even from our simple example, however, we see that we cannot understand a pattern merely with the feature extraction techniques described in Chapter 4. In order to know what exists in a given pattern, we need to build a pattern understanding system based on knowledge.

(5) *Knowledge representation for pattern understanding 2*

Now, let us consider a more realistic example of pattern understanding.

Consider the colored scene shown in Figure 5.7(a). First, we do feature extraction for the original pattern based on color and divide it into smaller regions as shown in Figure 5.7(b). By merging smaller regions around each bigger region, we obtain the final partition of regions shown in Figure 5.7(c).

If we represent each region obtained so far as a class, we obtain the symbolic representation of the pattern shown in Figure 5.7(d).

(a) A pattern of a scene

(b) Division into smaller regions

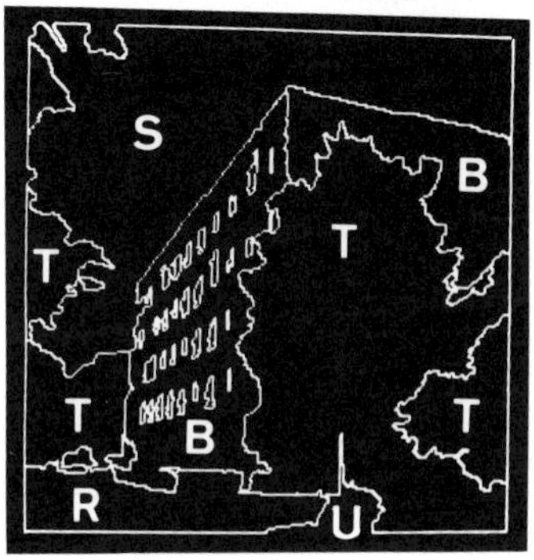

(c) The final division into regions
S: sky, T: tree, R: road,
B: building, U: unknown

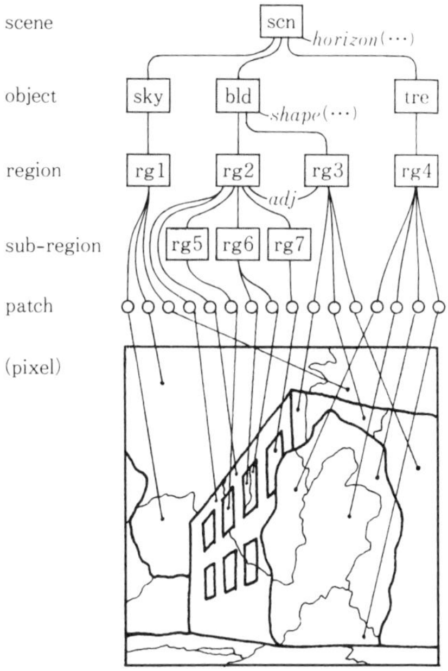

(d) The symbolic representation of the region

Figure 5.7 Pattern understanding based on knowledge (Ohta, 1985).

Next, based on knowledge, we try to label the regions partitioned as in Figure 5.7(c). We suppose that knowledge is represented by the semantic network and production rules shown in Figure 5.8. The semantic network represents declarative knowledge of the properties of objects and the relations among objects, whereas the production rules represent the procedural knowledge used for labeling.

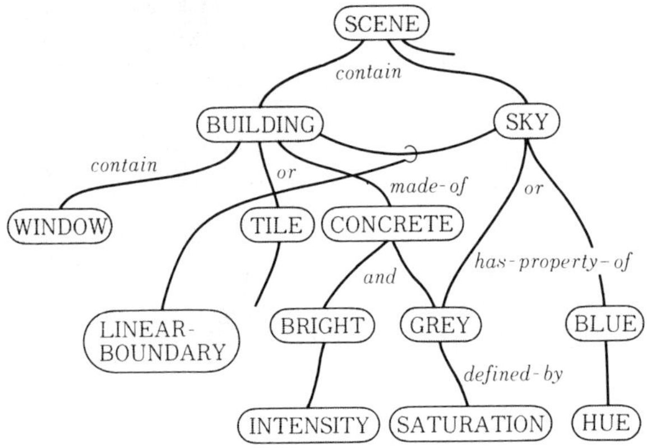

(a) Semantic network

[(*gen* (*or* (**blue* **sky*)(**grey* **sky*))(1.0 · 0.2))(**sky*)]
[(*gen* (*and* (**linear-boundary* **build* **sky*)
(*not* (*position up* **build* **sky*)))
*(1.0 · 0.5) *for sky*)(**build* **sky*)]

(b) Production rules

Figure 5.8 Knowledge for understanding the pattern in Figure 5.7 (Ohta, 1985).

In this case the pattern understanding system applies the production rules to the set of regions and, based on the knowledge in the semantic network, finds a plausible labeling of each region. That is, if we let $n_1, \ldots, n_k$ be the possible labelings for the region A, the plausibility of a labeling is is given by

$$label(A) = ((n_1\ \mu_1)(n_2\ \mu_2) \cdots (n_k\ \mu_k))$$
$$\mu_i \geq 0 \quad (i = 1, \ldots, k)$$
$$\sum_i \mu_i = 1$$

Concretely, the plausibility is represented, for example, by $label(A) = ((sky\ 0.7)(tree\ 0.2)(building\ 0.1))$.

Next, by using a production rule (for example, the last rule in Figure 5.8), we select the labeling with the highest plausibility, generate the pair of a region and its label, and attach it to the partially constructed semantic network shown in Figure 5.7. In Figure 5.7, (...) means the parts to be attached.

5.2 Pattern Matching and the Relaxation Method

A pattern understanding system tries to find the attributes of the objects in a pattern or relations among such objects using knowledge represented by the methods explained in Section 3.1 and the features extracted from the pattern. In this section, we will describe an algorithm for matching knowledge against features.

(a) Properties of pattern matching in pattern understanding

Matching in pattern understanding, unlike matching in symbolic processing, needs to take the following points into consideration:

(1) Since local features of a pattern usually match many different pieces of knowledge, we need to do matching based on the global structure obtained from local features.

(2) We need to attempt matching at various representation levels of a pattern.

(3) Since features of a pattern usually include noise, we need a matching algorithm applicable to data including noise.

(b) The relaxation method

Let us look at a relaxation method that is a representative algorithm for obtaining global structure from a set of local features. The purpose of the relaxation method is to find a consistent labeling of features, such as regions and boundaries, based on a set of local features. Although the relaxation method itself is an algorithm for finding the global structure of a pattern, it is also important as a preprocessing method for matching at the structure level. Now let $X = \{x_1, \ldots, x_n\}$ be the set of given features and $M = \{\mu_1, \ldots, \mu_m\}$ the set of possible labels. The relaxation algorithm is given a set of features as its input and outputs a globally consistent labeling of them.

There are two well-known kinds of relaxation methods:

(1) *The discrete relaxation method*

This method determines whether a feature can be labeled or not using the two discrete values 0 and 1. The method uses an algorithm for obtaining the value of f for all x_i and μ_j, when

$$f(x_i, \mu_j) = \begin{cases} 1 & \text{when a feature } x_i \text{ can be labeled as } \mu_j \\ 0 & \text{when a feature } x_i \text{ cannot be labeled as } \mu_j \end{cases}$$

(2) *The stochastic relaxation method*

This method represents the labeling of a feature as a probability vector P on M. That is, the possible labeling for a feature x_i is written as

$$P(x_i) = (p(x_i, \mu_1), \ldots, p(x_i, \mu_m))$$
$$\text{where } p(x_i, \mu_j) \geq 0 \ (j = 1, \ldots, m), \sum_j \mu_j = 1$$

This method uses an algorithm for obtaining the value of the vector $P(x_i)$ for all x_i.

Let us describe these two algorithms below.

(c) The discrete relaxation method

First, we describe an algorithm for the discrete relaxation method. The function f defined in (b) is for labeling one feature. So we also define a coefficient called the *compatibility coefficient*, which is a measure of how compatible the combination of features x_i and x_j is with the labels μ_k and μ_l, as

$$g(x_i, x_j, \mu_k, \mu_l) = \begin{cases} 1 & \text{when the features } x_i, x_j \text{ each} \\ & \text{can be labeled as } \mu_k, \mu_l \\ 0 & \text{when the features } x_i, x_j \text{ each} \\ & \text{cannot be labeled as } \mu_k, \mu_l \end{cases}$$

Whether a feature can be labeled or not depends on the pattern, so the actual definition of the function g will be different for each problem.

Let us consider the following algorithm:

Algorithm 5.1 (discrete relaxation method)

[1] Let X be a set of features. Enumerate locally possible labelings for each $x_i \in X$. Let $L(x_i)$ be the set of enumerated labelings for x_i $(i = 1, \ldots, n)$. (Local labeling)

[2] If there is an x_i such that $L(x_i) = \emptyset$, stop. A compatible labeling does not exist. Otherwise, go to [3]. (Termination condition)

[3] Let $f(x_i, \mu_j) = 1$ for all $\mu_j \in L(x_i)$, and let $f(x_i, \mu_j) = 0$ for all $\mu_j \notin L(x_i)$. (Setting the initial values of the labeling function f)

[4] Select any $x_i \in X$. (Setting the starting point for one relaxation cycle)

[5] Do the following substep for each feature x_j that is a neighbor of x_i. (Starting the relaxation cycle)

  [5.1] Do the following for all $\mu_k \in L(x_i)$: if $f(x_j, \mu_l) g(x_i, x_j, \mu_k, \mu_l) = 0$ for $\mu_k \in L(x_i)$ and all μ_l, then set $f(x_i, \mu_k) = 0$.

[6] Set $X = X - \{x_i\}$. (Ending the relaxation cycle)

[7] If $X = \emptyset$, stop. For each x_i, any μ with $f(x_i, \mu) = 1$ can be given to x_i as its label. If $X \neq \emptyset$, go to [4]. (Condition for terminating one relaxation cycle)

Algorithm 5.1 is conceptual. In practice we need to determine things like the compatibility coefficient g based on the actual problem. Also, this algorithm looks for a consistent labeling by using only the compatibility coefficient for local features, meaning that the labeling may not be globally consistent. In this case, when we are done, we still need to check combinatorially whether the labeling found by this algorithm is globally consistent.

A well-known discrete relaxation algorithm is the Waltz method for interpreting line drawings, which is described in Section 4.9(c). We will explain this algorithm once more using the formulation described here.

As an example, let us try to label each vertex $x_1, \ldots, x_4$ in the line drawing shown in Figure 5.9(a) using Algorithm 5.1. In this case labels are the vertex elements given in Section 4.9 and the compatibility coefficients are defined as follows:

$$g(x_i, x_j, \mu_k, \mu_l) = \begin{cases} 1 & \text{when the label } \mu_k \text{ for the vertex } x_i \\ & \text{and the label } \mu_l \text{ for the vertex } x_j \text{ assign} \\ & \text{the same symbol (among } +, -, >, <) \text{ to the} \\ & \text{line segment between } x_i \text{ and } x_j \\ 0 & \text{otherwise} \end{cases}$$

[Iteration 1]

[1] Let $X = \{x_1, x_2, x_3, x_4\}$. The following is a list of possible labels for each vertex (Local labeling):

$$L(x_1) = \{\text{angle}{<}{<}, \text{angle}{+}{<}, \text{angle}{<}{+}, \text{angle}{-}{>}, \text{angle}{>}{>}, \text{angle}{>}{-}\}$$
$$L(x_2) = \{\text{fork}{-}{+}{-}, \text{fork}{>}{+}{>}, \text{fork}{+}{-}{+}\}$$
$$L(x_3) = \{\text{angle}{<}{<}, \text{angle}{+}{<}, \text{angle}{<}{+}, \text{angle}{-}{>}, \text{angle}{>}{>}, \text{angle}{>}{-}\}$$
$$L(x_4) = \{\text{fork}{-}{+}{-}, \text{fork}{>}{+}{>}, \text{fork}{+}{-}{+}\}$$

[2] None of $L(x_i)$ are empty. (Termination condition)

[3] Set the value of $f(x_i, \mu_j)$ to 1 or 0. (Setting the initial value of the labeling function f)

[4] Pick the vertex $x_1 \in X$ arbitrarily. (Setting the starting point for one relaxation cycle)

[5] For the vertices x_2, x_4 that are neighbors of x_1 (Starting the relaxation cycle),

$$f(x_2, \mu_j) = 1, \quad \mu_j \in L(x_2)$$
$$f(x_4, \mu_j) = 1, \quad \mu_j \in L(x_4)$$

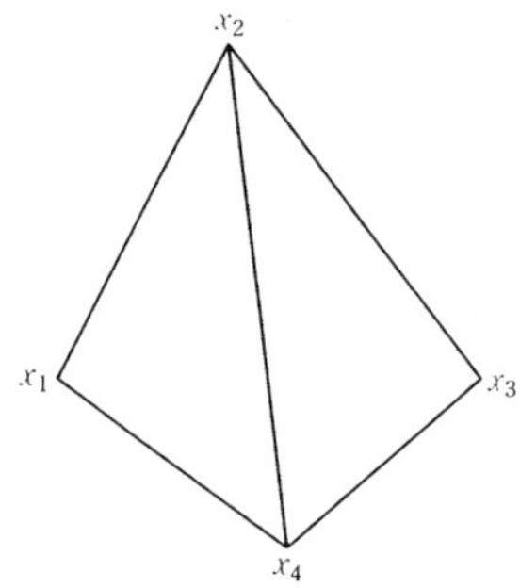

(a) A line drawing

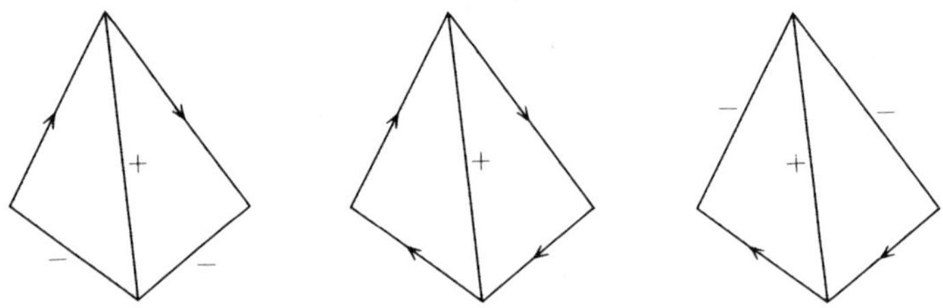

(b) A globally noncontradictory labeling

Figure 5.9 Interpreting a line drawing using the Waltz method.

and for all $\mu \in L(x_2)$,

$$g(x_1, x_2, \text{angle} <<, \mu) = 0, \quad \text{angle} << \in L(x_1)$$

Thus, set $f(x_1, \text{angle}<<) = 0$. Similarly, set $f(x_1, \text{angle}<+) = 0$. Also,

$$g(x_1, x_4, \text{angle}+<, \mu) = 0, \quad \text{angle}+< \in L(x_1)$$

So, set $f(x_1, \text{angle}+<) = 0$. As a result, we find that we cannot assign the label angle$<<$, angle$<+$, or angle$+<$ to the vertex x_1.

[6] Let $X = \{x_2, x_3, x_4\}$. (Ending the relaxation cycle)

[7] If $X \neq \emptyset$, go to [4]. (Condition for terminating one relaxation cycle)

[Iteration 2]

[4] Select the vertex $x_2 \in X$ arbitrarily. (Setting the starting point of one relaxation cycle)

[5] For the vertices x_1, x_3 that are neighbors of x_2 (Starting the relaxation cycle),

$$f(x_1, \text{angle}->) = f(x_1, \text{angle}>>) = f(x_1, \text{angle}>-) = 1$$
$$f(x_3, \mu_j) = 1, \quad \mu_j \in L(x_3)$$

Since there is no pair $y \in \{x_1, x_3\}$ and $\mu_k \in L(x_2)$ that makes $g(x_2, y, \mu_k, \mu) = 0$ for all of those labels μ making the value of f 1, no label can be found that can be assigned to x_2.

[6] Set $X = \{x_3, x_4\}$. (Ending the relaxation cycle)

[7] Since $X \neq \emptyset$, go to [4]. (Condition for terminating one relaxation cycle)

[Iteration 3]

[4] Select the vertex $x_3 \in X$. (Setting the starting point of one relaxation cycle)

[5] For the vertices x_2, x_4 that are neighbors of x_3 (Starting the relaxation cycle),

$$f(x_2, \mu_j) = 1, \quad \mu_j \in L(x_2)$$
$$f(x_4, \mu_j) = 1, \quad \mu_j \in L(x_4)$$

and for all $\mu \in L(x_3)$,

$$g(x_3, x_2, \text{angle>+}, \mu) = 0, \quad \text{angle>+} \in L(x_3)$$

So set $f(x_3, \text{angle>+}) = 0$. Similarly, set $f(x_3, \text{angle>>}) = 0$. Thus we find that the vertex x_3 cannot be labeled by either angle>+ or angle>>.

[6] Set $X = \{x_4\}$. (Ending the relaxation cycle)

[7] Since $X \neq \emptyset$, go to [4]. (Condition for terminating one relaxation cycle)

[Iteration 4]

[4] Select the vertex $x_4 \in X$. (Setting the starting point of one relaxation cycle)

[5] For the vertices x_3, x_1 that are neighbors of x_4 (Starting the relaxation cycle),

$$\begin{aligned} f(x_3, \text{angle+>}) &= f(x_3, \text{angle<}-) = f(x_3, \text{angle <<}) \\ &= f(x_3, \mathit{angle}-<) = 1 \\ f(x_1, \text{angle}->) &= f(x_1, \text{angle>>}) = f(x_1, \text{angle>}-) = 1 \end{aligned}$$

and for any $\mu \in \{\text{angle+>}, \text{angle<}-, \text{angle<<}, \mathit{angle}-<\}$

$$g(x_4, x_3, \text{fork+}-+, \mu) = 0, \quad \text{fork+}-+ \in L(x_4)$$

So, set $f(x_4, \text{fork+}-+) = 0$. In other words, the vertex x_4 cannot be labeled by fork+−+.

[6] Set $X = \emptyset$. (Ending the relaxation cycle)

[7] Since $X \neq \emptyset$, stop. The possible labels for each vertex are the following (Condition for terminating one relaxation cycle):

$$x_1 \ldots \text{angle}{>}{-}, \text{angle}{-}{>}, \text{angle}{>}{>}$$
$$x_2 \ldots \text{fork}{+}{-}{+}, \text{fork}{-}{+}{-}, \text{fork}{>}{+}{>}$$
$$x_3 \ldots \text{angle}{<}{-}, \text{angle}{-}{<}, \text{angle}{<}{<}$$
$$x_4 \ldots \text{fork}{-}{+}{-}, \text{fork}{>}{+}{>}$$

In this way, we have obtained all the possible labelings. From these labelings, we can construct $3 \times 3 \times 3 \times 2 = 54$ possible combinations of global labeling for the four vertices. However, they might include combinations of labeling that are globally inconsistent. For this reason, we need to check each of the 54 combinations for global inconsistency.

When we check, we find that the three combinations shown in Figure 5.9(b) are the only ones that are not globally inconsistent. As we saw, we need to enumerate for global inconsistency, but we can reduce a large number of inconsistent combinations by the discrete relaxation method above. In our example, the number of possible labels for each vertex is $6, 3, 6, 3$, respectively, so there are $6 \times 3 \times 6 \times 3 = 324$ possibilities. The above method reduced the number to 54. As a pattern becomes more complex, the relaxation method usually becomes more effective.

(d) The stochastic relaxation method

Suppose we have a set of features, X, extracted from a pattern and a set of possible labels, M. For any $x_i, x_j \in X$, $\mu_k, \mu_l \in M$, let $p(x_i, \mu_k | x_j, \mu_l)$ be the probability that the label of x_j is μ_l and the label of x_i is μ_k. For $p(x_i, \mu_k | x_j, \mu_l)$, the following holds: For any x_i, x_j, μ_l,

$$p(x_i, \mu_k | x_i, \mu_l) = \begin{cases} 1 & \text{when } \mu_k = \mu_l \\ 0 & \text{otherwise} \end{cases}$$

$$\sum_k \mu_k p(x_i, \mu_k | x_j, \mu_l) = 1$$

$p(x_i, \mu_k | x_j, \mu_l)$ can be thought of as the extent to which labeling x_i with μ_k and x_j with μ_l does not contribute to an inconsistent labeling, so it can be considered as a stochastic parameter that represents the compatibility of labels.

Below we assume, either statistically or from previous knowledge, that the value of $p(x_i, \mu_k | x_j, \mu_l)$ is given for all $x_i, x_j \in X$, $\mu_k, \mu_l \in M$. In this case, we can use the following algorithm:

Algorithm 5.2 (the stochastic relaxation method)

[1] Set $n = 0$. (Initialization of the iteration)

[2] For iteration n, from the probability, $P_n(x_i, \mu)$, that the label $\mu \in M$ is a label for each feature $x_i \in X$, obtain the probability vector for a labeling, $P_n(x_i) = (p_n(x_i, \mu_1), \ldots, p_n(x_i, \mu_m))$. (Computation of the probability vector)

[3] Using the following formula, compute $P_{n+1}(x_i) = (p_{n+1}(x_i, \mu_1), \ldots, P_{n+1}(x_i, \mu_m))$. (Updating the probability vector)

$$p_{n+1}(x_i, \mu_k) = \sum_j \gamma_{ij} \left\{ \sum_l p(x_i, \mu_k | x_j, \mu_l) p_n(x_j, \mu_l) \right\}$$

$$\text{where } \gamma_{ij} \geq 0, \quad \sum_j \gamma_{ij} = 1$$

[4] Stop if $\|P_n(x_i)\| \approx \|P_{n+1}(x_i)\|$ for all $x_i \in X$. If $\max_{\mu_k} p_{n+1}(x_i, \mu_k) = p_{n+1}(x_i, \mu_{k_i})(x_i \in X)$, select μ_{k_i} as the label for x_i. Otherwise, go to [5]. (Termination condition)

[5] Let $n = n + 1$ and go to [3]. (Repeating the iteration)

In Algorithm 5.2, γ_{ij} represents the degree to which the label μ_l contributes to x_j in the change of the labeling probability $p(x_i, \mu_k)$.

Updating the probability vector ([3] in Algorithm 5.2), in an actual problem, consists of repeating the multiplication of the matrix whose elements are $\gamma_{ij} p(x_i, \mu_k | x_j, \mu_l)$ and the vector $P_n(x_j)$. Thus efficient parallel computation is possible. The convergence of this process is not generally guaranteed, but if the matrix (linear operator for relaxation method) satisfies appropriate conditions, it can be proved to converge globally, that is, independent of the initial value of the probability vector $P_0(x_i)$ $(x_i \in X)$.

This method can be used for matching a pattern with noise or other defects because it treats the labeling as a probability distribution. Since, like the discrete relaxation method, it is based on only the local compatibility of the labeling, it does not always result in a globally consistent labeling. It still requires a test of global consistency of the labeling.

(e) Graph matching and its evaluation measure

Results from the relaxation method can easily be represented by graphs. Also, if we use graphs to represent knowledge for pattern understanding, such as semantic networks, we can generally make the amount of memory needed small. As a result, graph matching methods become important for matching two patterns or for matching a pattern against such knowledge.

First, let us consider evaluation measures for matching. Matching two graphs can be divided into three cases as in Figure 5.10: when they completely match, when they do not match, and when they partially match. Of these cases, partial matching is important here, because in pattern understanding graphs corresponding to two patterns will usually only partially match.

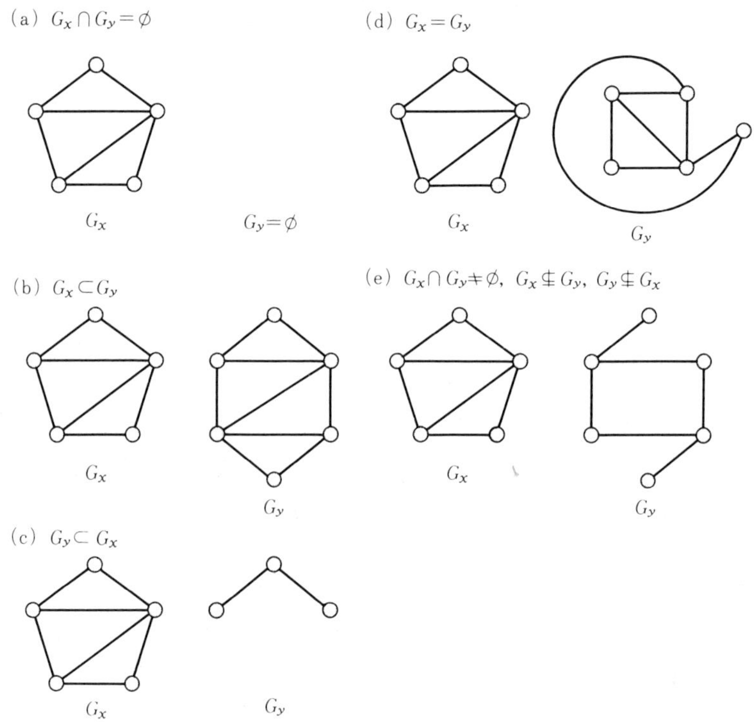

Figure 5.10 Cases in matching two graphs.

In partial matching, there are two problems:

(i) We need to evaluate the similarity of two graphs.
(ii) The computing time for such matching algorithms increases exponentially with the size of the graph (for example, with the sum of the numbers of nodes and edges).

Here, let us consider (i), the evaluation measure.

Suppose two patterns X and Y are represented by two directed graphs G_x and G_y. Let V_x and V_y be the sets of nodes of G_x and G_y, respectively, and suppose the elements of V_x and V_y correspond to some features, like vertices, boundaries, and regions, of X and Y. Also, let E_x and E_y be the sets of (directed) edges of G_x and G_y, respectively, and suppose the elements of E_x and E_y correspond to relations between two features of X or Y.

First, let us consider an evaluation measure for the similarity of two graphs. When the names of the nodes of two directed graphs G_x and G_y are appropriately overlapped, we can express the degree of similarity using $O = |V| + |E|$ where $|V|$ is the number of overlapping nodes and $|E|$ is the number of overlapping edges.

For example, five kinds of overlapping for the graphs G_x and G_y are, as shown in Figure 5.10,

(a) $G_x \cap G_y = \emptyset$
(b) $G_x \subset G_y$
(c) $G_y \subset G_x$
(d) $G_x = G_y$
(e) $G_x \cap G_y \neq \emptyset$, $G_x \not\subseteq G_y$, $G_y \not\subseteq G_x$

The values of O for (a)–(d) are, if we take the names of the nodes appropriately, $|V_x| + |E_x|$, $|V_y| + |E_y|$, $|V_x| + |E_x|$, respectively. For (e), the value satisfies $0 < O < \min\{|V_x| + |E_x|, |V_y| + |E_y|\}$.

The measure O can be thought of as one measure of the size of the maximum subgraph isomorphism of two graphs.

An algorithm that finds a subgraph isomorphism with the largest O (in other words, the maximum subgraph isomorphism) for two directed graphs X and Y basically has to check every possible pair of subgraphs. Improving the efficiency of such an algorithm requires heuristic knowledge. For example, in pattern understanding, a node of a graph usually corresponds to a feature, to which attribute-values such as texture and color are often provided. In a graph, these attribute-value pairs may be represented by a self-loop at a node. We can introduce the heuristic knowledge that, when matching two patterns, features need to have the same attribute-value pairs, represented by the self-loops, in order to match. Then we can limit the search for a subgraph isomorphism to nodes whose self-loop labels are the same. This can reduce the time needed for the search.

If we only want to find such a graph with the locally largest value of O, that is, a locally maximal subgraph isomorphism rather than the globally maximum subgraph isomorphism, we may possibly find a solution in a short time. However, the graph search usually attains many local maxima, and there is no guarantee that a local maximum value of the evaluation measure is close to the global maximum.

5.3 Maximal Subgraph Isomorphism and Clique Method

In this section we will explain a method from graph theory that provides an algorithm for obtaining a maximal subgraph isomorphism of two labeled directed graphs. This method can easily be applied to a graph without labels. First, let us consider the labeled directed graphs $G_x = (V_x, E_x, C_x)$, $G_y = (V_y, E_y, C_y)$, where C_x and C_y are the sets of labels of the edges of G_x, G_y, respectively. We define the association graph of G_x and G_y as follows:

Definition 1 (association graph) Suppose two labeled directed graphs $G_x = (V_x, E_x, C_x)$ and $G_y(V_y, E_y, C_y)$ are given. For $E = \{(v_i, v_j)|v_i \in V_x, v_j \in V_y\}$, let $U = \{\{e_1, e_2\}|e_1 = (v_{i1}, v_{j1}) \in E,\ e_2 = (v_{i2}, v_{j2}) \in E,$ $(v_{i1}, v_{i2}) \in E_x, (v_{j1}, v_{j2}) \in E_y, (v_{i1}, v_{i2})$ and (v_{j1}, v_{j2}) have the same label$\}$, and $S = \{e_i|\{e_i, e_j\} \in U\}$. The undirected graph $A = (S, U)$ is called the *association graph* for G_x and G_y.

In this definition, it is possible to restrict the elements in the set E using heuristic knowledge. For example, as we noted in Section 5.2(e), it is possible to define E by only collecting pairs of nodes representing features with the same attribute-value pairs.

Now, a maximal subgraph isomorphism of two graphs G_x and G_y corresponds to a maximum clique of the association graph for G_x and G_y. For example, let us consider the two graphs shown in Figure 5.11(a). Their association graph G is shown in Figure 5.11(b). There are three maximum cliques in G, each shown as a solid line. (In order to make the illustration simpler, we did not show most of the edges.) Each of these corresponds to a maximal subgraph isomorphism.

From these, we can formulate the following algorithm for detecting the maximum cliques of the association graph as a method for finding maximal subgraph isomorphisms of two given graphs.

Algorithm 5.3 (detecting maximum cliques for finding maximal subgraph isomorphisms)

[Detection of cliques]

- Suppose there is a procedure $C(H, K)$ that takes as inputs $H = (V_h, E_h)$, a clique of the graph G, and $K = (V_k, E_k)$, a subgraph of G that includes the nodes of H, and outputs all the cliques included in K. In particular, $C(\emptyset, G)$ returns all the cliques of G. $C(H, K)$ can be defined recursively as follows:

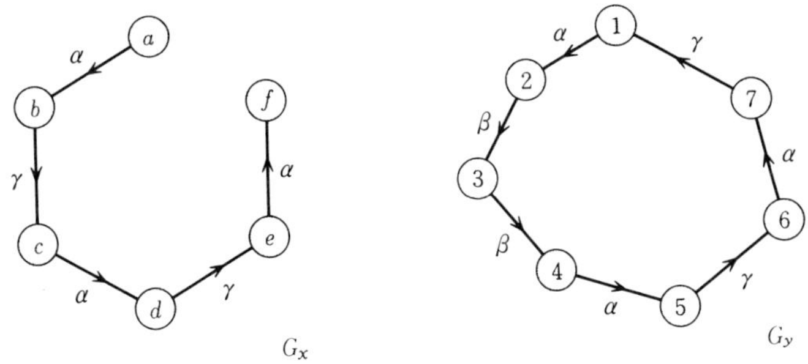

(a) Two graphs, G_x and G_y

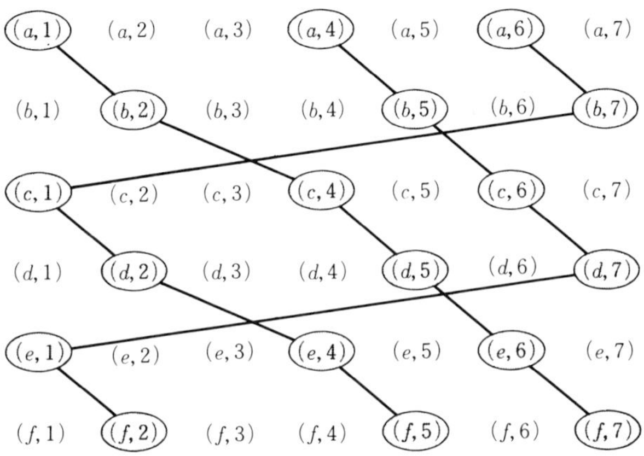

(b) An association graph of G_x and G_y

(The circled nodes represent a pair of nodes of G_x and G_y that have the same attribute, and the branches represent the fact that the pair of such nodes is not contradictory. (Most of the branches are omitted.))

Figure 5.11 Detection of maximal subgraph isomorphisms of two graphs.

(1) If for any $v \in V_k - V_h$ there exists a $v' \in V_h$ such that $(v, v') \notin E_k$, then return H.

(2) Otherwise, there is a $v^* \in V_k$ such that $(v^*, v') \in E_k$ for all $v' \in V_h$. Find v^*. Then compute $C(H^*, K) \cup C(H, K^*)$, where H^* is the graph obtained by adding the node v^* and all the $(v^*, v) \in E_k$ (where $v \in V_k - V_h$) to H and K^* is the graph that is obtained by deleting the node v^* and all the $(v^*, v) \in E_k$ (where $v \in V_k - V_h$) from K.

[Detection of maximum cliques]

- In order to find a maximum clique, compute $C(H^*, K) \cup C(H, K^*)$ recursively in (2) for all possible v^*.

As an example, suppose we obtained the two graphs shown in Figure 5.11(a) from the two patterns shown in Figure 5.12. The association graph for these two graphs is shown in Figure 5.11(b). If we use the above method [detection of maximum cliques], we find the three maximal cliques shown in Figure 5.11(b).

In this section we described methods of pattern matching using graph matching. These methods are clear and easy to see as they are based on the algorithms of graph theory. However, they are only for structures that are completely represented by graphs, so they are sometimes not so effective for patterns that include noise or defects.

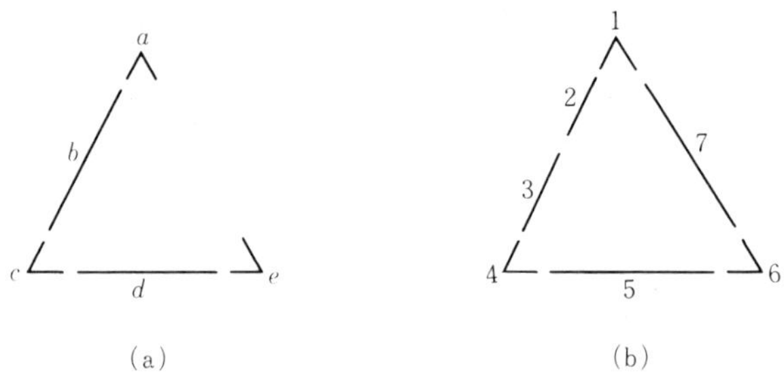

Figure 5.12 Patterns that yield the graphs G_x and G_y in Figure 5.11.

5.4 Control in Pattern Understanding

To understand patterns, we need to combine many different processes. The efficiency of pattern understanding depends on how we control various processes. Also, there are many problems we have not yet covered, such as interpolating incomplete patterns based on knowledge, integrating processing of different levels, and so on.

In this section we will look at these problems from the viewpoint of control in pattern understanding.

(a) Bottom-up and top-down processing

First, as an example, let us look at the pattern of a "hammer" shown in Figure 5.3(a). Figure 1.5 shows the result of feature extraction from the pattern of a "hammer" other than the one in Figure 5.3(a). Furthermore, Figure 1.6 shows the result of matching knowledge against the extracted features.

Since matching algorithms do not usually look into the details of features, matching against knowledge does not always work correctly. Sometimes it results in a contradiction with past analysis. Therefore, an algorithm needs a flexible method of control that can use feature extraction and knowledge utilization alternatively. We can summarize this in the following conceptual algorithm:

Algorithm 5.4 (bidirectional control in pattern understanding)
[1] Let $f(x)$ be a given pattern function.
[2] Do feature extraction on $f(x)$ and let the result be $g(x)$. Parts with more than one interpretation are left as they are.
[3] Match $g(x)$ against our knowledge. If we do not find knowledge k that matches $g(x)$ well, then stop. Output $g(x)$. Otherwise, go to [4].
[4] Using inference based on k, make the incomplete or ambiguous (multiply interpreted) parts of $g(x)$ more complete and call the result $g(x)$ again. If the result is satisfactory, then stop. Output $g(x)$. Otherwise, go to [2].

In Algorithm 5.4, [2] is called *bottom-up processing* or *data-driven processing*; [3] and [4] are called *top-down processing* or *model-driven processing*.

In pattern understanding based on knowledge, it would be ideal to perform bottom-up and top-down processing bidirectionally. However, we need to note that, since knowledge is generally incomplete, there is no general guarantee that the new pattern obtained in [4] gives a better result than previous iterations.

In Algorithm 5.4, bottom-up and top-down processing are executed in the following way:

Algorithm 5.5 (bottom-up processing)
[1] Preprocess the input data with techniques like the elimination of noise using smoothing.
[2] Extract local features of the pattern such as fragments of boundaries, small regions, color, or texture.
[3] Extract global features from local features.
[4] Generate a global representation of the pattern like a line drawing.

Algorithm 5.6 (top-down processing)
[1] Find a consistent labeling for the global features of the pattern.
[2] Match the labeled features against our knowledge.
[3] Interpolate the object's representation based on the knowledge.

As an example, consider a pattern understanding system for finding a tumor in an X-ray photograph. First, bottom-up processing is used to extract features from a given X-ray photograph.

Next, if the system knows that tumors are likely to grow in a lung, it can try to find the outline of the lung and its inside from fragmentary features extracted from the X-ray photograph by top-down processing using knowledge of the structure of a lung.

On the other hand, even if the system obtained the outline of the lung, knowledge about where we might find a tumor in the lung does not exist. The system needs to narrow down candidates for a tumor using bottom-up processing.

Furthermore, in order to select the most likely candidate for a tumor, top-down processing using knowledge of the lung's structure may be effective.

As in this example, a pattern understanding system can concentrate its attention on a selected candidate and analyze it in detail by controlling bottom-up and top-down processing bidirectionally. Also, at each point of processing it can combine appropriate methods of feature extraction and pattern matching.

(b) Interpolating representation based on knowledge

We now explain more concretely some methods of accomplishing the control described conceptually in (a). First, we describe a method for interpolating a representation based on knowledge.

Consider understanding the pattern of a polyhedron shown in Figure 5.13(a). We assume that we have obtained the boundary lines of the polyhedron as shown in Figure 5.13(b), using bottom-up processing.

If we know the heuristic "When there is a concave angle on the boundary, each side of this angle becomes part of the boundary of different objects," we can predict that there are boundary lines around the angles G and J and find new boundaries from fragmentary features around G and J. The result is shown in Figure 5.13(c).

Furthermore, if we use two other heuristics—"The end point of a boundary line connects to another boundary line" and "If two vertices are close each other, they are actually one vertex"—then we can interpolate the structures as shown in Figure 5.13(d) and (e) and can, in the end, obtain the structure shown in Figure 5.13(a).

(c) Control of modules using the blackboard model

Suppose we have several independent computation modules and one memory shared by those modules. A computing model for problem solving by

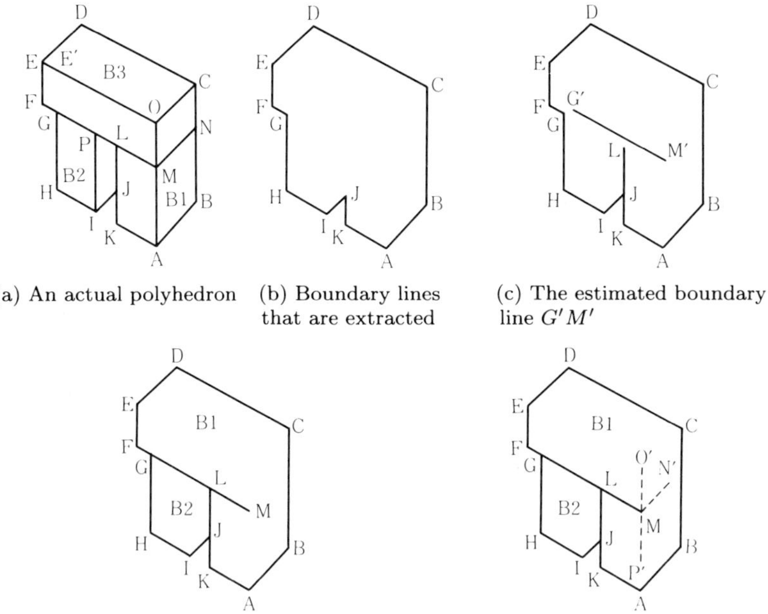

(a) An actual polyhedron (b) Boundary lines that are extracted (c) The estimated boundary line $G'M'$

(d) Considering end points G and G' as the same point (e) Estimating other boundary lines

Figure 5.13 Interpolating representations using top-down processing with heuristic knowledge (Shirai, 1975).

repeated execution of modules, each of which gets its input from the memory and writes its results to the memory, is called the *blackboard model.*

We now describe a method of control for pattern understanding using the blackboard model. As an example, let's look at an understanding system for aerial photographs based on the blackboard model. Figure 5.14 shows a summary. This system has both a region extraction module and an object recognition module. The former analyzes the pattern spectrum, shape, texture, and so on to extract regions and writes them to memory. The latter takes regions found by the former from the memory and does further analysis to estimate larger regions.

The memory keeps such information as the density of features, threshold values, the directional angle of the sun, various values of attributes for regions, shapes of regions, labels for spatial relations, semantic networks representing conceptual relations among objects, and so on.

For pattern understanding, we can formulate, as independent computing modules, various algorithms for extracting features at various levels and algorithms for labeling and matching based on knowledge. Although the blackboard model is a cooperative computing system using multiple

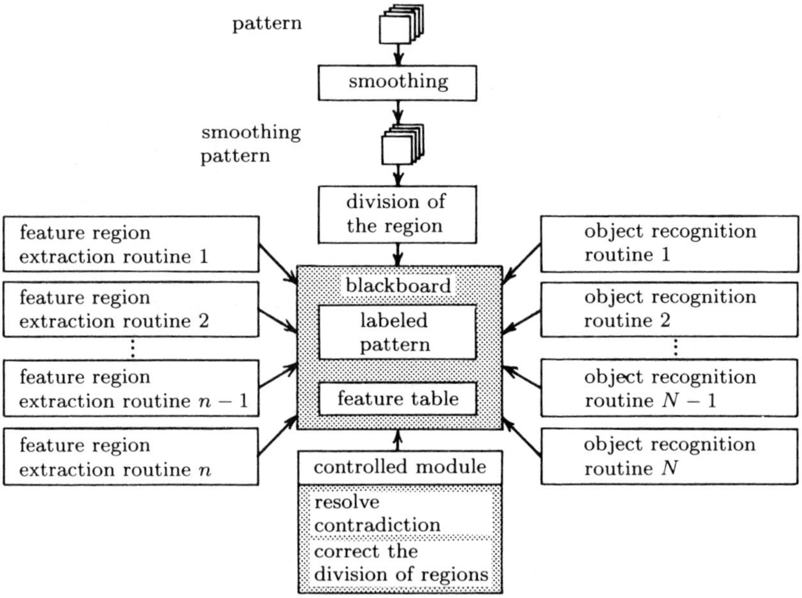

(a) Pattern understanding system

(b) Pattern of an aerial photograph

(c) Division into regions

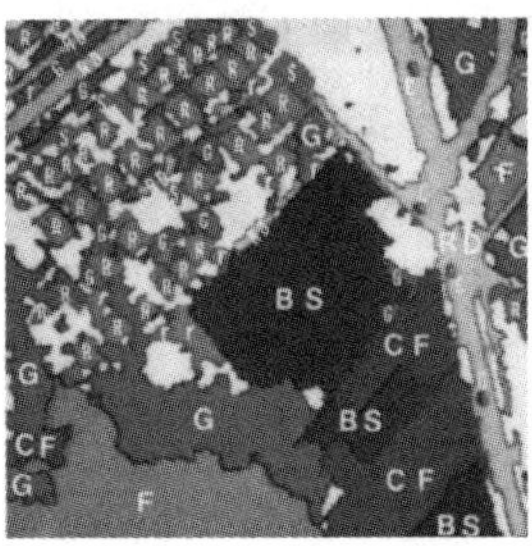

CF: fields
BS: bare land
G: grassland
F: forest
RD: road
C: car
R: roof
r: misrecognized roof
S: shadow

(d) Result of the pattern understanding

Figure 5.14 An understanding system and its analysis of an aerial photograph using the blackboard model (Matsuyama and Nagao, 1980 (in Japanese)).

modules, each module is independent, so contradictory data can exist in memory at the same time. Also, information that may negatively affect problem solving can possibly be written out to memory.

In the control of the blackboard model, we need not only to schedule the priority to give to modules but also to resolve contradictions in the data and eliminate meaningless data. Therefore, a system based on a blackboard model often has, in the control module, a routine for finding and resolving contradictory data and a routine for correcting the estimated partition of regions.

(d) Constraint satisfaction by back constraint

When we try to match a representation obtained by feature extraction using bottom-up processing against knowledge, ambiguities frequently remain. For example, in the analysis of a photographic portrait using the generalized cylinder method, the length, L, and the direction, D, of a generalized cylinder are often hard to determine because the camera angle or the direction of the sun is often not clear. For such cases, we can represent knowledge using a set of inequalities like $L_{\min} \leq L \leq L_{\max}$, $D_{\min} \leq D \leq D_{\max}$ as constraints.

Checking whether the length, L^*, and the direction, D^*, of a generalized cylinder obtained from feature extraction satisfy these inequalities or not corresponds to pattern matching. Furthermore, if L^* and D^* satisfy the inequalities, it is possible to estimate conditions when taking the photograph from the values of L^* and D^*. For instance, if knowledge of conditions when taking a photograph is represented as a set of inequalities about, for example, light rays in three-dimensional space, actual conditions for a given photograph can often be estimated by the values of L^* and D^*.

In this way, by propagating attributes of features satisfying constraints, we can often do consistent matching at various levels. This method is generally called constraint satisfaction by *back constraint.*

(e) Pattern understanding using production systems

By using production systems, we can often have flexible control over pattern understanding by combining declarative and procedural knowledge.

For example, we can keep a set of rules at each node of a semantic network and make them execute when the corresponding node is inferred. The scene understanding system described in Section 5.1(c)(4) is an example of a pattern understanding system based on a production system where the rules are localized.

There are two main differences between production systems and the blackboard model:

(1) Differences in modularization of knowledge

In a production system, procedural knowledge is represented by relatively small rules, and it is necessary to represent declarative knowledge of objects somewhere else, using frames, a semantic network, or some other declarative representation. In the blackboard model, we frequently use relatively large computing modules that join declarative and procedural knowledge together.

(2) Differences in inference method

In a production system, matching the condition side of a rule and the content of memory is the basic inference process. In the blackboard model, more complicated matching between a module and memory content is possible.

From these differences, we can say that a production system is useful for detailed control using a set of relatively small procedures, whereas the blackboard model is more appropriate when knowledge is too complicated to be divided into rules. However, in an actual problem, what kind of computing model is appropriate depends on the problem domain, and it is hard to determine what control method is best in general.

(f) Pattern understanding by plan generation

If we uniformly analyze every part of the pattern, it may sometimes take too much computing to find a specific object X in a pattern that includes many objects. It is convenient if we have some method of control for the priority we give to analyzing features of X.

Here, we consider *plan generation* as an example of this method of control. For example, in order to check, in a short amount of time, whether an aerial photograph of an airport includes a runway with a service road, we can execute the following procedure:

Procedure for plan generation

Generate the following plan to find a runway with a service road.

- goal: find a runway with a service road
  - subgoal[1] Find a runway

[1.1] Find the convex hulls (a convex hull of a set of points is the minimum convex set including those points) of a set of sample points with some particular density, which approximates a region with a narrow belt shape.

[1.1.1] Take a lot of sample points on the photograph and find the density of each point.

- subgoal[2] Find a service road that crosses the runway.
  - [2.1] Find the convex hulls of a set of sample points with some particular density, which approximates a region with a narrow belt shape.
    - [2.1.1] Take a lot of sample points on the photograph and find the density of each point.
  - [2.2] Of the results from subgoal [2.1], find the one that intersects a result from subgoal [1.1].

In the above plan, subgoals [1] and [2] are *AND goals.* For a goal above those subgoals to be attained, both subgoals need to be accomplished. Subgoals [2.1] and [2.2] are *SEQUENCE goals* and need to be attained in that order. Furthermore, subgoal [1.1] needs to be accomplished before [2.2]. Also, since subgoals [1.1.1] and [2.1.1] are attained by the same procedure, it is sufficient if either one of them is accomplished.

Thus, the above plan has chronological constraints on subgoals and is generally called a *nonlinear plan.* If a system has enough information to generate a nonlinear plan like the example, it has the possibility of finding an object in a short time by paying attention only to the necessary parts of a complex pattern. Sometimes generating a plan itself requires complicated inference, so if plan generation is used to control pattern understanding, the computation time as a whole may not always be improved.

(g) Expert vision

As we continue to study control in pattern understanding, we realize that a system for pattern understanding basically consists of a set of modules with various kinds of technical knowledge and the interaction among such modules. This makes it possible to construct a support system that organizes these modules to make them easier to use and makes it possible for a user who is not a specialist in pattern understanding systems to do pattern understanding by combining modules in an appropriate way. A support system that functions like this is called an *expert vision* system.

The knowledge that a pattern understanding system needs is mainly divided into two kinds:

(1) Knowledge necessary for extracting features from a pattern and generating some representation.
(2) Knowledge for combining and controlling various methods for pattern understanding.

In an expert vision system, the latter knowledge is systematized and is used in applications to determine automatically what method to use for visual image processing and so on.

Summary

In this chapter, we described methods of understanding patterns using knowledge.

5.1 Pattern understanding is the generation, using knowledge, of a representation of what objects are included in a pattern, what are their attributes and values, and what are the relations among those objects.

5.2 Two important methods of knowledge representation used in pattern understanding are the superordinate/subordinate relation and the whole/part relation for classes of objects.

5.3 Symbolic representations such as semantic networks, frames, and rules can be used as knowledge representations for pattern understanding.

5.4 The relaxation method is a method for matching features extracted from a pattern against knowledge. Pattern understanding can use both the discrete relaxation method and the stochastic relaxation method.

5.5 If we represent, as graphs, the results of feature extraction and labeling by relaxation and represent knowledge also as graphs, graph matching algorithms become an important method for pattern understanding.

5.6 A maximal subgraph isomorphism of two labeled directed graphs can be obtained by finding a maximum clique in the association graph for the two graphs.

5.7 In order to control the process of pattern understanding, both bottom-up processing (data-driven processing) and top-down processing (model-driven processing) can be used.

5.8 The method of interpolating a representation based on heuristic knowledge can be used for top-down processing.

5.9 Control of computing modules using the blackboard model, constraint satisfaction using back constraint, and plan generation are methods of control in pattern understanding systems.

5.10 An expert vision system is a support system for performing pattern understanding by intelligently combining knowledge modules and control modules.

Keywords

pattern understanding, knowledge representation, semantic network representation, frame representation, rule representation, labeling, pattern matching, discrete relaxation method, stochastic relaxation method, graph matching, subgraph isomorphism, association graph, clique, bottom-up processing, data-driven processing, top-down processing, model-driven processing, blackboard model, back constraint, plan generation, expert vision

Exercises

5.1 Describe the difference between extracting features of a pattern and understanding a pattern. Also enumerate the information necessary for pattern understanding.

5.2 We say that two graphs $G_1 = (V_1, E_1)$ and $G_2 = (V_2, E_2)$ are graph isomorphic when there is a one-to-one correspondence between the elements of V_1 and V_2 and the elements of E_1 and E_2, and that this correspondence extends to any edges $\{v_{11}, v_{12}\} \in E_1$, $\{v_{21}, v_{22}\} \in E_2$ in corresponding nodes $\langle v_{11}, v_{21}\rangle$, $\langle v_{12}, v_{22}\rangle$. Describe an algorithm for judging if two given graphs are graph isomorphic or not. Using this algorithm, show that the graphs given in Figure 5.10(d), G_x and G_y, are graph isomorphic.

5.3 In pattern understanding using plan generation, a set of subgoals that has the property that if any one of the subgoals is accomplished, we consider the set to be accomplished, are called *OR goals*. Show examples of pattern understanding where it is necessary to generate a plan including both OR goals and AND goals. Also describe an algorithm for plan generation including both OR goals and AND goals.

6 Learning Concepts

This chapter will discuss algorithms for learning concepts from examples. Learning concepts is the most basic kind of learning on a computer, so we need to understand it fully. We will first give the definition of a concept and general methods of learning concepts and algorithms. We will then give algorithms for version space and concept clustering.

6.1 Definition of a Concept

(a) Extensional and intensional meanings

Words such as "a triangle," "a coffee cup," and "a hammer" indicate a concept. An individual triangle is considered to be an *example* of the concept called a triangle. It is important to know how various concepts and their examples are represented in a computer when we formulate algorithms for pattern recognition and learning on a computer. In previous chapters, we represented a concept and its examples using representation techniques like class and instance; however, there we hardly defined terms such as concept and example. So, let us first define the notion of a concept.

There are two different ways of defining the meaning of a concept: extensional meaning and intensional meaning.

Definition 1 (extensional meaning) Various examples exist first and the meaning of a concept is defined by the set of these examples. This is the extensional meaning of a concept.

Definition 2 (intensional meaning) Various properties exist first and the meaning of a concept is defined by a set of these attributes. This is the intensional meaning of a concept.

Suppose we collect together all the triangles we have seen or have imagined and make the set of them. The extensional meaning of the concept "triangle" is this set. The intensional meaning of "triangle" is the set of its properties such that a triangle is surrounded by three line segments or that it is a plane figure. The extensional meaning and the intensional meaning of the same object are not necessarily the same. For example, "the brightest star in the evening (the evening star)" and "the brightest star in the morning (the morning star)" mean the same thing, Venus, in their extensional meaning, but they are different in their intensional meaning.

When we try to define a concept using extensional meaning, we need to list all its examples (it is impossible in an actual life but is possible conceptually). Using the intensional meaning, we can define a concept as a list of attributes, but, once again in real life, it is impossible to list all the possible attributes of a concept. In this book, we determine a set of attributes first and consider objects that satisfy such a set as examples of the concept. This type of definition can be considered as an approximation of a definition for the meaning of a concept that is both extensional and intensional.

The word "concept," like "knowledge" and "learning," has been used in philosophy and psychology. Although it is important to know the meaning of "concept" in these fields, we limit ourselves to the above approximate definition when we are dealing with learning on a computer.

(b) Representing a concept

A typical method for representing the meaning of a concept is to use a list containing the name of the concept followed by elements that are attribute-value pairs:

$$(\langle\text{name of a concept}\rangle(\langle\text{attribute}\rangle_1\ \langle\text{value}\rangle_1)\\ (\langle\text{attribute}\rangle_2\ \langle\text{value}\rangle_2)\ldots(\langle\text{attribute}\rangle_n\ \langle\text{value}\rangle_n))$$

For example, the concept c "something big, red, and round," can be expressed as follows using the three attributes, *size*, *color*, *shape*:

$$(c\ (\mathit{size}\ \mathit{large})(\mathit{color}\ \mathit{red})(\mathit{shape}\ \mathit{round}))$$

where *size*, *color*, and *shape* are the attributes representing a size, a color, and a shape, respectively, and *large*, *red*, and *round* are the values representing big, red, and round, respectively.

On the other hand, we also can represent the meaning of a concept using first-order predicate logic. In this case, each attribute corresponds to a predicate symbol and the name of the concept and the value correspond to arguments of the predicate. If we use the conjunction operator, a concept can generally be represented as a logical conjunction:

$$\begin{aligned}
&\quad \text{attribute}_1(\langle\text{name of a concept}\rangle,\ \langle\text{value}\rangle_1)\\
&\wedge\ \text{attribute}_2(\langle\text{name of a concept}\rangle,\ \langle\text{value}\rangle_2)\\
&\dots\\
&\wedge\ \text{attribute}_{n-1}(\langle\text{name of a concept}\rangle,\ \langle\text{value}\rangle_{n-1})\\
&\wedge\ \text{attribute}_n(\langle\text{name of a concept}\rangle,\ \langle\text{value}\rangle_n)
\end{aligned}$$

When a variable symbol is included in the above well-formed formula, the variable symbol is considered to be bound by the universal quantifier, $\forall$. If we omit the conjunction operators for simplicity, the definition of a concept can be represented as follows:

$$\{\text{attribute}_i(\langle\text{name of a concept}\rangle, \langle\text{value}\rangle_i)\ |i = 1, \dots, n\}$$

We also assume that the variable symbols in this set are bounded by universal quantifiers.

As an example, let us consider the concept c, "something big, red, and round." If the predicate symbols for size, color, and shape are *size*, *color*, and *shape*, c can be represented as follows:

$$\{\mathit{size}(c, \mathit{large}), \mathit{color}(c, \mathit{red}), \mathit{shape}(c, \mathit{round})\}$$

where *large*, *red*, and *round* are the constant symbols for big, red, and round, respectively. If we consider c, which we used as the name of the concept, to be a variable and use a variable symbol X, then the concept "something big, red, and round" can be represented by the well-formed formula

$$(\forall X)(\mathit{size}(X, \mathit{large}) \wedge \mathit{color}(X, \mathit{red}) \wedge \mathit{shape}(X, \mathit{round}))$$

In this chapter, we will use a predicate logic representation for concepts unless otherwise noted.

The definition of a concept in predicate logic can vary depending on which logical operators we choose to combine predicates. We often use literals instead of general predicates to define a concept:

Definition 3 (a single concept) Suppose $p_1, \dots, p_m$ are literals. Then $p = p_1 \wedge \dots \wedge p_m$, in other words, a concept defined by the logical conjunction of literals, is called *a simple concept* or a *conjunctive concept.* A simple concept is sometimes represented as a set of literals such as $p = \{p_1, \dots, p_m\}$.

Definition 4 (multiple concepts) Suppose $q_1, \ldots, q_n$ are simple concepts. Then $q = q_1 \vee \ldots \vee q_n$, in other words, a concept defined by the logical disjunction of concepts, is called a *multiple concept* or a *disjunctive concept.*

The predicate logic representation of "something big, red, and round" is an example of a simple concept. "something big and red or small and blue" is a multiple concept and can be represented as

$$(\forall X)(size(X, large) \wedge color(X, red) \vee size(X, small) \wedge color(X, blue))$$

Besides these two kinds of concepts, there are also exclusive multiple concepts that combine simple concepts using the exclusive disjunction operator, and implicative concepts that combine concepts by an implication symbol. These concepts are not used often since their logical meaning is simple. In this book, unless otherwise noted, we will mean a simple concept when we say a concept.

(c) A concept and its instances

We can generate various instances of a concept by substituting constants for variable symbols in the definition of the concept. Let us look at the relationship between a concept and its instances. We will define an instance later in Definition 5.

First, let us look at a figure shown in Figure 6.1. Suppose we have six literals

$$p_1 = shape(X_1, U_1), \quad p_2 = size(X_1, V_1), \quad p_3 = position(X_1, W_1)$$
$$p_4 = shape(X_2, U_2), \quad p_5 = size(X_2, V_2), \quad p_6 = position(X_2, W_2)$$

where the domain of each variable is

$$X_i \in \{a, b, c, d, e, f\}, \ U_i \in \{square, circle\}$$
$$V_i \in \{large, small\}, \ W_i \in \{upper, lower\} \quad (i = 1, 2)$$

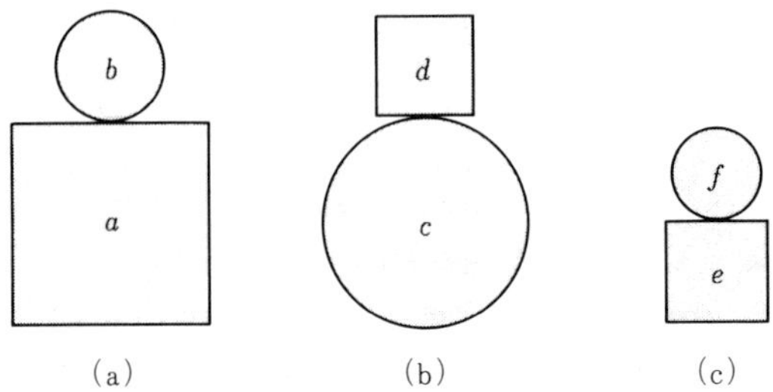

Figure 6.1 Examples of a simple concept.

The conjunction of the literals

$$p = p_1 \wedge p_2 \wedge \ldots \wedge p_6$$

is the simple concept "two things with some kind of shape, size, and position." Each of the three figures shown in Figure 6.1 can be regarded as representing an instance of the concept p. This is because each figure (a), (b), (c) corresponds to one of the logical expressions

$$\begin{aligned}
p\theta_1 =& \mathit{shape}(a, \mathit{square}) \wedge \mathit{size}(a, \mathit{large}) \wedge \mathit{position}(a, \mathit{lower}) \\
& \wedge \mathit{shape}(b, \mathit{circle}) \wedge \mathit{size}(b, \mathit{small}) \wedge \mathit{position}(b, \mathit{upper}) \\
p\theta_2 =& \mathit{shape}(c, \mathit{circle}) \wedge \mathit{size}(c, \mathit{large}) \wedge \mathit{position}(c, \mathit{lower}) \\
& \wedge \mathit{shape}(d, \mathit{square}) \wedge \mathit{size}(d, \mathit{small}) \wedge \mathit{position}(d, \mathit{upper}) \\
p\xi_1 =& \mathit{shape}(e, \mathit{square} \wedge \mathit{size}(e, \mathit{small}) \wedge \mathit{position}(e, \mathit{lower}) \\
& \wedge \mathit{shape}(f, \mathit{circle}) \wedge \mathit{size}(f, \mathit{small}) \wedge \mathit{position}(f, \mathit{upper})
\end{aligned}$$

that are obtained from p by applying the substitutions

$$\begin{aligned}
\theta_1 &= \{a_1/X_1, \mathit{square}/U_1, \mathit{large}/V_1, \mathit{lower}/W_1, \\
&\qquad b/X_2, \mathit{circle}/U_2, \mathit{small}/V_2, \mathit{upper}/W_2\} \\
\theta_2 &= \{c/X_1, \mathit{circle}/U_1, \mathit{large}/V_1, \mathit{lower}/W_1, \\
&\qquad d/X_2, \mathit{square}/U_2, \mathit{small}/V_2, \mathit{upper}/W_2\} \\
\xi_1 &= \{e/X_1, \mathit{square}/U_1, \mathit{small}/V_1, \mathit{lower}/W_1, \\
&\qquad f/X_2, \mathit{circle}/U_2, \mathit{small}/V_2, \mathit{upper}/W_2\}
\end{aligned}$$

Let us look at another example. Suppose, of the above six literals, we take only p_2 and p_3. Their conjunction is

$$p' = p_2 \wedge p_3$$

The expression

$$p'\eta = \mathit{size}(X_1, \mathit{large}) \wedge \mathit{position}(X_1, \mathit{lower})$$

that can be obtained by applying the substitution

$$\eta = \{\mathit{large}/V_1, \mathit{lower}/W_1\}$$

to p' is the concept meaning "something big is in a lower position." Now, consider the substitutions $\tau_1 = \{a/X_1\}$, $\tau_2 = \{c/X_1\}$, and $\tau_3 = \{e/X_1\}$. Then $p\theta_1, p\theta_2$ are special cases of the logical expressions

$$\begin{aligned}
p'\eta\tau_1 &= \mathit{size}(a, \mathit{large}) \wedge \mathit{position}(a, \mathit{lower}) \\
p'\eta\tau_2 &= \mathit{size}(c, \mathit{large}) \wedge \mathit{position}(c, \mathit{lower})
\end{aligned}$$

respectively.

On the other hand,

$$p'\eta\tau_3 = size(e, large) \wedge position(e, lower)$$

contradicts $p\xi_1$.

The conjunction of literals which is an instance obtained by applying substitutions to an original concept is called a positive instance of the original concept. A conjunction of literals which is not a positive instance is called a negative instance of the original concept. $p\theta_1, p\theta_2$, and $p\xi_1$ are positive instances of the concept p, and $p'\eta\tau_1$, $p'\eta\tau_2$, and $p'\eta\tau_3$ are positive instances of $p'\eta$. $p\theta_1$ and $p\theta_2$ are positive instances of p', but $p\xi_1$ is a negative instance of p'. Also, $size(a, large) \wedge position(a, upper)$ is a negative instance of p'. We will define positive and negative instances more accurately in Definition 5 below.

Next, let us pay attention to the fact that there are generally many concepts that have some particular conjunction of literals as a positive or negative instance. For example, for the substitution

$$\zeta = \{large/V_1, lower/W_1, small/V_2, upper/W_2\}$$

$p'\eta$ and $p\zeta$ are both concepts that have $p\theta_1$ and $p\theta_2$ as positive instances and have $p\xi_1$ as a negative instance.

Although it is true that a positive (negative) instance of $p\zeta$ always is a positive (negative) instance of $p'\eta$, the reverse is not true, because when we look at the concepts p and p' as a set of literals, we have $p' \subset p$ and we have $\eta \subset \zeta$ for the substitution. In other words, the concepts associated with some particular instance are divided into more general concepts and more specific concepts depending on how we make conjunction and substitution.

To summarize what we have explained so far, let us now define an instance of a concept.

Definition 5 (positive instance and negative instance) We represent a concept, p, as the set, $\{p_1, \ldots, p_n\}$, of literals constituting the concept. Suppose q is a finite set of ground literals. If $p\theta \subseteq q$ holds for some substitution θ that replaces all the variable symbols included in p with constant symbols, we say that q is a *positive instance* of p. On the other hand, when r is a finite set of ground literals, if $p\xi \not\subseteq r$ is true for any substitution ξ that replaces all the variable symbols with constant symbols, we say that r is a *negative instance* of p. We put together a positive instance and a negative instance and call them an instance. Also, when the above conditions $p\theta \subset q$ and $p\xi \not\subseteq r$ are replaced by $q \vdash p\theta$ and $r \not\vdash p\xi$, respectively, we sometimes call q and r a positive instance and a negative instance of p, respectively.

Definition 6 (generalization) Suppose we regard each of the given positive instances $p_1, \ldots, p_n$ as a set of literals. If there exists a set of literals, p, such that for all $i = 1, \ldots, n$, $p \subseteq p_i\theta_i$ holds for some θ_i, a substitution that replaces constant symbols with variable symbols, we call p a *generalization* of the positive instances $p_1, \ldots, p_n$ (based on $\theta_1, \ldots, \theta_n$). If we want to emphasize that p is represented by the conjunction of its elements, we specifically say that p is a *conjunctive generalization.* We also call it a generalization if we replace the conditions $p \subset p_i\theta_i$ by $p_i\theta_i \vdash p$ $(i = 1, \ldots, n)$.

We sometimes identify a concept whose positive instances are $\{p_1, \ldots, p_n\}$ with their generalization. There are usually many generalizations for a given set of positive instances of a concept. Each of those generalizations is one concept. When there are two generalizations $p\theta_1$ and $p\theta_2$ for the same set of positive instances, we determine which is more specific or more general using the following definition.

Definition 7 (specialization) We call $p\theta_2$ a *specialization* of $p\theta_1$ when $p\theta_1 = p\theta_2\xi$ holds for some substitution ξ that replaces constant symbols with variable symbols. In this case we also say that $p\theta_1$ is a generalization of $p\theta_2$.

We will return to the generalization and specialization of concepts in Section 6.3.

6.2 Methods for Concept Learning

Here we will explain some methods for learning a concept from a given set of instances. These methods use algorithms that take a set of instances as input and output a concept. We need to be careful because there are generally many concepts that can be derived from the same set of well-formed formulas that make up a set of instances. So an algorithm for learning concepts cannot help but include heuristic evaluation of which concept to choose. Here, as the basic method of concept learning, we describe an application of heuristic search in problem solving.

(a) Information necessary for learning concepts

In this section we consider what is necessary in an algorithm for learning concepts. First, let us focus on what we mean by learning a concept.

Definition 8 (learning a concept) Suppose we have some positive instances $p_1, \ldots, p_m$ and negative instances $q_1, \ldots, q_n$ ($m \geq 0, n \geq 0$). We say we have *learned a concept* for the instances $p_1, \ldots, p_m, q_1, \ldots, q_n$ if we have found a well-formed formula, r, for which there is a substitution θ_i ($i = 1, \ldots, m$) that replaces constant symbols with variable symbols so that $r \subseteq p_i\theta_i$ ($i = 1, \ldots, m$) and for which there is no substitution ξ_j ($j = 1, \ldots, n$) that replaces constant symbols with variable symbols so that $r \subseteq q_j\xi_j$ ($j = 1, \ldots, n$).

We say that r is a concept for the instances $p_1, \ldots, p_m, q_1, \ldots, q_n$. Learning a concept for a set of instances is called *induction* of the concept. Concept learning is learning by induction.

We need to pay attention to the following four things in order to improve the computational efficiency of learning concepts by a computer.

(1) Algorithms for learning concepts.

We will explain in subsection (b) algorithms for learning a concept from a given set of instances.

(2) Background knowledge and the introduction of new literals.

We need background knowledge to choose a specific concept for a given set of instances. We will explain in subsection (c) how we make use of such knowledge and how we make use of new literals when literals not included in the original set of instances appear in background knowledge.

(3) A set of instances and how they are given.

There are many ways in which a set of instances can be given to a system trying to learn a concept. For example, there are cases where only a small number of instances can be obtained or, to the contrary, where a large number of instances is given. There are cases where only positive instances are given. There are also cases where instances are obtained all at once or where they are obtained one by one.

A method that inputs all given instances at once into an algorithm for learning concepts is called *simultaneous presentation*; a method that inputs given instances one by one or incrementally is called *incremental presentation*. Simultaneous presentation is used, for example, in predicting weather from a large amount of given weather forecasting data. An example of this method is explained in Chapter 9. In an intelligent robot that is capable of learning, data for learning are usually obtained incrementally in real time. It is an example of incremental presentation.

(4) Representation of an instance and a concept.

We need to consider what representation language we can use to describe an instance and a concept. In this chapter, we use first-order predicate logic.

(b) Algorithms for learning concepts

Learning a concept from a given set of instances is generally done by replacing a constant included in the instance representation with a variable or by removing some literals from the instance. These transformations can be formalized as a problem solving process that involves generating and transforming predicates using some heuristic rules to obtain an appropriate well-formed formula. Let us define learning a concept as a problem solving process.

Definition 9 (problem solving) Suppose we have a set of positive instances, E_T, a set of negative instances E_F, and a set of rules, O, for transforming one well-formed formula to another. In the state space, S, where a set of well-formed formulas corresponds to a state, a rule $o \in O$ can be considered to be a state transition rule on S. When we move through S to state $s \in S$ using a rule $o \in O$, both $(\forall p \in s)(\exists \theta)(\exists q \in E_T)(q \vdash p\theta)$ and $(\forall p \in s)(\forall \xi)(\forall r \in E_F)(r \not\vdash p\xi)$ can be used as a constraint G, where θ and ξ are substitutions for replacing variable symbols with constant symbols. If we let c be the concept we are trying to find, then solving the problem $P = \langle S, O, G, E_T, \{c\} \rangle$ is called learning the concept c.

Although the concept c itself is used in the above definition, the structure of c is not usually known beforehand. Also, not all the elements of the state space S are known. So, in order to solve a problem P, we need to start from an initial state E_T, apply a state transition rule to the current state, and generate a new state. By repeating this operation, if we find among the generated states a concept c for the original set of instances, we stop the search. In the problem solving framework, this can be done using an algorithm for heuristic search.

As an example, let us look at the three instances shown in Figure 6.2:

$$
\begin{aligned}
p_1 &= on(b,a) \land cleartop(b) \land cleartop(c) \land ontable(a) \land ontable(c) \\
p_2 &= on(e,d) \land on(f,e) \land cleartop(f) \land ontable(d) \\
p_3 &= cleartop(g) \land cleartop(h) \land cleartop(i) \land ontable(g) \\
&\quad \land ontable(h) \land ontable(i)
\end{aligned}
$$

where p_1 and p_2 are positive instances and p_3 is a negative instance.

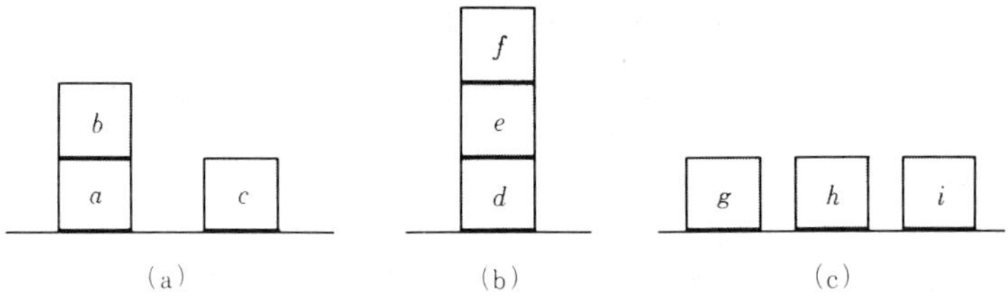

Figure 6.2 The concept of "a tower."

We regard $E_T = \{p_1, p_2\}$ as the initial state and $O = \{o_1, o_2\}$ as the set of state transition rules:

o_1: (a rule for changing a constant into a variable)
Let p be one of the well-formed formulas included in the current state $s \in S$ and p' be the new well-formed formula obtained by replacing a constant symbol (or constant symbols) in p with a variable symbol (or variable symbols). In this case, the new state $s' \in S$ generated from s is $s' = s \cup \{p'\} - \{p\}$.

o_2: (a rule for removing literals)
When q is one of the well-formed formulas included in the current state $s \in S$, we can obtain a new well-formed formula q' by removing one of the literals in q. In this case, the new state $s' \in S$ generated from s is $s' = s \cup \{q'\} - \{q\}$.

First, let us apply the rule o_1 to the state E_T. For example, if we apply the substitution $\theta_1 = \{X/a\}$ to $p_1 \in E_T$, we get the following state s_1:

$$\begin{aligned} s_1 &= \{p_1^1, p_2^1\} \\ p_1^1 &= p_1\theta_1 = on(b, X) \wedge cleartop(b) \wedge cleartop(c) \\ &\quad \wedge ontable(X) \wedge ontable(c) \\ p_2^1 &= p_2 \end{aligned}$$

Now, for state s_1, we have $p_1 \vdash p_1^1$, $p_2 \vdash p_2^1$, $(\forall\xi)(p_3 \not\vdash p_i^1\xi)(i = 1, 2)$, so the state transition from E_T to s_1 satisfies the constraint. Next, we apply rule o_1 to s_1. For example, if we apply the substitution $\theta_2 = \{X/e\}$ to $p_2^1 \in s_1$, we obtain the following state, s_2:

$$\begin{aligned} s_2 &= \{p_1^2, p_2^2\} \\ p_1^2 &= p_1^1 \\ p_2^2 &= p_2^1\theta_2 = on(X, d) \wedge on(f, X) \wedge cleartop(f) \wedge ontable(d) \end{aligned}$$

This state also satisfies the constraint. Now, let us apply the rule o_2 to the

Table 6.1 Generating a state using a state transition rule

s_3
$\Downarrow$ remove *cleartop*(c) from p_1^3 using o_2.
$s_4 = \{p_1^4, p_2^4\}, p_1^4 = on(b, X) \wedge cleartop(b) \wedge ontable(X) \wedge ontable(c), p_2^4 = p_2^3$
$\Downarrow$ remove *ontable*(X) from p_1^4 from using o_2
$s_5 = \{p_1^5, p_2^5\}, p_1^5 = on(b, X) \wedge cleartop(b) \wedge ontable(c), p_2^5 = p_2^4$
$\Downarrow$ remove *ontable*(c) from p_1^5 using o_1
$s_6 = \{p_1^6, p_2^6\}, p_1^6 = on(b, X) \wedge cleartop(b), p_2^6 = p_2^5$
$\Downarrow$ apply the substitution $\theta_6 = \{Y/b\}$ to p_1^6 using o_1
$s_7 = \{p_1^7, p_2^7\}, p_1^7 = p_1^6\theta_6 = on(Y, X) \wedge cleartop(Y), p_2^7 = p_2^6$
$\Downarrow$ remove *ontable*(a) from p_2^7 using o_2
$s_8 = \{p_1^8, p_2^8\}, p_1^8 = p_1^7, p_2^8 = on(c, X) \wedge cleartop(c)$
$\Downarrow$ apply the substitution $\theta_8 = \{Y/C\}$ to p_1^8 using o_1
$s_9 = \{p_1^9, p_2^9\}, p_1^9 = p_1^8, p_2^9 = on(Y, X) \wedge cleartop(Y)$

state s_2. For example, if we remove the literal $on(X, d)$ included in p_2^2, we obtain the following state that satisfies our constraint:

$$s_3 = \{p_1^3, p_2^3\}$$
$$p_1^3 = p_1^2$$
$$p_2^3 = on(f, X) \wedge cleartop(f) \wedge ontable(d)$$

Furthermore, if we apply the rules in the order shown in Table 6.1 and continue with state transitions that satisfy our constraint, we finally obtain $c = p_1^9 = p_2^9 = on(Y, X) \wedge cleartop(Y)$. This c is, according to Definition 9, a concept for the instances p_1, p_2, and p_3.

This example shows heuristic search in only one direction. Generally, more than one concept can be found by induction from a given set of instances, but this example does not cover the problem of how to choose one of the multiple concepts found by search. We will discuss this problem in Section 6.3.

(c) Background knowledge and introduction of new literals

There are cases when we can use background knowledge that includes literals not contained in instances. For example, suppose we have the background knowledge M

$$on(Y, Z) \wedge cleartop(Y) \rightarrow tower(Y, X)$$
$$on(Y, X) \wedge on(Z, Y) \rightarrow tower(Z, Y)$$

about the sample problem shown in Figure 6.2. Now if, from p_1 and p_2, we conclude

$$p'_1 = tower(b,a) \wedge cleartop(c) \wedge ontable(a) \wedge ontable(c)$$
$$p'_2 = tower(f,e) \wedge cleartop(f) \wedge ontable(d)$$

then $\{p_1\} \cup M \vdash p'_1$ and $\{p_2\} \cup M \vdash p'_2$ become true. So, if we repeatedly apply rules o_2 and o_1 to states, starting from the initial state $\{p'_1, p'_2\}$ and paying attention to the negative instance p_3, we can obtain $tower(Y, X)$ as a concept.

Background knowledge is often useful for improving the efficiency of search; however, background knowledge can include literals that are not part of the original instances, as in the above example. Learning in which a new literal that does not appear in the original set of instances is included in the generated concept is called *constructive* learning of a concept. Learning that does not involve new literals is called *selective* learning of a concept.

6.3 Generalization of Well-Formed Formulas

The transition rules, o_1, o_2, for well-formed formules described in Section 6.2(b) are considered to be rules that generalize a well-formed formula. In this section, we will discuss the generalization of well-formed formulas, which is one of the most important problems in concept learning.

(a) MSC generalization

Let us look at the example in Figure 6.3. The three instances in Figure 6.3 can be represented as follows:

$$\begin{aligned} p_1 = {} & shape(a, square) \wedge shape(b, square) \wedge size(a, large) \\ & \wedge size(b, small) \wedge on(b, a) \\ p_2 = {} & shape(c, square) \wedge shape(b, square) \wedge size(c, large) \\ & \wedge size(b, small) \wedge on(b, c) \\ p_3 = {} & shape(d, circle) \wedge shape(b, square) \wedge size(d, large) \\ & \wedge size(b, small) \wedge on(b, d) \end{aligned}$$

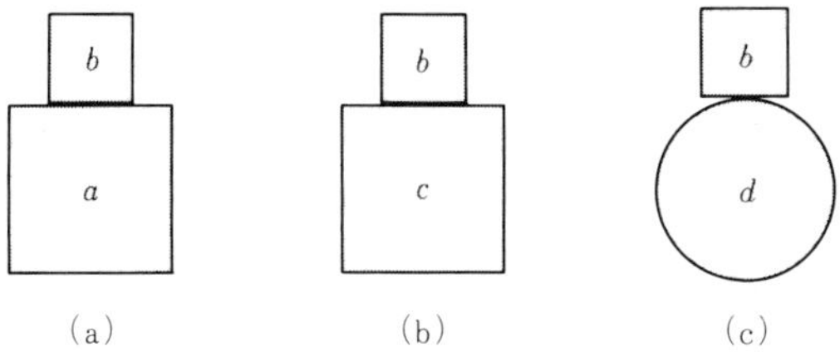

Figure 6.3 Sample problems of generalization of a predicate.

Now, let us consider four concepts

$$\begin{aligned}
c_1 &= shape(X, Z) \wedge shape(b, square) \wedge size(X, large) \\
&\quad \wedge size(b, small) \wedge on(b, X) \\
c_2 &= shape(X, Z) \wedge shape(Y, square) \wedge size(X, large) \\
&\quad \wedge size(Y, small) \wedge on(Y, X) \\
c_3 &= shape(b, square) \wedge size(X, large) \wedge size(b, small) \\
c_4 &= shape(Y, square) \wedge on(Y, X)
\end{aligned}$$

for which p_1, p_2, and p_3 are positive instances. In c_1 and c_2, the number of literals is the same, but the number of variables in c_2 is larger. The number of literals in c_3 is smaller than the number of literals in c_1. As you can see, there are differences in degree in the generalization and specialization of a concept for some given set of instances. We have already defined generalization and specialization in Definitions 6 and 7. Usually, we are interested in the most specific concepts for a given set of instances. We will explain what "the most specific" generalization is.

Let us look at generalization in the sense of Definition 6. Using the example in Figure 6.3, any one of $c_1, \ldots, c_4$ is a generalization of p_1, p_2, and p_3. For example, for c_2, if we use the substitutions

$$\begin{aligned}
\theta_1 &= \{X/a, Y/b, Z/square\} \\
\theta_2 &= \{X/c, Y/b, Z/square\} \\
\theta_3 &= \{X/d, Y/b, Z/circle\}
\end{aligned}$$

the following is true:

$$\begin{aligned}
c_2 = \{&shape(X, Z), shape(Y, square), size(X, large), \\
&size(Y, small), on(Y, X)\} \subseteq p_i\theta_i \quad (i = 1, 2, 3)
\end{aligned}$$

Next, based on the definition of generalization given in Definition 6, we can define "the most specific" generalization.

Definition 10 (MSC generalization) Let p be the generalization obtained by applying substitutions $\theta_1, \ldots, \theta_n$ to a given set of positive instances $\{p_1, \ldots, p_n\}$. Then, if there do not exist substitutions ξ_i, ρ_i $(i = 1, \ldots, n)$ that replace constant symbols with variable symbols and a generalization p' of $\{p_1, \ldots, p_n\}$ such that $p \subseteq p_i\xi_i\rho_i, p' \subseteq p_i\xi_i$, $p \subseteq p'\rho_i$ $(i = 1, \ldots, n)$, we call p an *MSC generalization* (maximally specific conjunctive generalization) of $p_1, \ldots, p_n$.

For example, in the previous example, if we consider $c_1, \ldots, c_4$, p_1, p_2, p_3 each as a set of literals, then there do not exist substitutions ξ_i, ρ_i $(i = 1, 2, 3)$ and a generalization c' where $c_1 = p_i\theta_i$ $(i = 1, 2, 3)$ for the following substitutions and θ_i $(i - 1, 2, 3)$ and $c_1 \subseteq p_i\xi_i\rho_i$, $c' \subseteq p_i\xi_i$, $c_1 \subseteq c'\rho_i$ $(i = 1, 2, 3)$:

$$\theta_1 = \{X/a, Z/square\}$$
$$\theta_2 = \{X/c, Z/square\}$$
$$\theta_3 = \{X/d, Z/circle\}$$

Therefore, c_1 is an MSC generalization of p_1, p_2, and p_3. On the other hand, c_2, c_3, c_4 are not MSC generalizations of p_1, p_2, and p_3. Even though an MSC generalization can be regarded as the most specific generalization, it is not always uniquely determined. However, since learning a concept often requires finding a concept that generalizes the set of instances as specifically as possible (for example, to include as few variables as possible), we usually choose one of the MSC generalizations from all the generalizations.

(b) Methods of generalization

In this section we provide methods for generalizing well-formed formulas. Rule o_1 described in Section 6.2(b) can be considered a special case of the method described below.

(1) *Changing a constant into a variable*

This method replaces a constant symbol in a well-formed formula with a variable symbol. For example, if we consider the substitutions

$$\nu_1 = \{X/a, Y/small\}$$
$$\nu_2 = \{X/b, Y/large\}$$

for the two well-formed formulas

$$q_1 = shape(a, square) \wedge size(a, small)$$
$$q_2 = shape(b, square) \wedge size(b, large)$$

we will obtain the following generalization of q_1 and q_2:

$$q = shape(X, square) \wedge size(X, Y)$$

(2) *Generalization of a constant in a given structure*

If relations among constants are given by a semantic network that inherits the characteristics of predicates, we can make a generalization by replacing a constant by another constant that corresponds to a node above the nodes of the original constants in the semantic network. For example, if the relations among *square*, *triangle*, and *polygon* are given by the semantic network shown in Figure 6.4, then for

$$p_1 = shape(a, square)$$
$$p_2 = shape(b, triangle)$$

by replacing the nodes *square* and *triangle* with their parent node *polygon*, we can obtain the generalization

$$p = shape(X, polygon)$$

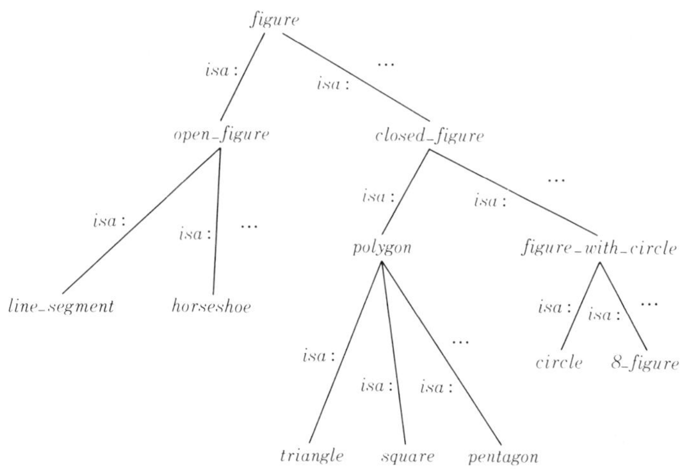

Figure 6.4 A semantic network for "figures."

(3) *Removing a literal included in a well-formed formula*

When a well-formed formula is a conjunction of more than one literal, remove one or some number of literals. For example, let

$$p = shape(a, square) \wedge size(a, medium) \wedge color(a, red)$$

Then the following is a generalization of p:

$$q = shape(a, square) \wedge color(a, red)$$

(4) *Deductive transformation of part of a well-formed formula*

Replace some of the literals in a well-formed formula with a literal that can be deduced from those literals and, if available, background knowledge. For example, if, as background knowledge, we can use the formula

$$\begin{aligned} &\mathit{shape}(X, \mathit{triangle}) \wedge \mathit{color}(X, \mathit{red}) \wedge \mathit{location}(X, \mathit{intersection}) \\ &\qquad \rightarrow \mathit{object}(X, \mathit{stop\_sign}) \end{aligned}$$

we can generalize the expression

$$\begin{aligned} p = {} & \mathit{shape}(a, \mathit{triangle}) \wedge \mathit{size}(a, \mathit{large}) \wedge \mathit{color}(a, \mathit{red}) \\ & \wedge \mathit{location}(a, \mathit{intersection}) \end{aligned}$$

to the following:

$$q = \mathit{object}(a, \mathit{stop\_sign}) \wedge \mathit{size}(a, \mathit{large})$$

(Here we use the fact that we can prove q from p and the background knowledge.)

(5) *Generalization using resolution*

Simplifying a well-formed formula by using the inference rule $(p \rightarrow q_1) \wedge (\sim p \rightarrow q_2) \rightarrow q_1 \vee q_2$, for any well-formed formulas p, q_1, and q_2, is called resolution. (The notion of resolution we described in Section 3.7 is an example of this kind of resolution.) Using resolution, we can generalize a given well-formed formula. For example, by extending the above rule a little, we obtain $(p \wedge q_1 \rightarrow r) \wedge (\sim p \wedge q_2 \rightarrow r) \rightarrow (q_1 \vee q_2 \rightarrow r)$ for any well-formed formula p, q_1, q_2, r. Using this rule, for example, on the well-formed formula

$$\begin{aligned} p_1 = {} & \{\mathit{shape}(a, \mathit{triangle}) \wedge \mathit{size}(a, \mathit{large}) \rightarrow \mathit{color}(a, \mathit{red})\} \\ & \wedge \{\sim \mathit{shape}(a, \mathit{triangle}) \wedge \mathit{size}(a, \mathit{medium}) \rightarrow \mathit{color}(a, \mathit{red})\} \end{aligned}$$

produces the following generalization:

$$p_1' = \mathit{size}(a, \mathit{large}) \vee \mathit{size}(a, \mathit{medium}) \rightarrow \mathit{color}(a, \mathit{red})$$

This is an example of a multiple concept rather than a simple concept.

By using this method as a state transition rule for learning concepts as described in Section 6.2(b), we can mechanically obtain a concept for a given set of instances. The above method, however, is a heuristic method and does not guarantee that we can always find an MSC generalization.

6.4 Version Space

As we described above, there may be many concepts for a given set of instances. To find these concepts, we can use heuristic search. Here, as an effective method for improving the efficiency of heuristic search, we will explain the method of version space, a search method that depends on the structure of the state space.

(a) An example of version space

Suppose we have four predicates representing the attributes of an object u:

$$\begin{array}{ll} \mathit{shape}(U,W), & W \in \{\mathit{triangle}, \mathit{circle}, \ldots\} \\ \mathit{size}(U,X), & X \in \{\mathit{small}, \mathit{large}, \ldots\} \\ \mathit{color}(U,Y), & Y \in \{\mathit{white}, \mathit{black}, \ldots\} \\ \mathit{texture}(U,Z), & Z \in \{\mathit{fine}, \mathit{coarse}, \ldots\} \end{array}$$

We consider the following concepts, represented by a set of these predicates:

$$p_1 = \{\mathit{shape}(U, \mathit{triangle}), \mathit{size}(U, \mathit{small}), \mathit{color}(U, \mathit{white}), \mathit{texture}(U, \mathit{fine})\}$$
$$p_2 = \{\mathit{shape}(U, W), \mathit{size}(U, X), \mathit{color}(U, Y), \mathit{texture}(U, \mathit{fine})\}$$
$$p_3 = \{\mathit{shape}(U, W), \mathit{size}(U, X), \mathit{color}(U, Y), \mathit{texture}(U, Z)\}$$

Now we leave the variable U in p_1, p_2, p_3 as is and either substitute the constant symbol *triangle*, *small*, *white*, *fine* into W, X, Y, Z or leave W, X, Y, Z as is. We let Q be the set of concepts generated from p_1, p_2, p_3. For example, the well-formed formula

$$p_2' = \{\mathit{shape}(U, \mathit{triangle}), \mathit{size}(U, \mathit{small}), \mathit{color}(U, Y), \mathit{texture}(U, \mathit{fine})\}$$

that can be obtained by replacing W and X of p_2 with *triangle* and *small*, respectively, is an element of Q. In this case, the number of elements in Q is $2^4 = 16$. Now, we represent the elements of Q using a bit array of four 0s or 1s and let each bit correspond to one of the predicates *shape*, *size*, *color*, and *texture*. If a constant symbol has been substituted for one of the variables, W, X, Y, Z, then we make the corresponding bit 1; and if it stays as a variable symbol, we make it 0. For example, the formula p_2' is represented by 1101.

Using this representation, the relations among the elements of Qs can be represented by the graph shown in Figure 6.5, where each edge in the graph represents a substitution, the top node n_1 represents the most "specific" concept, and the lowest node n_3 represents the most "general" concept.

Edges or paths in the graph shown in Figure 6.5 represent substitutions. More concretely, the graph corresponds to a generalization of a well-formed formula by making constants into variables. For example, n_3 is a generalization of n_1, and n_2 is a generalization of n_1. A version space, intuitively, is

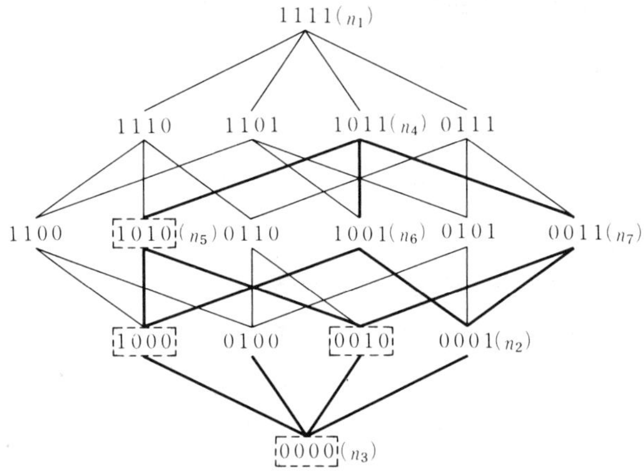

Figure 6.5 An example of version space.

a set of well-formed formulas that are related each other by generalizations as exemplified in the graph in Figure 6.5.

(b) The partial order of generalizations and version space

To explain concept learning using version space, let us give a more exact definition to version space. First, notice the fact that, as we noted in Definition 6, a generalization orders two well-formed formulas. We can describe this more generally as follows:

Definition 11 (partial order of generalizations) Let Q be a set of well-formed formulas each defined by a conjunction of literals. For q_i and $q_j \in Q$, we write $q_i \leq q_j$ if and only if q_i is a generalization of q_j. Then $\leq$ is a partial order on Q.* We call $\leq$ the *partial order of generalizations.*

In Definition 11, an MSC generalization corresponds to a maximal element in the partial order of generalizations.

Next, let us define version space using the partial order of generalizations.

*For a given set A and a binary relation $\leq$ on the elements of A, $\leq$ is a partial order on A if and only if the reflection law ($a_i \leq a_i$), the symmetry law (if $a_i \leq a_j$ and $a_j \leq a_i$, then $a_i = a_j$), and the transitive law (if $a_i \leq a_j$ and $a_j \leq a_k$, then $a_i \leq a_k$) are true for all $a_i, a_j, a_k \in A$. For $a_j \in A$, if $a_i \leq a_j$ is true for all $a_i \in A$ where $a_j \neq a_i$, then a_j is called a *maximal element* of the partial order $\leq$. If $a_j \in A$ and if $a_j \geq a_i$ is true for all $a_j \neq a_i$, then a_i is a *minimal element.*

Definition 12 (version space) Suppose the partial order of generalizations, $\leq$, is defined for a set of concepts, Q, and Q is a complete lattice** under $\leq$. In particular, there are an element $q \in Q$ (the minimum element) that makes $q \leq q_i$ and $q \leq q_j$ true and an element $q' \in Q$ (the maximum element) that makes $q_i \leq q'$ and $q_j \leq q'$ true for all $q_i, q_j \in Q$. We assume that the maximal element of the complete lattice Q corresponds to a given positive instance p. We call Q the *version space* for the positive example p.

(c) Concept learning using the version space method

In a version space Q, relations among elements represent generalization relations among concepts. So we can narrow the search for a goal concept using the following rules:

(1) When a new positive example is given, only a concept obtained from that example or a concept that is more general than the example can be a goal concept.
(2) When a new negative example is given, no concept more general than the example can be the goal concept.
(3) Starting from the maximum element (the most specific case; in Figure 6.5, the top node) and the minimum element (the most general element; in Figure 6.5, the lowest node) of Q, we can narrow the possible subset including the goal concept using (1) and (2) together.

Finding a concept for a given set of examples using these rules is called concept learning by the version space method.

Let us use the version space method for the example in Figure 6.5. The concept

$$p_4 = \{shape(U, triangle), size(U, X), color(U, white), texture(U, fine)\}$$

that is, "a white, fine-textured triangle," is given as a new concept. Node n_4 in Figure 6.5 corresponds to this concept. So, possible concepts that can be found by the version space method are n_4 and the part of the graph connected by paths under n_4. In Figure 6.5, this part is shown with bold lines.

Next, suppose

$$p_5 = \{shape(U, triangle), size(U, X), color(U, white), texture(U, Z)\}$$

**If, for each subset D of a partially ordered set Q, there exist q and q' such that $q \leq q_i$ and $q_i \leq q'$ for all $q_i \in D$, then we say that Q is a *complete lattice*. We call q and q' a lower bound and an upper bound of D, respectively. When $D = Q$, we call them the minimum and maximum elements of Q.

in other words, "a white triangle," is given as the concept corresponding to a negative instance. The node for this concept is n_5 in Figure 6.5. Then the concept we are looking for does not exist in the part of the graph that includes n_5 and that is connected by paths under n_5. That is, the nodes surrounded by broken lines cannot correspond to the concept we are looking for. Now, if

$$p_6 = \{shape(U, triangle), size(U, X), color(U, Y), texture(U, fine)\}$$

that is, "a fine-textured triangle" (node n_6 in Figure 6.5), is the concept for a negative instance, n_6, then n_2 cannot be the concept we are looking for. So, the concept we want is narrowed down to just one:

$$p_7 = \{shape(U, W), size(U, X), color(U, white), texture(U, fine)\}$$

This concept corresponds to node n_7 in Figure 6.5.

This example uses a small graph, but the version space method can be applied to graphs with many more nodes. The method can be used even when the elements of the space, in other words, the well-formed formulas that are candidates for the goal concept, are not known beforehand. This is true since a node of a graph can be generated every time an instance is given. In summary, concept learning using the version space method has the following features:

(1) If the maximum element and the minimum element of a version space and a method of generalization are given, we do not need to know the structure of the space beforehand.
(2) Learning a concept is possible not only when instances are input simultaneously but also when they are given one by one.
(3) When a variable is included in each element of a version space, the amount of computation can be very large.
(4) It does not always work for noisy or defective data.

Of these features, (1) and (2) are the most important in real use. For (3), notice that many concept relations can be formulated using a version space that does not involve variables at all.

6.5 Conceptual Clustering

So far we have described methods for concept learning from a given set of instances. On the other hand, classifying instances by finding some relation among them and separating them into several clusters so that each cluster corresponds to a concept is also an important problem in concept

Table 6.2 Data for the example of conceptual clustering using attributes

attribute \ object	o_1	o_2	o_3	o_4	o_5	o_6	o_7	o_8
speed x_1	h	m	h	l	m	l	h	m
color x_2	r	r	g	b	b	g	b	r
price x_3	h	l	h	rh	rl	l	rh	rh

learning. Classifying a given set of instances into clusters so that each cluster corresponds to a different concept is called *conceptual clustering.*

(a) Conceptual clustering using attributes

Let us consider a conceptual clustering method that classifies instances based on attributes. Suppose that there are n objects $o_1, \ldots, o_n$, and each has some attributes represented by m variables $x_1, \ldots, x_m$. For example, there are eight automobiles $o_1, \ldots, o_8$, and each has the values shown in Table 6.2 for the three attributes, speed $x_1 \in \{high, medium, low\}$, color $x_2 \in \{red, blue, green\}$, and price $x_3 \in \{high,$ *relatively-high*, *relatively-low*, $low\}$. Below, using this example problem, we will explain conceptual clustering.

We now try to classify n given objects into several different clusters by whether their attribute-value pairs are similar or not. Suppose that the number of clusters k is given beforehand and that we have an evaluation function f that can tell us how close objects are (of course, this depends on the method of classification). Conceptual clustering by attributes can be characterized as classifying n objects into k different clusters so that the value of f is minimum. Let us look at Table 6.2. It can be rewritten as Figure 6.6 when based on attributes. Now, let us define the evaluation function f as follows:

First, to determine the area surrounding some attribute-value pairs, we can specify part of the matrix shown in Figure 6.6. For example, $(x_1 = h) \wedge (x_2 \in \{b, g\}) \wedge (x_3 \in \{h, rh, rl\})$ specifies the gray area in Figure 6.6. An area around attribute-value pairs determined in this way is called an *attribute complex.* The number of matrix elements that are included in an attribute complex α, but do not contain an object, is called the *sparseness* of α and is written $s(\alpha)$. For example, the sparseness of the attribute complex corresponding to the gray part of Figure 6.6 is $s(\alpha) = 4$. We can imagine that the higher the sparseness of an attribute complex is, the

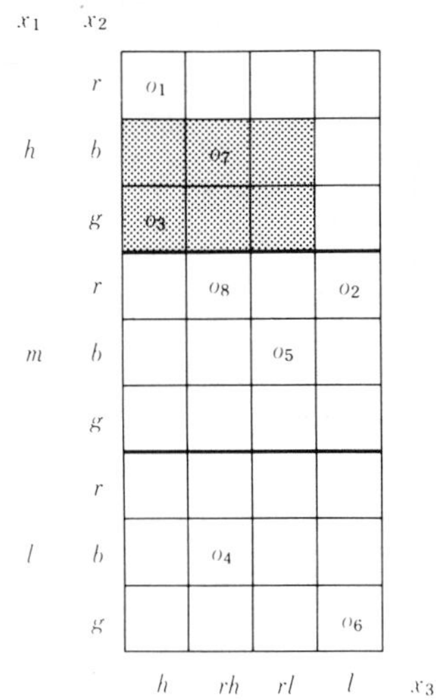

Figure 6.6 A matrix for objects $o_1, \ldots, o_8$ and their attributes.

larger it will be as a cluster for classifying given objects. Suppose we have found a set of attribute complexes that can classify k objects, $\{\alpha_1, \ldots, \alpha_k\}$, where α_i $(i = 1, \ldots, k)$ is the attribute complex that separates the objects in the ith cluster from the other objects. We now define f as

$$f = \sum_{i=1}^{k} s(\alpha_i)$$

Also, we agree that f is minimized over sets of attribute complexes that can classify k different objects. For example, in the problem in Figure 6.6, if we assume $k = 2$, conceptual clustering by attributes becomes the problem of finding two attribute complexes α_1, α_2 that divide $o_1, \ldots, o_8$ into different clusters and that make $f = s(\alpha_1) + s(\alpha_2)$ minimum.

Below, we will describe an algorithm for solving this kind of problem. At the heart of this algorithm is a clustering algorithm for dividing a set of objects into k clusters. By applying it recursively, we can generate a representation where clusters are hierarchically structured. Below we will show an algorithm for clustering including an algorithm for generating a cluster hierarchy. By a *cover* of a set of objects O, we mean a set of sets $\alpha = \{Q_1, \ldots, Q_m\}$ that satisfies the property $O \subseteq \bigcup_{i=1}^{m} Q_i$, $Q_i \cap Q_j = \emptyset$ $(i \neq j)$. Also, if $O = \bigcup_{i=1}^{m} O_i$, $O_i \subseteq Q_i$, $Q_i \cap Q_j = \emptyset$ $(i \neq j)$ $(i, j = 1, \ldots, m)$ hold for a cover of the set O, $\alpha = \{Q_1, \ldots, Q_m\}$, $\{O_1, \ldots, O_m\}$ is called a *partition* of O by the cover α.

Algorithm 6.1 (conceptual clustering by attributes)

[I] Clustering

[1] Let I be the upper limit of the number of iterations. Set $iteration = 1, f_0 = \infty, \hat{\alpha} = \emptyset$. (Setting parameter values)

[2] Extract k objects $o_1, \ldots, o_k$ from the given objects. (Extracting cluster seeds)

[3] Obtain a set of attribute complexes $\{\alpha_i{}^1, \ldots, \alpha_i{}^{n_i}\}$ that distinguishes o_i from $o_1, \ldots, o_{i-1}, o_{i+1}, \ldots, o_k$ for each i $(i = 1, \ldots, k)$.

[4] For the attribute complexes obtained in [3]:

$$\begin{array}{ccc} \alpha_1^1, & \ldots, & \alpha_1^{n_1} \\ \alpha_2^1, & \ldots, & \alpha_2^{n_2} \\ \vdots & \vdots & \vdots \\ \alpha_k^1, & \ldots, & \alpha_k^{n_k} \end{array}$$

find $f_{\min} = \min_{\{\alpha_1^{j_1}, \ldots, \alpha_k^{j_k}\}} f = \sum_{h=1}^{k} s(\alpha_h^{j_h})$ (where $\{\alpha_1^{j_1}, \ldots, \alpha_k^{j_k}\}$ ranges over only the covers of $\{o_1, \ldots, o_k\}$). If $f_{\min} \le f_0$, then set $f_0 = f_{\min}$. Pick one of $\{\alpha_1^{j_1}, \ldots, \alpha_k^{j_k}\}(1 \le j_1 \le n_1, \ldots, 1 \le j_k \le n_k)$ that give $f_{\min}$, and call it $\hat{\alpha} = \{\hat{\alpha}_1^{j_1}, \ldots, \hat{\alpha}_k^{j_k}\}$. Go to [5]. If $f_{\min} \le f_0$, then go to [6]. (Selecting an attribute complex that makes the evaluation function value minimum)

[5] If $iteration \ge I$, go to [6]. Otherwise, go to [7]. (Checking the number of iterations)

[6] Stop. The partition of $\{o_1, \ldots, o_k\}$ by the cover $\hat{\alpha}$ is a solution to the clustering. (Termination condition)

[7] Select one of the objects included in each of the k attribute complexes $\hat{\alpha}_i^{j_i}$ $(i = 1, \ldots, k)$, in $\hat{\alpha}$, and call it o_i $(i = 1, \ldots, k)$. These objects are selected by the following substeps. (Selecting new cluster seeds)

[7.1] Do the following for each $\hat{\alpha}_i$ $(i = 1, \ldots, k)$. Let p be the vector of values for attributes of objects o in $\hat{\alpha}_i^{j_i}$ p. If there are two of these vectors, p and q, define the distance between p and q by the number of their elements that are not the same (called the Hamming distance). Obtain, as follows, the *median vector* $g(\hat{\alpha}_i^{j_i})$ for the vectors, p_j $(j = i_1, \ldots, j_{n_j})$, corresponding to objects included in $\hat{\alpha}_i^{j_i}$:
For each dimension of the vector p_j $(j = i_1, \ldots, i_{n_j})$, pick the value that appears most often. Then let $g(\hat{\alpha}_i^{j_i})$ be the vector of those values.

[7.2] Pick the vector that has the smallest Hamming distance to $g(\hat{\alpha}_i^{j_i})$ from the vectors p_j $(j = i_1, \ldots, i_{n_j})$ corresponding to objects in $\hat{\alpha}_i^{j_i}$ $(i = 1, \ldots, k)$. Let the objects corresponding to this vector be the objects selected from $\hat{\alpha}_i^{j_i}$.

When all the objects were selected by the substeps, let *iteration* = *iteration* + 1 and go to [3].

[II] Generating the hierarchy

[1] Divide the given objects into k clusters using the clustering algorithm. (Application of clustering)

[2] If the hierarchy of clusters reaches a given depth, stop. Otherwise, go to [3]. (Termination condition)

[3] Generate subclusters by applying [1] to each cluster generated in [1]. This increments the depth of the cluster hierarchy. Go to [2]. (Recursive application)

Let us apply the clustering algorithm to the example in Figure 6.6, where the upper limit of the number of iterations is set to 2.

[1] Let $I = 2$, $iteration = 1$, $f_0 = \infty$, $\hat{\alpha} = \emptyset$.

[2] Pick o_1 and o_2 from $o_1, \ldots, o_8$ (which object is chosen influences the efficiency of the computation).

[3] Suppose we found the following attribute complexes that include o_1 but do not include o_2:

$$\alpha_1^1 = (x_2 = r \vee b) \wedge (x_3 = h \vee rh \vee rl)$$
$$\alpha_1^2 = (x_1 = h \vee l)$$

In this case, $\{o_1, o_4, o_5, o_7, o_8\} \in \alpha_1^1$ and $\{o_1, p_3, o_4, o_6, o_7\} \in \alpha_1^2$. Suppose we found the following attribute complexes that include o_2 but do not include o_1:

$$\alpha_2^1 = (x_1 = h) \wedge (x_2 = g) \vee (x_3 = 1)$$
$$\alpha_2^2 = (x_1 = m)$$

In this case, $\{o_2, o_3, o_6\} \in \alpha_2^1$ and $\{o_2, o_5, o_8\} \in \alpha_2^2$. (There are many other sets of attribute complexes that satisfy the conditions, but we limit ourselves here to these two.)

[4] If we let $\alpha_A = \{\alpha_1^1, \alpha_2^1\}$, $\alpha_B = \{\alpha_1^1, \alpha_2^2\}$, $\alpha_C = \{\alpha_1^2, \alpha_2^1\}$, $\alpha_D = \{\alpha_1^2, \alpha_2^2\}$ for $\alpha_1^1, \alpha_1^2, \alpha_2^1, \alpha_2^2$, only α_A and α_D are a cover of $\{o_1, \ldots, o_8\}$. For these, using

$$f(\alpha_A) = s(\alpha_1^1) + s(\alpha_2^1) = 13 + 9 = 22$$
$$f(\alpha_D) = s(\alpha_1^2) + s(\alpha_2^2) = 19 + 9 = 28$$

the minimum value of f is $f_{\min} = 22$ and $f_{\min} < f_0$. The cover that gives $f_{\min}$ is α_A, so let $\hat{\alpha} = \alpha_A = \{\alpha_1^1, \alpha_2^1\}$.

[5] Since *iteration* < 2, go to [7].

[7] The objects included in α_1^1, o_1, o_4, o_5, o_7, o_8, can be represented by the following three-dimensional vectors for the values of the attributes x_1, x_2, x_3.

$$o_1 : (h, r, h) \qquad o_7 : (h, b, rh)$$
$$o_4 : (l, b, rh) \qquad o_8 : (m, r, rh)$$
$$o_5 : (m, b, rl)$$

Then we can pick $g(\hat{\alpha}_1^1) = (h, b, rh)$ as the median vector. In this case, o_7 is the object that is closest to g. Similarly, if we pick $g(\hat{\alpha}_2^1) = (l, g, l)$ as the median vector, we find that o_6 is the object that is closest to g. Set *iteration* $= 2$.

[3] If we found the following attribute complexes that include o_7 but do not include o_6:

$$\alpha_1^1 = (x_3 = h \vee rh)$$
$$\alpha_1^2 = (x_1 = h \vee m) \wedge (x_2 = r \vee b) \wedge (x_3 = h \vee rh)$$

we have $\{o_1, o_3, o_4, o_7, o_8\} \in \alpha_1^1$, and $\{o_1, o_4, o_7, o_8\} \in \alpha_1^2$. Also, if we found the following attribute complexes that include o_6 but do not include o_7:

$$\alpha_2^1 = (x_1 = m \vee l) \wedge (x_3 = rl \vee l)$$

we have $\{o_2, o_5, o_6\} \in \alpha_2^1$.

[4] For $\alpha_A = \{\alpha_1^1, \alpha_2^1\}$, $\alpha_B = \{\alpha_1^2, \alpha_2^1\}$, only α_A is a cover of $\{o_1, \ldots, o_8\}$. For α_A we have

$$f(\alpha_A) = s(\alpha_1^1) + s(\alpha_2^1) = 13 + 9 = 22$$

and $f_{\min} = f(\alpha_A)$. Since $f_{\min} \leq f_0$, we let $f_0 = f_{\min}$ and $\hat{\alpha} = \alpha_A$. Go to [5].

[5] Since *iteration* $= 2$, go to [6].

[6] Stop. The partition $\{o_1, o_3, o_4, o_7, o_8\}$, $\{o_2, o_5, o_6\}$ by the cover $\hat{\alpha} = \{\alpha_1^1, \alpha_2^1\}$ is a solution of the clustering.

The two clusters found in the above example turn out to be the cluster of the objects where the value of the attribute x_3 is h or rh and the cluster of the objects where the value of the attribute x_3 is rl or l.

The algorithm for conceptual clustering described here is a heuristic method and does not always find a clustering that makes f, the sum of the sparseness, minimum. However, not many conceptual clustering methods have been proposed where the clusters are unknown. Besides algorithms using the attribute values, as we described here, there are other conceptual clustering methods where the data are input one by one.

(b) Conceptual clustering and cluster analysis

Cluster analysis is a clustering method similar to conceptual clustering. Conceptual clustering is different from cluster analysis in that it classifies clusters according to the semantic structures of concepts. Cluster analysis cannot usually take global attributes of the data set into consideration, since it represents the value of an attribute of the data as a single number. On the other hand, conceptual clustering finds clusters based on the type of concepts it is given. Therefore, even if the distance between two objects is small in the sense of cluster analysis, if the two objects are examples of different concepts, conceptual clustering can possibly do the classification.

When we think about classification based on concepts, the goal of the classification and background knowledge are necessary elements in the classification. Although we have not defined background knowledge, we can understand its importance. For example, even variables that are not included in the attribute descriptions of a given object can be used for clustering as long as the variables and the given attributes are related by background knowledge.

Summary

In this chapter, we defined the notion of concept and its instances. We also described algorithms for learning concepts.

6.1 (Simple) concepts can be defined by the conjunction of literals, and their instances can be obtained as the conjunction of ground literals where constant symbols are substituted into variable symbols in a concept.

6.2 To learn concepts, we need to decide on an algorithm, background knowledge and its representation, a method for introducing new literals, a set of instances and a way to input them, and a method of representing instances and concepts.

6.3 Learning concepts can be done by generalizing well-formed formulas. Generalization of well-formed formulas is based on the notion of MSC generalization. Generalization can be done by heuristically applying methods like replacing constant symbols with variable symbols and applying deductive transformation.

6.4 Concept learning can be done based on an algorithm for heuristic search in problem solving. A popular method of this kind is the version space method.

6.5 One algorithm for conceptual clustering is to classify a set of instances into exclusive clusters, each corresponding to a different concept.

Keywords

concept, concept learning, simple concept, multiple concept, example, positive example, negative example, induction, background knowledge, generalization, specialization, partial order of generalization, MSC generalization, version space, conceptual clustering, attribute complex

Exercises

6.1 Enumerate decisions that you have to make when learning concepts on a computer.

6.2 For the example problem (Figure 6.1) in Section 6.1(c), consider the conjunction of literals

$$p'' = p_2 \wedge p_3 \wedge p_5 \wedge p_6$$

and the substitution

$$\eta'' = \{large/V_1, upper/W_2\}$$

Then show that p'' and η'' are concepts for the positive instances $p\theta_1, p\theta_2$ and the negative instance $p\xi_1$.

6.3 Find an MSC generalization of positive instances:

$$\begin{aligned} p_1 = \{&temperature(burma, high),\ humidity(burma, high),\\ &mechanization(burma, low)\}\\ p_2 = \{&temperature(japan, high),\ humidity(japan, high),\\ &mechanization(japan, medium)\} \end{aligned}$$

Also, give an example of a generalization that is not an MSC generalization. Furthermore, check if the found MSC generalization is an overgeneralization according to our knowledge. If so, devise a method for improving it.

6.4 Write a learning algorithm for integration by parts of indefinite integrals using the version space method.

7 Learning Procedures

In this chapter we will explain methods of learning procedures for transforming information, such as operators in problem solving, production rules, and computer programs. Representations of these procedures not only are more complex than those of concepts but also have a deep relation to inference methods. Therefore, learning procedures require different methods than learning concepts. In this chapter we will learn basic methods for learning procedures by explaining several popular algorithms.

7.1 Learning Operators in Problem Solving

A solution to a problem in problem solving can be represented as a sequence of operators for moving from the initial state to the goal state. By solving one problem, generating a sequence of operators necessary in solving a problem, and generalizing such a sequence, we have the possibility of solving other problems. Learning, in this sense, is a typical example of learning procedures and is called learning operators in problem solving. We will explain methods of operator learning in problem solving in this section.

(a) Problem solving by theorem proving

Suppose we have a problem $P = \langle S, O, F, s_o, s_d \rangle$. First, we will describe a method of finding a solution for P using the technique of theorem proving. We represent a state $s \in S$ by the conjunction of predicates, or equivalently a set of predicates. Also, we represent an operator $o \in O$ by the triple $\langle p, d, a \rangle$ of *preconditions* p, a *delete list* d, and an *add list* a, where p, d, and a are each a set of predicates. Moving from a state s to another state s' by applying an operator o is equivalent to generating $s' = s \cup a\eta - d\eta$ under the condition that the constraint $s \rightarrow p\eta$ holds for some substitution η. If we consider the initial state s_o as a set of axioms and the goal state s_d as a set of theorems, we can say that we have solved P when we have proved all the elements of s_d, starting from s_o.

Let us represent by $s \vdash t$ the fact that all the elements of a set of predicates t can be proved from a set of predicates. Given that we can use the method described in Chapter 3 as an algorithm for theorem proving, we can give an algorithm for solving a problem P using theorem proving as follows:

Algorithm 7.1 (problem solving based on theorem proving)

[1] Let $g = s_d$.

[2] Try to solve $s_o \vdash g$. If it is proved, then stop. We take the sequence of operators applied so far as a solution to the problem. If it is not proved, let g be the set of predicates necessary for the proof and go to [3].

[3] Pick an operator where the add list and g match. If we find such an operator, let g be its preconditions and go to [2]. Otherwise, stop. A solution to the problem does not exist.

Let us consider the problem, P, of how a robot, *robot1*, in a room, *room1*, can bring the box *box1* from another room, *room2*, to the room, *room1*. The arrangement of the rooms is shown in Figure 7.1.

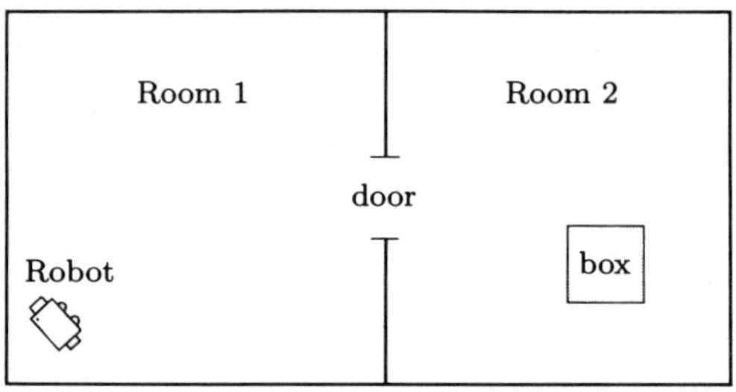

Figure 7.1 Robot problem solving.

We assume that the initial state of P, s_o, the goal state, s_d, and the three available operators represented as a triple are given as follows:

initial state s_o: $in(robot1, room1)$
$in(box1, room2)$
$connect(door1, room1, room2)$
$connect(door1, room2, room1)$
$robot(robot1)$
$box(box1)$
$door(door1)$
$room(room1)$
$room(room2)$

goal state s_d: $in(robot1, Y)$
$in(box1, room1)$
$connect(D, X, Y)$
$connect(D, Y, X)$
$robot(robot1)$
$box(box1)$
$door(door1)$
$room(room1)$
$room(room2)$

Operators

$walkto(R, W, X, Y)$

preconditions p_1: $in(R, X)$, $connect(W, X, Y)$, $robot(R)$
delete list d_1: $in(R, X)$
add list a_1: $in(R, Y)$

$carryto(R, B, W, X, Y)$

preconditions p_2: $in(R, X)$, $in(B, X)$, $connect(W, X, Y)$, $robot(R)$, $box(B)$
delete list d_2: $in(R, X)$, $in(B, X)$
add list a_2: $in(R, Y)$, $in(B, Y)$

The rule $walkto(R, W, X, Y)$ means to delete the condition that R is in X and add the condition that R is in Y, provided that a robot R is in X and that X and Y are connected by W. This rule can be read as "R moves from X to Y through W." The rule $carryto(R, B, W, X, Y)$ similarly can be read as "if R is in the same room as the box B, R moves to the connecting room carrying B."

To prove the theorem, we need to prove that all the predicates in s_d are true. Let us describe only the proof of $in(box1, room1)$ to save space. For simplicity, we suppose $s_d = \{in(box1, room1)\}$.

[1] Set $g = s_d = \{in(box1, room1)\}$.
[2] Since $s_0 \vdash g$ cannot be proven directly, go to [3].

[3] Of all the operators, the add list a_2 of *carryto* matches g by the substitution $\theta_1 = \{box1/B, room1/Y\}$. So, set $g = p_2\theta_1 = \{in(R, X), in(box1, X), connect(W, X, room1), robot(R), box(box1)\}$.

[2] Try to prove $s_o \vdash g$. The process of proof by resolution is shown in Figure 7.2(a). As shown in Figure 7.2(a), in order to prove $s_0 \vdash g$, we only need to prove $in(robot1, room2)$ in order to prove $s_0 \vdash g$. So, set

$$g = \{in(robot1, room2)\}$$

[3] Of all the operators, the add list a_1 of *walkto* matches g by the substitution $\theta_2 = \{robot1/R, room2/Y\}$. So, set

$$g = p_1\theta_2 = \{in(robot1, X), connect(W, X, room2), robot(robot1)\}$$

[2] $s_o \vdash g$ can be proven. The proof is shown in Figure 7.2(b). As a result, a solution to the problem can be represented as the sequence of operators:

$$\begin{aligned} & walkto(robot1, door1, room1, room2) \\ & \quad = walkto(R, W, X, Y)\theta_2\{door1/W, room1/X\} \\ & carryto(robot1, box1, door1, room2, room1) \\ & \quad = carryto(R, B, W, X, Y)\theta_1\{robot1/R\}\{door1/W, room2/X\} \end{aligned}$$

In other words, if we apply these rules to the initial state in order, we obtain the goal state. The above solution can be interpreted as "*robot1* moves from *room1* to *room2* and goes back to *room1* with the box *box1*."

(b) Generalization of operators

A sequence of the operators obtained by theorem proving exemplified in (a) can be regarded as a procedure for transferring a given initial state to a goal state. However, such a procedure can be used only in a specific problem and cannot be used in different problems even with as simple a change as renaming a room. For example, if we change *room1* and *room2* to other symbols, we cannot be sure that the original procedure is usable.

One method of removing this restriction is to generalize the procedure that was found so that it can be used in other problems. Below, we describe a method for generalizing a sequence of operators obtained by solving the problem P.

First, we represent the sequence of operators we found by solving the problem P in a *triangular table.* A triangular table represents states of the problem and applicable operators using the lower left triangular part (including the diagonal line) of a square matrix of size $n+1$, where n is the length of the sequence. Each row of a triangular table represents a state

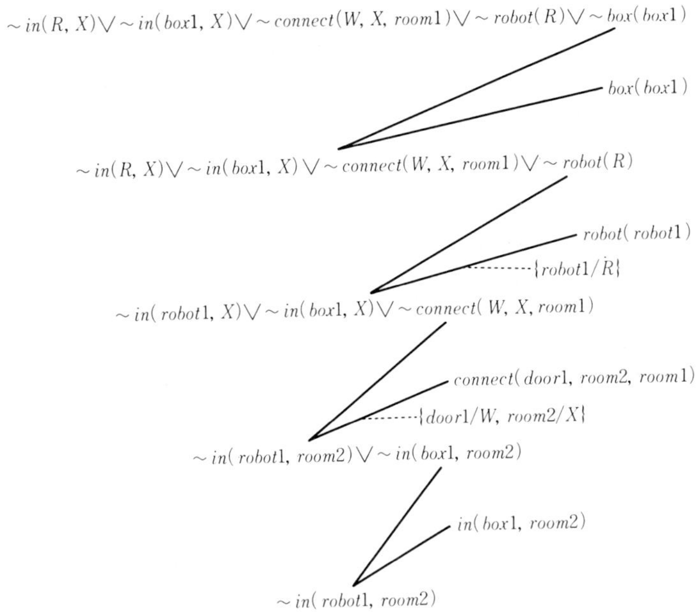

(a) A proof process by resolution (1)

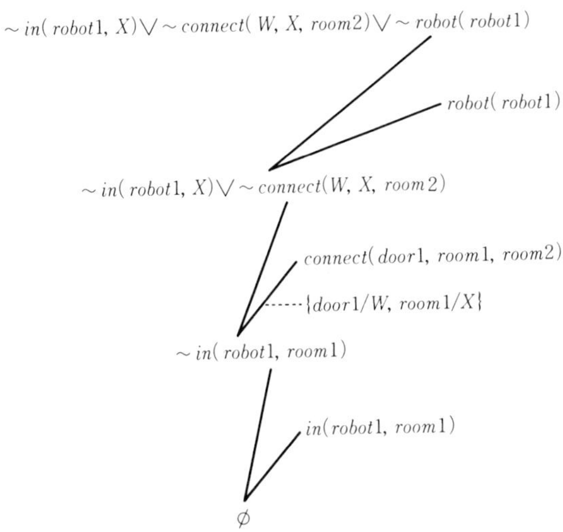

(b) A proof process by resolution (2)

Figure 7.2 Theorem proving used in problem solving.

transition in order from the top. To the right of the row we put the operator that was used in the state transition. The leftmost end of the row contains the set of the predicates that were included in the initial state and used as preconditions when applying the operator. The predicates that are added to the preconditions by the operator in the $i-1$th row are written in the intersection of the ith column and ith row $(2 \leq i \leq n+1)$. Similarly, the predicates that were not deleted from the preconditions by the operator in the $j-1$th row are written in the ith column and jth row $(i < j \leq n+1)$. For example, the sequence of operators obtained in the example described in (a) can be represented as the triangular table shown in Figure 7.3.

predicates that are used as preconditions in the initial state		
① *in*(*robot*1, *room*1) *connect*(*door*1, *room*1, *room*2) *robot*(*robot*1)	operator 1 *walkto*(*robot*1, *door*1, *room*1, *room*2)	
② *in*(*box*1, *room*2) *connect*(*door*1, *room*2, *room*1) *robot*(*robot*1) *box* (*box*1)	④ predicates that are added by the operator 1 *in*(*robot*1, *room*2)	operator 2 *carryto*(*robot*1, *box*1, *door*1, *room*2, *room*1)
③	⑤ predicates that are not deleted by the operator 2 in ④ none	⑥ predicates that are added by the operator 2 *in*(*robot*1, *room*1) *in*(*box*1, *room*1)

Figure 7.3 Representation of operators by a triangular table.

Next, we generalize the sequence of operators represented by the triangular table in the following steps:

Algorithm 7.2 (generalizing a sequence of operators)

[1] Replace constant symbols with variable symbols in the predicates that are in the leftmost column of the triangular table (①, ②, ③, in Figure 7.3), where if the same constant symbol is used in two or more places, replace each of them with a different variable.

[2] Replace the arguments of each operator with different variable symbols. Let θ be the substitution for the replacements.

[3] Using θ, replace the arguments of the add list with variable symbols.

[4] Using the rules that are generalized in [1]–[3], repeat the proof of the original problem once more. This can be done by using the fact that the predicates in the ith row of the triangular table are used to prove the preconditions of the operator that will be used at the ith step. In this second proof, we use the predicates in the same way as in the original proof. The reason for doing the proof once more is to prevent inconsistent substitutions for the variables in the predicates.

[5] The operators that are found in this way are possibly overgeneralized. To prevent this, redo the substitution of variables by applying the sequence of new operators to the original problem.

As an example, let us find a sequence of generalized operators from the triangular table shown in Figure 7.3. First, if we apply [1]–[3] to the triangular table in Figure 7.3, we obtain the generalized triangular table shown in Figure 7.4.

① *in*(X1, X2) *connect*(X3, X4, X5) *robot*(X6)	*walkto*(X14, X15, X16, X17)	
② *in*(X7, X8) *connect*(X9, X10, X11) *robot*(X12) *box*(X13)	④ *in*(X14, X17)	*carryto*(X18, X19, X20, X21, X22)
③	⑤	⑥ *in*(X18, X22) *in*(X19, X22)

Figure 7.4 Replacing constant symbols with variable symbols in a triangular table.

Next, as stated in [4], redo the proof using the table in Figure 7.4. This proof proceeds as follows:

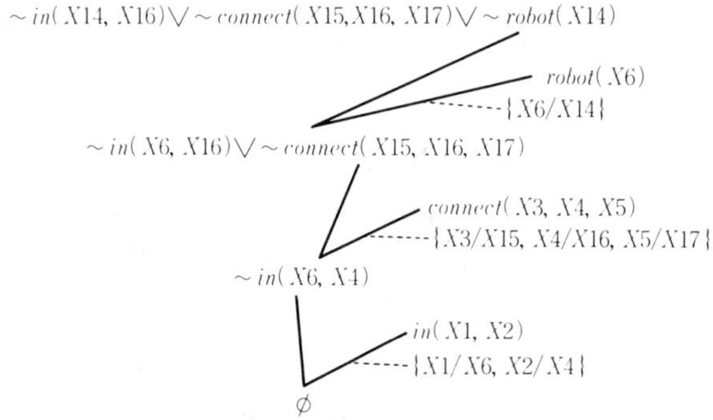

(a) Generating the substitution by theorem proving

① in(X6, X2) connect(X3, X2, X5) robot(X6)	walkto(X6, X3, X2, X5)	
② in(X7, X8) connect(X9, X10, X11) robot(X12) box(X13)	④ in(X6, X5)	carryto(X18, X19, X20, X21, X22)
③	⑤	⑥ in(X18, X22) in(X19, X22)

(b) The triangular table obtained by substitution

Figure 7.5 A triangular table with consistent variables (1).

(1) Prove the preconditions of *walkto*$(X14, X15, X16, X17)$ using Figure 7.4 ①. (Figure 7.5(a)). Apply the substitution obtained by this to the triangular table of Figure 7.4 to obtain a new triangular table (Figure 7.5(b)).

(2) Prove the preconditions of *carryto*$(X18, X19, X20, X21, X22)$ using Figure 7.5(b) ②, ④ (Figure 7.6(a)). Apply the substitution obtained by this to Figure 7.5(b) to obtain a new triangular table (Figure 7.6(b)).

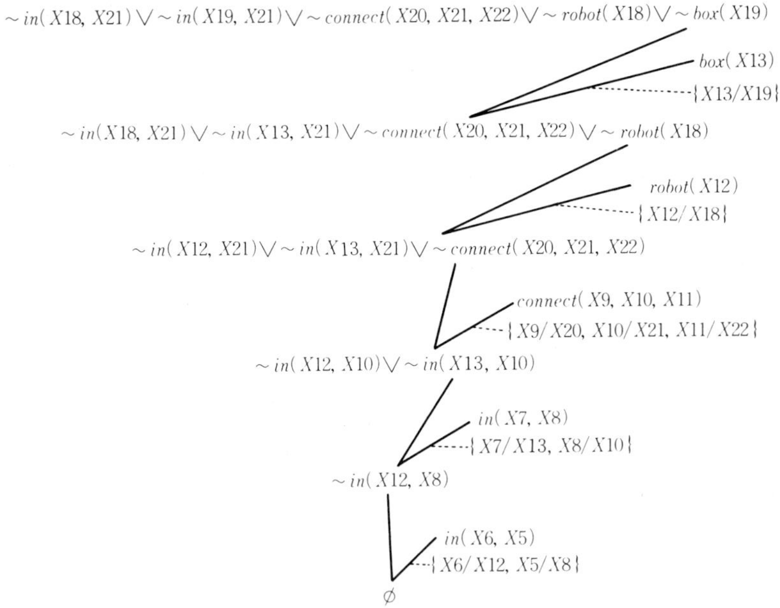

(a) Generating the substitution by theorem proving

① *in*(X6, X2) *connect*(X3, X2, X5) *robot*(X6)	*walkto*(X6, X3, X2, X5)	
② *in*(X7, X5) *connect*(X9, X5, X11) *robot*(X6) *box*(X7)	④ *in*(X6, X5)	*carryto*(X6, X7, X9, X5, X11)
③	⑤	⑥ *in*(X12, X11) *in*(X13, X11)

(b) The triangular table obtained by substitution

Figure 7.6 A triangular table with consistent variables (2).

From Figure 7.6(b), we learn that the sequence of generated operators

$$walkto(X6, X3, X2, X5)$$
$$carryto(X6, X7, X9, X5, X11)$$

is a generalization of the one shown in Figure 7.3. We can interpret the sequence of generalized operators as: "The robot $X6$ moves from the room $X2$ to the room $X5$ through door $X3$. Next, $X6$ carries the box $X7$ and moves from the room $X5$ to the room $X11$ through the door $X9$." Since the same symbol does not have to be substituted for $X2$ and $X11$, the robot can move to a room different from the one where it was originally located.

As you can see, the goal state obtained by the sequence of generalized operators can be different from the goal state of the original problem. In the above example, the difference occurs because the variable, $X22$, in ⑥ is different from the variable, $X2$, in ① in the triangular table of Figure 7.4. One method of preventing this overgeneralization is to apply the sequence of generated operators in Figure 7.6(b) to the original problem and redo the substitution of the variables, as described in [5] of the algorithm. Doing that, we see that we should do the substitution $\{X2/X11\}$ in *carryto*. We can obtain a sequence of new operators from this substitution:

$$walkto(X6, X3, X2, X5)$$
$$carryto(X6, X7, X9, X5, X2)$$

If we apply this sequence of operators to the initial state of the original problem, the robot $X6$ goes from the room $X2$ to the room $X5$, takes the box $X7$, and goes back to the original room $X2$ with the box, where the names of the doors between $X2$ and $X5$ are represented by the two variables $X3$ and $X9$. This means that the robot does not have to go though the same door between the two rooms as it goes back and forth. In this sense, the sequence of operators obtained above is generalized not only in the sense that constant symbols are replaced by variable symbols but also as a method of problem solving.

This algorithm is heuristic and the generated sequence of operators can be redundant or provide inconsistent solutions. In such cases, we need to modify the operators to eliminate redundancy or resolve inconsistency by using some heuristics.

Also, in this technique one state transition is done by one operator, but sometimes more than one consecutive state transition could be done by one operator. Such an operator is called a *macro-operator*. A macro-operator can be generated by learning. In the above example, a generalized macro-operator can be synthesized from the operators *walkto* and *carryto*.

7.2 Learning Rules

In this section, we will describe a method for learning procedures represented as production rules. Production rules can be learned by giving a production system the capability of generating a new rule by itself and adding it to the set of rules. Below, we will describe general methods for learning and generalizing rules, and later we will describe examples of learning rules.

(a) Methods of rule learning

A new production rule can be learned by giving to the action side of a rule in a production system the capability of generating new rules and the action of adding these new rules to the original set of rules. A production system with the capability of generating rules is called an *adaptive production system.* Now we will describe methods of generating new rules used in adaptive production systems. Here by a production system we mean a production system with ordered rules. The following methods can be used in combination with each other.

(1) *Independent addition of rules*

This method generates a new rule all at once in the action side of one rule and adds it to the original set of rules. This method of learning is called the *independent addition* of rules, because such rules are independent of the original ones. For example, let us consider the following set of rules:

$$\begin{array}{ll} r_1 & (a\ b)(c\ d\ e) \rightarrow (*build\ ((a\ b) \rightarrow (a\ c)\ (*delete\ (a\ b)))) \\ r_2 & (a\ b) \rightarrow (*add\ (c\ d\ e)) \end{array}$$

Here **build* is a function for adding its value to the top of the set of original rules. **delete* and **add* are functions that delete the value of its argument from working memory and add the value of its argument to working memory, respectively.

We assume that **add* can be omitted. In other words, when the action side of a rule has a list without a function name as its first element, we assume that such a list has **add* as its first element. Also, we represent working memory as a list of lists. If we assume the initial state of working memory is $((a\ b))$, these rules are executed as shown in Figure 7.7. In the execution of **build*, the name of the rule to be generated is automatically created, and the list (⟨name of the rule⟩ *built*) is added to working memory. Also, in the above example, the rule does not include any variables, but a similar method can be used when the rule includes variables.

Iteration 1:
working memory: $((a\ b))$
set of rules: r_1 $(a\ b)(c\ d\ e) \to (*build((a\ b) \to (a\ c)(*delete(a\ b))))$
r_2 $(a\ b) \to (c\ d\ e)$
Iteration 2: execution of r_2
working memory: $((c\ d\ e)(a\ b))$
set of rules: r_1 $(a\ b)(c\ d\ e) \to (*build((a\ b) \to (a\ c)(*delete(a\ b))))$
r_2 $(a\ b) \to (c\ d\ e)$
Iteration 3: execution of r_1
working memory: $(rg1\ built)(c\ d\ e)(a\ b))$
set of rules: rg_1 $(a\ b) \to (a\ c)(*delete(a\ b))$
r_1 $(a\ b)(c\ d\ e) \to (*build((a\ b) \to (a\ c)(*delete(a\ b))))$
r_2 $(a\ b) \to (c\ d\ e)$
Iteration 4: execution of rg_1
working memory: $((a\ c)(rg1\ built)(c\ d\ e))$
set of rules: rg_1 $(a\ b) \to (a\ c)(*delete(a\ b))$
r_1 $(a\ b)(c\ d\ e) \to (*build((a\ b) \to (a\ c)(*delete(a\ b))))$
r_2 $(a\ b) \to (c\ d\ e)$
Iteration 5: stop

Figure 7.7 The independent addition of a rule

(2) *Dependent addition of rules*

This method first generates components of the rule to be learned (each condition and action) separately and maintains them with a marker in working memory. When all the components are ready, it makes a new rule and adds it to the original set of rules. This method is called *dependent addition* in a sense that the rule learning is dependent on several rules. Section 7.2(c) will describe an example of learning by the dependent addition of rules.

(3) *Generalization of rules*

As in generalization of concepts, there are several methods for generalizing rules.

(i) Replacing constants with variables

This method generalizes a rule by replacing constants by variables within one rule. An example of this method is shown in Figure 7.8. **generalize* in Figure 7.8 is the function that, for the rule whose name is given in its first argument, generalizes constants bound to its second argument to new variables. When **generalize* is executed, constants are replaced by variables in a specific rule and the rule is added to the top of the original set of rules.

initial state:
  working memory: ( )
  set of rules:
    r_1 *(pronoun i)(verb love)(object you)* → *(sentence (i love you) r1)*
        *(*delete (pronoun i))*
        *(*delete (verb love))*
        *(*delete (object you))*
    r_2 $(\textit{sentence}\ (\$x\ \$y\ \$z\ \$r) \rightarrow (*\textit{generalize}\ \$r\ (\$y))$
    r_3 → *(pronoun i)(verb love)(object you)*
iteration 1: execution of r_3
  working memory: *((object you)(verb love)(pronoun i))*
  set of rules:
    r_1 *(pronoun i)(verb love)(object you)* → *(sentence (i love you) r1)*
        *(*delete (pronoun i))*
        *(*delete (verb love))*
        *(*delete (object you))*
    r_2 $(\textit{sentence}\ (\$x\ \$y\ \$z\ \$r) \rightarrow (*\textit{generalize}\ \$r\ (\$y))$
    r_3 → *(pronoun i)(verb love)(object you)*
iteration 2: execution of r_1
  working memory: *((sentence (i love you) r1))*
  set of rules:
    r_1 *(pronoun i)(verb love)(object you)* → *(sentence (i love you) r1)*
        *(*delete (pronoun i))*
        *(*delete (verb love))*
        *(*delete (object you))*
    r_2 $(\textit{sentence}\ (\$x\ \$y\ \$z\ \$r) \rightarrow (*\textit{generalize}\ \$r\ (\$y))$
    r_3 → *(pronoun i)(verb love)(object you)*
iteration 3: execution of r_2
  working memory: *((rg1 generalized_from r1)(sentence (i love you) r1))*
  set of rules:
    rg_1 $(\textit{pronoun i})(\textit{verb}\ \$a1)(\textit{object you}) \rightarrow (\textit{sentence}\ (i\ \$a1\ \textit{you})\ rg1)$
        *(*delete (pronoun i))*
        $(*\textit{delete}\ (\textit{verb}\ \$a1))$
        *(*delete (object you))*
    r_1 *(pronoun i)(verb love)(object you)* → *(sentence (i love you) r1)*
        *(*delete (pronoun i))*
        *(*delete (verb love))*
        *(*delete (object you))*
    r_2 $(\textit{sentence}\ (\$x\ \$y\ \$z\ \$r) \rightarrow (*\textit{generalize}\ \$r\ (\$y))$
    r_3 → *(pronoun i)(verb love)(object you)*

Figure 7.8 Rule learning by replacing constants with variables.

(ii) Replacing constants with functions

This method generalizes a rule by replacing constants with functions within one rule. For example, it can generate the new rule

$$rg_1 \quad (symbol\ \$x)(symbol\ (next\ \$x)) \rightarrow (list\ (\$x\ (next\ \$x)))$$

from the rule

$$r_1 \quad (symbol\ a)(symbol\ b) \rightarrow (list\ (a\ b))$$

by replacing a and b with $\$x$ and $(next\ \$x)$, respectively, and adding the new rule to the top of the original set of rules.

(iii) Generalizing from two rules

This method generates a new rule that is executable whenever either one of two rules can be executed and adds it to the top of the original set of rules. This is done by making the set of conditions for the new rule $C_1 \cap C_2$ or its subset (ignoring differences in the names of variables) when the original sets of conditions for the two rules are C_1 and C_2, respectively. For example, we generate

$$rg_1 \quad (a\ \$x)(b\ \$y\ c) \rightarrow (rg1\ fired)$$

from

$$r_1 \quad (a\ \$s)(b\ \$t\ c)(d\ \$u\ \$v\ \$w) \rightarrow (r1\ fired)$$
$$r_2 \quad (a\ \$m)(b\ \$n\ c)(e\ \$o\ \$p\ \$q) \rightarrow (r2\ fired)$$

where rg_1 is a generalization of r_1 and r_2 in the sense that rg_1 is executed when either r_1 or r_2 is executed. However, since this method is likely to result in *overgeneralization*, it usually selects a most specific rule among the generalized rules, as in an MSC generalization for concept learning.

For example,

$$rg_2 \quad (a\ \$x) \rightarrow (rg2\ fired)$$

is a generalized rule for r_1 and r_2, but rg_1 is a more specific rule than rg_2. Actually, in this example, rg_1 is the most specific rule, and rg_1, not rg_2, would be generated.

(4) *Specialization of rules*

In addition to generalization, we can generate new rules by specializing an already existing rule.

(i) Replacing variables with constants

One method is to make a more specific rule by replacing variables with constants within one rule and adding the new rule to the original set of rules.

(ii) Replacing functions with constants

Another method is to make a more specific rule by replacing functions with constants within one rule and adding the new rule to the original set of rules.

(iii) Specializing one rule from two rules

Given two rules r_1 and r_2, we make a new rule rs_1. This method constructs rs_1 so that r_1 and r_2 are both executable whenever rs_1 is executable. The newly made rule is added to the top of the original set of rules. For example, we can generate

$$rs_1 \quad (a\ \$x)(c\ \$v\ \$w)(g\ \$n) \rightarrow (rs1\ \textit{fired})$$

from

$$r_1 \quad (a\ \$u)(c\ \$v\ \$w) \rightarrow (r1\ \textit{fired})$$
$$r_2 \quad (a\ \$m)(g\ \$n) \rightarrow (r2\ \textit{fired})$$

Here rs_1 is a specialization of r_1 and r_2.

As in generalization, *overspecialization* can happen when specializing a pair of rules. For example,

$$rs_2 \quad (a\ \$x)(b\ \$y)(c\ \$v\ \$w)(g\ \$n) \rightarrow (rs2\ \textit{fired})$$

is a specialization of r_1 and r_2, but it is a more specific rule than rs_1. Usually we select a *maximally general specialization* as the new rule.

(5) *Composing rules*

This method generates a new rule whose execution has the same result as the consecutive execution of two existing rules and adds the new rule to the top of the original set of rules. For example, suppose A and C are the sets of conditions and B and D are the sets of actions for each rule. If we know that two rules

$$r_1 \quad A \rightarrow B$$
$$r_2 \quad C \rightarrow D$$

are always executed in this order, we can generate the new rule

$$rc_1 \quad A, C\text{–}B \rightarrow B, D$$

and add it to the top of the original set of rules. After rc_1 is added to the set of rules, rc_1 is executed whenever r_1 and r_2 would be executed consecutively. As a result, the state of working memory would be the same as if r_1 and r_2 had been executed.

Composition of rules is a learning method similar to generating macro-operators, described in Section 7.1.

(b) Learning by generalizing rules

Here we will explain learning by generalization of rules in detail. We will assume that we have a production system that satisfies the following conditions:

(1) The only actions allowed by a rule are storing and deleting lists in working memory.
(2) Conditions are all lists.
(3) In any rule, lists that are deleted by executing the action side of the rule appear explicitly in the condition side of the rule.

For a production system satisfying (1)–(3), each rule can be represented as

$$a_2 \rightarrow b_2 b_1 \tag{I}$$

where a_2 is a set of conditions, and b_1 and b_2 are actions for deleting lists from and adding lists to working memory, respectively. Here we are assuming that all the actions for deleting lists are executed before the actions for adding lists.

If we let c be the set of lists that are included in a_2 but not included in b_2 and let $a_1 = a_2 - c$, we can write the rule (I) as

$$[c]a_1 \rightarrow b_1$$

The set c is called the *context.* We use σ to denote the content of working memory. A necessary condition for $[c]a_1 \rightarrow b_1$ to be executable for σ is that there exists a substitution θ satisfying

$$a_1\theta \subseteq \sigma \quad \text{and} \quad c\theta \subset \sigma$$

In this case if $[c]a_1 \rightarrow b_2$ is executed for σ, the content of working memory is replaced by $\sigma' = (\sigma - a_1\theta) \cup b_1\theta$.

Below we define generalization of rules, assuming that all of the rules have the form $[c]a_1 \rightarrow b_1$.

Definition 1 (generalization) If, for the rules r_1 and r_2,

$$(\sigma \overset{r_1}{\Rightarrow} \sigma') \quad \text{whenever} \quad (\sigma \overset{r_2}{\Rightarrow} \sigma')$$

for any working memory σ and σ', we call r_1 a generalization of r_2, where $\mu \overset{r}{\Rightarrow} \mu'$ denotes transforming the content of working memory from μ to μ' by executing the rule r. Let $r_1 \leq r_2$ denote that r_1 is a generalization of r_2.

Definition 2 (strong generalization) Assume $r_1 \leq r_2$ for some rules r_1 and r_2. If there is no substitution θ that makes $r_1 = r_2\theta$, we call r_1 a *strong generalization* of r_2 and write $r_1 < r_2$.

In generalizing a rule, the following holds: suppose that for two rules $r_x : ([c_x]a_x \rightarrow b_x)$ and $r_y : ([c_y]a_y \rightarrow b_y)$, there is a substitution θ such that $a_x\theta \cap b_x\theta = \emptyset$ and $a_y\theta \cap b_y\theta = \emptyset$. In this case, a necessary condition for $r_x \leq r_y$ is that a substitution ξ exists for which $c_x\xi \subseteq c_y, a_x\xi = a_y, b_x\xi = b_y$.

Next, let us define the following for creating a rule by generalizing two rules:

Definition 3 (common generalization) For two rules r_1 and r_2, we call a rule r_3 such that $r_3 \leq r_1$ and $r_3 \leq r_2$ a *common generalization* of r_1 and r_2.

There may be many common generalizations of two rules. Just as in the case of MSC generalizations in learning concepts, it is generally better to choose a common generalization that is "close" to the original rules (here, r_1 and r_2). To do that, we introduce the following definition:

Definition 4 (maximal common generalization) When rules r_1, r_2, and r_3 satisfy the following condition, we call r_3 a *maximal common generalization* of r_1 and r_2: there does not exist a rule r_3' such that (1) $r_3 \leq r_1$ and $r_3 \leq r_2$ and (2) $r_3 \leq r_3'$, $r_3' \leq r_1$, and $r_3' \leq r_2$.

For example, let us look at the following four rules:

$$
\begin{array}{ll}
r_1 & [(\textit{temperature hot})](\textit{season } X) \rightarrow (\textit{season } Y) \\
r_2 & [(\textit{temperature hot})](\textit{season spring}) \rightarrow (\textit{season summer}) \\
r_3 & [(\textit{temperature hot})](\textit{season winter}) \rightarrow (\textit{season spring}) \\
r_4 & [\ ](\textit{season } X) \rightarrow (\textit{season } Y)
\end{array}
$$

Here $r_1 \leq r_2$, $r_1 \leq r_3$, $r_4 \leq r_2$, and $r_4 \leq r_3$. Therefore, r_1 and r_4 are common generalizations of r_2 and r_3, respectively. However, since $r_4 < r_1$, r_4 is not a maximal common generalization of r_2 and r_3. On the other hand, r_1 is a maximal common generalization of r_2 and r_3. Note that a maximal common generalization is not always unique even if we identify different ways of making substitutions.

Now, when a rule r_1 is a maximal common generalization of r_2 and r_3, there exist substitutions θ_a and θ_b such that

$$
\begin{array}{ll}
c_1\theta_a \subseteq c_2, & c_1\theta_b \subseteq c_3 \\
a_1\theta_a = a_2, & a_1\theta_b = a_3 \\
b_1\theta_a = b_2, & b_1\theta_b = b_3
\end{array}
$$

because of the statements given below Definition 2. If $|\cdot|$ is the number of elements included in a finite set $\cdot$ and $|a_1| \neq |a_3|$ or $|b_2| \neq |b_3|$ for r_2 and r_3, then a maximal common generalization of r_2 and r_3 cannot exist. As we can see from this example, in obtaining a maximal common generalization for two rules, the condition that $|a_2| \neq |a_3|$ or $|b_2| \neq |b_3|$ for the number of the elements of a_2, a_3, b_2, b_3 in these rules becomes an easily identifiable termination condition.

A maximal common generalization of two rules, if it exists, can be obtained by finding the substitutions θ_a, θ_b by an appropriate pattern matching algorithm. Also, a set of maximal common generalizations for three or more rules can be obtained by repeating the operation of obtaining a maximal common generalization for two rules.

(c) Learning by rule addition

Rule addition is one of the simplest learning methods for production systems, and because of its simplicity, it is widely applicable. Here we will describe learning by dependent addition of rules.

Let us consider a method of learning called *paired-associate learning.* This is a simple method of associative memory to remember pairs of information and recall one of a pair of information when the other is presented. For example, suppose we want to remember pairs of symbol strings that are made of three letters such as `(rej qin)`, `(ruk nac)`, ... Remembering such pairs and recalling the three letters on the right side of a pair when the three letters on the left side of the pair are given can be easily done by searching a table of these pairs. Here, let us consider the case of answering with three letters from the right side when only one or two letters from the left side are given. For a learning system that is able to search using only partial information, we need to *index* the symbol strings to be remembered. Below, we describe a method using dependent addition of rules as a learning algorithm for doing indexing automatically.

First, let us look at the case of answering `qin` whenever the first letter of the left side of a pair is `r`. This procedure can be said to be learned if the learning system generates the rule by itself

> **if** the first letter is `r`
> **then** output `qin`

and adds this rule to the original set of rules. In order to do this learning, let us consider the program for a production system that uses the nine rules `p1`–`p9` shown in Figure 7.9. Here the rules are in the order `p1` through `p9` and the program is an ordered production system. Also, we assume that not only lists but also predicates can be given in the condition side of a rule. A list condition is satisfied when it matches working memory. A predicate condition is satisfied when its value is T.

First, we will explain the predicates and functions in Figure 7.9. `*abs` is the predicate that takes T if and only if the list in its argument does not

(a) The initial state of the set of the rules

```
p1 (ready ok)->(*write (***** type input *****))(input is (*read))
p2 (ready ok)(input is $x)->(*delete (ready ok))(*perceive $x ?)
p3 (system response is $x)(*abs (response is $x))(*abs_list
   response)->(*write (***** type response *****))(response is
   (*read))
p4 (system response is $x)(*abs (response is $x))->
   (*delete (system response is $x))($x is error)
p5 ($x was used already)($y is error)(response is $z)->
   (*delete ($x was used already))(condition $x)(action (@*delete $x))
   (action ($x was used already))
p6 (input is $x)(*abs_list response)-> (system response is ?)
   (*write (?))
   (*write (***** type response *****))(response is (*read))
p7 (is $x -th letter $y ?)(response is $z)($w is error) ->
   (condition (is $x -th letter $y ?))
   (action (@*delete (is $x -th letter $y ?)))
   (action ((is $x -th letter $y ?) was used already))
   (action (system response is $z))(action (@*write ($z)))
   (*build (*newsym)(*collectlist condition)(*collectlist action))
   (*deletelist all)
   (*write (***** type (ready ok) if continue -- type (stop) if
   terminate))
   (*read)
p8 (system response is $z)(response is ok)->
   (*write (***** system response was correct *****))(*deletelist all)
   (*write (***** type (ready ok) if continue -- type (stop) if
   terminate))
   (*read)
p9 (stop)->(*halt)
```

(b) The initial state of working memory

```
((ready ok))
```

Figure 7.9 A production system for paired-associate learning by dependent addition of rules.

match working memory. **abs_list* is the predicate that takes a symbol as an argument and is T if and only if no list in working memory contains that symbol as its first element. `*delete` is a function that deletes lists from the working memory. `*deletelist` is a function for clearing working memory when its argument is the atom `all`. `*collectlist` is a function for collecting all the lists in working memory that have its argument as their first element, making a new list of these lists, and adding it to working memory. `*read` and `*write` are functions for input and output, respectively. `*newsym` is a function that generates a new atom.

`*perceive` is a function for dividing a symbol string that appears as its first argument into its constituent symbols, generating three lists (i ⟨ith symbol⟩ ⟨the second argument of `perceive`⟩) ($i = 1, 2, 3$), and adding the lists to working memory in the order $i = 2, 3, 1$. Finally, `*build` is a function that generates a rule, which has the rule's name as its first argument, conditions, as elements of the second argument, and adds the rule to the original set of rules. For an atom that contains the character @ in the program, @ will be deleted when the atom is stored in working memory.

Next, we will explain each rule in Figure 7.9. First, p1 is a rule for reading the information in the left side of each pair. p2 is a rule for dividing the string read in p1 into separate symbols, p3 is a rule for reading the information in the right side of each pair. p4 is a rule that is activated when the response from the system is not the correct response. p5 is a rule for collecting data in order to generate a new rule. p6 is a rule for reading the first response. p7 is a rule for generating a new rule. p8 is a rule that is activated when the response from the system is correct. p9 is a rule for terminating the execution.

Furthermore we assume that the initial state of working memory consists of one list, `(ready ok)`, as is shown in Figure 7.9.

Figure 7.10 shows the result of executing the program. When the first information `rej` is input, p1 and p2 are executed consecutively, then p6 is executed, and the information `qin` that forms a pair with `rej` is input. After the execution of p4, a new rule `g0184` is generated by p7. `g0184` can be interpreted as

> **if** if the first symbol of the right side of the pair is `r`
> **then** output `qin`

Next, `ruk`, the left side of a second pair, is input by p1. Then, right after p2, `g0184` is executed, and `qin` is returned as the answer. This is a wrong answer due to the accidental fact that the first symbol of `ruk` is `r`. So, `nac` is now read as the right side of `ruk` by p3. Through p4 and p5, a new rule `g0186` is created by p7. `g0186` can be interpreted as

> **if** the first symbol in the right side of the pair is `r`
> **and** the third symbol is `k`
> **then** output `nac`

As a result, after the rules `g0814` and `g0186` are generated and added to the set of rules, the correct answers, `gin` and `nac`, are returned for `rej` and `ruk`, respectively. The last half of Figure 7.10 shows such answers.

```
>>(execute)
***** type input ***** >> rej
p1 ((input is rej)(ready ok))
p2 ((is 1 -th letter r ?)(is 3 -th letter j ?)
   (is 2 -th letter e ?)(input is rej))
?
***** type response ***** >> qin
p6 ((response is qin)(system response is ?)(is 1 -th letter r ?)
   (is 3 -th letter j ?)(is 2 -th letter e ?)(input is rej))
p4 ((? is error)(response is qin)(is 1 -th letter r ?)
   (is 3 -th letter j ?)(is 2 -th letter e ?)(input is rej))
***** new production g0184 was built *****
g0184 (is 1 -th letter r ?)->(*delete (is 1 -th letter r ?))
      ((is 1 -th letter r ?) was used already)
      (system response is qin)(*write (qin))
***** type (ready ok) if continue -- type (stop) if terminate *****
   >> (ready ok)
p7 ((ready ok))
***** type input ***** >> ruk
p1 ((input is ruk)(ready ok))
p2 ((is 1 -th letter r ?)(is 3 -th letter k)
   (is 2 -th letter u ?)(input is ruk))
qin
g1084 ((system response is qin)(is 1 -th letter r ?)
      (is 3 -th letter k ?)(is 2 -th letter u ?)(input is ruk))
***** type response ***** >> nac
p3 ((response is nac)(system response is qin)((is 1 -th letter r ?)
   was used already)
   (is 3 -th letter k ?)(is 2 -th letter u ?)(input is ruk))
p4 ((qin is error)(response is nac)((is 1 -th letter r ?)
  was used already)(is 3 -th letter k ?)(is 2 -th letter u ?)
  (input is ruk))
p5 ((action ((is 1 -th letter r ?) was used already))
  (action (*delete (is 1 -th letter r ?)))
  (condition (is 1 -th letter r ?))(qin is error)(response is nac)
  (is 3 -th letter k ?)(is 2 -th letter u ?)(input is ruk))
***** new production g0186 was built *****
g0186 (is 1 -th letter r ?)(is 3 -th letter k ?)-> (*delete
      (is 1 -th letter r ?))
      ((is 1 -th letter r ?) was used already)
```

(*continued*)

Figure 7.10 Execution of learning for the production system shown in Figure 7.9 (underlined words are input).

```
      (*delete (is 3 -th letter k ?))
      ((is 3 -th letter k) was used already)
      (system response is nac)(*write (nac))
***** type (ready ok) if continue -- type (stop) if terminate *****
  >> (ready ok)
p7 ((ready ok))
***** type input ***** >> rej
p1 ((input is rej)(ready ok))
p2 ((is 1 -th letter r?)(is 3 -th letter j ?)
   (is 2 -th letter e ?)(input is rej))
qin
g0184 ((system response is qin)
      ((is 1 -th letter r?) was used already)(is 3 -th letter j ?)
      (is 2 -th letter e ?)(input is rej))
***** type response *****>> ok
p3 ((response is k)(system response is qin)((is 1 -th letter r ?)
   was used already)(is 3 -th letter j ?)
   (is 2 -th letter e ?)(input is rej))
***** system response was correct *****
***** type (ready ok) if continue -- type (stop) if terminate *****
  >> (ready ok)
p8 ((ready ok))
***** type input ***** >> ruk
p1 ((input is ruk)(ready ok))
p2 ((is 1 -th letter r ?)(is 3 -th letter k ?)
   (is 2 -th letter u ?)(input is ruk))
nac
g1086 ((system response is nac)
      ((is 3 -th letter k ?) was used already)
      (is 2 -th letter u)(input is ruk))
***** type response ***** >> ok
p3 ((response is ok)(system response is nac)((is 3 -th letter k ?)
   was used already)(is 2 -th letter u ?)(input is ruk))
***** system response was correct *****
***** type (ready ok) is continue -- type (stop) if terminate *****
  >> (stop)
p8 ((stop))
p9 ((stop))
halt
```

Figure 7.10 *Continued.*

7.3 Learning Programs

In this section we describe learning procedures that are represented in the form of programs. Examples of learning complicated procedures include constructing algebraic functions and Lisp functions or constructing computer programs from input-output examples. Currently it is very difficult for a system to learn automatically complicated functions or programs. Some people are doing research on systems that enable a user to make a program by interacting with the computer. However, when a program is complicated, the system that supports this interactive programming requires a lot of knowledge about programs and programming. Thus how to represent this information in a computer becomes an important problem.

In this section, we will concentrate on a system for learning problem solving procedures in the form of programs.

(a) Learning a problem solving program based on knowledge

Consider problem solving in the world of blocks shown in Figure 7.11. The problem is to find a sequence of operators that transforms the initial state s_o to the goal state s_d. Let us first represent the states in the form of lists.

$$s_o : ((on\ c\ a)(cleartop\ c)(on\ a\ table)(on\ b\ table)(cleartop\ b))$$
$$s_d : ((on\ b\ a)(on\ c\ b)(on\ a\ table)(cleartop\ c))$$

We call the set s_d–s_o the *goal* and represent it using the function:

$$goal : (make\ (and\ (on\ b\ a)\ (on\ c\ b)))$$

We can think of this problem as one of finding a procedure for deriving the *goal* from the initial state, s_o (under the condition that $s_d \cap s_o$ is included in the goal state). To solve the problem, we need only search for an appropriate procedure leading to the *goal* from s_o using a knowledge base about such procedures. However, there is no guarantee of finding such a procedure directly. So, in case the procedure cannot be found, we should search a procedure leading to a similar goal.

Next, when a problem cannot be solved by the procedure we found during the search, we need to find the cause of the failure, in other words, a *bug* in the program. We then examine the type of bug and search for a procedure for removing this type of bug using the knowledge base. Then we correct the procedure for reaching the goal using the procedure obtained for removing bugs. If we could solve the problem using the corrected procedure, we make the procedure a subroutine and add it to the knowledge base.

This method is summarized in Figure 7.12

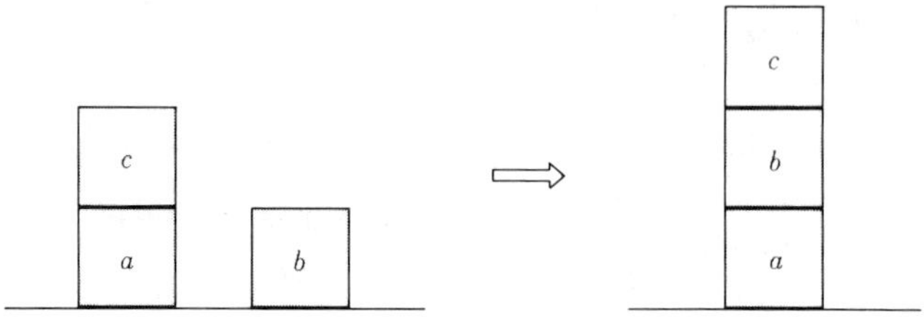

Figure 7.11 Learning an operator in problem solving.

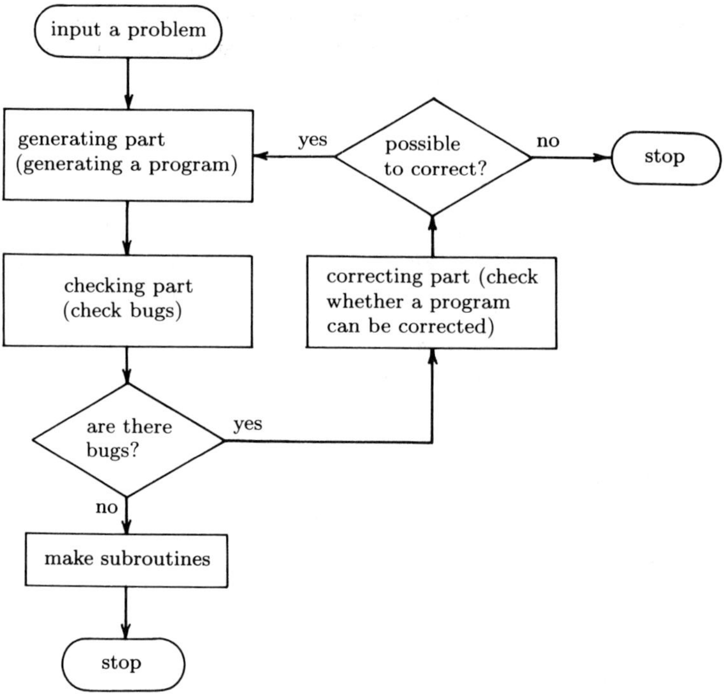

Figure 7.12 Learning a problem solving program.

One common kind of bug is in the order of satisfying subgoals. For example, in the problem of Figure 7.11, suppose there are two *subgoals*, (*on b a*) and (*on c b*), and we reach (*on c b*) first and then try to reach (*on b a*). If we move *c* that is on *b* onto *a*, we return to the initial state that causes a loop in the state transition. This is due to the fact that each subgoal is regarded as an independent goal. In order to avoid this, there are search methods that change the order of subgoals and a method called *goal regression* that tests whether the result of attaining a subgoal contradicts some other subgoals.

(b) An example of learning

Here we describe how a system learns a problem solving program based on the method described in (a), using the example shown in Figure 7.13. In this example, appropriate procedures are immediately obtained from the knowledge base; however, in more complex cases, we generally need to do backtracking if the search finds inappropriate procedures.

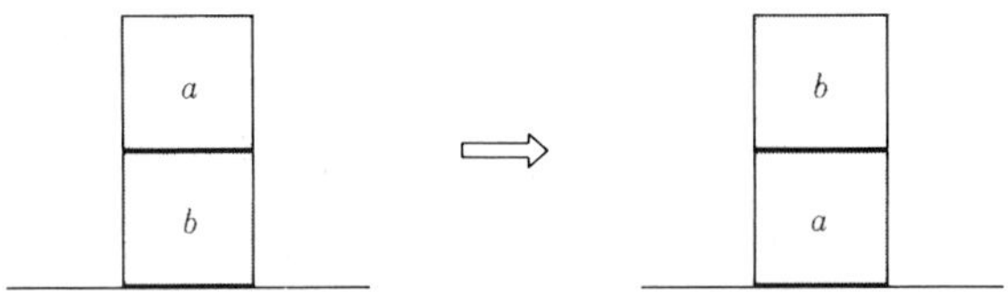

initial state s_o — goal *goal*

((*on a b*) (*cleartop a*) (*on b table*)) — (*make* (*on b a*))

Figure 7.13 An example of learning a problem solving program.

(1) *Executing the generation part*

Suppose we found the following function in the knowledge base that is a procedure for reaching the goal, (*make* (*on b a*)), in the problem of Figure 7.13:

(*to* (*make* (*on X Y*))
  (*hprog make_on* (*statement g*01 (*puton X Y*)))) (7.1)

where *hprog* is a function that explains what the function *to* does, gives *make_on* as the name of the subroutine *to*, and shows that the function (*puton X Y*) is defined on line *g*01.

Also, when this function is in the knowledge base, the lists

(*goal make_on* (*make* (*on X Y*))) (7.2)

(*purpose g*01 (*make* (*on X Y*)) *make_on*) (7.3)

are also stored in the knowledge base. The program (7.2) indicates that the goal of the subroutine shown in (7.1), *make_on*, is (*make* (*on X Y*)). The program (7.3) indicates that the purpose of g01, the statement of the subroutine *make_on*, is to (*make* (*on X Y*)), Now, suppose that a program like (7.1) was found in the generation part of Figure 7.12.

(2) *Execution of the checking part*

The checking part of Figure 7.12 executes the program (7.1) using the substitution $\{b/X, a/Y\}$. However, in the example in Figure 7.13, (7.1) cannot be applied to the initial state, so (7.1) is sent to the correcting part of Figure 7.12.

(3) *Execution of the correction part*

The correction part discovers bugs and determines their types. Suppose the reason why the program (7.1) cannot be executed on the initial state is that the function *puton* inside (7.1) does not work since (*on a b*) cannot be found in the initial state. This bug can be described as

$$(bug\ unsatisfied\_prerequisite\ (not\ (on\ a\ b))) \tag{7.4}$$

Next, suppose we search the knowledge base for the conditions that will allow us to remove the bug in (7.4) and we find

$$\begin{aligned} &(fact\ (prerequisite\ V\ (cleartop\ W)) \\ &\qquad (have\ (\ )\ (moves\ V\ W))) \end{aligned} \tag{7.5}$$

$$(fact\ (moves\ (puton\ X\ Y)\ X)) \tag{7.6}$$

The program (7.5) says that, if V is a function for moving a block W, we cannot execute V unless there is nothing on W. Since the program (7.6) can be substituted into (7.5) by the substitution $\{(puton\ X\ Y)/V, X/W\}$, we only need to check whether (*cleartop* X) is true in order to remove the bugs.

We now check if

$$(test\ (cleartop\ X)) \tag{7.7}$$

is true for the substitution $\{b/X\}$. Since (7.7) is not true for the initial state, the type of the bug can be determined to be

$$(prerequisite\_missing\ make\_on\ g01\ (cleartop\ b)) \tag{7.8}$$

Next, we need to correct the original program (7.1) to eliminate bugs of type (7.8). Suppose we found the following knowledge in the knowledge base as a procedure for correcting a program:

$$\begin{aligned} &(fact\ (patch\ (prerequisite\_missing\ P\ Q\ R) \\ &\qquad\qquad (newline\ P \\ &\qquad\qquad\qquad (achieve\ R) \\ &\qquad\qquad\qquad (((achieve\ R)\ Q))))) \end{aligned} \tag{7.9}$$

Program (7.9) tells us how to insert a new statement right before the statement Q where the bug is found in the original program P so that the new program satisfies the unsatisfied condition R.

(4) *Re-execution of the generation part*

Using (7.9), program (7.1) can be rewritten as follows:

$$\begin{array}{l}(to\ (make\ (on\ X\ Y))\\ \quad (hprog\ make\_on\\ \quad\quad (line\ g02\ (achieve\ cleartop\ Y)))\\ \quad\quad (line\ g01\ (puton\ X\ Y))))\end{array} \tag{7.10}$$

We also augment the knowledge base with the following knowledge about the newly inserted statement:

$$(purpose\ g02\ (achieve\ cleartop\ Y))\ g01) \tag{7.11}$$

(5) *Re-execution of the checking part*

The newly generated program (7.10) checks whether the original problem can be solved or not. If the problem is solved using (7.10), then (7.1) is added to the knowledge base and the execution of the learning program is terminated.

(c) Learning by detecting and deleting bugs

The system we explained in (b) is an example of a system for learning a new program by detecting and deleting bugs during problem solving. As you can see from this example, the learning of complicated programs needs to have a large amount of information in the knowledge base. Also, we assumed in this example that a bug can be easily detected, but it is often not easy to identify the bug that causes a program error. Furthermore, even if the system generates a program that has no bugs, we do not know much about what kinds of problems this new program will solve. What we explained in this section is a simple example of learning based on knowledge. When we apply these techniques to larger problems, we need to solve many supplementary problems.

Summary

In this chapter we learned methods that can be used to learn procedures that are used in inference and problem solving.

7.1 If a sequence of operators for solving a problem can be found using a theorem proving algorithm, a system can learn a sequence of operators for solving more general problems by generalizing the proof process.

7.2 A production system can learn production rules in various ways.

7.3 We can construct a system that learns problem solving procedures in the form of a program.

Keywords

procedure, problem solving, triangular table, learning of operators, theorem proving, macro-operator, production system, learning of production rules, generalization , specialization, common generalization, maximal common generalization, paired-associate learning, indexing, learning of programs, bugs, generating programs, goal regression

Exercises

7.1 Suppose in the problem solving of the robot (Figure 7.1), which is described in Section 7.1(a), the goal state s_d is "the box *box1* is in room *room1* and the robot *robot1* is in room *room2*." Find a sequence of operators for reaching s_d.

7.2 Make a triangular table using the answer of Exercise 7.1, and generalize it and find a sequence of generalized operators.

7.3 Write a program for an adaptive production system that performs dependent addition of rules described in Section 7.2(a)(2), where the system is assumed to be an ordered production system. You can use any programming language.

7.4 In the problem in Figure 7.14, suppose the goal is given as

$$goal: \ (make \ (and \ (on \ a \ b) \ (on \ a \ c)))$$

Then a loop occurs if subgoals are attained as follows:

subgoal : (*on a b*)
  subgoal : (*clear b*)
    subgoal : (*move c table*)
    attained
  attained
  subgoal : (*puton a b*)
  attained
attained
subgoal : (*on b c*)
  subgoal : (*clear b*)
    subgoal : (*move b table*)
    attained
  attained

Describe how to eliminate this loop.

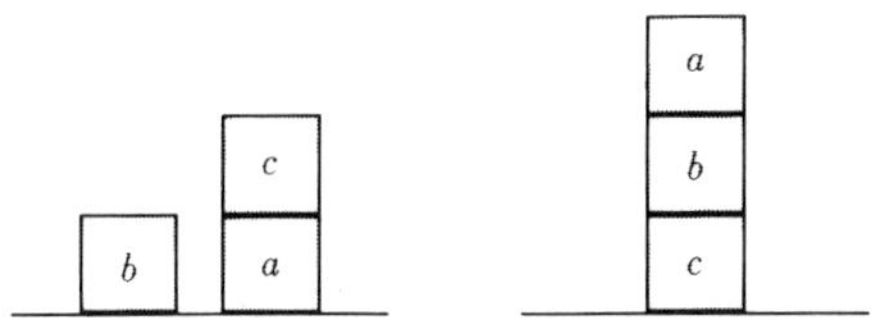

initial state s_o	goal state s_d
(*on c a*)	(*on a b*)
(*cleartop c*)	(*on b c*)
(*ontable a*)	(*cleartop a*)
(*cleartop b*)	(*ontable c*)
(*ontable b*)	

Figure 7.14

8 Learning Based on Logic

Logical inference using knowledge represented by predicate logic and inference rules does not seem to generate any new information or have anything to do with learning. However, when we try to understand the structure that is buried in a large amount of complicated knowledge, we can regard a system for organizing knowledge by logical inference as generating new knowledge that we have not seen before. Also, a system based on logic can be used for algorithms that actually generate new information by embedding learning methods, such as generalization and specialization, into logical inference. We generally refer to learning based on logical inference as learning based on logic. In this chapter, we will explain various learning algorithms based on logic.

8.1 Explanation-Based Learning

Suppose we have a concept c and its positive instance, a. The fact that a is a positive instance of c corresponds, from the viewpoint of logic, to the fact that c can be proved from a. For example, with well-formed formulas

$$\begin{aligned} &\mathit{mammal}(X) \rightarrow \mathit{animal}(X) \\ &\mathit{human}(\mathit{taro}) \rightarrow \mathit{mammal}(\mathit{taro}) \end{aligned} \tag{8.1}$$

the fact that taro is an animal is proved from the fact that taro is a human being, so we can think of taro as a positive instance of an animal. This logical relation between concepts and instances can be looked at as saying that the formulas (8.1) are a logical "explanation" of the concept $animal(X)$. Also, if we rewrite (8.1) using the substitution $\{T/taro\}$ as

$$\begin{aligned} &mammal(X) \rightarrow animal(X) \\ &human(Y) \rightarrow mammal(Y) \end{aligned} \tag{8.2}$$

we have the generalization that not only taro but also any human being is a positive instance of an animal.

Generalizing a logical explanation like this can be thought of as a kind of learning. Learning in this sense is called *explanation-based learning.* We will describe this kind of learning in this section.

(a) Explanation-based generalization

Explanation-based generalization is intuitively, as suggested in (8.1) and (8.2), the process of generalizing the logical relation between a concept and its positive instance by replacing constant symbols in well-formed formulas with variable symbols.

Explanation-based generalization can be formulated as a general algorithm using an algorithm for theorem proving. Let us first explain such an algorithm by an example.

Suppose the system wants to learn the relation between the concept "resort" and its positive instance. Suppose further that it knows that a resort is a place with nice weather and is good for a vacation. In other words

$$resort\_place(X) \leftrightarrow isa(X, place) \wedge refreshing(X) \wedge amusing(X) \tag{8.3}$$

is given as a *goal concept.* Here $\leftrightarrow$ is the logic symbol representing $\rightarrow$ and $\leftarrow$. Next, suppose that a description of one positive instance of the goal concept is given. For example, suppose we give a description of "sapporo" as a positive instance of "resort." The following conjunction (or equivalently a set) of ground literals is given:

$$\begin{aligned} &isa(sapporo, city) \\ &average\_temperature(sapporo, 18) \\ &average\_humidity(sapporo, 20) \\ &population\_density(sapporo, 100) \\ &average\_age(sapporo, 28) \\ &location(sapporo, north) \\ &facilities(sports, sapporo, best) \end{aligned} \tag{8.4}$$

Furthermore, as the *domain theory*, we give the following set of logic formulas:

$$
\begin{aligned}
& isa(X, city) \rightarrow isa(X, place) \\
& isa(X, place) \wedge average\_humidity(X, H) \wedge between(10, H, 30) \\
& \quad \rightarrow refreshing(X) \\
& isa(X, place) \wedge average\_age(X, A) \wedge between(20, A, 30) \\
& \quad \rightarrow place\_for\_young(X) \qquad (8.5) \\
& place\_for\_young(X) \wedge facilities(sports, X, best) \\
& \quad \rightarrow amusing(X) \\
& between(10, 20, 30) \\
& between(20, 28, 30) \\
& between(15, 18, 22)
\end{aligned}
$$

Using the formulas in (8.5) we can prove *resort_place*(*sapporo*) (the left side of (8.3)) from the description of "sapporo" given in (8.4). In other words, "sapporo" satisfies the goal concept "resort." Figure 8.1 shows the proof process using a proof tree.

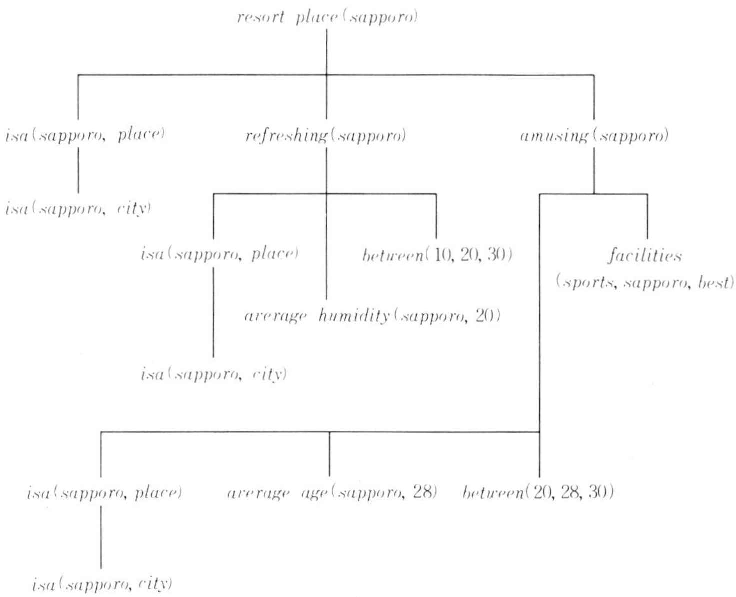

Figure 8.1 A proof tree for explanation

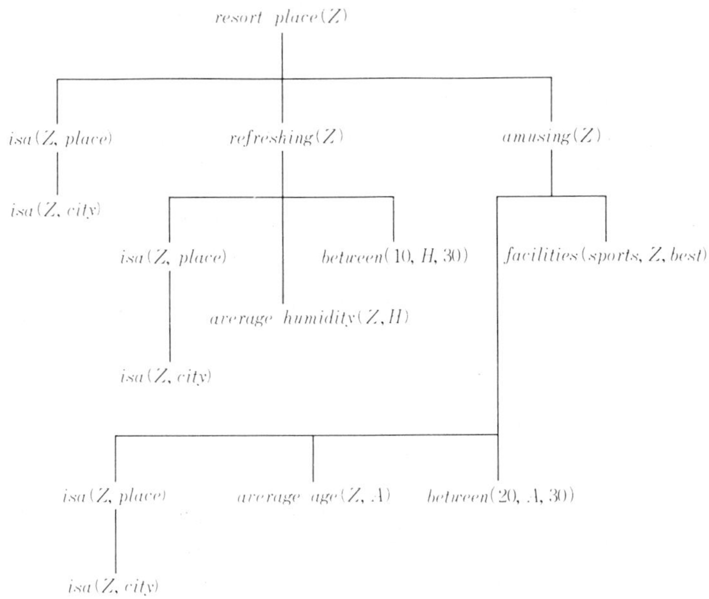

Figure 8.2 A generalized proof tree

A proof tree that shows the logical relation between a goal concept and one of its positive instances is called an *explanation structure* for the goal concept. In order to do generalization based on explanation, we first replace constant symbols in this explanation structure with variable symbols. For example, we propagate the substitution $\{Z/sapporo\}$ downward from the root node of the tree in Figure 8.1 in order to generalize the constant symbol "sapporo" to Z. For example, $resort\_place(sapporo)$ is generalized to $resort\_place(Z)$, and in the lower nodes we get $isa(Z, place)$, $refreshing(Z)$, $amusing(Z)$ as shown in Figure 8.2, where at each node the substitution into the formulas (8.3), (8.4), (8.5) is repeated. For example, at nodes under the node $refreshing(Z)$ in Figure 8.2, (8.5) provides the substitution $\{H/20\}$. As a result, the necessary substitution for obtaining a generalization of the whole proof tree shown in Figure 8.2 is $\{Z/sapporo, H/20, A/28\}$.

The proof tree shown in Figure 8.2 demonstrates that the well-formed formula at the root node can be proven from the conjunction of its leaves. That is,

$$\begin{aligned} &isa(Z, city) \wedge average\_humidity(Z, H) \wedge between(10, H, 30) \\ &\wedge average\_age(Z, A) \wedge between(20, A, 30) \\ &\wedge facilities(sports, Z, best) \rightarrow resort\_place(Z) \end{aligned} \tag{8.6}$$

Formula (8.6) generalizes and explains the goal concept *resort_place*(Z) using only predicates included in the description of the positive instance (8.4) (except for the predicate *between*). (8.6) can be read as "a city where the average humidity is between 10% and 30% and the average age of the residents is between 20 and 30 years old and there are good sports facilities is called a resort." The description (8.4) of the positive instance "sapporo" satisfies (8.6). (8.6) gives a sufficient condition for given data to be a positive instance of the goal concept.

In the above example, as in (8.6), the original concept can be described using only the predicates that appear in the description of the positive instance (except for the predicate *between*). However, this is generally not the case. Rather, in most cases the goal concept can only be explained using predicates that appear in the domain theory, but not in the positive instance. Finding these predicates is an interesting learning problem on a computer. The relation between the goal concept and a positive instance can be seen as a constraint on using some data as a positive instance of the goal concept. This constraint is generally called an *operationality criterion* (for the goal concept).

Let us formulate, in general terms, the algorithm for the explanation-based generalization that we explained above. First, let us make the problem clear.

[The problem of explanation-based generalization]

When the following are given:

(1) goal concept: a well-formed formula that describes the concept to be learned
(2) positive instance: a set of ground literals that describe a positive instance of the goal concept
(3) domain theory: a set of well-formed formulas that are related to the positive instance and the goal concept
(4) operationality criterion: a constraint on the positive instance for being usable as a positive instance of the goal concept,

the problem is to find

(5) a sufficient condition: a sufficient condition that is a well-formed formula satisfying the operational criterion and makes the given positive instance a positive instance of the goal concept.

For example, the operationality criterion of the problem in the "resort" example specifies that "a sufficient condition should be described only by the predicates that correspond to literals appearing in the positive instance."

Now, the basic algorithm for solving the above problem is described below. However, the following algorithm can sometimes fail. An example of this failure and its recovery will be explained in (b).

Algorithm 8.1 (explanation-based generalization)

[1] If the well-formed formula describing the goal concept satisfies the operational criterion, then stop. In this case, we do not need to generate a new sufficient condition by generalizing the positive instance. Otherwise, go to [2].

[2] Generate the explanation structure E of the goal concept c using the set of ground literals describing the positive instance, L, and the domain theory, M. E is the proof tree that corresponds to the proof of $L \cup M \vdash c$, where $L \cup M$ is a set of axioms.

[3] Find a substitution θ that makes $c = n_0\theta$ for c and the root node n_0 of E, and propagate this substitution downward from n_o to all the nodes of E.

[4] Do [3] for each node of E (other than the root node). If, for the literal l at each node, there is a literal X in M such that a substitution θ exists that makes $l = X\theta$, propagate the substitution using those literals. If such a literal X does not exist, then leave l as is.

[5] Construct the well-formed formula

$$C \rightarrow c$$

where C is the conjunction of the leaves in the generalized explanation structure that was obtained in [4]. This well-formed formula describes a desired sufficient condition.

(b) Generalization using upward propagation

The algorithm for explanation-based generalization described in (a) repeats the substitution at each node downward from the root node of the proof tree. There are some cases where this algorithm does not work.

We will consider these cases and explain how to deal with them using an example. Suppose we have the following explanation-based generalization problem.

[Example problem]

When the following are given:

(1) goal concept: $love(A, B)$

(2) positive example: $selfish(hanako)$
$good\_point(good\_proportion)$
$get(hanako, good\_proportion)$

(3) domain theory: $sympathetic(P,Q) \wedge attractive(R) \wedge have(P,R)$
$\rightarrow love(P,Q)$
$selfish(X) \rightarrow sympathetic(X,X)$
$good\_point(Y) \rightarrow attractive(Y)$
$get(Z,W) \rightarrow have(Z,W)$

(4) operationality criterion: The sufficient condition is described only using predicates that correspond to literals appearing in positive instances,

find

(5) sufficient condition: A well-formed formula that satisfies the operational criterion and gives a sufficient condition for the positive instance to be a positive instance of the goal concept.

First, if we apply Algorithm 8.1, we obtain in [2] the explanation structure shown in Figure 8.3. Then, in [3] and [4], we try to generate a generalized explanation structure. For example, $c = n_o\theta$ holds with the substitution $\theta = \{A/hanako, B/hanako\}$ for the goal concept of the problem, $c = love(A,B)$, and the root node of the proof tree shown in Figure 8.3, $n_o = love(hanako, hanako)$. So, we propagate the substitution downward using θ. Similarly, if we generalize the explanation structure in Figure 8.3, we obtain the generalized explanation structure shown in Figure 8.4 using the substitution $\{A/hanako, B/hanako, R/good\_proportion\}$. Figure 8.4 also shows the substitutions for deriving the tree. Note that the substitution is repeated at each node, making use of the domain theory.

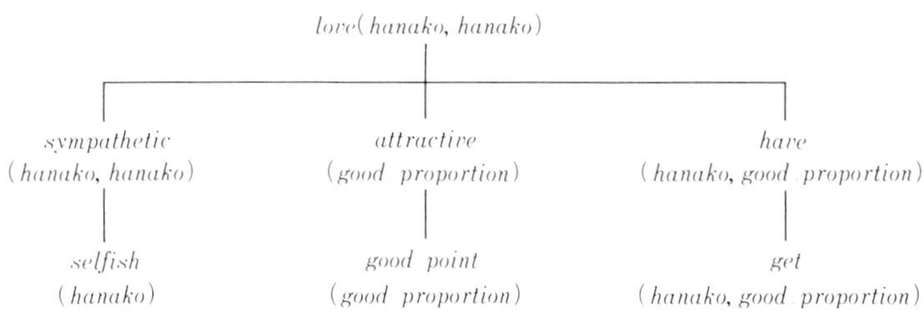

Figure 8.3 Explanation structure of the example problem.

Next, from the conjunction of the leaves of the generalized explanation structure in Figure 8.4, we obtain the following well-formed formula:

$$selfish(B) \wedge good\_point(R) \wedge get(B,R) \rightarrow love(A,B) \qquad (8.7)$$

However, the interpretation of (8.7) is "if B is selfish and has some good point, any A loves B." This is not what we expected.

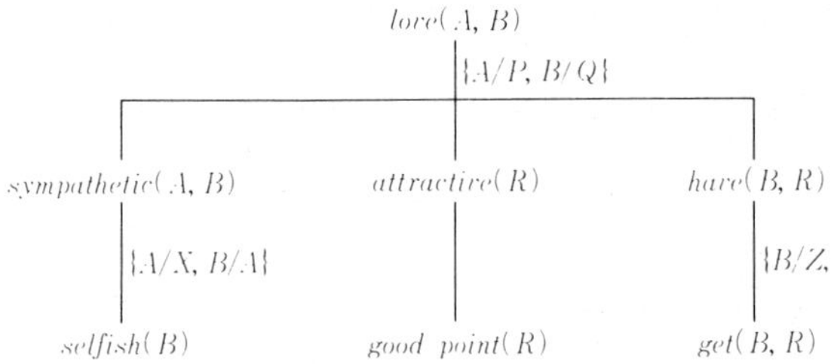

Figure 8.4 Generalized explanation structure ({ } shows substitutions into the domain theory).

This result is due to the fact that the goal concept, *love*(A, B), is too general compared to the domain theory used in generating the explanation structure in Figure 8.3. So, we try to generalize the appropriate goal concept by propagating the substitution upward from the leaves of the explanation structure, inverting the direction of propagation in [3], [4] in Algorithm 8.1.

For example, if we apply the domain theory to the leaves of the explanation structure in Figure 8.3 and propagate the substitution $\{X/hanako, Y/good\_proportion\}$ upward, we get the explanation structure shown in Figure 8.5. By using this explanation structure, we get the following new well-formed formula representing the relation between the goal concept and the positive instances:

$$selfish(X) \wedge good\_point(Y) \wedge get(X, Y) \rightarrow love(X, X) \tag{8.8}$$

This expression can be interpreted as "If X is selfish and has some good point, X loves himself." Also, using the formula (8.8), the goal concept, *love*(X, X), can be explained only using the predicates appearing in the description of the positive instance, and thus (8.8) satisfies the operationality criterion.

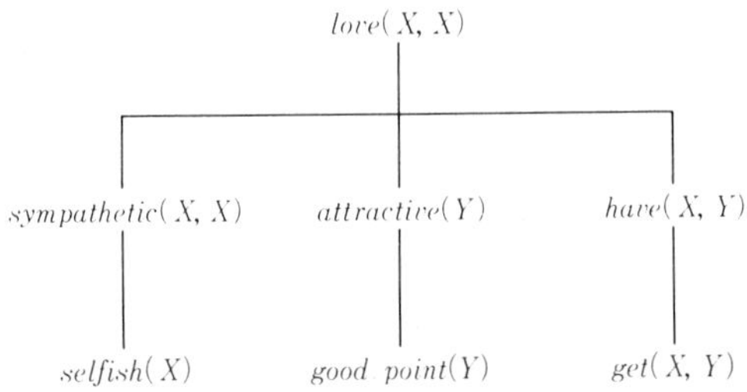

Figure 8.5 An explanation structure obtained by the upward propagation of substitution.

By generalizing the method explained above by example, we can change the algorithm in the following way:

Algorithm 8.2 (improved algorithm for explanation-based generalization)

We change [3] and [4] in Algorithm 8.1 to the following:

[3]′ Find a substitution θ that makes $X = l\theta$ for each leaf, l, of E and literal X in $L \cup M$, and propagate θ to all the nodes of E upward from l. If such a substitution does not exist, leave l as is.

[4]′ Do [3] to each node of E (other than leaves).

(c) Generalization by unification of Horn clauses

Upward propagation of substitutions in a proof tree is actually a special case of unification used in logical inference. On the other hand, unification can easily be done by executing a Prolog program if we limit the representation of formulas to Horn clause logic. Actually, full explanation-based generalization can easily be done using Prolog as long as we limit our representation to Horn clauses. We will describe a method of explanation-based generalization under Horn clause logic, using unification in Prolog.

First, let us remember that the following two trees were generated in our algorithm for the explanation-based generalization:

(i) A proof tree for proving the goal concept from a positive instance and domain theory. This tree does not contain variables.

(ii) A generalized proof tree that replaces the goal concept for the root node of the proof tree (i) with the original goal concept (that includes variables) and propagates this substitution to all the nodes of the tree.

These trees can be generated all at once using the Prolog program shown Figure 8.6. By executing this program, the proof trees (i) and (ii) are substituted into *ProofTree* and *GeneralizedProofTree*, respectively. Then, the desired sufficient condition can be obtained as the Horn clause whose head is the root node and whose body consists of the leaves of the proof tree that is substituted into *GeneralizedProofTree*. For example, the problem explained in (b) can be represented in Horn clause logic and can be rewritten as the Prolog program in Figure 8.7.

Now, for this program, let us compare the goal concept with constants, *love*(*hanako*, *hanako*), and the goal concept with variables *love*(A, B). For that, it is sufficient to generate the proof trees (i) and (ii) at the same time

```
explain(X,GeneralX,[X],[GeneralX]):-clause(X,true).
explain((X,Y),(GeneralX,GeneralY),ProofTree,
   GeneralizedProofTree):-
  explain(X,GeneralX,XProofTree,GeneralizedXProofTree),
  explain(Y,GeneralY,YProofTree,GeneralizedYProofTree),
  append(XProofTree,YProofTree,ProofTree),
  append(GeneralizedXProofTree,GeneralizedYProofTree,
     GeneralizedProofTree).
explain(X,GeneralX,[ProofTree[,[GeneralizedProofTree]):-
  clause(GeneralX,GeneralY),copy((GeneralX:-GeneralY),(X:-Y)),
  explain(Y,GeneralY,YProofTree,GeneralizedYProofTree),
  append([X].[YProofTree],ProofTree),
  append([GeneralX],[GeneralYProofTree],GeneralizeProofTree),
copy(OldTree,NewTree):-
  assert('$marker'(OldTree)),retract('$marker'(NewTree)).
```

Figure 8.6 A Prolog program for explanation-based generalization.

```
selfish(hanako).
good_point(good_proportion).
get(hanako,good_proportion).
love(P,Q):-sympathetic(P,Q),attractive( R),have(P,R).
sympathetic(X,X):-selfish(X).
attractive(Y):-good_point(Y).
have(Z,W):-get(Z,W).
```

Figure 8.7 A Prolog program for an example of explanation-based generalization.

by using the unification $\{A/hanako, B/hanako\}$. We use the following goal:

$$explain(love(hanako, hanako), love(A, B), ProofTree, GeneralizedProofTree) \tag{8.9}$$

If we generate the two proof trees (i) and (ii) using the goal (8.9) and the programs in Figure 8.6 and 8.7, we obtain the output shown in Figure 8.8. $\_4$ and $\_36$ are Prolog variables. From Figure 8.8, we notice that the variables in (8.9), A and B, are unified to the same variable $\_4$ and there occurred no problem of substitution such as described in (b). Using the leaves of the proof tree (ii) obtained in Figure 8.8 and the goal concept after the unification, we obtain the following Horn clause:

$$love(\_4,\_4) :- selfish(\_4), good\_point(\_36), get(\_4,\_36)$$

This is the same as the sufficient condition (8.8) that was obtained in (b).

```
|?-explain(love(hanako,hanako),love(A,B),ProofTree,
  GeneralizedProofTree).                                   ...goal

A=_4
B=_4                                                       ...unification

ProofTree=[[love(hanako,hanako),
            [sympathetic(hanako,hanako),[selfish(hanako)]],
            [attractive(good_proportion),
              [good_point(good_proportion)]],
            [have(hanako,good_proportion),
              [get(hanako,good_proportion)]]]]             ... proof tree (i)

GeneralizedProofTree=
            [[love(_4,_4),
              [sympathetic(_4,_4),[selfish(_4)]],
              [attractive(_36),[good_point(_36)]],
              [have(_4,_36),[get(_4,_36)]]]]               .... proof tree (ii)
```

Figure 8.8 Output from the Prolog program for explanation-based generalization.

8.2 Analogical Learning

(a) Analogical reasoning

Just as a cat eats a rat, a lion eats a zebra. We can represent this relation as follows where *eat* and *smaller_than* are predicate names:

$$eat(cat, rat) \tag{8.10}$$

$$eat(lion, zebra) \tag{8.11}$$

$$smaller\_than(cat, lion) \tag{8.12}$$

$$smaller\_than(rat, ?) \tag{8.13}$$

What should be in the place of ? in (8.13) can be easily inferred from the other three predicates. From (8.10) and (8.11), a cat corresponds to a lion and a rat corresponds to a zebra. From (8.12) a cat and a lion are related by "smaller-than," so we can infer that a zebra is related to a rat by "smaller-than." This kind of inference based on relations among objects is called *analogical reasoning*.

In analogical reasoning, we can make an inference even when there is not sufficient knowledge about an object to be inferred. Actually, we can generate new knowledge as the result of analogical reasoning. For example, though we have no knowledge of the size of a rat and a zebra before the above reasoning, the fact that a rat is smaller than a zebra can be inferred. This characteristic of analogical reasoning suggests that such reasoning is a kind of learning for obtaining new knowledge. If analogical reasoning is done in order to obtain new knowledge, such reasoning is called *learning by analogy*.

(b) Framework for learning by analogy

Let us make a relatively formal definition of learning by analogy. First, suppose we have two knowledge bases, $\mathcal{B}$ and $\mathcal{T}$. We assume that each element of $\mathcal{B}$ and $\mathcal{T}$ can be represented as a finite set of ground literals. For example, let $\mathcal{B}$ be the world of the solar system and $\mathcal{T}$ the world of atoms, and let us choose an element of $\mathcal{B}$, *earth*, and an element of $\mathcal{T}$, *electron*. These elements can be represented as the following sets of ground literals:

$$\begin{aligned} D_1 = \{&round\_body(earth), attracted(earth, sun), \\ &move\_around(earth, sun), trajectory(earth, circle)\} \\ D_2 = \{&round\_body(electron), attracted(electron, nucleus), \\ &probabilistic\_existence(electron)\} \end{aligned}$$

Now, let us give the following definition:

Definition 1 (similarity relation) Suppose P_1 and P_2 are finite sets of predicates and $q_1 \in P_1$, $q_2 \in P_2$ are predicates whose names are the same. Then the pair $\langle q_1, q_2 \rangle$ is said to be in a *similarity relation* on $P_1 \times P_2$.

For example, $\langle attracted(earth, sun), attracted(electron, nucleus) \rangle$ is in a similarity relation on $D_1 \times D_2$.

Now, for $\beta \in \mathcal{B}$ and $\tau \in \mathcal{T}$, the set of the predicates that are in a similarity relation on $\mathcal{B} \times \mathcal{T}$ can be written as

$$\begin{aligned} P_{\beta\times\tau} =\{&\langle p_1(x_{11}, \ldots, x_{1m_1}), p_1(y_{11}, \ldots, y_{1m_1}) \rangle, \\ &\langle p_2(x_{21}, \ldots, x_{2m_2}), p_2(y_{21}, \ldots, y_{2m_2}) \rangle, \\ &\ldots \\ &\langle p_n(x_{n1}, \ldots, x_{nm_n}), p_n(y_{n1}, \ldots, y_{nm_n}) \rangle\} \end{aligned} \tag{8.14}$$

where x_{jk}, y_{jk} $(1 \leq k \leq m_j, 1 \leq j \leq n)$ are terms. For example, in the above example, for $D_1 \in \mathcal{B}$, $D_2 \in \mathcal{T}$,

$$\begin{aligned} P_{D_1\times D_2} =\{&\langle round\_body(earth), round\_body(electron) \rangle \\ &\langle attracted(earth, sun), attracted(electron, nucleus) \rangle\} \end{aligned}$$

There are corresponding relations between the pairs of terms x_{jk} and y_{jk} ($k = 1, \ldots, m_j$) for each pair of predicates in the similarity relation, $p(x_{j1}, \ldots, x_{jm_j})$ and $p(y_{j1}, \ldots, y_{jm_j})$, $j = 1, \ldots, n$. For example, in $\langle$*attracted*(*earth*, *sun*), *attracted*(*electron*, *nucleus*)$\rangle$, the constant *earth* corresponds to *electron* and *sun* corresponds to *nucleus*.

If we substitute the same variable A_{jk} into the corresponding terms x_{jk} and y_{jk}, (8.14) becomes

$$Q_{\beta\times\tau} = \{p_1(A_{11}, \ldots, A_{1m_1}), p_2(A_{21}, \ldots, A_{2m_2}), \ldots, p_n(A_{n1}, \ldots, A_{nm_n})\}$$

For example, for $P_{D_1 \times D_2}$, we have

$$Q_{D_1\times D_2} = \{round\_body(X), attracted(X, Y)\} \tag{8.15}$$

where in order to restore $Q_{D_1\times D_2}$ to $P_{D_1\times D_2}$, we can use the pair of substitutions

$$\langle\{earth/X, sun/Y\}, \{electron/X, nucleus/Y\}\rangle \tag{8.16}$$

Now, let's summarize all of this. Let us write $Q_{\beta\times\tau}$ simply as Q and let $v(Q)$ be the set of variable symbols included in Q. Also, let us define the substitution θ as

$$\begin{aligned} \theta =& \langle\theta_1, \theta_2\rangle \\ \theta =& \{x_{jk}/A_{jk} | 1 \le k \le m_j, 1 \le j \le n\} \\ \theta_2 =& \{y_{jk}/A_{jk} | 1 \le k \le m_j, 1 \le j \le n\} \end{aligned}$$

We give the following definition:

Definition 2 (partial match) Suppose, for $\beta \in \mathcal{B}$ and $\tau \in \mathcal{T}$, β and τ are finite sets of ground literals without common constant symbols. If, for a set of literals in Q, $Q\theta \subseteq \beta \times \tau$ and $Q\theta$ and $v(Q)\theta$ are one-to-one relations, (Q, θ) is called a *generalized partial match* or simply a *partial match* of β and τ, or $\beta \times \tau$.

For example, in the previous example, if we let (8.15) and (8.16) be Q and θ, respectively, (Q, θ) is a partial match for $D_1 \times D_2$. For a given pair of sets, $\beta \times \tau$, there can be more than one partial match. A partial match is a (generalized) common part of the two sets; however, it can be a small part or a bigger part including the small part. Suppose we have

$$Q' = \{attracted(U, V)\} \tag{8.17}$$

$$\theta' = \langle\{earth/U, sun/V\}, \{electron/U, nucleus/V\}\rangle \tag{8.18}$$

Then $(Q'\theta')$ is a partial match for $D_1 \times D_2$, but intuitively it is smaller than (Q, θ). Now, let us define a partial order on partial matches as follows:

Definition 3 (partial ordering) Let (Q, θ) and (Q', θ') be two partial matches for a pair of given sets, $\beta \times \tau$. If there exists a substitution ξ such that $Q'\xi \subseteq Q$, and $W\theta' = W\xi\theta$ for any $W \in v(Q')$, we say that (Q, θ) is *bigger* than (Q', θ') and write $(Q, \theta) \geq (Q', \theta')$.

Definition 4 (maximal partial match) If, for partial matches (Q, θ) and (Q', θ') for $\beta \times \tau$, $(Q, \theta) \geq (Q', \theta')$ whenever $(Q', \theta') \geq (Q, \theta)$, we say that (Q, θ) is a (generalized) *maximal partial match* for $\beta \times \tau$.

In the example above, the partial match (Q, θ) defined in (8.15) and (8.16) is a maximal partial match for $D_1 \times D_2$. But the partial match (Q', θ') given in (8.17) and (8.18) is not maximal. Note that a maximal partial match for the same pair of sets is not unique.

Now, let us extend the notion of a partial match for a pair of sets, $\beta \times \tau \in \mathcal{B} \times \mathcal{T}$, to a partial match for a pair of relations. Suppose $\beta_1, \beta_2 \in \mathcal{B}$ are in relation b_{12}. For example, if we have

$$\begin{aligned} \beta_1 &= \{\mathit{move\_around}(\mathit{earth}, \mathit{sun}), \mathit{small}(\mathit{earth})\} \\ \beta_2 &= \{\mathit{large}(\mathit{sun})\} \\ b_{12} &= \{\mathit{move\_around}(X, Y), \mathit{small}(X)\} \times \{\mathit{large}(Y)\} \end{aligned} \tag{8.19}$$

b_{12} is the relation "A small object is moving around a big object."

Suppose, for $\tau_1 \in \mathcal{T}$ and $\beta_1 \in \mathcal{B}$, we know a maximal partial match m for $\beta_1 \times \tau_1$. Let us consider another set $\tau_2 \in \mathcal{T}$ such that m also is a maximal partial match for $\beta_2 \times \tau_2$ and the relation between τ_1 and τ_2 can be replaced by the relation b_{12}. We now define learning by analogy formally as follows:

Definition 5 (learning by analogy) Suppose, for $\beta_1, \beta_2 \in \mathcal{B}$, $\tau_1 \in \mathcal{T}$, and a relation b_{12} on $\mathcal{B} \times \mathcal{B}$, $\beta_1 \times \beta_2 \in b_{12}$ and a maximal partial match m for $\beta_1 \times \tau_1$ is known. Then, finding $\tau_2 \in \mathcal{T}$ such that $\tau_1 \times \tau_2 \in b_{12}$ and m is a maximal partial match for $\beta_2 \times \tau_2$ is called learning by analogy.

The relation among β_1, β_2, τ_1, and τ_2 in Definition 5 is shown in Figure 8.9. According to the above definition, learning by analogy looks for knowledge τ_2 in $\mathcal{T}$, which can be newly related to the already known knowledge b_{12} and m. As shown in Figure 8.9, we call the already known knowledge domain $\mathcal{B}$ the *base domain* and the unknown knowledge domain $\mathcal{T}$ the *target domain.*

For instance, in the previous example (8.19), let us make

$$\begin{aligned} \tau_1 = \{&\mathit{move\_around}(\mathit{electron}, \mathit{nucleus}), \mathit{small}(\mathit{electron}), \\ &\mathit{attracted}(\mathit{electron}, \mathit{nucleus})\} \end{aligned}$$

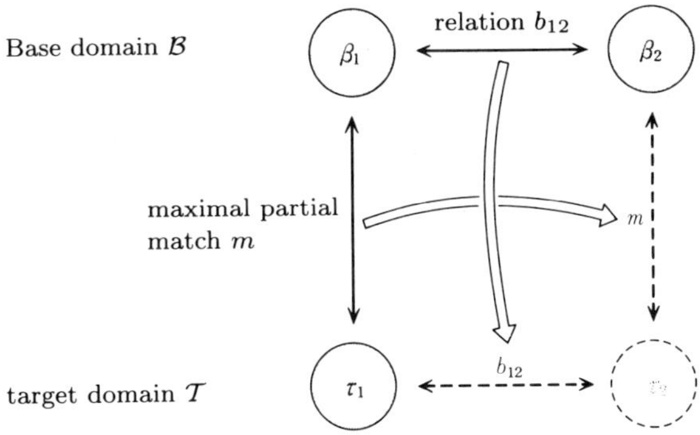

Figure 8.9 Learning by analogy.

and consider the following maximal partial match for $\beta_1 \times \tau_1$:

$$\begin{aligned} m &= (Q, \theta) = (Q, \langle \theta_1, \theta_2 \rangle) \\ &= (\{move\_around(X, Y), small(X)\}, \\ &\quad \langle \{earth/X, sun/Y\}, \{electron/X, nucleus/Y\} \rangle) \end{aligned}$$

By computing $b_{12}\theta_2$, we obtain

$$\{move\_around(electron, nucleus)\} \times \{large(nucleus)\}$$

So, we can set

$$\tau_2 = \{large(nucleus)\}$$

In Definition 5 we defined learning by analogy as operations that mapped a relation on sets in the base domain to the target domain based on partial match, m. There are many other methods of learning by analogy that are not based on this operation.

(c) Examples of learning by analogy

Let us consider an example of learning by analogy where the base domain $\mathcal{B}$ and the target domain $\mathcal{T}$ are state spaces in problem solving and a relation b_{12} on $\beta_1, \beta_2 \in \mathcal{B}$ is defined by transition rules from the state β_1 to the state β_2.

Consider the blocks world shown in Figure 8.10. If state $\langle 1 \rangle$ changes into state $\langle 2 \rangle$, what state may $\langle 3 \rangle$ change into?

If each state is given by a finite set of ground literals as in Figure 8.10, a maximal partial match of $\langle 1 \rangle$ and $\langle 3 \rangle$ would be, for example,

$$\begin{aligned} &(\{on(X, Y), cleartop(X), square(X), square(Y)\}, \\ &\langle \{a/X, b/Y\}, \{e/X, f/Y\} \rangle) \end{aligned} \tag{8.20}$$

Certainly there are other maximal partial matches. For example, both

$$(\{on(X,Y), ontable(Y), square(X), square(Y)\},$$
$$\langle\{a/X, b/Y\}, \{f/X, g/Y\}\rangle)$$

and

$$(\{cleartop(X), ontable(Y), square(X), square(Y)\},$$
$$\langle\{a/X, b/Y\}, \{e/X, g/Y\}\rangle)$$

are also maximal partial matches of $\langle 1\rangle$ and $\langle 3\rangle$.

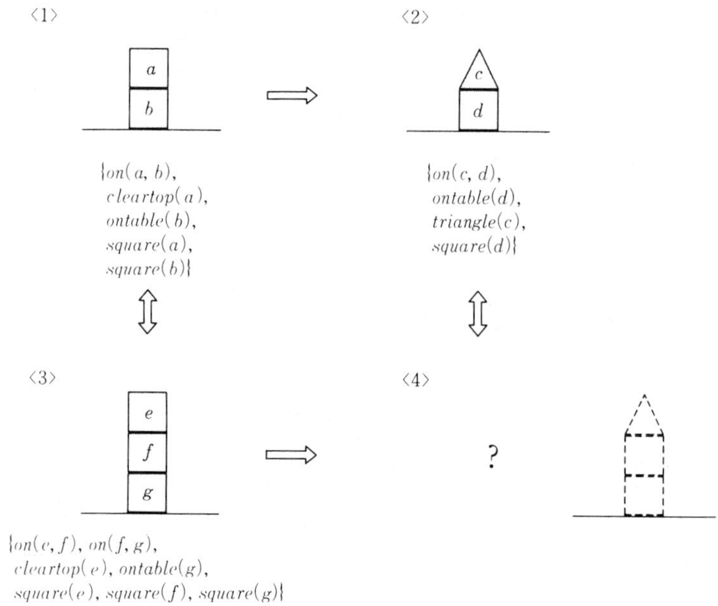

Figure 8.10 Example of learning by analogy.

Next, let us represent the state change from $\langle 1\rangle$ to $\langle 2\rangle$ by the transformation

$$\langle 1\rangle\text{-}(\langle 1\rangle \cap \langle 2\rangle) \Rightarrow \langle 2\rangle\text{-}(\langle 2\rangle \cap \langle 1\rangle) \qquad (8.21)$$

where $\langle i\rangle$-$(\langle i\rangle \cap \langle j\rangle)$ can generally be found using the following steps:

[1] Suppose $(Q, \langle\theta_1, \theta_2\rangle)$ is one of the maximal partial matches of $\langle i\rangle$ and $\langle j\rangle$. Then let $Q = \langle i\rangle \cap \langle j\rangle$.
[2] Do the substitution θ_1 to $\langle i\rangle$-$(\langle i\rangle \cap \langle j\rangle)$.
[3] Use for (8.21) the set of generalized literals obtained in [2].

For example, suppose we use the formula (8.20) as a maximal partial match. If we apply the substitution $\{a/X, b/Y\}$ to $\langle 1 \rangle$ (including literals other than those in (8.20)), $\langle 1 \rangle$ is generalized to

$$\{on(X,Y), cleartop(X), ontable(Y), square(X), square(Y)\} \tag{8.22}$$

Similarly, $\langle 2 \rangle$ is generalized to

$$\{on(X,Y), ontable(Y), triangle(X), square(Y)\}$$

by the substitution $\{c/X, d/Y\}$. Therefore, (8.21) can be written as

$$\{cleartop(X), square(X)\} \Rightarrow \{triangle(X)\} \tag{8.23}$$

If we apply the substitution given in (8.20) to parts other than the maximal partial match in $\langle 3 \rangle$, $\langle 3 \rangle$ is generalized to

$$\{on(X,Y), on(Y,Z), cleartop(X), ontable(Z), square(X), \\ square(Y), square(Z)\} \tag{8.24}$$

If we replace the part in (8.24) that matches the left side of (8.23) with the right side of (8.23), we obtain

$$\{on(X,Y), triangle(X), square(Y), on(Y,Z), \\ ontable(Z), square(Z)\} \tag{8.25}$$

(8.25) represents state $\langle 4 \rangle$ that can be found based on learning by analogy. (8.25) can be illustrated as the broken lines in Figure 8.10.

Let us summarize the above description as a general algorithm. We assume that $\beta_1, \beta_2 \in \mathcal{B}$ and $\tau_1 \in \mathcal{T}$ are given for the base domain $\mathcal{B}$ and the target domain $\mathcal{T}$, and β_1, β_2, τ_1 do not have common constant symbols.

Algorithm 8.3 (learning by analogy)

[1] Find a maximal partial match m of β_1 and τ_1. (In the example, (8.22))
[2] Find a relation b_{12} of β_1 and β_2. (In the example, (8.23))
[3] Let τ_1' be the generalization of τ_1 using m. (In the example, (8.24))
[4] Find the element τ_2 of $\mathcal{T}$ that corresponds to β_2 using τ_1' and b_{12}. (In the example, (8.25))

As we noted in (b), the important aspects of learning by analogy are that there is generally more than one maximal partial match for sets of literals and that a different analogy is found based on which maximal partial match is used. In the above example, a different analogy will be produced if we use another common part.

8.3 Nonmonotonic Logic and Learning

(a) Inference by nonmonotonic logic

Predicate logic is a just one kind of formal logic, but it sometimes cannot represent commonsense knowledge. Let us look at an example.

Let us represent the facts "tweety is a fish," "a fish breathes through a gill," "a mermaid is a fish," "a mermaid does not breathe through a gill" by the set of axioms

$$\begin{aligned} A = \{ & \mathit{fish}(\mathit{tweety}), \\ & \forall X(\mathit{fish}(X) \rightarrow \mathit{respiration}(X, \mathit{gills}(X))), \\ & \forall X(\mathit{mermaid}(X) \rightarrow \mathit{fish}(X)), \\ & \forall X(\mathit{mermaid}(X) \rightarrow {\sim}\mathit{respiration}(X, \mathit{gills}(X)))\} \end{aligned}$$

where *gills* is a function symbol. Also, let us consider the set consisting only of *modus ponens*

$$\frac{P, P \rightarrow Q}{Q} \tag{8.26}$$

as the set of inference rules. Now if we apply (8.26) to A, we can prove as a theorem

$$\mathit{respiration}(\mathit{tweety}, \mathit{gills}(\mathit{tweety})) \tag{8.27}$$

that is, the fact "tweety breathes through the gills." However, suppose we later learn that "tweety is a mermaid." If we add this to A and make the new set of axioms

$$A' = A \cup \{\mathit{mermaid}(\mathit{tweety})\}$$

(8.27) no longer holds and we have two inconsistent theorems:

$$\mathit{respiration}(\mathit{tweety}, \mathit{gills}(\mathit{tweety}))$$
$${\sim}\mathit{respiration}(\mathit{tweety}, \mathit{gills}(\mathit{tweety}))$$

(This implies that any well-formed formula is a logical consequence of A'.)

This contradiction occurs because a fact included in A' has exceptions. In other words, the fact that a fish "usually" breathes through a gill but that a mermaid does not breathe through a gill even if it is a fish leads to a contradiction. The commonsense knowledge of human beings contains many such exceptions, and as the above example shows, a fact often stops being a fact when new knowledge is added. In this case, $S(A) \subseteq S(A \cup B)$ does not hold, where $S(X)$ is the set of theorems that can be proved from a set of axioms X. This kind of logical inference is called inference by *nonmonotonic logic.*

On the other hand, in ordinary predicate logic, $S(A) \subseteq S(A \cup B)$ always holds. In other words, if a theorem g can be proved from A by I, then g

can also be proved by I from $A \cup \{a\}$ if a is a well-formed formula with the value of T. Logical inference with this monotonicity property is called inference by *monotonic logic.*

Inference by nonmonotonic logic checks if a contradiction occurs with the already proved theorems every time a new fact is added to the set of axioms. If a contradiction occurred, the system needs to correct and generate a new set of theorems. This can be considered to be learning in the sense that existing knowledge changes due to new information.

(b) Default reasoning

First we will explain default reasoning, a kind of reasoning using nonmonotonic logic. Consider the following inference rule:

$$\frac{P(X_1, \ldots, X_n) : Q(X_1, \ldots, X_n)}{R(X_1, \ldots, X_n)}$$

where P, Q, and R are n-place predicates, and $X_1, \ldots, X_n$ are variable symbols. The above rule can be read as "if $P(X_1, \ldots, X_n)$ is true and $Q(X_1, \ldots, X_n)$ does not contradict other knowledge, then we assume that $R(X_1, \ldots, X_n)$ is true." Such a rule is generally called a *default inference rule.*

In the default inference rule, we call P the premise, Q the assumption, and R the *hypothesis.* Note that we call it an hypothesis rather than a theorem. This is because the truth value of well-formed formulas obtained so far can change when a new fact is introduced. The set of hypotheses that are obtained using a set of default inference rules is called the *extension* of default reasoning.

Suppose we have a set of axioms A, a set of inference rules of ordinary predicate logic I, and a set of default inference rules K. Then, generating from A a set of hypotheses that contain the well-formed formula g using $I \cup K$ is called *default reasoning.*

In the example in (a), default reasoning means deriving

$$respiration(X, gills(X))$$

as a hypothesis using the default inference rule

$$\frac{fish(X) : respiration(X, gills(X))}{respiration(X, gills(X))} \tag{8.28}$$

In this example, $respiration(X, gills(X))$ is assumed not to contradict $\sim mermaid(X)$. Default inference rules often have the form where the assumption and hypothesis are identical, as in (8.28). This kind of default inference rule is generally called a *normal default inference rule*, and default reasoning based on a normal default inference rule is called reasoning based on *normal default theory.*

In default reasoning, the set of hypotheses to be found varies according to the order of application of default inference rules that generate hypotheses. For example, suppose "a substance is either a gas, a liquid, or a solid" is given as a fact. We represent this fact as the set of axioms

$$A = \{gas(X) \vee liquid(X) \vee solid(X)\}$$

Furthermore, we define the inference rule "if a solid cannot be determined to be a gas (liquid or solid), assume that it is not a gas (liquid or solid)" as the following three default inference rules:

$$\underset{\text{(i)}}{\frac{: \sim gas(X)}{\sim gas(X)}} \qquad \underset{\text{(ii)}}{\frac{: \sim liquid(X)}{\sim liquid(X)}} \qquad \underset{\text{(iii)}}{\frac{: \sim solid(X)}{\sim solid(X)}}$$

The set of hypotheses derived from A depends on which rule is applied first. For example,

If (i) is applied ... $\{\sim gas(X), liquid(X) \vee solid(X)\}$
If (ii) is applied ... $\{\sim liquid(X), gas(X) \vee solid(X)\}$
If (iii) is applied ... $\{\sim solid(X), gas(X) \vee liquid(X)\}$

As you can see from this example, default reasoning often generates more than one extension. Which extension to use cannot be determined purely by logical inference. It is determined by the purpose of the inference system and its interaction with the outside world.

The inference rules (i)–(iii) above are special cases of the rule

$$\frac{: \sim P(X_1, \dots, X_n)}{\sim P(X_1, \dots, X_n)} \tag{8.29}$$

for an n-place predicate $P(X_1, \dots, X_n)$. (8.29) can be read "If the value of $P(X_1, \dots, X_n)$ cannot be determined to be T, we assume the value is F." Logical inference on a computer sometimes assumes that $\sim P$ is proved if it cannot find a proof that P is T. This assumption is called the *closed world assumption.* We can use an inference rule like (8.29) to make the closed world assumption part of a default reasoning system.

Now we give an algorithm for default reasoning using normal default theory. Let A be a set of axioms, I a set of inference rules of predicate logic, K a set of normal default rules, and g the well-formed formula to be proved. We use $f(k)$ and $h(k)$ for the premise and the hypothesis of a rule k, respectively. For any $k \in K$, we define the subset $L \subseteq K$ as

$$f(L) = \wedge_{k \in L} f(k)$$
$$h(L) = \wedge_{k \in L} h(k)$$

where $\wedge_{k \in L}$ means the conjunction of all k in L. Furthermore, for A, g, and any $L \subseteq K$, we assume that $f(L)$ and $h(L)$ are represented as a set of clauses. Now, let us consider the following algorithm:

Algorithm 8.4 (default reasoning)

[1] Assume the value of $h(K)$ is T and set $D = A \wedge h(K)$ where A is regarded as a conjunction. Try to prove $D \vdash g$. We can do this by trying to prove $D \cup \{\sim g\}$ using the theorem proving algorithm based on the resolution principle.

[2] Let L be the subset of K, the set of default inference rules, whose hypothesis appears in the formulas used during the proof process of [1]. If $L = \emptyset$, go to [4]. Otherwise, set $N = N \cup h(L)$ and go to [3].

[3] Do the proof $A \cup h(L) \vdash f(L)$. Go to [2].

[4] Prove that N is satisfiable.

To find the set L in Algorithm 8.4 [2] we should keep the list of the default inference rules that were used in each theorem proving step. In the framework of first-order predicate logic, it is known that there does not exist a procedure that can determine the consistency of the set N as required in [4]. Therefore, in [4], we need to use some heuristic method to determine consistency.

Let us assume that, when [4] is executed in the above algorithm, g is found as a hypothesis from A, I, and K. The conditions that g is found as a hypothesis can be summarized as follows (this is another way of explaining the algorithm):

(i) $A \cup h(K) \vdash g$.

(ii) Subsets $L_1, \ldots, L_m$ of K exist and $A \cup h(L_i) \vdash f(L_i)$.

(iii) $L_m = \emptyset$.

(iv) $A \cup h(L_1) \cup h(L_2) \cup \ldots \cup h(L_m)$ is satisfiable in the sense of first-order predicate logic.

We can rephrase the definition of default reasoning to be reasoning that satisfies (i)–(iv) above. Generating hypotheses from incomplete knowledge using default reasoning is an example of learning based on knowledge. We also need to remember that there may be more than one extension, that is, the set of hypotheses generated by default reasoning, depending on the order of using the default inference rules.

(c) Truth maintenance system (TMS)

The default reasoning described in (b) is a method of inference for generating hypotheses from incomplete knowledge. If we consider cases where new knowledge is incrementally added to the knowledge base, we sometimes need to change hypotheses that have already been added. For example, as in the example shown in (a), when the new fact

$$mermaid(tweety)$$

is added to the set of axioms

$$\begin{aligned} A = \{&fish(tweety),\\ &\forall X(fish(X) \to respiration(X, gills(X))),\\ &\forall X(mermaid(X) \to fish(X)),\\ &\forall X(mermaid(X) \to \sim respiration(X, gills(X)))\} \end{aligned}$$

the hypothesis that had been obtained

$$respiration(X, gills(X))$$

no longer holds as a hypothesis.

Let us look at a *truth maintenance system* (we will call it a TMS) as an algorithm for changing hypotheses and maintaining the consistency of hypotheses. The TMS is related to default reasoning in the sense that both change hypotheses, but, as we show below, the former can be formalized as an algorithm that is seemingly unrelated to the latter. In order to avoid confusion, we will use the term *belief* rather than hypothesis below.

We consider an abstract object called belief that has two states, the *In state* and the *Out state*. Whether the state of a belief is In or Out depends on the states of other beliefs. More concretely, we say that the state of a belief b_0 is In only when other beliefs $b_1, \ldots, b_i$ are all in the In state and $b_{i+1}, \ldots b_j$ are all in the Out state. If we interpret the In state as "believe" and the Out state as "do not believe," the above can be read as "we believe b_0 only when we believe $b_1, \ldots, b_i$ and do not believe $b_{i+1}, \ldots, b_j$."

When a new state of a belief is given, a TMS finds beliefs that can be justified by this state and, at the same time, computes all the state changes of other beliefs due to this justification.

A TMS is a system that nonmonotonically keeps consistency of dependency relations among current beliefs: a new belief state is inferred by another inference system and sent to the TMS. The relation between a TMS and an inference system is shown in Figure 8.11.

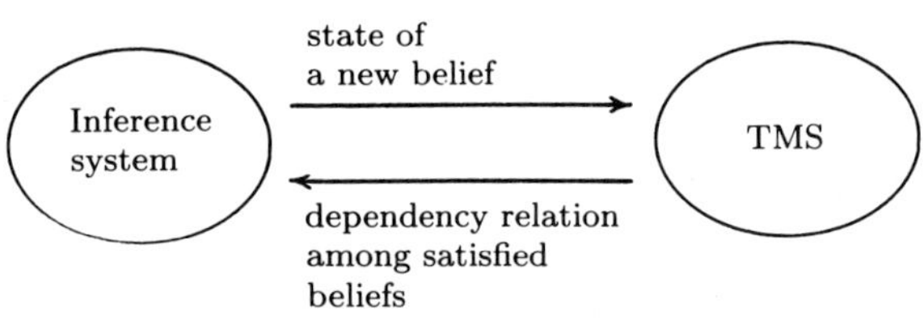

Figure 8.11 Relation between a TMS and an inference system.

Below we explain the representation of belief in a TMS and an algorithm for keeping the consistency of belief states. Note that an algorithm for a TMS is not related to what kind of knowledge representation is used for inference.

We represent a belief as a pair of a node and a *justification*:

$$\langle \text{node name} \rangle : \langle \text{justification} \rangle$$

A node name is the label for a belief. A justification is defined as a list with the meaning of (1) or (2) described below. Below $\langle In\ \text{list}\rangle$ and $\langle Out\ \text{list}\rangle$ are lists of node names, and $\langle\text{result}\rangle$ is a node name. A pair of $\langle In\ \text{list}\rangle$ and $\langle Out\ \text{list}\rangle$ described in a justification is called a *support list.*

(1) *Support list justification: SL*

$$(SL\ \langle In\ \text{list}\rangle\ \langle Out\ \text{list}\rangle)$$

The state of a node becomes In only when all the nodes included in its in list, $\langle In\ \text{list}\rangle$, are in the In state and all the nodes in its out list, $\langle Out\ \text{list}\rangle$, are in the Out state.

(2) *Conditional proof justification: CP*

$$(CP\ \langle\text{result}\rangle\ \langle In\ \text{list}\rangle\ \langle Out\ \text{list}\rangle)$$

The state of a node becomes In only when the states of the nodes in $\langle\text{result}\rangle$ become In under the condition that the states of all the nodes of $\langle In\ \text{list}\rangle$ are In and the states of all the nodes of $\langle Out\ \text{list}\rangle$ are Out.

For example,

$$N1:\ (SL\ (N3\ N5)\ (N4\ N7))$$

means that, when $N3$ and $N5$ are in the In state and $N4$ and $N7$ are in the Out state, the node $N1$ is in the In state, and otherwise $N1$ is in the Out state. Also,

$$N4:\ (CP\ N6\ (N1\ N5)\ (N8))$$

means that, if an inference system believes $N6$ under the condition that it believes $N1$ and $N5$ but does not believe $N8$, then $N4$ is in the In state, and otherwise $N4$ is in the Out state.

There are three kinds of support list justifications:

(i) When $\langle In\ \text{list}\rangle = \langle Out\ \text{list}\rangle = \emptyset$. The state of the corresponding node is always In. A belief with this justification is called a *premise.*

(ii) When $\langle In\ \text{list}\rangle \neq \emptyset$ and $\langle Out\ \text{list}\rangle = \emptyset$. A belief with this justification is monotonic in the sense that the state of the corresponding node does not change even when the nodes in the In state are added.

(iii) When ⟨*Out* list⟩ $\neq \emptyset$. For a belief with this justification, the state of the corresponding node can change as nodes in the *In* state are added. This belief is called an *assumption.*

A TMS holds beliefs and their states as defined above. Every time a new belief is input, it generates the states that do not contradict each other and outputs these states. In order to change the state of a belief, we can use some search algorithm. What we need to be careful of is that a nonmonotonic change can happen due to the fact that the state of a belief in a support list changes, or a new belief is entered into the support list and the corresponding justification can no longer be supported.

As an example, let us consider the set of beliefs shown in Figure 8.12. Figure 8.12 shows the states of beliefs about starting times and the type of transportation to use. These are input from an inference system for managing business trip schedules.

node name	meaning	justification	state of belief
N_1	use a train:	$(SL\ (\ )\ (N2))$	*In*
N_2	use an air plane:		*Out*
N_3	time=8:00:	$(SL\ (\ )\ (N4))$	*In*
N_4	time≠8:00:		*Out*

Figure 8.12 An example problem for TMS.

Suppose that the inference system found a contradiction between beliefs $N1$ and $N3$. (For example, it found that there is no train leaving at 8:00 due to a change in the train schedule.) The TMS adds the following two beliefs to the set of the original beliefs, and makes the states of both beliefs *In*:

$$N5\ CONTRADICTION:\ (SL\ (N1,\ N3)\ (\ )) \tag{8.30}$$

$$N6\ (NOGOOD\ (N1\ N3):\ (CP\ N5\ (N1\ N3)\ (\ )) \tag{8.31}$$

where (8.31) can also be described as

$$N6\ (NOGOOD\ N1\ N3):\ (SL\ (\ )\ (\ ))$$

Next, the TMS sets the state of (8.30) to *Out* and changes the state so that the states of the beliefs $N1$–$N6$ are consistent. The result is shown in Figure 8.13(a).

Now let us imagine that the inference system finds that $N2$ cannot be believed (for example, due to the information that dense fog has shut the

(a) Belief and its state 1

$N1$	use a train: $(SL\ (\ )\ (N2))$	*Out*
$N2$	use an air plane: $(SL\ (N6\ N1)\ (\ ))$	*In*
$N3$	time=8:00: $(SL\ (\ )\ (N4))$	*In*
$N4$	time≠8:00:	*Out*
$N5$	*CONTRADICTION*: $(SL\ (N1\ N3)\ (\ ))$	*Out*
$N6$	(*NOGOOD* N1 N3): $(CP\ N5\ (N1\ N3)\ (\ ))$	*In*

(b) Belief and its state 2

$N1$	use train: $(SL\ (\ )\ (N2))$	*In*
$N2$	use an air plane: $(SL\ (N6\ N1)\ (\ ))$	*Out*
$N3$	time=8:00: $(SL\ (\ )\ (N4))$	*Out*
$N4$	time≠8:00: $(SL\ (N8)\ (\ ))$	*In*
$N5$	*CONTRADICTION*: $(SL\ (N1\ N3)\ (\ ))$	*Out*
$N6$	(*NOGOOD* N1 N3): $(CP\ N5\ (N1\ N3)\ (\ ))$	*In*
$N7$	*CONTRADICTION*: $(SL\ (N2)\ (\ ))$	*Out*
$N8$	(*NOGOOD* N3): $(CP\ N7\ (N3)\ (\ ))$	*In*

Figure 8.13 Execution result of the example problem for TMS.

airport). Then, the TMS generates the new beliefs with the *In* state,

$$N7\ CONTRADICTION:\ (SL\ (N2)\ (\ )) \tag{8.32}$$

$$N8\ (NOGOOD\ N3):\ (CP\ N7\ (N3)\ (\ )) \tag{8.33}$$

and adds them to the set of beliefs in Figure 8.13(a). Here (8.33) can also be described as

$$N8\ (NOGOOD\ N3):\ (SL\ (N6)\ (\ ))$$

Next, the TMS sets the state of (8.32) to *Out* and changes the state so that the states $N1$–$N8$ are consistent. The result is shown in Figure 8.13(b). The result shows that, since $N1$ and $N4$ are *In* and $N2$ and $N3$ are *Out*, we can keep the dependency relations among beliefs consistent if we use a train that leaves at any time other than 8:00.

(d) Assumption-based truth maintenance system (ATMS)

In the TMS described in (c), the only information associated with each node is its justification. Such justifications can only refer to local belief relations in order to maintain global consistency among beliefs. As a result, the computation is generally slow and the search for state change might get into a loop when using relations among nodes described only in the justifications. In order to eliminate these problems, it is sufficient to compute the set of hypotheses globally covering all the nodes from justifications. A system for computing the set of global hypotheses and, at the same time, maintaining dependency relations among beliefs is called an *assumption-based truth maintenance system* (*ATMS* hereafter).

Like a TMS, an ATMS receives information on relations among beliefs from an inference system and changes the dependency relations of beliefs so that they are consistent. However, unlike a TMS, it does not use the concept of the state of a belief. Instead, it always maintains and can change the whole set of hypotheses for keeping consistency among beliefs.

A node in an ATMS is represented as follows:

$$\text{node name: } \langle \text{the name of data, label, justification} \rangle$$

Here "the name of data" is information about a belief that is handled by the inference system and is given to the ATMS as data. Also, a justification is sent from the inference system in the form of

$$a_1, a_2, \ldots, a_m \Rightarrow b$$

where $a_1, \ldots, a_m$ (called the *antecedents*) are names of data, and b (called the *consequent*) is the name of a node of the ATMS. Furthermore, a special node called the *contradiction node* is defined in the ATMS, and if antecedents contradict each other, b becomes the contradiction node.

For any node, we call the set of names of data that can maintain consistency of beliefs a *hypothesis*. A hypothesis is computed from justifications using the algorithm given below. A set of possible hypotheses is called a *label*.

When a name of data and a justification are sent to the ATMS from the inference system, the label of the node that appears in the consequent of the justification is updated using the following algorithm:

Algorithm 8.5 (updating a label in an ATMS)

[1] Using [1.1]–[1.4], repeat updating the label for a node given in the consequent for each of the justifications sent from the inference system. There, first update the labels of nodes that include the node whose label is changed in the antecedents of the justification.

- [1.1] Obtain a label for $\vee_k \wedge_i L_{ik}$ and compute L_{ik}. Here L_{ik} is the kth hypothesis at the node corresponding to the ith element in the antecedents of the justification.
- [1.2] Of elements in the label obtained in [1.1], remove redundant or contradictory ones.
- [1.3] When the new label is equal to the original label, stop. Otherwise, go to [1.4].
- [1.4] When the node is the contradictory node, add the hypotheses

to the database called *NOGOOD*, and remove all the contradictory hypotheses from the labels of all nodes.

As an example, let us consider the problem described in (c) (Figure 8.12). The node representations of the inference system and the ATMS for this problem are given in Figure 8.14(a) and (b).

(a) nodes of the inference system	(b) nodes of the ATMS
I1: use a train	$N1 : \langle I1, \{\{I1\}\}, \{(I1)\}\rangle$
I2: use an air plane	$N2 : \langle I2, \{\{I2\}\}, \{(I2)\}\rangle$
I3: time=8:00	$N3 : \langle I3, \{\{I3\}\}, \{(I3)\}\rangle$
I4: time≠8:00	$N4 : \langle I4, \{\{I4\}\}, \{(I4)\}\rangle$

Figure 8.14 An example problem for ATMS.

Suppose the information that nodes $I1$ and $I2$ and nodes $I3$ and $I4$ are contradictory is sent to the ATMS from the inference system. Then the ATMS generates the following *NOGOOD* database:

$$NOGOOD\{\{I1, I2\}, \{I3, I4\}\}$$

where the information from the inference system is given in the form of the justifications

$$I1 \wedge I2 \Rightarrow \perp$$
$$I3 \wedge I4 \Rightarrow \perp$$

Here $\perp$ represents the contradictory node. As a result, of the 16 possible combinations of the hypotheses, there are nine consistent hypotheses that are circled in Figure 8.15. These nine hypotheses constitute the set of hypotheses at this time. Now, if the information that $I1$ and $I3$ are contradictory is sent to the ATMS using the justification

$$I1 \wedge I3 \Rightarrow \perp$$

the hypothesis $\{I1, I3\}$ becomes contradictory and is removed from the set of hypotheses. Also, $\{I1, I3\}$ is added to the *NOGOOD* database. Furthermore, if the justification

$$I2 \Rightarrow \perp$$

is sent to the ATMS, the hypothesis $\{I2\}$ and any hypothesis including $I2$ are removed from the set of hypotheses, and $\{I2\}$ is added to the *NOGOOD* database.

The set of hypotheses obtained so far is

$$\{\{\ \}, \{I1\}, \{I3\}, \{I4\}, \{I1, I4\}\}$$

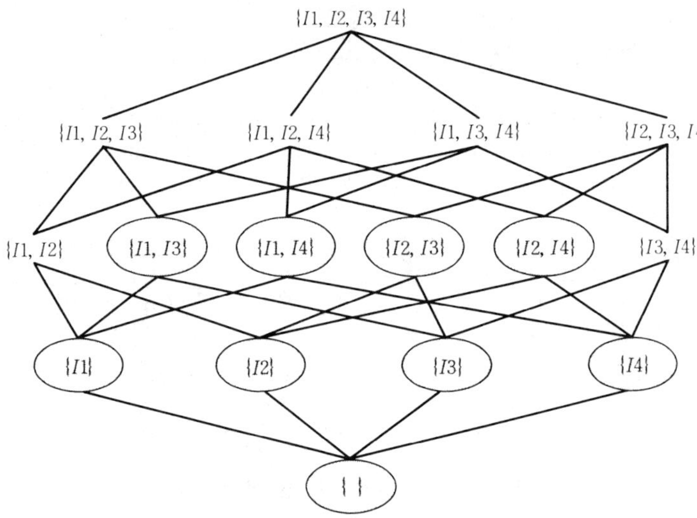

Figure 8.15 A set of hypotheses for the ATMS example.

This shows that the nodes $I1$ and $I4$ are not contradictory; in other words, using a train that leaves at any time other than 8:00 does not contradict the schedule.

As we can see from the above example, an ATMS uses an algorithm based on the updating of the set of hypotheses that are not contradictory or redundant, not the states of beliefs. This algorithm only requires removing hypotheses that cause contradiction from the set of hypotheses. It does not require local search of justifications as in a TMS.

Summary

In this chapter, we described algorithms for learning by generalization based on logical inference and methods of truth maintenance of hypotheses based on nonmonotonic logic.

8.1 Explanation-based generalization is a method of finding an explanation for how an instance is a positive instance of a given concept using the concept and one positive instance of it and generalizing a proof tree that is found by theorem proving.

8.2 If we restrict the representation to Horn clause logic, we can write a program for explanation-based generalization in Prolog.

8.3 Learning by analogy is done by finding a maximal partial match for two sets of literals.

8.4 Nonmonotonic logic can be used for learning based on logical inference. Default reasoning using default inference rules is one popular example.

8.5 A truth maintenance system (TMS) is a system for generating a set of new hypotheses by checking local consistency of existing hypotheses, when new facts are incrementally added to the knowledge base.

8.6 An assumption-based truth maintenance system (ATMS) is a system that generates a set of new hypotheses by checking the global consistency of the set of hypotheses.

Keywords

explanation-based generalization, goal concept, domain theory, operationality criterion, Horn clause logic, unification, analogy, learning by analogy, partial match, maximal partial match, nonmonotonic logic, default reasoning, truth maintenance system, belief, support list, justification, assumption-based truth maintenance system, set of hypotheses

Exercises

8.1 In the example of explanation-based generalization described in Section 8.1(b), when the positive instance is

$$sympathetic(hanako, hanako)$$
$$good\_point(good\_proportion)$$
$$get(hanako, good\_proportion)$$

and the domain theory is

$$sympathetic(P, Q) \wedge attractive(R) \wedge have(P, R) \rightarrow love(P, Q)$$
$$good\_point(Y) \rightarrow attractive(Y)$$
$$get(Z, W) \rightarrow have(Z, W)$$

what result do we get if we use a Prolog program in Figure 8.6? Find a proof tree and a generalized proof tree like the ones shown in Figure 8.8 and a sufficiency condition such as formula (8.8). How is the sufficiency condition generalized compared to the original positive instance?

8.2 Suppose we have the finite sets of ground literals

$$\beta_1 = \{square(a), triangle(b), ontable(a), ontable(b)\}$$
$$\beta_2 = \{square(c), square(d), ontable(c), ontable(d)\}$$
$$\tau_1 = \{circle(e), triangle(f), ontable(e), ontable(f)\}$$

8.3 Then

(i) Find a maximal partial match, m, of β_1 and τ_1.

(ii) Express the state change from β_1 to β_2 in the form of a transformation as in (8.21).

(iii) Find τ_1', a generalization of τ_1, by applying the substitution in m to τ_1.

(iv) Do the transformation of (ii) on τ_1' and let the result be τ_2. (Then τ_2 is the result of learning by analogy that uses $\{\beta_1, \beta_2\}$ as the base domain and $\{\tau_1\}$ as the target domain.)

8.4 Suppose we are given the facts that a swallow, a sparrow, a robin, and a hawk are birds. What inference rule do we need to make logical inference that the only birds are (or equivalently birds are circumscribed to be) a swallow, a sparrow, a robin, and a hawk? Generalizing the obtained rule, describe an inference rule that says "if an object x has a property p, the objects that have property p are circumscribed to be x." This generalized rule is a well-formed formula in second-order predicate logic. (Logical inference using this kind of inference rule is called *circumscription*. Circumscription is known to be a method of nonmonotonic reasoning.)

9 Learning by Classification and Discovery

This chapter will explain methods for learning by classification and discovery. The first half of this chapter describes a classification method using decision trees and Bayesian statistics. A decision tree can be generated by a simple algorithm and is an efficient method of finding regularities of massive data. Bayesian statistics can be applied to a learning algorithm for data that include noise.

The second half of this chapter explains learning by discovery as a method for problems with unknown goals. Learning by discovery can be formalized as the problem of generating new representations from data and knowledge.

9.1 Representing Instances by a Decision Tree

Let us consider the classification of objects into classes that are defined by a set of attribute-value pairs. This can be done by generating a decision tree where each class corresponds to a leaf and the classes are discriminated by tests at intermediate nodes. In order to explain how to learn to classify objects by generating a decision tree, first let us consider a method of representing objects using a decision tree.

We assume that a positive instance of a concept is represented by a set of attribute-value pairs. For example, if we want to represent "it is fair weather, low temperature, low humidity, and no wind" as a positive instance of the concept "weather," we can use

instance name	attribute	value
instance1	weather	fair
	temperature	low
	humidity	low
	wind	no

When such instances are given as data, we can represent the data as a tree structure. Below we call instances data.

For example, the set of data shown in Figure 9.1(a) can be represented as the tree shown in Figure 9.1(b). In this tree, an intermediate node of the tree corresponds to the test of whether an attribute is included in the data or not, and an edge corresponds to a value. Each leaf of the tree represents some particular subset of data. Nodes and edges that correspond to attribute-value pairs not included in the data are omitted in Figure 9.1(b).

A substructure of the data represented by a tree like Figure 9.1(b) can be represented by an appropriate subtree. For example, Figure 9.1(c) is a subtree of the tree shown in Figure 9.1(b). The leaves of this subtree correspond to a subset of the given set of data. The leaf shown with the oblique line in Figure 9.1(c) corresponds to the set of data that satisfy the condition "it is fair weather and low temperature," in other words, the set of data 1 and 10. In this way, we can concisely represent the characteristics of massive data using subtrees.

The tree representation of a concept as shown above is generally called a representation by a *decision tree.*

On one hand, a decision tree is one of the methods for representing a set of data declaratively. On the other hand, if we regard the procedure for following a path from the root of the tree to a leaf as representing the leaf, a decision tree can be thought of as a procedural representation of a set of data. For example, Figure 9.2 is the procedural form of the decision tree representation in Figure 9.1(c). However, note that, in this representation, the order of testing attributes is from the root of the decision tree to the leaves and is determined beforehand.

One advantage of considering a decision tree as a procedural representation is that we can easily represent a procedure for adding new data to the decision tree. When a procedure like Figure 9.2 is given, all we need to do to add new data, d, is to apply the procedure to d, and when d is found to

data no. \ attribute	weather	temperature	humidity	wind
1	clear	low	low	no
2	clear	medium	low	yes
3	cloudy	medium	medium	yes
4	rain	low	high	no
5	rain	low	high	no
6	clear	high	medium	no
7	clear	high	medium	no
8	cloudy	medium	medium	yes
9	cloudy	low	high	yes
10	clear	low	low	no

(a) The set of data

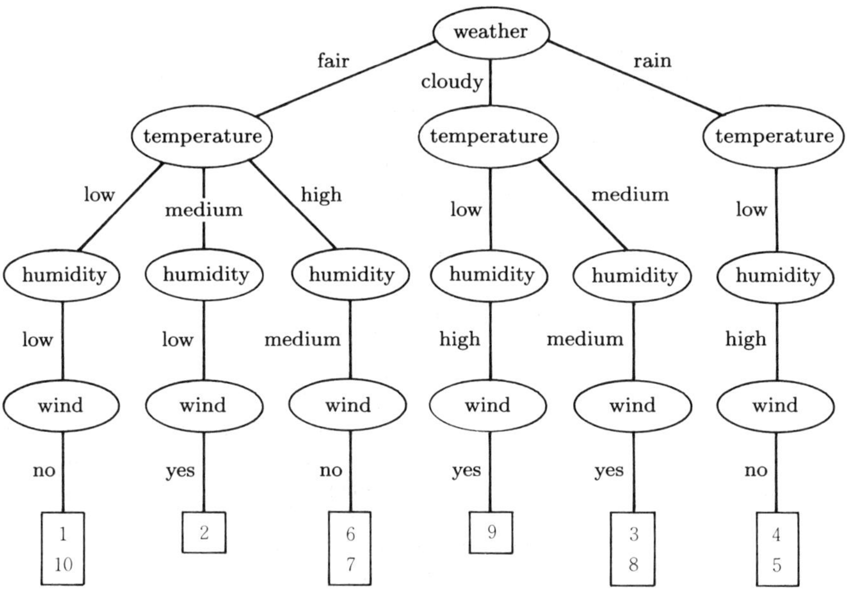

(b) The decision tree representation of (a)

Figure 9.1 Representing data by a decision tree.

be classified into leaf D, update D to $D = D \cup \{d\}$. Also, we can test by checking if $d \in D$ whether d is new data and whether it matches already given data. A decision tree is useful both as a representation of massive data and as a procedure for adding new data.

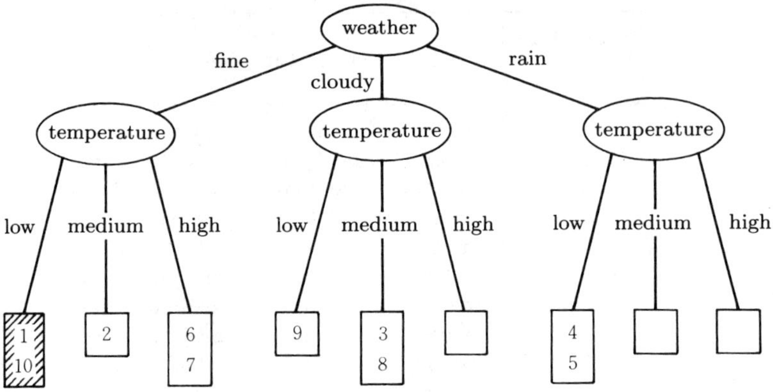

(c) A sub-tree of the tree representation (b)

Figure 9.1 *Continued.*

```
if weather = clear
  then if temperature = low
         then data = {1, 10},
         else if temperature = medium
                then data= {2},
                else if temperature=high
                       then data= {6, 7},
                       else error,
  else if weather = cloudy
         then if temperature = low
                then data = {9},
                else if temperature = medium
                       then data = {3, 8},
                       else if temperature = high
                              then data = { },
                              else error,
         else if weather = rain
                then if temperature = low
                       then data = {4, 5},
                       else if temperature = medium
                              then data = { },
                              else if temperature = high
                                     then data = { },
                                     else error.
```

Figure 9.2 A procedural representation of the decision tree shown in Figure 9.1(c)

9.2 An Algorithm for Generating a Decision Tree

In order to classify a set of data that is defined by a set of attribute-value pairs into several mutually exclusive clusters, it is sufficient to generate a decision tree representation for the data in which each leaf corresponds to some cluster. In this section we will explain a method for doing this.

As an example, let us consider the 16 objects shown in Table 9.1. This data is the information on 16 cars and consists of four attributes—the amount of exhaust, the type, existence of automatic transmission, and the color—and their corresponding values. Also, in Table 9.1, each object is classified into one of the two classes, positive instances (P) or negative instances (N). To classify the data into P or N, we can use, for example, the well-formed formula

$$\begin{aligned}&\text{amount of exhaust}(2800)\\ &\vee \{\text{amount of exhaust}(2000) \wedge \text{automatic}(\text{yes}) \wedge \text{color}(\text{bright})\}\\ &\vee \{\text{amount of exhaust}(1600) \wedge \text{type}(\text{two\_door})\}\end{aligned} \tag{9.1}$$

and label the data with value T by P and the other data by N. Here we represent the data as a decision tree.

The decision tree in Figure 9.3(a) is equivalent to the representation in (9.1) in the sense that all data can be divided into P or N. The number of branches at each node in this tree is three for the amount of exhaust and the type, two for automatic transmission, and two for the color, 10 in total. Also, the decision tree in Figure 9.3(b) describes the same classification as (9.1). However, the number of branches in this tree is 24. There are generally many decision trees that classify the same set of data into clusters. This suggests that we need to generate a decision tree that can classify data efficiently.

Generally, the efficiency of a decision tree for classification depends on how simple the tree structure is. The simplicity of the tree structure can be evaluated by applying information theory. Below, we describe an algorithm for generating a decision tree for efficient data classification based on elementary information theory.

Suppose we are given a finite set of data D. Furthermore, suppose that there is a finite number of tests common to all data, $t_1, \ldots, t_n$, and that the value v_{ip} for each attribute $p \in \{q_1, \ldots, q_i\}$ is obtained by giving the test t_i to the data d. For example, for the data in Table 9.1, we set t_i to be the function that gives the value v_{ip} to the ith attribute. As an example, taking data1 and the amount of exhaust as t_1, we get $v_{11} = 2000$. If we define $v = f(d, t)$, using a function f to make the data d and the test t correspond

Table 9.1 Data for classification

data no.	attribute				class
	amount of exhaust	type	automatic	color	
1	2000	2 door	yes	bright	P
2	2800	4 door	yes	bright	P
3	2000	2 door	no	dark	N
4	1600	4 door	yes	dark	N
5	1600	4 door	yes	bright	N
6	2800	4 door	yes	dark	P
7	2000	4 door	yes	bright	P
8	2000	van	no	bright	N
9	1600	2 door	no	bright	P
10	2800	van	yes	bright	P
11	2800	van	no	dark	P
12	2000	4 door	yes	dark	N
13	1600	2 door	no	dark	P
14	2800	2 door	no	dark	P
15	1600	4 door	no	bright	N
16	2000	van	yes	dark	N

to v, then in this example, $2000 = f(\text{data1, amount of exhaust})$.

Suppose a finite number of *classes* $c_1, \ldots, c_m$ are given and each datum d falls into one of the $c_1, \ldots, c_m$. For example, for the data in Table 9.1, there are two classes, P and N, and the data1 falls into P. Here, we can define $c = g(d)$, using a function g that makes a class correspond to the data. For instance, $P = g(\text{data1})$ in the above example. For the set D of these data, let us consider an algorithm for generating a decision tree.

First we consider a list of three items: the node number, an edge from this node, and the node number of the child node connected by the edge. We represent a decision tree using a set of these lists. For example, the decision tree in Figure 9.3(a) can be represented as

$$H = \{(1\ 2800\ 2)(1\ 20000\ 3)(1\ 1600\ 4)(3\ \text{yes}\ 5)(3\ \text{no}\ 6)$$
$$(4\ \text{two\_door}\ 7)(4\ \text{four\_door}\ 8)(4\ \text{van}\ 9)(5\ \text{bright}\ 10)(5\ \text{dark}\ 11)\}$$

Since using node numbers makes things complicated, we will use a test at a node instead of its node number. For example, in the decision tree in Figure 9.3(a), we will use the list (amount of exhaust 2800 P) instead of (1 2800 2). This sometimes creates two identical lists in a decision tree, but here we assume that there is only one instance of a list in a decision tree. When two identical lists exist, we can argue similarly by attaching different numbers to them.

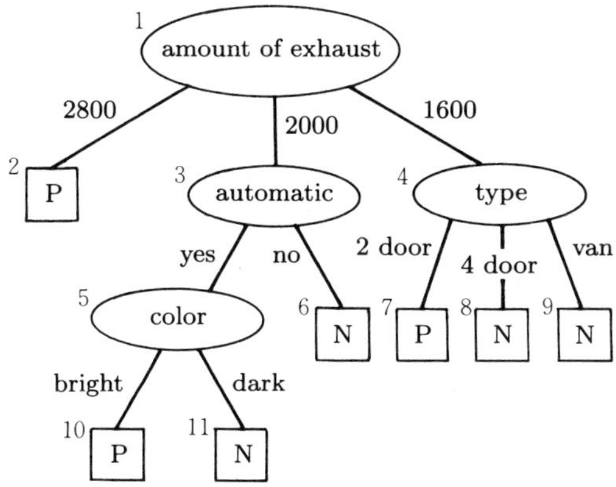

(a) Data classification with 10 branches

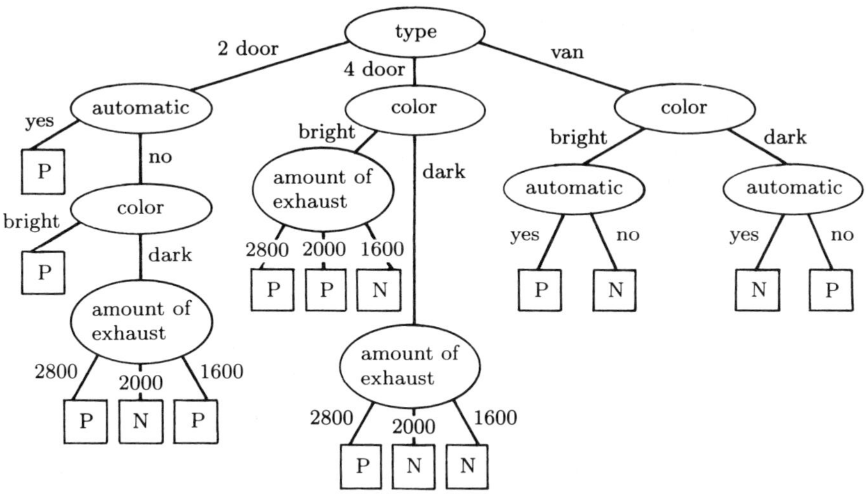

(b) Data classification with 24 branches

Figure 9.3 Examples of decision trees for classifying data.

For the data in Table 9.1, the set of tests is

$$\{t_1, t_2, t_3, t_4\} = \{\text{amount of exhaust, type, automatic, color}\}$$

The set of values for each test is

$$\begin{array}{ll}
\text{for } t_1 & \{v_{11}, v_{12}, v_{13}\} = \{2800, 2000, 1600\} \\
\text{for } t_2 & \{v_{21}, v_{22}, v_{23}\} = \{\text{two_door, four_door, van}\} \\
\text{for } t_3 & \{v_{31}, v_{32}\} = \{\text{yes, no}\} \\
\text{for } t_4 & \{v_{41}, v_{42}\} = \{\text{bright, dark}\}
\end{array}$$

The set of classes is

$$\{c_1, c_2\} = \{P, N\}$$

Also, we represent the set of data D by a set of data numbers. For the data in Table 9.1 we use

$$D = \{1, 2, \ldots, 16\}$$

When a leaf corresponds to a test in a decision tree, such a leaf is called an *active node*. The trees in Figure 9.3(a) and (b) do not have active nodes. A path from the root of a decision tree, s_0, to a node s is represented as the list of nodes, $Q(s) = (s_o, \ldots, s)$, where we use tests, or the values of tests, instead of node numbers. Consider the following algorithm:

Algorithm 9.1 (generating a decision tree for data classification)

[1] If $D = \emptyset$, then stop. $H = \emptyset$ is the decision tree we want.

[2] If $c = g(d_k)$ for all $d_k \in D$, in other words, if all $d_k \in D$ are classified into the same class, set $H = \{(nil\ nil\ c)\}$ and stop. H is the decision tree we want. Here $\{(nil\ nil\ c)\}$ means the tree with only the root node c.

[3] Choose a test $t_i \in \{t_1, \ldots, t_n\}$ and set $H = \{(nil\ nil\ t_i)\}$. (By definition, t_1 becomes an active node.)

[4] If an active node does not exist in H, stop. H is the decision tree we want.

[5] Choose one active node in H, and let it be s_i. Let D_{ij} $(j = 1, \ldots, q_i)$ be the set of $d_k \in D(s_i)$ such that $v_{ij} = f(d_k, s_i)$, where $D(s_i)$ is the subset of D in which the values of the tests corresponding to elements of $Q(s_i) - \{s_i\}$ are fixed. For each D_{ij}, do (1) and (2):

(1) When all $d \in D_{ij}$ are classified into the same class c_{ij}, set $H = H \cup \{(t_i\ v_{ij}\ c_{ij})\}$.

(2) In cases other than (1), choose a new test $t_k \in \{t_1, \ldots, t_n\} - Q(t_i)$ and set $H = H \cup \{(t_i\ v_{ij}\ t_k)\}$. (Here if such a t_k does not exist, it means that inconsistent classification occurs for the data.)

When (1) and (2) have been executed for all d_{ij}, go to [4].

As an example, let us generate using Algorithm 9.1 the decision tree in Figure 9.3(a) from the data in Table 9.1.

[Iteration 1]

Since conditions [1] and [2] of Algorithm 9.1 do not hold, go to [3].

[3] Choose the test "amount of exhaust." Set $H = \{(nil\ nil$ amount of exhaust$)\}$.

[4] Since the conditions are not satisfied, go to [5].

[5] If we choose "amount of exhaust" as the active node of H, then $D(\text{amount of exhaust}) \equiv D$. So, consider the following three cases:

(i) for $d = 2, 6, 10, 11, 14 \quad 2800 = f(d, \text{amount of exhaust})$
(ii) for $d = 1, 3, 7, 8, 12, 16 \quad 2000 = f(d, \text{amount of exhaust})$
(iii) for $d = 4, 5, 9, 13, 15 \quad 1600 = f(d, \text{amount of exhaust})$

For (i), $g(d) = P$ for all d. Therefore, set $H = \{(\textit{nil nil}$ amount of exhaust), (amount of exhaust 2800 $P)\}$. Next, for (ii), all d's cannot be classified into one class. So, choose a new test from {amount of exhaust, type, automatic, color} – {amount of exhaust}, where $Q(\text{amount of exhaust}) = \{\text{amount of exhaust}\}$ was used.
Now choose "automatic" as the test and set

$$H = \{(\textit{nil nil} \text{ amount of exhaust}), (\text{amount of exhaust } 2800\ P), \\ (\text{amount of exhaust } 2000 \text{ automatic})\}$$

For (iii), as in (ii), choose a new test from {amount of exhaust, type, automatic,color} – {amount of exhaust}. Suppose we pick "type" here. In this case, we have

$$H = \{(\textit{nil nil} \text{ amount of exhaust}), (\text{amount of exhaust } 2800\ P), \\ (\text{amount of exhaust } 2000 \text{ automatic}), \\ (\text{amount of exhaust } 1600 \text{ type})\}$$

[Iteration 2]

[4] Since the conditions are not satisfied, go to [5].
[5] The active nodes of H are "automatic" and "type." If we choose "automatic," $D(\text{automatic}) = \{1, 3, 7, 8, 12, 16\}$. So, consider the following two cases:
(i) for $d = 1, 7, 12, 16 \quad \text{yes} = f(d, \text{automatic})$
(ii) for $d = 3, 8 \quad \text{no} = f(d, \text{automatic})$
For (i), choose a new test from {amount of exhaust, type, automatic, color} – {amount of exhaust, automatic}. Now, suppose we choose "color." We set $H = H \cup \{(\text{automatic yes color})\}$. For (ii), since $g(d) = N$ $(d = 3, 8)$, set $H = H \cup \{(\text{automatic no } N)\}$.

[Iteration 3]

[4] Since the conditions are not satisfied, go to [5].
[5] Suppose we choose "type" from active nodes of H. Then $D(\text{type}) = \{4, 5, 9, 13, 15\}$. Consider the following:
(i) $d = 9, 13 \quad \text{two\_door} = f(d, \text{type})$
(ii) $d = 4, 5, 15 \quad \text{four\_door} = f(d, \text{type})$

In (i), since $g(d) = P$, set $H = H \cup \{(\text{type two\_door } P)\}$. In case (ii), since $g(d) = N$, set $H = H \cup \{(\text{type two\_door } P)\}$. Also, since a d that makes $f(d, \text{type}) = \text{van}$ does not exist, define $g(\emptyset) = N$ and set $H = H \cup \{(\text{type van } N)\}$.

[Iteration 4]

[4] Since the conditions are not satisfied, go to [5].
[5] For the active node of H "color," update $H = H \cup \{(\text{color bright } P)$ $(\text{color dark } N)\}$ using the same method as described above.

[Iteration 5]

[4] Since no active node exists in H, stop. H we obtained is the decision tree we want.

The H at the end is the decision tree in Figure 9.3(a) itself. If we use the decision tree generated by Algorithm 9.1, we can classify new data. For example, if we want to classify the following new data:

amount of exhaust	type	automatic	color
2000	four_door	no	bright

using the decision tree in Figure 9.3(a), we find that these data can be classified as N. Also, if this classification is a mistake and the data should be classified as P, rewrite (automatic new N) in the decision tree H to (automatic new type) or (automatic no color) and reexecute [5]. By doing this, we can expand H and classify data correctly. The expansion of a decision tree is generally done using the following algorithm.

Algorithm 9.2 (adding new data to a decision tree)
[1′] If the decision tree H already exists and new data d whose class is known is given, go to [6].
[6] If the class c that is obtained by letting d go though H matches the correct class of d, then stop. Otherwise, choose a new test $t_i \in \{t_1, \ldots, t_n\} - Q(c)$. Also, let $(t\ v\ c)$ be the last edge in the path $Q(c)$. In this case, set $H = H \cup \{(t\ v\ t_i)\} - \{(t\ v\ c)\}$ and go to [5] in Algorithm 9.1.

9.3 Selecting a Test in Generating a Decision Tree

In the algorithm for generating a decision tree that was described in Section 9.2, what to choose as a new test changes the complexity of the decision tree. This is easily seen if we compare (a) and (b) in Figure 9.3. Below, we will describe a method for generating the simplest (by one measure) decision tree possible.

Suppose the data in a data set D are classified into different classes $c_1, \ldots, c_m$ by the decision tree H. Also, suppose that the number of data that fall into c_i is d^i. We assume that the probability of new data being classified into c_i is $d^i / \sum_{i=1}^{m} d^i$. In other words, we regard the size of the data subset to be classified to be the same as the probability. Under this assumption, we can look at H as a stochastic information-processing machine. In other words, H can be considered to be a machine for transmitting a message c_i with probability $d^i / \sum_{i=1}^{m} d^i$. In this case, the amount of information that the machine H transmits is given by

$$E(d^1, \ldots, d^m) = -\sum_{i=1}^{m} \frac{d^i}{\sum_{l=1}^{m} d^l} \ln \frac{d^i}{\sum_{l=1}^{m} d^l} \tag{9.2}$$

Now suppose, for the same decision tree H, the root node corresponds to the test t_j and t_j may take n_j different values $v_{j1}, \ldots, v_{jn_j}$. We set $D_{jk} = \{d \in D | f(d, t_j) = v_{jk}\}$ $(k = 1, \ldots, n_j)$ for these values. Furthermore, suppose each D_{jk} includes d^i_{jk} items of data that fall into the class c_i. The partial tree H_{jk} that corresponds to D_{jk} can be considered to be a stochastic machine where the amount of information is given by $E(d^1_{jk}, \ldots, d^m_{jk})$, as in (9.2). Therefore, the amount of information is

$$E'(t_j) = \sum_{k=1}^{n_j} \frac{\sum_{l=1}^{m} d^l_{jk}}{\sum_{l=1}^{m} d^l} E(d^1_{jk}, \ldots, d^m_{jk}) \tag{9.3}$$

Of (9.2) and (9.3), (9.2) is the amount of information for the decision tree H; (9.3) is the amount of information for the decision tree when we choose a test t_j for the root node of H. Therefore, the increase in the amount of information as a result of choosing t_j is

$$G(t_j) = E(d^1, \ldots, d^m) - E'(t_j) \tag{9.4}$$

So, as a method for choosing a test when generating a decision tree, we can use a method that chooses t_j so that

$$\max_j G(t_j)$$

This method can be applied not only to the root node but also to any node in the decision tree. Since $E(d^1, \ldots, d^m)$ is a constant independent of the choice of the test, from (9.4), maximizing $G(t_j)$ and minimizing $E'(t_j)$ yield the same value.

We will now explain a method for choosing a test by maximizing $G(t_j)$ using the data in Table 9.1. We will only show what to choose as the test for the root node; however, we can repeat this method for the intermediate nodes. First, nine data are in the class P and seven data are in the class N, so if we set $d^1 = 9$, $d^2 = 7$, we have

$$\begin{aligned} E(d^1, d^2) &= -\frac{d^1}{d^1 + d^2}\ln\frac{d^1}{d^1 + d^2} - \frac{d^2}{d^1 + d^2}\ln\frac{d^2}{d^1 + d^2} \\ &= -\frac{9}{16}\ln\frac{9}{16} - \frac{7}{16}\ln\frac{7}{16} \\ &= 0.989 \text{ bit} \end{aligned}$$

Next, we compute $G(t_j)$ as follows for the four tests "amount of exhaust," "type," "automatic," "color."

(1) $t_1 =$ "amount of exhaust"

$$\begin{aligned} &d^1_{11} = 5, d^2_{11} = 0, \\ &\quad D(d^1_{11}, d^2_{11}) = -\frac{5}{5+0}\ln\frac{5}{5+0} - \frac{0}{5+0}\ln\frac{0}{5+0} = 0 \text{ bit} \\ &d^1_{12} = 2, d^2_{12} = 4, \\ &\quad E(d^1_{12}, d^2_{12}) = -\frac{2}{2+4}\ln\frac{2}{2+4} - \frac{4}{2+4}\ln\frac{4}{2+4} = 0.918 \text{ bit} \\ &d^1_{13} = 2, d^2_{13} = 3, \\ &\quad E(d^1_{13}, d^2_{13}) = -\frac{2}{2+3}\ln\frac{2}{2+3} - \frac{3}{2+3}\ln\frac{3}{2+3} = 0.971 \text{ bit} \end{aligned}$$

Therefore, from (9.3),

$$\begin{aligned} E'(\text{amount of exhaust}) &= \frac{5}{9+7}E(d^1_{11}, d^2_{11}) + \frac{6}{9+7}E(d^1_{12}, d^2_{12}) \\ &\quad + \frac{5}{9+7}E(d^1_{13}, d^2_{13}) \\ &= 0.648 \text{ bit} \end{aligned}$$

So,

$$G(t_1) = 0.989 - 0.648 = 0.341 \text{ bit}$$

(2) $t_2 =$ "type"
Similarly to (1), $G(t_2) = 0.082$ bit

(3) t_3 = "automatic"
Similarly to (1), $G(t_3) = 0.001$ bit

(4) t_4 = "color"
Similarly to (1), $G(t_4) = 0.012$ bit

From these, we can obtain the maximum of $G(t_j)$ for t_1 = "amount of exhaust." So, in generating the decision tree, if we choose "amount of exhaust" as the test at the root node, we can increase the amount of information at the root node to a maximum, as in the decision tree in Figure 9.3(a). As opposed to this, the tree in Figure 9.3(b) chooses as the test at the root node, "type," which results in only a small increase in the amount of information.

In the method above, when choosing a test at each node, we need to check the classes of all the data for each possible test. Therefore, the computational complexity of the above procedure is on the order of $O(x \cdot y \cdot z)$ where x is the amount of data, y is the maximum number of possible tests, and z is the number of times we choose a test. This is not an exponential function of x, so it is possible to classify massive data efficiently.

9.4 Learning from Noisy Data

As we described in Section 9.3, in learning by generating a decision tree, the amount of computation necessary to generate a decision tree depends a lot on which test is chosen at each node. This becomes a serious problem particularly when there is noisy data, and data can be classified into wrong classes. Not only when using decision trees but also in dealing with massive data in general, learning from noisy data is an important problem. In this section we treat learning from noisy data.

(a) Generating a decision tree from noisy data

First, let us describe briefly learning by generating a decision tree with data containing noise. We look at whether the amount of information in the decision tree increases significantly when choosing a test t_j at a node. In order to do this, let us consider the probability that the value of t_j is independent of the class distribution $d^1, \ldots, d^m$ of the data set D:

$$p_k^i = d^i \frac{\sum_{l=1}^{m} d_{jk}^l}{\sum_{l=1}^{m} d^l} \quad (k = 1, \ldots, n_j)$$

Also we consider the χ^2 distribution of degree of freedom $n_j - 1$

$$\sum_{k=1}^{n_j} \sum_{l=1}^{m} \frac{(d_{jk}^i - p_k^i)}{p_k^i} \tag{9.5}$$

If the value of p_k^i $(i = 1, \ldots, m)$ is not small, we can test the hypothesis "t_j is independent of the class distribution of D" using expression (9.5). In other words, if we do the χ^2-test at the 1% condidence level and the hypothesis is not rejected, we should not choose t_j as a test. However, in the case that no t_j is chosen, another method that chooses the class c_h giving $d^h = \max\{d^1, \ldots, d^m\}$ instead of a test is also possible.

We can generate a decision tree efficiently to some extent even if the data include noise. The above method is effective when all the data are presented simultaneously. It is difficult to apply this method when the data are presented incrementally.

(b) Processing errors in incrementally presented data

Let us consider a learning method when data are presented incrementally and include noise (in other words, the data are classified erroneously). First, we will discuss a method of processing errors for data presented incrementally based on *Bayes' theorem.*

Suppose we classify data obtained by observations and experiments into several classes. To simplify, we suppose there are two classes, 0 and 1. Possible errors occur when the data that are supposed to be classified into 0 are classified into 1 and when the data that are supposed to be classified into 1 are classified into 0.*

To avoid these errors, let us represent a class statistically as one point on the interval [0,1]. For example, we allow a classification such that the (stochastic) class for the data "is 0.2." In this case, if the true class of the data is 0, the error rate is 0.2; if the true class is 1, the error rate is 0.8. Furthermore, suppose we have a set of data D consisting of d_0 items in class 0 and d_1 items in class 0. The (stochastic) class that minimizes the square sum of the error rate for the classification of each datum in D is given by $d_1/(d_0 + d_1)$. (There is another method where, for the set D, if $d_0 > d_1$, then the class is 0, and if $d_0 \leq d_1$, then the class is 1. These classes minimize the sum of the rate of errors in the classification of the data.)

*In statistics, the former error is generally called an error of the first kind and the latter error is called an error of the second kind, from the standpoint of class 0.

This method is the same as the one described in Section 9.3. The method is simple, but effective when massive amounts of data are presented simultaneously. However, in actual observations and experiments, data are usually presented incrementally rather than simultaneously. In this case, we can use Bayes' theorem as a method for dealing with errors in classification.

Let us suppose we need to judge whether a given datum is a positive instance of a concept c or not when c is represented as a set of attribute-value pairs. If we let x be the stochastic event that the datum is a positive instance of c, and let a be the event that A is an attribute of c, we can define the ratio that the expected value of the probability that x occurs is enhanced by A as

$$s_1(a,x) = \frac{p(a|x)}{p(a|\overline{x})} \tag{9.6}$$

where $\overline{e}$ is a complementary event of a stochastic event, e.

On the other hand, the ratio that the expected value of the probability that x occurs is reduced by A can be defined as

$$s_2(a,x) = \frac{p(\overline{a}|x)}{p(\overline{a}|\overline{x})}. \tag{9.7}$$

Now, if we can compute s_1 and s_2 for all attributes A of c, their product represents a measure for judging whether the datum is a positive instance of c or not. In other words, the bigger the value of the product, the bigger the chance of being a positive instance. Actually, we cannot compute $s_1(a,x), s_2(a,x)$ directly using the above definition. However, there is a simple approximation method described below.

First, note there are four kinds of matching of a datum and an attribute:

(1) When the datum is a positive instance,
  (1-1) it matches an attribute
  (1-2) it does not match an attribute
(2) When the datum is a negative instance,
  (2-1) it matches an attribute
  (2-2) it does not match an attribute

Of these, (1-2) and (2-1) are the cases that cause error. (1-2) causes errors of the first kind and (2-1) causes errors of the second kind.

Now let us consider matching a datum to a concept, and let m_p, u_p, m_n, u_n be the number of items for (1-1), (1-2), (2-1), (2-2), respectively. Then, $s_1(a,x)$ and $s_2(a,x)$ that are defined by (9.6) and (9.7) can be approximated by

$$s_1(a,x) \approx \frac{m_p(m_n+u_n)}{m_n(m_p+u_p)}, \quad s_2(a,x) \approx \frac{u_p(m_n+u_n)}{u_n(m_p+u_p)} \tag{9.8}$$

Let us prove this.

First, from Bayes' theorem, $p(e_1|e_2) = p(e_1 \cap e_2)/p(e_2)$ for any stochastic events e_1 and e_2. This can be applied to (9.6) and (9.7) as follows:

$$s_1(a,x) = \frac{p(a \cap x)/p(x)}{p(a \cap \overline{x})/p(\overline{x})}, \quad s_2(a,x) = \frac{p(\overline{a} \cap x)/p(x)}{p(\overline{a} \cap \overline{x})/p(\overline{x})} \tag{9.9}$$

On the other hand, if we set $N = m_p + u_p + m_n + u_n$, by the definitions of m_p, u_p, m_n, u_n we have

$$\begin{aligned} p(a \cap x) &\approx m_p/N, \quad p(a \cap \overline{x}) \approx m_n/N \\ p(\overline{a} \cap x) &\approx u_p/N, \quad p(\overline{a} \cap \overline{x}) \approx u_n/N \end{aligned} \tag{9.10}$$

Also, if we use $p(e_1) = p(e_1 \cap e_2) \cup p(e_1 \cap \overline{e}_2)$, we have

$$\begin{aligned} p(a) &\approx (m_p + m_n)/N, \quad p(\overline{a}) \approx (u_p + u_n)/N \\ p(x) &\approx (m_p + u_p)/N, \quad p(\overline{x}) \approx (m_n + u_n)/N \end{aligned} \tag{9.11}$$

By substituting (9.10), (9.11) into (9.9), we obtain the expressions (9.8).

Since m_p, u_p, m_n, u_n can be incremented each time a new datum is provided, the expressions in (9.8) can be recomputed easily each time a new datum is given.

Now, as a parameter for checking whether the concept c itself is a concept for some "positive instance" or not, we introduce

$$c_p = \frac{m_p + u_p}{m_n + u_n} \tag{9.12}$$

The computation of c_p can be done easily each time a new datum is given.

If we use (9.8) and (9.12), the parameter for checking whether the datum x is a positive instance of the concept c or not can be given by

$$x_p = c_p \times \prod_{a\text{:matched attribute}} s_1(a,x) \times \prod_{a\text{:unmatched attribute}} s_2(a,x) \tag{9.13}$$

Also, from what we explained above, x_p can be recomputed each time a new datum is given.

(c) Learning by incremental presentation of noisy data

We will explain a method for learning to classify data when noisy data are given incrementally. First, let us consider a method for judging whether the datum x presented incrementally is a positive instance of a concept c or not, when c is represented as a set of attribute-value pairs. Such a method needs at least the following functions:

(1) determine the initial representation of the concept
(2) match a concept with the datum
(3) evaluate the concept
(4) correct the concept

Below, we consider a method of learning using the functions (1)–(4). First, let us look at (1). Suppose we are given the attributes $A_1, \ldots, A_n$ and the values that A_i can take are $a_{i1}, \ldots, a_{ik_i}$. Then we define the representation of a concept as follows:

(i) We represent as α_{ij} a possible value that the attribute A_i can take. Then, a *characterization* generally means the predicate $A_i(\alpha_{ij})$, its logical conjunction, or disjunction.
(ii) A *concept description element* is a triple consisting of a characterization and two parameters, w_p and w_n, where w_p and w_n each are weight parameters whose value becomes larger as the characterization of positive and negative instances becomes better.
(iii) A concept is a finite set of conceptual description elements.

For example, suppose the attributes of various liquids and their possible values are given. Then, $temperature(hot)$, $temperature(hot) \vee viscosity(low)$, $color(orange) \vee color(red)$, $temperature(warm) \wedge color(orange) \vee color(red) \vee viscosity(medium)$ are characterizations. Since the set of an attribute's possible values is given beforehand, the negation of an attribute's value can be represented using a disjunction. For example, a description of the characteristic "viscosity is not high" can be represented as

$$viscosity(medium) \vee viscosity(low)$$

Therefore, all well-formed formulas using $\wedge$, $\vee$, $\sim$ for a given value of an attribute can be represented using definition (iii).

When the representation of a concept is defined like this, we need to give the initial representation of the concept at the beginning in order to be able to judge whether an incrementally presented datum is a positive instance of the concept or not. For example, let us choose the following as the initial representation. First, consider the concept description element $(A_i(a_{ij}), 1, 1)$ where $w_p = 1, w_n = 1$, and $A_i(\alpha_{ij})$, the predicate representation of any attribute-value pair that does not include a conjunction or disjunction, is a characterization. Then, we let the set consisting of all of those elements, $\{(A_i(a_{ij}), 1, 1) | (j = 1, \ldots, k; i = 1, \ldots, n)\}$, be the initial representation. For example, the initial representation for the attribute-value pairs in Figure 9.4(a) can be given by Figure 9.4(b).

attribute	value
temperature	*hot*
	warm
	cold
viscosity	*high*
	medium
	low
color	*yellow*
	orange
	red

(a) Attributes and their values

characterization	weight parameter w_p	w_n
temperature(hot)	1	1
temperature(warm)	1	1
temperature(cold)	1	1
viscosity(high)	1	1
viscosity(medium)	1	1
viscosity(low)	1	1
color(white)	1	1
color(yellow)	1	1
color(orange)	1	1
color(red)	1	1

(b) Example of initial representation for a concept

Figure 9.4 Representing a concept in learning from noisy data.

Now, let us assume we have the initial representation of a concept. Then, suppose we are presented with the first datum x. What we will do is (2), in other words, match the concept with the datum. This can be done by the method described in (b) by obtaining c_p, m_p, u_p, m_n, u_n in the following way:

Algorithm 9.3 (matching a concept with a datum)

[1] Check whether the attribute of the datum d matches with each concept description element that makes up the concept.

[2] If they match, increase by 1 the value of w_p that corresponds to this attribute. If not, increase by 1 the value of w_n.

[3] In addition, find c_p, m_p, u_p, m_n, u_n from the result of matching for each description element, and compute the value of the parameter x_p suggesting that x is a positive instance from c_p, m_p, u_p, m_n, u_n using (9.13).

Since the datum x has the possibility of including noise, this method does not always correctly determine whether a datum is a positive instance or not. What it can do is to determine the probability of being a positive instance. It is important for this kind of stochastic method to have an evaluation function that judges whether the representation of the concept is appropriate or not. This function is in (3). (3) is computed by updating the values of weight parameters as in [2] of Algorithm 9.3.

Finally let us look at (4), the correction of a concept. In (4), not only are the weight parameters updated but also the representation for the concept itself is corrected. This is done by searching the the concept representation space. This space is not only finite but has the structure of a complete lattice. Using this structure, we can do generalization, specialization, and negation of a concept.

For example, Figure 9.5 shows a part of the concept representation consisting of the attributes and their values shown in Figure 9.4(a). In this graph, we do specialization by searching upward, i.e., by finding, for instance, a higher node for *viscosity*(*high*) and *color*(*white*), which is *viscosity*(*high*) $\wedge$ *color*(*white*). Generalization, on the other hand, searches the graph downward.

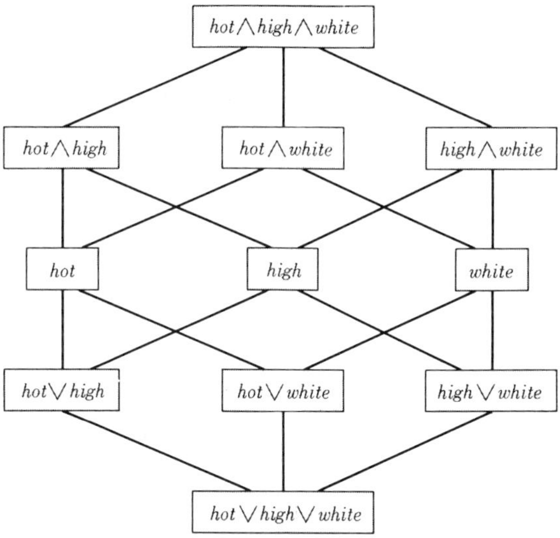

Figure 9.5 Part of the concept representation space defined by the data shown in Figure 9.4(a). (Predicate names are omitted.)

Search of the concept representation space depends on how the current concept representation and the datum are matched. For example, if the datum is misjudged, deciding that a negative instance is a positive instance, we can do specialization because the representation of the current concept is considered too general. Conversely, if the datum is misjudged to be a negative instance when it is actually a positive instance, we can do generalization since the representation is too specific. In either case we can try the negation of the well-formed formula. We can improve the efficiency of the search not only by choosing a generalization, specialization, or negation but also by combining them with various methods of heuristic search.

(d) A learning example

We explain an example of learning based on the above method. Let us consider the case where the data on cars shown in Table 1 are incrementally presented from the top. In this example, the attributes and their possible values for the data are

amount of exhaust: 2800, 2000, 1600
type: 2 door, 4 door, van
automatic: yes, no
color: bright, dark

If we match the data with numbers 1–7 in Table 9.1 with an initial representation similar to the one in Figure 9.4(b), we obtain the result shown in Figure 9.6(a). Here the initial value of m_p, u_p, m_n, u_n is set to 10, and each time the value is changed, we take 99% of the changed value as the new value. For example, in Figure 9.6, the value of $m_p = 11.77$ for the amount of exhaust (2000) means that, of the data that have been input so far, the number of positive instances where the value of "amount of exhaust" is "2000" is 11.77 using the conversion method above.

Suppose we are given a new datum, d: amount of exhaust(2000) $\wedge$ type(van) $\wedge$ automatic(no) $\wedge$ color(bright) (data number 8 in Table 9.1). For each attribute A_i, if we compute $s_1(a_i, d)$ and $s_2(a_i, d)$ based on (9.8), we get Figure 9.6(b). By (9.12), the value of the parameter c_p becomes $c_p = 1.00$ and, using (9.13) on these values, the probability of d being a positive instance is suggested by $x_p = 0.77$. (The values of s_1 and s_2 used to obtain x_p are in ( ) in Figure 9.6(b).)

As shown in Table 9.1, the datum d is a negative instance. In this case, first we need to update the values of m_n and u_n for each characterization. For example, since the characterization of the amount of exhaust(2000) matches d, we need to increase the value of m_n for the amount of exhaust(2000) using the above method. Since the amount of exhaust(1600) does not match d, the value of u_n is increased to account for the amount of exhaust(1600). Next, we correct the concept representation itself to a more specific one. For example, we find an a that makes $s_1(a, x)$ the minimum among characterizations that do not match the negative instance d and find an a' that makes $s_2(a', x)$ the minimum among the characterizations that match d. We then insert their conjunction explicitly into the representation of c. By this method, in this example, we add amount of exhaust(1600) $\wedge$ automatic(yes) to the original representation. The attribute-value pair where $s_1(a, x)$ takes the minimum value is

attribute(value) A_i	m_p	u_p	m_n	u_n	$s_1(a_i, x)$	$s_2(a_i, x)$
amount of exhaust(2800)	11.77	11.77	10.00	12.64	1.13	0.90
amount of exhaust(2000)	11.77	11.77	10.89	11.77	1.04	0.96
amount of exhaust(1600)	10.00	13.51	11.77	10.89	0.82	1.20
type(two_door)	10.89	12.64	10.89	11.77	0.96	1.03
type(four_door)	12.64	10.89	11.77	10.89	1.03	0.96
type(van)	10.00	13.51	10.00	12.64	0.96	1.03
automatic(yes)	13.51	10.00	11.77	10.89	1.11	0.89
automatic(no)	10.11	13.51	10.89	11.77	0.89	1.11
color(bright)	12.64	10.89	10.89	11.77	1.12	0.89
color(dark)	10.89	12.64	11.77	10.89	0.89	1.12

(a) Intermediate result of learning for the data 1–7 in Table 9.1

attribute(value) A_i	m_p	u_p	m_n	u_n	s_1	s_2
amount of exhaust(2800)	11.77	11.77	10.00	13.51	1.18	(0.87)
amount of exhaust(2000)	11.77	11.77	11.77	11.77	(1.00)	1.00
amount of exhaust(1600)	10.00	13.51	11.77	11.77	0.85	(1.15)
type(two_door)	10.89	12.64	10.89	11.77	1.07	(1.00)
type(four_door)	12.64	10.89	11.77	11.77	1.07	(0.93)
type(van)	10.00	13.51	10.00	13.51	(1.00)	1.00
automatic(yes)	13.51	10.00	11.77	11.77	1.15	(0.85)
automatic(no)	10.00	13.51	11.77	11.77	(0.85)	1.15
color(bright)	12.64	10.89	11.77	11.77	(1.07)	0.93
color(dark)	10.89	12.64	11.77	11.77	0.93	(1.07)

(b) Intermediate result of learning when a new datum is added to (a)

Figure 9.6 Learning example with data presented incrementally. (The data are shown in Table 9.1.)

automatic(no), and "automatic" takes only two values, "yes" and "no." Thus we can also add the negation, in other words, automatic(yes). In this example, since we can add automatic(yes) by the specialization previously stated, we can also use the heuristic of not adding automatic(yes) but removing automatic(no).

9.5 Learning by Discovery

In most of the learning algorithms we described so far, the goal of the learning is given beforehand. Let's now look at learning algorithms when the goal is not decided beforehand. Such learning is called *learning by discovery*. As we will explain below, learning by discovery can be used for finding regularity in massive amounts of data or generating new representations based on knowledge.

(a) Discovering regularities in data and attributes

In this section we provide an algorithm for finding relations among numeric data and representing these relations as variables. This problem, as we describe later, can be formulated as a problem whose goal state is not known beforehand. Its learning algorithm can be represented as an algorithm of search in problem solving. We start by defining a data-vector space and operations on data-vectors as follows:

Definition 1 (data-vector space) Suppose the values of n data x_i $(i = 1, \ldots, n)$ for each of the given attributes $a_1, \ldots, a_k$ are given by $v_{i1}, \ldots, v_{ik}$ $(i = 1, \ldots, n)$. Then the n-dimensional Euclidean space including the set of the n-dimensional vectors $V = \{(v_{1j,\ldots,v_{nj}})|j = 1, \ldots, k\}$ is called the (n-dimensional) *data-vector space.*

Definition 2 (product and quotient) We define the *product* $\circ$

$$z = x \circ y \Leftrightarrow z_i = x_i y_i \quad (i = 1, \ldots, n) \quad (x, y, z \in M)$$

and the quotient /

$$z = x/y \Leftrightarrow z_i = x_i/y_i \quad (i = 1, \ldots, n) \quad (x, y, z \in M)$$

as binary operations on the n-dimensional data-vector space M. Note that only the vectors y that make $y_i \neq 0$ $(i = 1, \ldots, n)$ are defined.

Let $X_0 = \{x_1, \ldots, x_n\}$, a set of data-vectors with more than two elements, and for two arbitrary elements of X_0, x^i, x^j, let $X_1 = \{x_1, \ldots, x_n, x^i \circ x^j\}$ and $X_2 = \{x_1, \ldots, x_n, x^i/x^j\}$. Repeating this operation for each of X_1 and X_2, we can generate an infinite list of sets, $X_0, X_1, X_2, \ldots$. Here we assume that in a quotient vector x^i/x^j all the elements of x^j are not 0. Let us call this condition $(*)$.

Let us consider $X = \{X_0, X_1, X_2, \ldots\}$ as the state space, X_0 as the initial state, each operation generating $X_1, X_2, \ldots$ as an operator, and the

Table 9.2 Data for the physical state of a gas

data no.	P(pressure)	V(volume)	T(temperature)
1	10.0	3.0	12.5
2	12.0	1.5	7.5
3	14.0	3.0	17.5
4	16.0	1.5	10.0
5	18.0	2.0	15.0

condition $(*)$ in generating the quotient vector $(*)$ as a constraint on operator application. Then finding a goal state $X_g \in X$ can be regarded as problem solving. In particular, when X_g is not given beforehand, finding the goal state becomes learning by discovery according to the above definition.

As an example, suppose we have data for the pressure P, volume V, and temperature T for some gas as shown in Table 9.2 (we ignore the units). The problem is to find some regularity among the attributes P, V, and T. Suppose the initial state of the problem is the set of the data-vectors $X_0 = \{p, v, t\}$ where

$$p = (10.0, 12.0, 14.0, 16.0, 18.0)$$
$$v = (3.0, 1.5, 3.0, 1.5, 2.0)$$
$$t = (12.5, 7.5, 17.5, 10.0, 15.0)$$

Then, if we generate new states by repeatedly applying the above operations to the elements of X_0, p, v, t, and obtain some interesting state, we can say that we discovered a relation among P, V, T.

If we use breadth-first search on this state space, the states shown in Figure 9.7 are generated. In this case the vector $p \circ v/t$ becomes a vector whose elements all have the same value (called a constant vector). A state including a vector whose elements have a constant value is an "interesting" state. Actually, the fact that $p \circ v/t$ is a constant vector means that $PV/T =$ constant; in other words, Boyle's law holds for the data in Table 9.2.

This algorithm is very simple, but it can be used to give a new name to a regularity that is found and to discover higher-order regularities by regarding this regularity as a new attribute. For example, suppose we get the data 1–9 as shown in Table 9.3 by measuring the weight of the components in some samples of three kinds of gas consisting of oxygen O and nitrogen N. Suppose we apply the above method for each of the three subsets of data 1–3, 4–6, and 7–9 and, as a result, we obtain the following

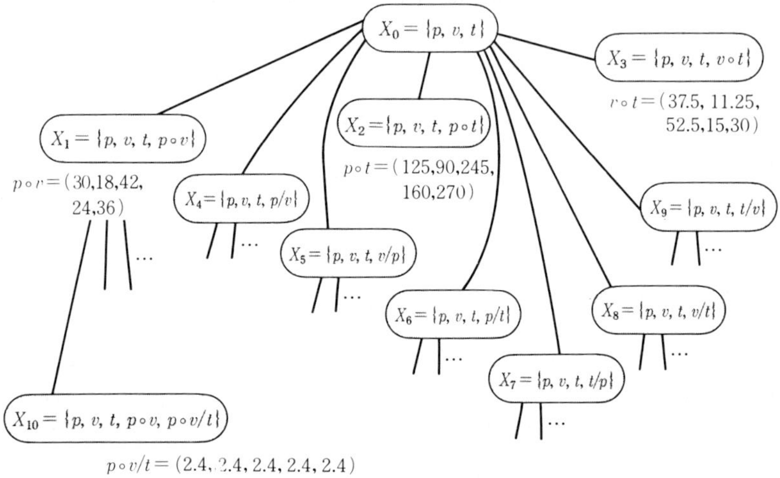

Figure 9.7 Part of the state space generated by breadth-first search from the data of Table 9.2.

Table 9.3 Data for the weight of ingredients of substances consisting of oxygen O and nitrogen N

data no.	total weight	N	O
1	350.0 mg	163.6 mg	186.4 mg
2	218.3	102.0	116.3
3	291.8	136.4	155.4
4	103.9	66.2	37.7
5	482.5	307.3	175.2
6	327.7	208.7	119.0
7	524.6	159.9	364.7
8	435.9	132.9	303.0
9	276.7	84.4	192.3

for the weight w_O for oxygen and the weight w_N for nitrogen:

$$\begin{aligned} w_O/w_N = & 1.14(\text{constant}) \quad (\text{data } 1\text{–}3) \\ & 0.57(\text{constant}) \quad (\text{data } 4\text{–}6) \\ & 2.28(\text{constant}) \quad (\text{data } 7\text{–}9) \end{aligned}$$

Then, if we define $\alpha = w_O/w_N$ as a new attribute common to the three kinds of gas, each gas can be said to have the characteristic that the values of the variable α differ by a multiple of an integer.

(b) A search method for discovering regularity

In this section we explain a method for discovering regularity in numeric data that is slightly different from the one explained in (a).

Suppose data are represented as the set of the pairs of attributes $a_1, \ldots, a_k$ and their values. A data-vector is defined as the vector of those k values for a datum. For such data, let us define the binary operations $\circ$ (product) and / (quotient) on the data-vector space. We define the graph G which has $a_1, \ldots, a_k$ as nodes and whose edges are joined only between the attributes when the data-vector becomes a constant vector by the operation of $\circ$ or /. This graph is called a *proportionality graph*, and we can consider the following search algorithm for G.

Algorithm 9.4 (proportionality graph search for discovering regularities)

[1] Set $M = \emptyset$.

[2] Of the maximal cliques for the graph G, find the maximum clique. Let N be the set of nodes in this clique.

[3] Pay attention only to attributes that correspond to the nodes of N and find a pair of attributes where a constant data-vector is generated by the operation $\circ$ or /. (For example, use depth-first search.) In this case, generate a new node $a_i \circ a_j$ or a_i/a_j corresponding to $\circ$ or / and add this node to N. Also, delete a_i and a_j from N. Set $M = M \cup \{a_i \circ a_j\}$ or $M = M \cup \{a_i/a_j\}$. If a pair of such attributes does not exist, then stop. The new nodes that were found so far provide the regularity in the original data.

[4] For the updated set of nodes, N, define edges only for pairs of attributes where a constant data-vector is generated using $\circ$ or /. Call the resulting graph G and go to [2].

As an example, let us consider a sphere that falls down freely in a viscous medium. Suppose given data have as attributes the mass of the sphere m, the radius r, the density ρ, the viscosity coefficient of the medium η, the wavelength of the color λ, and the velocity v. If the data do not include noise, the initial proportionality graph G in the above algorithm is the top graph in Figure 9.8. There are three maximal cliques for this graph, $\{\rho, r\}$, $\{m, r, v, \eta\}$, $\{\eta, \lambda\}$, describing them as sets of nodes. Let us pick $\{m, r, v, \eta\}$, which has the largest number of nodes. If we check the regularity of the data-vectors that correspond to the attributes m, r, v, η, and notice that the vector r/m becomes a constant vector, we obtain the second graph in Figure 9.8. By repeating this process, we finally reach $N = \{vr\eta/m\}$, and the algorithm stops. We have found the regularity that $vr\eta/m = \text{constant}$ for the original set of data.

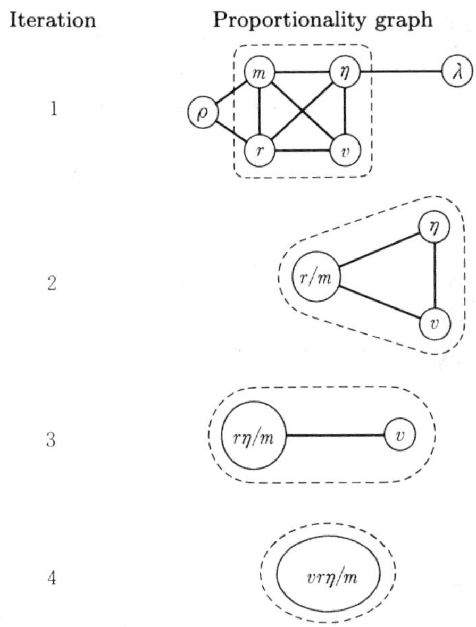

Figure 9.8 The proportionality graph search for a relation among attributes. (The maximum clique obtained during each iteration is shown inside each broken box.)

The discovered characteristic is equivalent to Stokes' law of the viscosity of a liquid as applied to an object that falls freely.

Since Algorithm 9.4 for the *proportionality graph search method* chooses only the maximum cliques in [2], it sometimes cannot find regularities that can be found from other maximal cliques. This can be avoided by extending Algorithm 9.4 and doing [3] and [4] for all the maximal cliques. For example, in the example of Figure 9.8, we can obtain the regularity $m/\rho r =$ constant if we choose $\{m, \rho, r\}$ instead of $\{m, r, v, \eta\}$ as the node set for the maximal clique.

On the other hand, this search method can cause computational explosion because it may generate and accumulate too many new nodes during the search. One method of solving this problem is the *suspension search method.* In this method, when the data at a generated node are not constant within predetermined intervals, no further search involving this node is performed. Such a node is called a *suspended node.* By doing the proportionality graph search only for nodes that are not suspended, we may avoid decreases in the search efficiency to some extent.

(c) Qualitative discovery and processing noise

So far we have described methods for discovering regularities in numeric data. There are also methods for discovering qualitative regularity of data. By classifying given numeric data into clusters, the set of data can be described by a set of rules, not just one rule. In this case, since each cluster can be thought of as a concept that is newly generated from the data, we can use for clustering the method of concept clustering described in Section 6.5. A method for finding regularities for this notion of concept is one example of qualitative discovery. Also, in this section we did not describe methods for processing noise. One method for processing noise is to allow an error range of some extent (for example, 1%) when we check the relation $\circ$ or $/$ among data-vectors.

9.6 Discovery of New Concepts and Rules

(a) Heuristic knowledge

No totally new and interesting concepts or rules have been discovered by applying the algorithm for discovering regularities described in Section 9.5. Three reasons can be given for this:

(1) Actual data include complicated noise, but the current discovery algorithms do not have powerful methods for dealing with noise.
(2) The amount of data is not sufficient or important attributes are missing.
(3) Knowledge for the processing data is lacking.

The most important reason is (3). Knowledge used for discovery is necessary not only for processing data but also for asking what data are missing and for removing noise.

One characteristic of discovery as problem solving is the fact that the goal is unknown. This suggests that the control of search requires a lot of specific knowledge, that is, heuristic knowledge. Having lots of heuristic knowledge is a necessary condition for discovering a new interesting concept or rule. In this section, we will describe an algorithm for discovery based on massive heuristic knowledge and a simple control mechanism.

(b) Discovering a concept based on knowledge

To discover a new concept based on massive heuristic knowledge, we first need to consider how to represent heuristic knowledge. To do that, we use a representation combining frames and rules.

As an example, let us consider the domain of simple arithmetic. The frame representation of a concept in arithmetic can be described, for example, as in Figure 9.9. A slot and its filler, as shown in this example, correspond to an attribute and its value. Some attributes have a value that is fixed at the time the frame is made; other attributes have values that can change.

name:	prime number
specialization:	curious prime number, small prime number, pair of prime numbers
isa:	set
example:	extreme positive instance: 2, 3 extreme negative instance: 0, 1 typical positive instance: 5, 7, 11, 13, 17, 19 typical negative instance: 34, 100
estimate:	promising estimate: uniqueness of factorization, expression of $d(n)$ unit of the promising estimate: time, is a divisor of ~, making an exponent, a number with three divisors, making it square
analogy:	simple group
worth:	800
history:	number of positive examples: 840 number of negative examples: 5000 number of estimates that have not been refuted: 3 number of estimates that have been refuted: 7

Figure 9.9 A frame representation of "prime number" (modified from Lenat, 1977).

The following is an example of heuristic rules:

> **if** f is a function that transforms an element of the object A into an element of the object B
> **then** consider only the elements of A that are transformed into extreme elements of B.

For example, if A and B are sets of natural numbers and f is a function for "is a divisor of ~," we try to generate as subsets of A "a set of numbers without divisors," "a set of numbers that has only one divisor," "a set of numbers that has two divisors," "a set of numbers that has three divisors," etc. Among them, "a set of numbers that has two divisors" is equivalent to "prime number."

Suppose we have the following heuristic rule:

> **if** f is an interesting function
> **then** consider the inverse function of f.

If we apply this rule to the function "is a divisor of $\sim$," the inverse function of "is a divisor of $\sim$," in other words, "multiplication," is considered. Then, if we apply other heuristic rules for "multiplication," we can obtain simpler functions.

As we can see, if we repeat the application of heuristic rules starting with known concepts, we might be able to find a new concept. For example, we may generate a concept such as "prime number" and "number with a maximal number of divisors"* from the concept "addition" and "direct product (of sets)."

The application of heuristic rules, as described in Section 9.5, uses frames for concepts and does search "where the goal state is not given beforehand" using best-first search. The direction of the search is determined by the value of the "worth" parameter that appears in each frame and heuristic rules for controlling search that have been set up separately. As the search proceeds, a new frame is generated based on the heuristic rules.

Now, many of the discovery algorithms that we have considered so far use search using heuristic rules. However, if the set of heuristic rules remains fixed, possibly only uninteresting concepts may be generated as new concepts by the search. In this case, a method for discovering heuristic rules enables us to find more interesting concepts using newly discovered rules.

As a method for discovering a heuristic rule itself, heuristic rules can be thought of as concepts and the methods described above can be used. Heuristic rules can be represented as a frame just as was done for concepts, and heuristic knowledge can be generated as a new concept using heuristic search. In this case, the original heuristic rules become meta rules that work themselves on heuristic rules.

For example, let us consider the following rule:

> **if** no good result can be obtained even if the rule f is applied repeatedly
> **then** consider generating a rule that is more specific than f.

The problem with using the above representation is that it is not clear what attributes to use in the frames representing heuristic rules. Generalization, specialization, analogy, and so on can also be used to generate new heuristic rules.

*That a natural number n is a number with the maximal number of divisors means that $\#(n) > \max_{1 \le i \le n-1} \#(i)$ where $\#(n)$ is the number of natural numbers that divides n. $1, 2, 4, 6, 12, \ldots$ are numbers with a maximal number of divisors.

Summary

This chapter described methods for learning regularities in data.

9.1 Data given as a set of attribute-value pairs can be represented efficiently using a decision tree.

9.2 By using a decision tree, we can easily add data that are provided incrementally to the original tree.

9.3 There are generally many decision tree representations for a given set of data. Of such possible trees, by applying information theory, the most efficient tree for discriminating the data can be generated.

9.4 In the case in which the data include noise or in the case of incremental presentation of noisy data, there are systems that can learn to classify by applying statistical methods or Bayes' theorem.

9.5 In the case of incremental presentation of noisy data, we can use search in the space of concept representations as an algorithm for learning the classification of data.

9.6 Learning by discovery can be formulated as problem solving whose goal state is not given.

9.7 Learning by discovery can make use of search methods such as breadth-first search, best-first search, and so on.

9.8 Discovery of heuristic rules can be done using methods for learning by discovery.

Keywords

massive data, decision tree, information theory, noisy data, simultaneous presentation, incremental presentation, Bayes' theorem, concept representation space, learning by discovery, problem solving, heuristic search, discovery of attributes, proportionality graph search, suspended node, heuristic knowledge, frame representation, heuristic rule, meta rule

Exercises

9.1 Give a decision tree representing the following set of data:

attribute/data no.	age	blood pressure (high)	blood pressure (low)	*class*
1	65	150	95	−
2	64	180	100	+
3	73	190	110	+
4	60	160	110	−
5	66	145	90	−
6	65	140	80	−
7	62	130	80	−
8	60	145	95	−
9	70	190	100	+
10	70	145	90	−
11	68	150	90	−
12	60	140	85	−
13	72	175	95	+
14	71	175	105	+
15	68	175	100	+

9.2 Find a decision tree that classifies the set of data shown in Exercise 9.1 into classes $\{+, -\}$ that maximizes the amount of information in the sense of (9.4).

9.3 Using the method shown in Section 9.5(a), discover regularities in the following set of data (each datum gives the energy E that a wall receives when an object with mass m hits the wall at velocity v).

data no.	m (mass)	v (velocity)	E (energy)
1	5.0	4.0	40.0
2	10.0	3.0	45.0
3	15.0	8.0	480.0
4	20.0	8.0	640.0
5	12.0	10.0	600.0
6	8.0	5.0	100.0

10 Learning by Neural Networks

In this chapter, we describe algorithms for learning using neural networks. A neural network is a kind of computation system in which a state of the system is represented as a numerical distribution pattern with many processing units and connections among those units. Learning by neural networks uses an algorithm for transforming distribution patterns, which is quite different from learning based on symbolic representations described in Chapters 6–9. We will describe popular neural networks and explain methods for representing and using them for learning.

10.1 Representing Neural Networks

If we abstract a brain or the central nervous system of an animal, we can construct a model as a network where many neurons are densely connected with excitatory and inhibitory synapses. Furthermore, each of the neurons corresponding to the nodes of this network can be thought of as a function for transforming input information to another form of output. The efficiency of information transmission of the synapses that correspond to the edges of the network can be thought of as plastic, in the sense that the efficiency can change as the input information to the network changes. A state of the network can be represented as a numerical distribution pattern of the neurons' states and the synapses' information transmission efficiency over the network.

Furthermore, in this network, computation of the input-output function at each neuron and computation of the transmission efficiency change at each synaptic union can be done as a parallel process. Also, even if some of the neurons are broken, the state of the network as a whole and the output may not be influenced.

We can consider this structure, where the connectivity relation of many parallel processing units changes plastically, as one of the basic characteristics of the nervous system. Generally a dynamic network with these characteristics is called a neural network. Neural networks can change the input-output relation by changing the state of a processing unit and the transmission efficiency of the unit. This is called learning in a neural network.

In this section, we will describe the representation of neural networks in preparation for explaining learning using neural networks. First, we define the general structure of the neural nets we are going to use in this chapter.

Definition 1 (neural network) Consider a set of processing units (called a *unit* from now on) $U = \{u_1, \ldots, u_n\}$ and (directed) links between two units (called a *link* from now on) $L = \{(i,j) | u_i \in U,\ u_j \in U\} \subseteq U \times U$. Each unit receives input from other units joined by a link or from the outside and sends outputs to other units joined by a link or to the outside. The input-output relation at each unit u_i can be defined as follows using the *output function* g_i and the *state transition function* f_i:

$$\begin{array}{ll} \text{Output function:} & o_j(t) = g_j(a_j(t)) \\ \text{State transition function:} & a_j(t+1) = f_j(\sum_i w_{ji} o_i(t)) \end{array}$$

where $a_j(t)$ and $o_j(t)$ represent the state of unit j at time t and the output from j at time t, respectively. w_{ji} represents the weight of the link from unit i to j. We include the input function to unit j in the state transition function in the above definition. We represent the above definition as a five-tuple $K = \langle U, L, W, O, F \rangle$, where W is the set of the links' weights, and O and F are the sets of the output and state transition functions. K is called a *neural network*.

The representation of units and links in a neural network is similar to the one for nodes and edges of a graph. Since each unit of a neural network is a function that depends on time, it can be regarded as an extended version of the graph representation described in Chapter 2.

[Example 1] One example of neural networks is shown in Figure 10.1(a). This example is a network made of five units and six links. The units u_1 and u_2 receive input only from the outside, u_5 is a unit that sends output to the outside, and u_3 and u_4 are other units. The links (1,3) and (2,4) have weight 1, (3,5) and (4,5) have weight 0.5, and (1.4) and (2,3) have weight −2. Next, let us classify units.

Definition 2 (various units) A unit that receives input from the outside is called an *input unit.* A unit that sends output to the outside is called an *output unit.* A unit that is neither input nor output unit is called a *hidden unit.*

Definition 3 (various links) A link whose weight is nonnegative is called an *excitatory link*, and a link whose weight is negative is called an *inhibitory link.*

In Figure 10.1, the excitatory links are expressed using → and the inhibitory links are expressed using ⊸. For example, the link from unit u_2 to u_3 is inhibitory and has the weight $w_{32} = -2$.

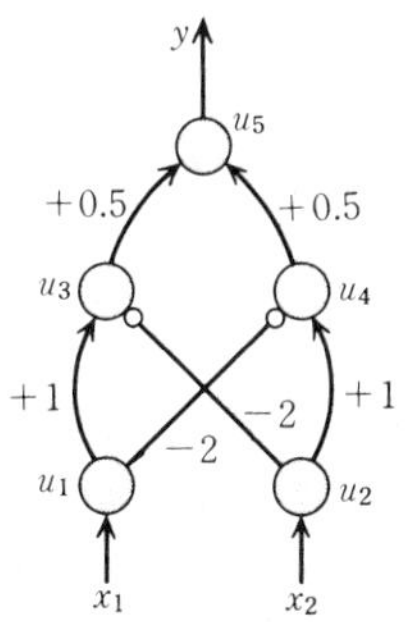

(a) Neural network for computing exclusive OR

input x_1	input x_2	output y
0	0	0
0	1	1
1	0	1
1	1	0

(b) The truth table of the two-input exclusive OR

Figure 10.1 An example of neural networks.

[Example 2] Consider a unit that has $o_i(t) = a_i(t)$ as an output function and has the following state transition function:

$$a_i(t+1) = \begin{cases} 1 & \text{when } \sum_j w_{ij} o_j - \theta_i > 0 \\ 0 & \text{otherwise} \end{cases}$$

This kind of unit is called a *linear threshold unit.* A neural network with layers of linear threshold units is known to possess computational power equivalent to that of a Turing machine. As an example, suppose the threshold value of each unit i in Figure 10.1(a) is $\theta_i = 0$ $(i = 1, \ldots, 5)$. Then we can compute the exclusive OR using this neural network. For example when the input is $x_1(0) = 1$, $x_2(0) = 1$, we get $a_1(1) = 1$, $a_2(1) = 1$, $a_3(1) = 0$, $a_4(1) = 0$, $a_5(1) = 0$, and the output $y(1) = 0$.

However, in the case of this version of exclusive OR, as the number of inputs increases, it becomes more and more difficult to find, within a practically reasonable time, the states and weights starting from arbitrarily given initial states and weights. The reason for this is that in the input-output relation of the exclusive OR, the input vector cannot be linearly separated according to the output values as intuitively shown in Figure 10.2.

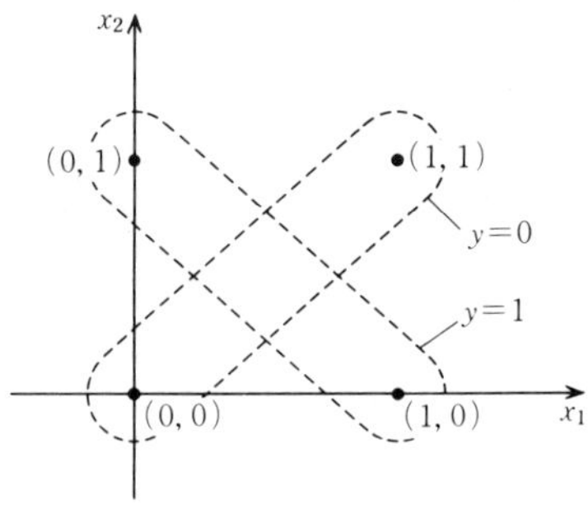

Figure 10.2 Exclusive OR cannot be linearly separated.

[Example 3] A simple three-layer *perceptron* is a network where a stimulus unit layer, an association unit layer, and one response unit are linked in series. Here we assume that the links from the stimulus unit layer to the association unit layer have random-valued weights and that all the association unit are linked to the response unit. Figure 10.3 shows an example. Let a_{ji} be the weight of the link from stimulus unit i to association unit j, w_{rj} be the weight of the link from association unit j to the response unit r, and y_j be the output from j to r. Furthermore, assume that the association units and the response unit are linear threshold units and that the threshold value of unit k is θ_k. Also, the output y_j of association unit j is assumed as follows when the output from stimulus unit i to j is x_{ji}:

$$y_j = \begin{cases} 1 & \text{when } \sum_i a_{ji}x_{ji} - \theta_j > 0 \\ 0 & \text{otherwise} \end{cases}$$

Also, we assume the following when the output of the response unit is o_r:

$$o_r = \begin{cases} 1 & \text{when } \sum_j w_{rj}y_j - \theta_r > 0 \\ 0 & \text{otherwise} \end{cases}$$

For the above neural network we want the response unit to output 1 when the input pattern is included in the set of patterns X and 0 when it

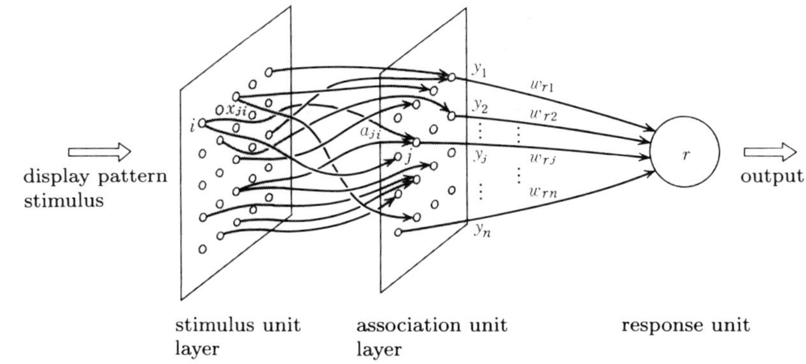

Figure 10.3 A simple three-layer perceptron.

is not included in X. This can be done by repeatedly changing the values of w_{rj} $(j = 1, \ldots, n)$ by the *fixed increment correction method* given below.

Given a set of patterns X and a set of classes C, finding the subsets $X_1, \ldots, X_k$ of X that correspond to $c_1, \ldots, c_k \in C$ respectively and satisfy $X = \cup_{i=1}^{k} X_i, X_i \cap X_j = \emptyset$ $(i \neq j)$ is called *pattern discrimination.* When not all the classes $c_1, \ldots, c_k$ are known, this is called *pattern classification.* The example we look at here is an example of pattern discrimination where the set of classes is $C = \{0, 1\}$.

Algorithm 10.1 (the fixed increment correction method)

[1] Suppose the set of patterns that can be input, $P = \{p_1, \ldots, p_n\}$, is given. Also, for all the association units j, assign random values to w_{rj} as the initial weights.

[2] Pick up an element of P, p, randomly and obtain the output from the response unit, o_p, for the input pattern p.

[3] When the ideal output for p is r_p, compute $\Delta w_{rj} = \epsilon(r_p - o_p)x_j$ for all the association units j, where ϵ is a positive constant that does not depend on the input pattern.

[4] Update the value of w_{rj} using $w_{rj} = w_{rj} + \Delta w_{rj}$ for all the association units j.

[5] If the value of w_{rj} no longer changes for all the input patterns $p \in P$, stop. The input patterns can be discriminated using w_{rj}. Otherwise, go to [2].

Now, let E_T be a subset of input patterns (whose ideal output from the response unit is 1), and let E_F be the complementary set of E_T for the set of all the possible input patterns (whose ideal output from the response unit is 0). Suppose E_T and E_F can be separated linearly. In other words, when an input pattern is represented by an n-dimensional vector, we assume that there is an $(n-1)$-dimensional hyperplane $a^T y = b$ that makes $a^T y > b$ for all $y \in E_T$, $a^T y \leq b$ for all $y \in E_F$. In this case, for a simple three-layer perceptron with the structure described above, if we take a small enough value of the step width ϵ when updating w_{rj} in Algorithm 10.1, the algorithm converges in a finite number of iterations and we can find the weights w_{rj} $(j = 1, \ldots, n)$ that make the discrimination of the input patterns possible. A rule for learning weights where the amount of change in the link weights is determined by the difference between the ideal output and the actual output is called a *delta rule*. The fixed increment correction method is a kind of delta rule.

10.2 Back Propagation

In the three-layer perceptron described in Section 10.1 [Example 3], it is difficult to learn to discriminate input patterns that cannot be separated linearly. More precisely, in such a three-layer perceptron, the number of units necessary for pattern discrimination depends on the size of the input pattern (for example, the dimension in a vector representation). However, there are many patterns that cannot be separated linearly, like the exclusive OR that was described in Example 2. We will explain the *back propagation error learning* algorithm as an algorithm for neural networks that learn to discriminate patterns that cannot be separated linearly.

(a) The structure of a neural network and an algorithm

Let us consider the neural network shown in Figure 10.4. This neural network has the following two features:

(1) It has a *multilayer structure* that has hidden-unit layers between the input-unit layer and the output-unit layer.
(2) It has a *feedforward structure* where links from the input-unit layer to the output-unit layer exist, but links in reverse directions do not exist.

Consider the following learning algorithm for neural networks with this structure. Suppose pairs of the input data and their ideal output are given in order. If we do the input-output computation for each unit using the neural network on these input data, we can obtain the actual output value. So, based on the error between the ideal output value and the actual output value for the same input datum, we change the weights of the links in the net so that the actual output value comes close to the ideal output value.

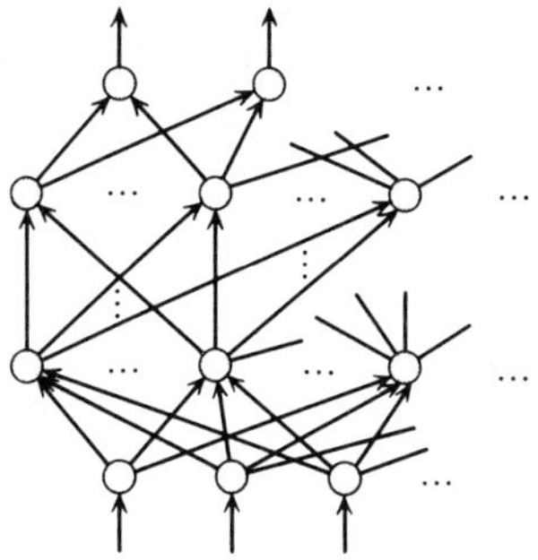

Figure 10.4 A neural network with feedforward links and hidden units.

The problem here is whether, when we do this operation for each input, we can eventually learn the weights that output the ideal output value for arbitrary inputs.

The following algorithm gives a "weak" answer to this problem, "weak" meaning that the algorithm gives the steepest descent direction* that makes the sum of the squares of the error local minimum for the weights of the links. This does not guarantee that the algorithm converges in a finite number of steps or that it converges to the global minimum. However, from experience we know that, for networks up to reasonable sizes, we often can obtain weights that make the error between the actual output value and the ideal output value small using this algorithm. This algorithm can be thought of as a kind of algorithm for *supervised learning* in the sense that the ideal output value is given from outside.

Definition 4 (symbols for the algorithm) First, we define the output error of the output unit f for the kth input-output data (the pair of the input datum and its ideal output value) by

$$\delta_{kj} = (r_{kj} - o_{kj})h'_j(i_{kj}) \tag{10.1}$$

where we assume that r_{kj} and o_{kj} are the ideal output value and the actual output value of the jth output unit for the kth input-output data,

*That a real-valued function $f(x)$ defined on n-dimensional Euclidean space E^n takes a *local minimum* at a point x^* means that there exists $\epsilon > 0$ such that, for the ϵ-neighborhood of x^*, $N(x^*, \epsilon) \subseteq E^n$, $f(x^*) \leq f(x)$ for all $x \in N(x^*, \epsilon)$. When $f(x^*) \leq f(x)$ for all $x \in E^n$, we say that $f(x)$ has a *global minimum* at x^*. When $f(x)$ is differentiable, $-\nabla f(\hat{x})$ is the direction where the value of $f(x)$ at $\hat{x}$ is decreasing the fastest. This direction is called the steepest descent direction of $f(x)$ at $\hat{x}$, and the method for obtaining a local minimum of $f(x)$ by successively obtaining the steepest descent direction is called the *steepest descent method*.

respectively, and that they take nonnegative values. i_{kj} is the weighted sum of the outputs from each unit that are input to the jth unit in learning using the kth input-output data and can be defined as

$$i_{kj} = \sum_i w_{ji} o_{ki} \tag{10.2}$$

where the ith unit is an input unit, and $w_{ki} = x_{ki}$ (x_{ki} is the value of the ith element of the input pattern in the kth input-output data).

The function h_j has the following meaning. When the output function of the unit j is simply

$$o_{kj} = g_j(a_{kj}) = a_{kj} \tag{10.3}$$

where a_{kj} is the state of unit j for the kth input-output data, and the state transition function is

$$a_{kj} = f_j(i_{kj}) \tag{10.4}$$

we incorporate all of this and write

$$o_{kj} = g_i(f_i(i_{kj})) = h_j(i_{kj}) \tag{10.5}$$

In other words, h_j is the composite function of the output function g_j and the state transition function f_j, and matches f_j exactly under the definition of (10.3) and (10.4). We assume that h_j (in other words f_j) is a nonlinear differentiable monotonically nondecreasing function and h'_j is the derivative of h_j. The condition of being nonlinear is necessary to make the propagation of the error become effective since the following algorithm is a method that is linear in the error.

Next, for a hidden unit, we define the output error of unit j for the kth input-output data as

$$\delta_{kj} = h'_j(i_{kj}) \sum_m \delta_{km} w_{mj} \tag{10.6}$$

(10.6) is a recursive expression where the output error of the hidden unit j is determined using the output error of other units that are directly linked to j. (10.1) and (10.6) together are called a *generalized delta rule.*

Using these definitions, the change in the link weight w_{ji} for the kth input-output data is given by

$$\Delta_k w_{ji} = \alpha \delta_{kj} o_{ki} \tag{10.7}$$

where α is a constant. Using (10.1), (10.6), and (10.7), the amount of change in the weights of all links can be computed using the following algorithm.

Algorithm 10.2 (back propagation error learning)

[1] Compute the output of each unit for the presented input in order from the input layer to the output layer (since the net does not include feedback links, this can be done easily).

[2] Compare the output o_{kj} of each output unit j against the presented ideal output value r_{kj} and compute the output error δ_{kj} for each output unit j using (10.1).

[3] For each output unit j, compute the amount of change to the link weights that are directly connected to j from δ_{kj} and the actual output o_{kj} using (10.7).

[4] Change the weights of all the links that enter each output unit j, w_{ji}, to $w_{ji} + \Delta_k w_{ji}$. Another method for obtaining the weight at time $t+1$, $w_{ji}(t+1)$, is to add the weight at time $t-1$, $w_{ji}(t-1)$, and set

$$w_{ji}(t+1) = w_{ji}(t) + \Delta_k w_{ji}(t) - \beta w_{ji}(t-1)$$

The latter method smooths the changes of the weights and often avoids oscillation.

[5] Compute the output error δ_{kj} using (10.6) for each hidden unit j that is in the layer one layer closer to the input layer from the output layer.

[6] Compute the changes in the weights of the links that directly enter j, $\Delta_k w_{ji}$, using (10.7) from δ_{kj} and the actual output o_{ki} for each hidden unit j computed in [5].

[7] Change the weights of all the links that enter j, w_{ji}, to $w_{ji} + \Delta_k w_{ji}$ for each hidden unit j computed in [6]. Similarly to [4], the weight at time $t+1$ can also be obtained by adding the weight at time $t-1$, $w_{ji}(t-1)$, and setting $w_{ji}(t+1) = w_{ji}(t) + \Delta_k w_{ji}(t) - \beta w_{ji}(t-1)$. In this way, we can smooth the changes of the weights.

[8] Do the same computation as in [5], [6], [7] for all the hidden units in order from the hidden layer closer to the output layer toward the input layer.

[9] Do [1]–[8] for each input-output data repeatedly changing the weights. The order of presenting the data can be fixed or can be random. When the square sum of the output error for the datum that is input last, $\sum_j \delta_{kj}^2$, is smaller than a given threshold value for each input-output data, stop. The learning is completed. Note that there are many other stopping criteria.

In Algorithm 10.2, since the error to be propagated is proportional to the weights of the links, if we make the initial values of the weights fixed for all the links, the algorithm may not converge. We can avoid this problem by initializing the weights with random values.

As mentioned in [9], we define the evaluation function for the output error as follows:

$$E = \sum_k E_k$$

$$E_k = \frac{1}{2} \sum_j (r_{kj} - o_{kj})^2 \tag{10.8}$$

where j denotes the jth output unit. E_k is the evaluation function for the kth input-output data. Thus, Algorithm 10.2 provides a computation procedure that gives the steepest descent direction to E (as a function of w_{ji}). Let us prove this. In the following proof, we assume that all the weights are kept fixed during the computation of w_{ji} for all input-output data. Since Algorithm 10.2 changes the weights as the input-output data are given, this assumption does not hold. However, in actual use, we expect the influence of this assumption on the algorithm will be small if we change the weights with a small step size, α.

[Proving convergence of the back propagation error algorithm]

The following two facts will be sufficient to prove that the back propagation error algorithm converges to a local minimum:

(1) $\Delta_k w_{ji} = -\frac{\partial E_k}{\partial w_{ji}}$ (10.9)

(2) Suppose j is an output unit. For the actual output value o_{kj} and the ideal output value r_{kj}, $\partial E_k / w_{ji} \geq 0$ when $o_{kj} > r_{kj}$; $\partial E_k / \partial w_{ji} \leq 0$ when $o_{kj} < r_{kj}$.

(1) guarantees that the amount of change of the weights is in the steepest direction of the evaluation function. (2) guarantees that the weight changes in a direction that makes the value of the evaluation function smaller. By combining these two, if we prove (1) and (2), we can prove that the amount of change of the weights is in the steepest descent direction, and therefore we can prove that the algorithm converges to a local minimum of the evaluation function. (In the above, we used the error of the kth input-output data, E_k, but the same thing can be said for $E = \sum_k E_k$.) First, let us prove (1).

Now,

$$\frac{\partial E_k}{\partial w_{ji}} = \frac{\partial E_k}{\partial i_{kj}} \frac{\partial i_{kj}}{\partial w_{ji}} \tag{10.10}$$

Here the first term on the right side of (10.10) represents the change of the error E_k for the kth input-output data due to the change of input i_{kj} to unit j. The second term represents the change of the whole input i_{kj} to the unit j due to the change of a particular weight w_{ji}. Then, by (10.2), we have

$$\frac{\partial i_{kj}}{\partial w_{ji}} = \frac{\partial}{\partial w_{ji}} \sum_m w_{jm} o_{km} = o_{ki} \tag{10.11}$$

Also, when the unit j is an output unit, we have

$$\begin{aligned} \frac{\partial E_k}{\partial i_{kj}} &= \frac{\partial E_k}{\partial o_{kj}} \frac{\partial o_{kj}}{\partial i_{kj}} \\ &= -(r_{kj} - o_{kj}) \frac{\partial o_{kj}}{\partial i_{kj}} \qquad (j \text{ is an output unit}) \\ &= -(r_{kj} - o_{kj}) h'_j(i_{kj}) \qquad (\text{from expression (10.5)}) \qquad (10.12) \end{aligned}$$

Since (10.12) (after we change variables on the right side) is equivalent to the right side of (10.1), we have, from (10.10), (10.11), and (10.12), the following for a given constant $\alpha > 0$:

$$\frac{\partial E_k}{\partial w_{ji}} = -a\delta_{kj} o_{kj} \tag{10.13}$$

If we compare this expression with (10.7), we get

$$\Delta_k w_{ji} = -\frac{\partial E_k}{\partial w_{ji}}$$

That is, we obtained (10.9).

On the other hand, if the unit j is not an output unit, we have

$$\begin{aligned} \frac{\partial E_k}{\partial o_{kj}} &= \sum_m \frac{\partial E_k}{\partial i_{km}} \frac{\partial i_{km}}{\partial o_{kj}} \\ &= \sum_m \frac{\partial E_k}{\partial i_{km}} \frac{\partial}{\partial o_{kj}} \sum_n w_{mn} o_{kn} \qquad (\text{from expression (10.2)}) \\ &= \sum_m \frac{\partial E_k}{\partial i_{km}} w_{mj} \end{aligned}$$

Thus, we have

$$\frac{\partial E_k}{\partial i_{kj}} = \left\{ \sum_m \frac{\partial E_k}{\partial i_{km}} w_{mj} \right\} h'_j(i_{kj}) \tag{10.14}$$

(10.14) and (10.6) match by setting

$$\frac{\partial E_k}{\partial i_{kj}} = \delta_{kj}, \quad \frac{\partial E_k}{\partial i_{km}} = \delta_{km}$$

Therefore, just as in the case of an output unit described above, we get from (10.7)

$$\Delta_k w_{ji} = -\frac{\partial E_k}{\partial w_{ji}}$$

and again we obtain the expression (10.9). Thus we have proved (1).

Now, let us prove (2). From (10.12) and (10.13), we have the following for an output unit j:

$$\frac{\partial E_k}{\partial w_{ji}} = -\alpha(r_{kj} - o_{kj})o_{kj}h'_j(i_{kj})$$

By assumption, h_j is a monotonically nondecreasing function, so we have $h'_j(i_{kj}) \geq 0$. Also, $o_{kj} \geq 0$ by assumption. Therefore, $\partial E_k/\partial w_{ji} \geq 0$ when $o_{kj} > r_{kj}$, and $\partial E_k/\partial w_{ji} \leq 0$ when $o_{kj} < r_{kj}$. This proves (2).

(b) Examples of back propagation error learning

Let us look at two examples of back propagation error learning.

[Example 4] The exclusive OR problem

We can construct a neural network for computing exclusive OR described in Section 10.1 [Example 2] using the back propagation error learning. First, define the state transition function for each unit j (including the output function: refer to expression (10.5)) using a sigmoid function:

$$o_{kj} = h_j(i_{kj}) = \frac{1}{1 + \exp(-i_{kj} + \theta_j)}$$

Its derivative $h'_j(i_{kj})$ is given by

$$h'_j(i_{kj}) = o_{kj}(1 - o_{kj})$$

With these functions, and using a network with the same structure as shown in Figure 10.1(a), we present it with the input-output data in Figure 10.1(b) a total of 3200 times in the order in which they are shown. Start by setting the value of the parameter α of (10.7) to 2.50, set all the initial threshold values to 0, and, assuming that there is an imaginary unit v that always outputs 1, we represent the threshold value of the unit j as the weight of the imaginary link from v to j. We give a random value between ± 0.3 as the initial values of the weights. Figure 10.5(a) shows the initial values of the weights that were actually used and the results are shown in Figures 10.5(b) and (c). Figure 10.5(c) shows how the outputs for the input (0,0) and (1,1) converge to 0 and the outputs for (0,1) and (1,0) converge to 1.

[Example 5] Pattern discrimination

Suppose we have the six 8×8 bit input patterns shown in Figure 10.6. Suppose, of these patterns, (a)–(c) represent an airplane and (d)–(f) represent a ship. We will build a neural network for discriminating whether a given input pattern is an airplane or a ship using back propagation error learning.

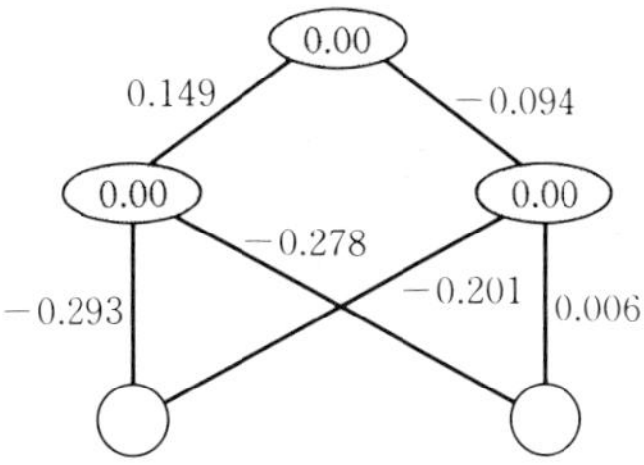

(a) The initial values of the weights and the threshold value

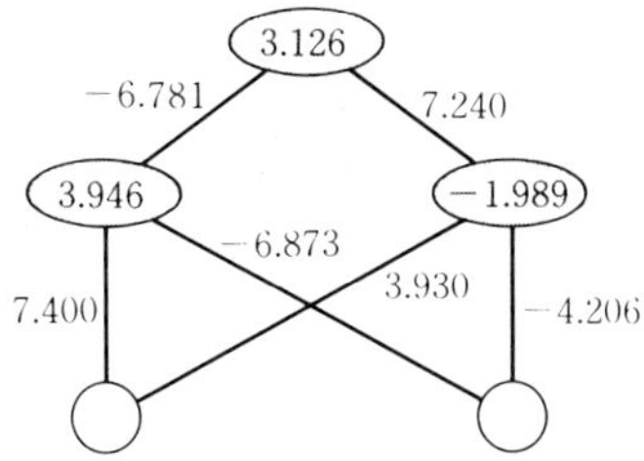

(b) The weights and the threshold value after the data are presented 3200 times

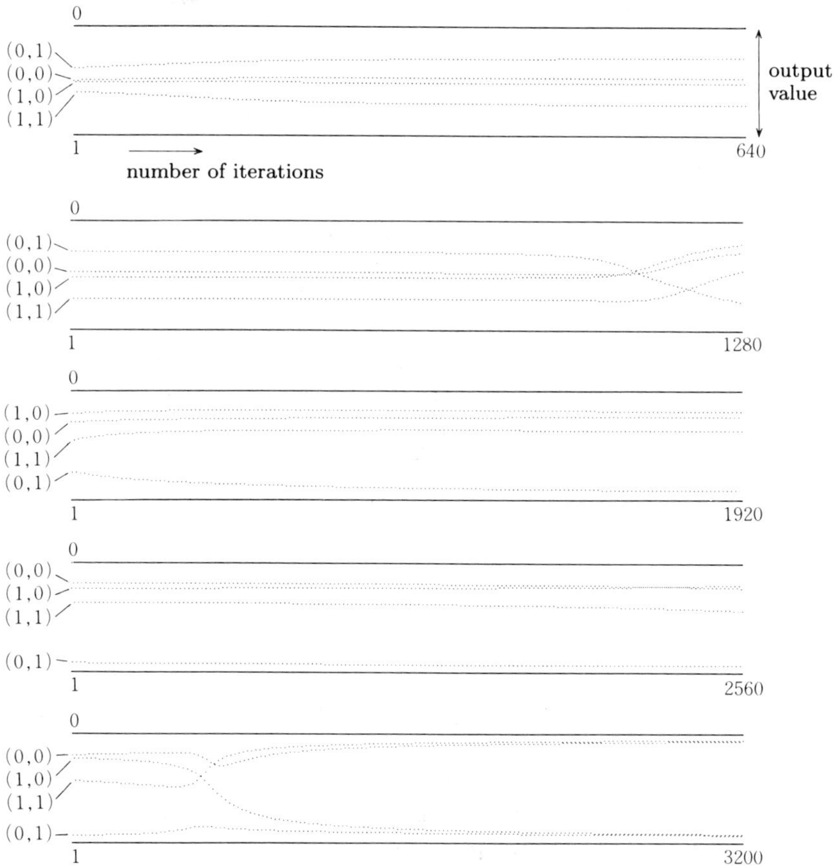

(c) Changes of the output value for each input datum

Figure 10.5 A solution to the exclusive OR problem using back propagation error learning.

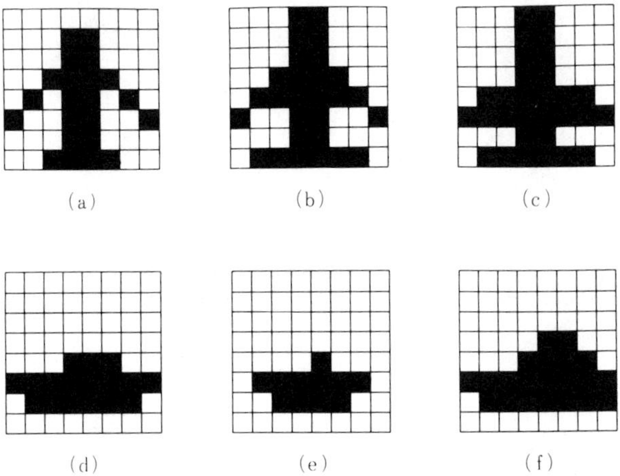

Figure 10.6 Training patterns for back propagation learning.

Let us consider a neural network with feedforward links in three layers of 64 input units, 32 hidden units, and 2 output units. Links are connected from each input unit to all the hidden units and from each hidden unit to all the output units. Also, we assume that θ_j, the threshold value for each unit u_j, can change, and we represent θ_j as the weight of a link from a special unit that always outputs 1 to u_j. We also assume that the initial value of θ_j is 0 and set the initial value of the weights randomly between ± 0.3.

The weights are updated using, as an example, a slightly different formula from the one described in Section 10.1:

$$w_{ji}(t+1) = w_{ji}(t) + \Delta w_{ji}(t)$$
$$\Delta w_{ji}(t) = \eta \delta_{kj} o_{kj} + \alpha \Delta w_{ji}(t-1)$$

In this example, the values of the coefficients are set to $\alpha = 0.80$, $\eta = 1.0$. Also, the algorithm is supposed to terminate when the sum of the values of the evaluation function that are obtained when each of the six patterns is presented once is less than 0.06, i.e., when $\sum_{k=1}^{6} E_k < 0.06$.

Using back propagation error learning with the six different input patterns in Figure 10.6 in the order (d), (a), (e), (b), (f), (c), the output converges in three cycles with the results shown in Figure 10.7. In other words, output unit u_1 responds to the patterns of airplanes (a)–(c), and output unit u_2 responds to the patterns of ships (d)–(e). ((a)–(f) are called the *training patterns*.)

If the two patterns (i) and (ii) (called *test patterns*) as shown in Figure 10.8(a) are input to the neural network obtained in this way, output unit u_1 responds to (i) and u_2 responds to (ii) as shown in Figure 10.8(b). Thus

presentation no.	input pattern	output value output unit u_1	output unit u_2	evaluation function value
1	d	0.540	0.525	
2	a	0.495	0.603	
3	e	0.552	0.536	
4	b	0.521	0.643	
5	f	0.557	0.543	
6	c	0.520	0.586	1.696
7	d	0.548	0.371	
8	a	0.876	0.138	
9	e	0.564	0.379	
10	b	0.894	0.147	
11	f	0.611	0.342	
12	c	0.843	0.164	1.163
13	d	0.025	0.968	
14	a	0.932	0.072	
15	e	0.038	0.958	
16	b	0.957	0.054	
17	f	0.040	0.954	
18	c	0.0898	0.106	0.022

Figure 10.7 Training patterns for back propagation error learning.

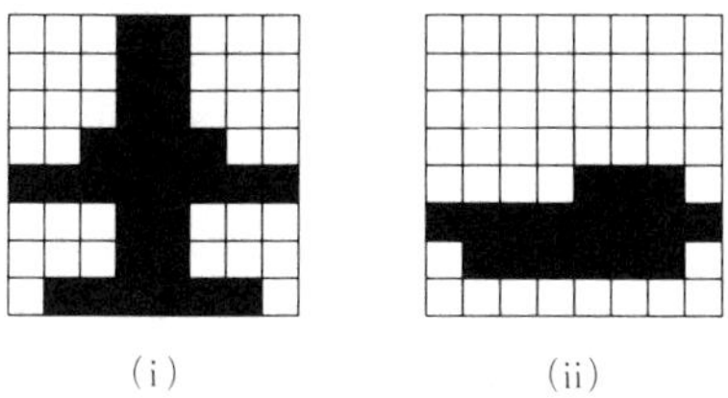

(a) test pattern

test pattern		output value output unit u_1	output unit u_2
(i)	→	0.952	0.059
(ii)	→	0.031	0.963

(b) test result

Figure 10.8 Test patterns for back propagation learning (Example 5) and output results.

we can assume that (i) is an airplane and (ii) is a ship.

People are trying to apply back propagation error learning to visual pattern recognition, as shown here, to voice recognition, voice synthesis, expert systems, and so on.

10.3 Competitive Learning

One of the characteristics of the back propagation error learning algorithm described in Section 10.2 is that it is supervised learning. As opposed to this, competitive learning is known as *unsupervised learning.* Unsupervised learning is a method of learning without giving ideal output values (sometimes called teacher signals). In this section, we will explain neural networks and an algorithm for competitive learning.

(a) The structure of the neural network and an algorithm

First, we will explain neural networks where the units are clustered.

Let us look at a network with the structure shown in Figure 10.9. In other words, the input layer appears as the leftmost, the output layer appears as the rightmost, and each of them is a set of clusters including units. (Generally, clusters can either be overlapped or not overlapped, but in this section we consider neural networks where they do not overlap.) Between these layers, there is a certain number of hidden layers, and each layer is also made up of a certain number of clusters. In this section, we assume that there are no links connecting units in different clusters within one layer and that links do not exist between units in one cluster within the input or output cluster. Also, in any cluster in a hidden layer, any two units are connected with an inhibitory link. Furthermore, only excitatory links may exist between two units in clusters in neighboring layers from the input layer toward the output layer (see Figure 10.9).

With these conditions, let us consider neural networks with the following characteristics:

(1) At any one time, only one of the units in any cluster of a hidden layer produces output; the other units in the cluster do not. For example, consider a circuit where only the unit whose input size is the maximum will produce an output (a maximum-value detection circuit).

(2) It only updates the weights of the links that enter the units that produced the output in (1). (Section 10.3 (b) [example 7] shows a method different from this.)

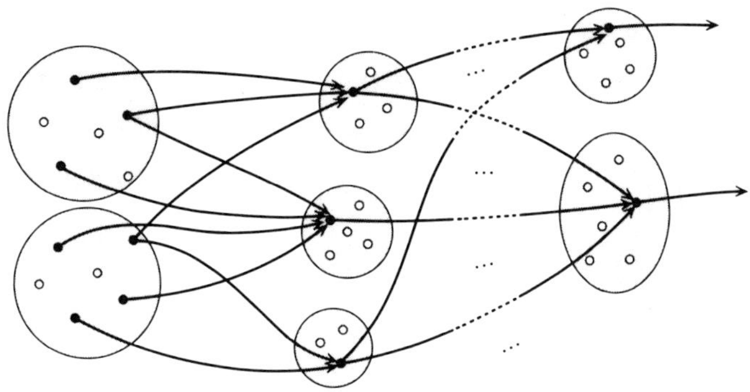

Figure 10.9 A neural network for competitive learning.

Learning weights by giving output from only one unit in a cluster in a hidden layer or the output layer within a clustered network as described above is called *competitive learning* since the output result is obtained by a competition among units within each cluster.

Next, let us look at an algorithm for competitive learning. Consider the following algorithm for the neural networks shown in Figure 10.9.

Algorithm 10.3 (competitive learning)

[1] Let w_{ji} be the weight of an excitatory link from unit i to unit j, where $\sum_i w_{ji} = 1$. Then, based on

$$\Delta w_{ji} = \begin{cases} \gamma(\frac{c_{ik}}{n_k} - w_{ji}) & \text{when unit } j \text{ gives output for the } k\text{th input pattern} \\ 0 & \text{otherwise} \end{cases} \qquad (10.15)$$

w_{ji} is changed by setting $w_{ji} = w_{ji} + \alpha \Delta w_{ji}$, where n_k is the number of input units that give outputs for the kth input pattern, α and γ are positive constants, and

$$c_{ik} = \begin{cases} 1 & \text{when unit } i \text{ gives output for the } k\text{th input datum} \\ 0 & \text{otherwise} \end{cases}$$

Let us consider a convergent state in the above algorithm, that is, an *equilibrium state* where the input and output values are equal for any unit. In this case, the link weight w_{ji} is in proportion to the conditional probability that the link from unit i to j is activated when unit j is responding. Let us prove this. Let p_k be the probability that the kth input pattern is given, and let v_{jk} be the probability that unit j responds to the kth input pattern. Then, from (10.15),

$$\sum_k \Delta w_{ji} v_{jk} p_k = \gamma \sum_k \left(\frac{c_{ik}}{n_k} - w_{ji}\right) v_{jk} p_k \tag{10.16}$$

Since the value of (10.16) is 0 in an equilibrium state, we have

$$\sum_k \frac{c_{ik} v_{jk} p_k}{n_k} = w_{ji} \sum_k v_{jk} p_k$$

Therefore

$$w_{ji} = \frac{\sum_k \frac{c_{ik} v_{jk} p_k}{n_k}}{\sum_k v_{jk} p_k} \tag{10.17}$$

Now, let us assume that the sizes of input patterns are the same. In other words, we assume $n_k = n$ for any k. Then, (10.17) becomes

$$\begin{aligned} w_{ji} &= \frac{\sum_k c_{ik} v_{jk} p_k}{n \sum_k v_{jk} p_k} \\ &= \frac{1}{n} P(\text{the link from the unit } i \text{ to } j \text{ is activated} | \text{unit } j \text{ is responding}) \end{aligned} \tag{10.18}$$

(10.18) shows that the weight of a link in an equilibrium state, w_{ji}, is in proportion to the conditional probability that the link from i to j is activated when j is responding.

We can say that, when the above algorithm reaches an equilibrium state, the network responds to similar input patterns more strongly and to non-similar input patterns more weakly. Let us prove this.

Suppose a new lth input pattern is given in the equilibrium state, and let i_{jl} be the input to unit j. Then we have

$$\begin{aligned} i_{jl} &= \sum_i w_{ji} c_{jl} \\ &= \frac{1}{n} \sum_i c_{il} \frac{\sum_k c_{ik} v_{jk} p_k}{\sum_k v_{jk} p_k} \end{aligned}$$

If we set

$$\xi_{kl} = \sum_m c_{mk} c_{ml} \tag{10.19}$$

we have

$$i_{jl} = \frac{1}{n} \frac{\sum_k \xi_{kl} v_{jk} p_k}{\sum_k v_{jk} p_k} \tag{10.20}$$

We can consider that (10.19) is the number of links that are activated for both the kth and lth input patterns, and it shows the similarity between the kth and lth input patterns. Therefore (10.20) shows that unit j, in an equilibrium state, responds more strongly to a similar input pattern and more weakly to an input pattern that is not so similar.

From these remarks an equilibrium state that can be reached using competitive learning by Algorithm 10.3 has some significance in processing similar patterns. Actually which equilibrium state can be reached is constrained depending on how output is chosen at each cluster. For example, if we use the maximum-value detection circuit, even when the equilibrium state mentioned above is reached, it has the following constraint:

$$v_{jk} = \begin{cases} 1 & \text{when } i_{jk} > i_{hk} \text{ for all } h \neq j \\ 0 & \text{otherwise} \end{cases}$$

(b) An example of competitive learning

[Example 6] A method of pattern classification

Suppose we have a carrot, an apple, a cucumber, a kiwi, an eggplant, and grapes as objects, and they are given as the 13-bit patterns shown in Figure 10.10. Each bit in these patterns shows the color red, green, or purple and whether it is a vegetable or a fruit, where the color in a pattern can be slightly different due to differences in density.

presented pattern	characteristics					meaning
	red	green	purple	vegetable	fruit	
carrot	101	000	000	11	00	red vegetable
apple	111	000	000	00	11	red fruit
cucumber	000	111	000	11	00	green vegetable
kiwi	000	110	000	00	11	green fruit
eggplant	000	000	011	11	00	purple vegetable
grapes	000	000	111	00	11	purple fruit

Figure 10.10 Patterns for classification using competitive learning.

Consider the two-layer network whose input layer consists of one cluster including 13 units and whose output layer consists of one cluster including two units and one cluster including three units. We assume there is no hidden layer. We set the parameters of (10.15), γ and α, to $\alpha\gamma = 1.0$.

The patterns of Figure 10.10 are input in order once for each cycle and repeat for 100 cycles. The result is the output from the output clusters shown in Figure 10.11. The result for output cluster 1 shows that the six

presentation pattern	output cluster 1 output unit 1	2	output cluster 2 output unit 1	2	3
carrot	0	1	0	1	0
apple	0	1	0	0	1
cucumber	1	0	0	1	0
kiwi	1	0	1	0	0
eggplant	1	0	0	1	0
grapes	1	0	1	0	0

Figure 10.11 The result of competitive learning for the training patterns

patterns are classified into {carrot, apple} and {cucumber, kiwi, eggplant, grapes}, in other words, red things and not red things. The result for output cluster 2 shows that they are classified into {kiwi, grapes} and {carrot, cucumber, eggplant}, {apple}, that is, green or purple fruits, vegetables, and red fruits.

Next, the test patterns shown in Figure 10.12(a) are input to the network learned in this way, and we obtain the output shown in Figure 10.12(b). In other words, a tomato and a red radish are considered to be members of the red things when patterns are classified under two categories, and they are considered to be members of the red fruits when patterns are classified under three categories. Also, a cauliflower and a fig are considered to be green or purple fruits when patterns are classified into two categories, and a cauliflower is considered to be a vegetable and a fig is considered to be a green or purple vegetable when patterns are classified into three categories.

[Example 7] There is a method that not only changes the weights of the links from the input units to units that have an output as in (10.15) but also changes the weights of the links connected to units that did not have an output. Although we did not say this in (a), the method uses the following formulas to change link weights:

$$\Delta w_{ji} = \begin{cases} \gamma'(\frac{c_{ik}}{n_k} - w_{ji}) & \text{when the unit } j \text{ does not give output for the } k\text{th input pattern} \\ 0 & \text{otherwise} \end{cases} \qquad (10.21)$$

$$w_{ji} = w_{ji} + \alpha' \Delta w_{ji}$$

Using the method of Example 6, the patterns in Figure 10.10 can be classified using both (10.21) and (10.15) by setting the parameters γ' and α' of (10.21) so that $\alpha'\gamma' = 0.01$. The results are shown in Figure 10.13(a).

(a) Test patterns

presented pattern	characteristics				
	red	green	purple	vegetable	fruit
tomato	111	010	000	01	10
red radish	101	010	000	10	01
cauliflower	000	111	011	01	10
fig	100	100	100	10	10

(b) Results from test

presented pattern	output cluster 1 output unit		output cluster 2 output unit		
	1	2	1	2	3
tomato	0	1	0	0	1
red cabbage	0	1	0	0	1
cauliflower	1	0	0	1	0
fig	1	0	1	0	0

Figure 10.12 Results of competitive learning of test patterns.

The results show that the network can distinguish whether a pattern is a vegetable or a fruit when it classifies patterns into two classes and whether a pattern is red, green, or purple when it classifies patterns into three classes.

If we input the test patterns of Figure 10.12(a) to this trained network, we obtain the results shown in Figure 10.13(b). A tomato and a red radish are classified as vegetables when patterns are classified into two classes, and they are classified as red things when patterns are classified into three classes. Overall, a tomato and a red radish are classified as red vegetables. A cauliflower and a fig are classified as a green vegetable and a green fruit, respectively. Overall, we can say that they are classified as green things.

Pattern classification by competitive learning not only uses an unsupervised learning technique but also works without prior knowledge of classes to distinguish. In the above example, we gave the meanings such as vegetable, fruit, color, and so on. We did that for convenience. It does not mean that the patterns we used as examples correctly reflect the meanings that we gave them. However, the above example shows us that competitive learning can be used as a method for classifying patterns whose meaning is unknown.

(a) Results for the training patterns

presented pattern	output cluster 1 output unit 1	output cluster 1 output unit 2	output cluster 2 output unit 1	output cluster 2 output unit 2	output cluster 2 output unit 3
tomato	0	1	0	0	1
apple	1	0	0	0	1
cucumber	0	1	0	1	0
kiwi	1	0	0	1	0
eggplant	0	1	1	0	0
grapes	1	0	1	0	0

(b) Results for the test patterns

presented pattern	output cluster 1 output unit 1	output cluster 1 output unit 2	output cluster 2 output unit 1	output cluster 2 output unit 2	output cluster 2 output unit 3
tomato	0	1	0	0	1
red radish	0	1	0	0	1
cauliflower	0	1	0	1	0
fig	1	0	0	1	0

Figure 10.13 Results of competitive learning using both (10.15) and (10.21).

10.4 Hopfield Networks

In a neural network where many units are linked to each other, if we limit the state of each unit to 0 or 1, we can represent the state of the whole network as a distribution pattern of local states each taking 0 or 1. In this global state, we can compare the state of each unit with the positive or negative direction of the spin of an electron using an analogy from physics. Under this comparison, if we let the potential of the global state of the network correspond to the energy of the spins, the thermodynamic process that tries to reach a state with the minimum spin energy corresponds to the process of finding an equilibrium state of the network.

Suppose we extend this idea and assume that the state of each unit can take a continuous value between [0,1]. Then, if we consider the spin glass model* in physics, we can also make the energy function's process of moving to a local minimum correspond to the neural network's process of reaching an equilibrium state.

Based on this physical analogy, we can construct a neural network called a Hopfield network. In this section, we will explain Hopfield networks. Though the Hopfield network below is not basically a network for learning, it is explained here since it is a basic neural network representation and is deeply related to the Boltzmann machine that will be described in Section 10.5.

(a) The structure of the neural network and the algorithm

Let us look at the structure of a Hopfield network. Suppose we have a neural network where many units are interconnected with each other. The interconnection means that, if unit i is linked to j, then there is a link from j to i. We write $a_j(t)$ for the state of unit j at time t. Suppose $a_j(t)$ takes a value in [0,1], and let $i_j(t)$ be the input to j and θ_j be the threshold value of j (note the sign of θ). If we let $o_i(t)$ be the output from unit i and w_{ji} the weight of the link from j to i, we have

$$i_j(t) = \sum_i w_{ji} o_i(t) + \theta_i \tag{10.22}$$

We assume that the state of unit j, $a_j(t)$, changes according to the following rule:

$$\frac{\mathrm{d}a_j(t)}{\mathrm{d}t} = -\frac{a_j(t)}{\tau} + i_j(t) \tag{10.23}$$

Here τ is the *time constant* of the state of j. We assume the output of j is given by the following output function:

$$o_j(t) = g(a_j(t)) = \frac{1}{2}\left(1 + \tan\tanh\frac{a_j(t)}{a_0}\right) \tag{10.24}$$

where a_0 is a constant called the *reference activation level.*

Now, we define the *energy* of this neural network as follows:

$$E = -\frac{1}{2}\sum_{i,j} w_{ji} a_i(t) a_j(t) - \sum_j \theta_j o_j(t) - \sum_j \int_{\frac{1}{2}}^{o_j(t)} g^{-1}(s)\mathrm{d}s \tag{10.25}$$

*An irregular magnetic substance whose magnetic interaction can be positive or negative and that has the order phase without long-distance order under a certain temperature is called spin glass. Under such a temperature, it is considered that there exist numerous semistable states that move gradually toward stable states as the temperature is reduced.

If we assume $w_{ji} = w_{ij}$ (symmetry of weights) for any i and j, we can bring the network to a local minimum value of E by computing the states of all units, $a_j(t)$, using (10.22), (10.23), and (10.24) repeatedly. The algorithm can be described simply as follows:

Algorithm 10.4 (minimization of the energy of a Hopfield network)
[1] Differentiate (10.23) and obtain the value of the difference Δt, the constant τ, and a_0, the constant in (10.24).
[2] Set the values of the link weights w_{ji} and the threshold value θ_j.
[3] Update the states of all units repeatedly using (10.22), (10.23), and (10.24).
[4] When the value of E that is defined in (10.25) becomes smaller than some given positive constant, stop. (There are other stopping criteria.)

(b) Example of Hopfield networks

An *optimization problem* that minimizes an evaluation function under some constraints is frequently solved using mathematical programming. Optimization problems such as finding an optimal path in a graph generally include variables that take only discrete values. It becomes difficult to solve such a problem when it contains a large number of variables. A Hopfield network can be used for finding a locally optimal solution to this kind of problem.

[Example 8] As an example, we will apply Hopfield networks to the *traveling salesperson problem.* The traveling salesperson problem is defined as the following optimization problem.

> "Suppose there are n towns. Find the shortest route that starts at some town, visits every other town once and only once, and returns to the original town."

Suppose the n towns are $1, \ldots, n$, and the distance between the towns i and j is d_{ij}. We define the variables

$$x_{ij} = \begin{cases} 1 & \text{when town } i \text{ is the } j\text{th town visited} \\ 0 & \text{otherwise} \end{cases}$$

Then, the problem can be formalized as a problem of finding x_{ij} $(i, j = 1, \ldots, n)$ that minimize the following function. We let the state of each unit be 0 or 1. The following can be applied when the state of each unit takes a continuous value from [0,1].

$$E = \frac{A}{2}\sum_{i=1}^{n}\Big(\sum_{j=1}^{n} x_{ij} - 1\Big)^2 + \frac{B}{2}\sum_{j=1}^{n}\Big(\sum_{i=1}^{n} x_{ij} - 1\Big)^2 + \frac{C}{2}\sum_{i=1}^{n}\sum_{k\neq i}^{n}\sum_{\substack{j=1 \\ j\neq i}}^{n} d_{ik}x_{ij}(x_{k,j-1} + x_{k,j+1}) \tag{10.26}$$

where A, B, and C are constants. The first term on the right side of (10.26) is the constraint that each town should be visited only once, the second term is the condition that the towns are visited one at a time, and the third term is to minimize the total distance. (10.26) assumes that there is no loop in any unit j. Let $w_{i2j2,i1j1}$ be the weight of the link from (i_1, j_1) to (i_2, j_2). Comparing (10.25) and (10.26) in the Hopfield network with n^2 units that represents the fact that town i is visited at time j with the unit (i, j), the weight and the threshold value are

$$\begin{aligned} w_{i2j2,i1j1} &= -A\delta_{i1i2}(1 - \delta_{j1,j2}) - B\delta_{j1,j2}(1 - \delta_{i1,j2}) \\ &\quad - Cd_{i1,i2}(\delta_{j1,j2-1} + \delta_{j1,j2+1}) \\ \theta_j &= \frac{A}{2} + \frac{B}{2} \end{aligned}$$

where

$$\delta_{kl} = \begin{cases} 1 & \text{when } k = l \\ 0 & \text{otherwise} \end{cases}$$

Then we can find a local minimum of E using Algorithm 10.4. A path that provides such value is a locally optimal solution to the original problem.

As an example, consider the 10 towns shown in Figure 10.14(a). These towns are the nodes of the strongly connected graph that allows movement between any two towns. The distance between towns is shown in Figure 10.14(a). For example, the distance between towns 5 and 8 is $3\sqrt{2}$. Assume $A = B = C = 1.0$ and $\Delta t = \tau = a_0 = 1.0$.

If we apply Algorithm 10.4 to this problem and its parameters, we get the result shown in Figure 10.14(b). The abscissa of the figure represents the name of a town and the ordinate represents the order of the visit on the route. The radius of the circle in the figure represents the state of the corresponding unit. The result in Figure 10.14(b) shows that, although there is still some noise, the route 10.14(c) starting from town 1 and going back to 1 was found by paying attention only to nodes whose radius is large.

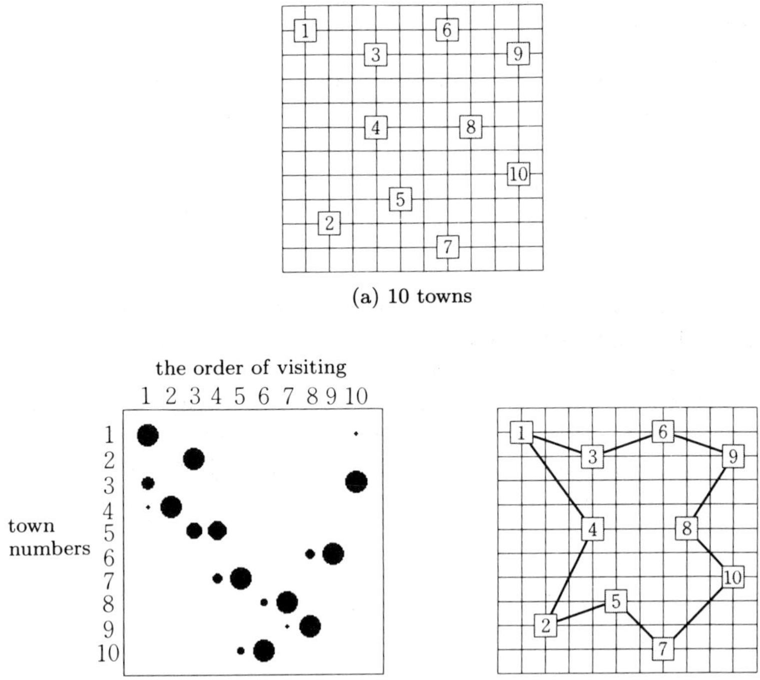

(a) 10 towns

(b) The computation result

(c) The shortest route

Figure 10.14 The traveling salesperson problem solved using a Hopfield network.

10.5 Boltzmann Machines

As we said about the Hopfield network in Section 10.4, the behavior of some kinds of neural networks have the analog of a physical system moving toward a state of energy equilibrium. Under some conditions, the behavior of a neural network, where the input is given stochastically, can be described as statistical thermodynamic behavior. Using this analogy, by adding stochastic fluctuation to the state change of each unit, it is possible to make the energy a little bigger, and the network escapes from a local energy minimum and reaches the global minimum as shown in Figure 10.15.

Boltzmann machines are neural networks with this feature.

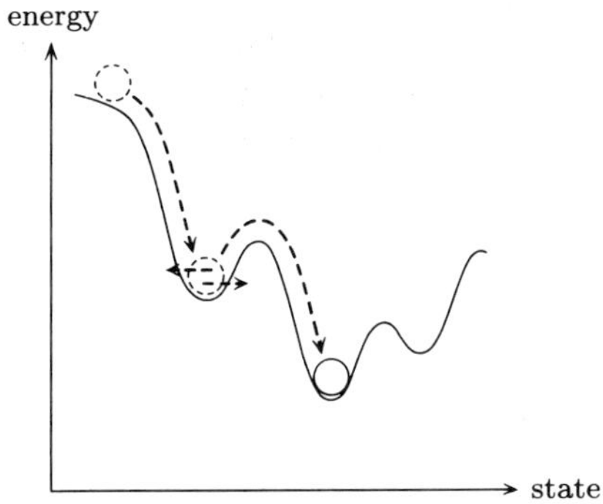

Figure 10.15 Escape from a local minimum using stochastic fluctuation.

(a) Structure of the neural network and its algorithm

Let us consider a neural network that works in a stochastic environment in which the input data follow a given probability distribution. In this neural network, it is natural to assume that the state transition of each unit and its output also follow some probability distributions. Let us consider the following problem: how could we find the link weights of a network that makes its input-output relation have a probability distribution "as close as possible" to the probability distribution of the input-output data given from the outside?

Solving this problem corresponds to generalizing a Hopfield network to be stochastic. Below, we will describe an algorithm for solving the problem under some conditions. Algorithms of this kind, along with neural networks that compute them, are called *Boltzmann machines.* Unlike Hopfield networks, Boltzmann machines can learn link weights such that they minimize the error between the probability distribution of the ideal output and the distribution of actual output values.

First, we assume that in a neural network K with n units, the state s_j of each unit j takes the value 0 or 1 stochastically. A state of K can be represented as an n-dimensional vector whose elements each stochastically take the value 0 or 1. We assume that for the weight of the link between units i and j, as in a Hopfield network, the symmetry $w_{ij} = w_{ji}$ holds.

Now let us regard K as a statistical thermodynamic system consisting of n particles. If we let E_α be the energy of a state of K, α, the probability of K taking the state α is given by the Maxwell-Boltzmann distribution:

$$P_\alpha = \frac{e^{-E_\alpha/kT}}{\sum_\lambda e^{-E_\lambda/kT}} = \frac{e^{-E_\alpha/T}}{\sum_\lambda e^{-E_\lambda/T}} \tag{10.27}$$

In (10.27), k is the Boltzmann constant. (When we consider K as a collection of particles that is in thermal equilibrium with an ideal gas having a large heat capacity, we can derive the above distribution using the idea of energy level.) T corresponds to temperature.

Corresponding to the energy function E defined in Section 10.4(a), we define energy E_α as follows:

$$E_\alpha = -\sum_{i<j} w_{ij} s_i^\alpha s_j^\alpha - \sum_j \theta_j s_j^\alpha \tag{10.28}$$

Here we assume $w_{ij} = w_{ji}$, and s_j^α and θ_j are the values of the state variable s_j and the threshold in the state α, respectively.

The problem is now to find the weight that realizes the probability distribution of the input-output data "as precisely as possible" without any input from outside. For this, below we divide the set of the units of K into two groups, the set of the input and output units (*visible units*) A and the set of other units (hidden units) B. Let P_α^- be the probability distribution for the state vector α of the set of visible units A, when there is no input and let $\alpha + \beta$ be the state vector of K for α and the state vector β of the set of the hidden units B. Then, similarly to (10.27), we have

$$P_\alpha^- = \sum_\beta P_{\alpha+\beta}^- = \frac{\sum_\beta e^{-E_{\alpha\beta}/T}}{\sum_{\lambda,\mu} e^{-E_{\lambda\mu}/T}} \tag{10.29}$$

where $E_{\alpha\beta}$ is the energy of K in the state $\alpha + \beta$. If we let $s_i^{\alpha\beta}$ be the state of K in $\alpha + \beta$, $E_{\alpha\beta}$ is given, as before, by

$$E_{\alpha\beta} = -\sum_{i<j} w_{ij} s_i^{\alpha\beta} s_j^{\alpha\beta} \tag{10.30}$$

In the network described above, the probability distributions of the states of the input units and those of the output units are not separated. This kind of Boltzmann machine is called an *autoassociative Boltzmann machine.* On the other hand, the probability distribution of the states of the input units can be considered separately from the probability distribution of those of the output units when some input is given. Such a machine is called an *mutually associative Boltzmann machine.* We consider only the autoassociative Boltzmann machines.

From (10.30),

$$\frac{\partial e^{-E_{\alpha\beta}/T}}{\partial w_{ij}} = \frac{1}{T} s_i^{\alpha\beta} s_j^{\alpha\beta} e^{-E_{\alpha\beta}/T}$$

Thus, from (10.29),

$$\frac{\partial P_\alpha^-}{\partial w_{ij}}$$
$$= \frac{\frac{1}{T}\sum_\beta s_i^{\alpha\beta} s_j^{\alpha\beta} e^{-E_{\alpha/\beta}/T}}{\sum_{\lambda,\mu} e^{-E_{\lambda\mu}/T}} - \frac{\sum_\beta e^{-E_{\alpha\beta}/T} \cdot \frac{1}{T}\sum_{\lambda,\mu} s_i^{\lambda\mu} s_j^{\lambda\mu} e^{-E_{\lambda\mu}/T}}{\{\sum_{\lambda,\mu} e^{-E_{\lambda\mu}/T}\}^2}$$
$$= \frac{1}{T}\left\{\sum_\beta s_i^{\alpha\beta} s_j^{\alpha\beta} P_{\alpha+\beta}^- - P_\alpha^- \sum_{\lambda,\mu} s_i^{\lambda\mu} s_j^{\lambda\mu} P_{\lambda+\mu}^-\right\} \tag{10.31}$$

When the input and output are given from outside of K, let P_α^+ be the probability distribution taken by α, the state vector of A. Since P_α^+ is determined only by the input and output, it is independent of w_{ij}. The problem here is to find w_{ij} that makes the difference between P_α^+ and P_α^- as small as possible. In order to do that, let us find w_{ji} that makes the Kullback information measure for P_α^+ and P_α^-

$$G = \sum_\alpha P_\alpha^+ \ln \frac{P_\alpha^+}{P_\alpha^-}$$

a local minimum. If we differentiate G with respect to w_{ij}, we get the following using (10.31):

$$\frac{\partial G}{\partial w_{ij}} = -\sum_\alpha \frac{P_\alpha^+}{P_\alpha^-}\frac{\partial P_\alpha^-}{\partial w_{ij}}$$
$$= -\frac{1}{T}\left\{\sum_\alpha \frac{P_\alpha^+}{P_\alpha^-}\sum_\beta s_i^{\alpha\beta} s_j^{\alpha\beta} P_{\alpha+\beta}^- \right.$$
$$\left. - \sum_\alpha P_\alpha^+ \sum_{\lambda,\mu} s_i^{\lambda\mu} s_j^{\lambda\mu} P_{\lambda+\mu}^-\right\} \tag{10.32}$$

Now if, in an equilibrium, we assume that the probability of the state β of B when the state of A is fixed at α is equal to the probability of β when the state of A is not fixed, we have

$$P_{\beta|\alpha}^- = P_{\beta|\alpha}^+ \tag{10.33}$$

However,

$$P_{\alpha+\beta}^+ = P_{\beta|\alpha}^+ P_\alpha^+$$
$$P_{\alpha+\beta}^- = P_{\beta|\alpha}^- P_\alpha^-$$

Therefore, from (10.33),

$$P^-_{\alpha+\beta}\frac{P^+_\alpha}{P^-_\alpha} = P^+_{\alpha+\beta} \tag{10.34}$$

Also, for the probability P^+_α,

$$\sum_\alpha P^+_\alpha = 1 \tag{10.35}$$

So, if we substitute (10.34) and (10.35) into (10.32), we get

$$\frac{\partial G}{\partial w_{ij}} = -\frac{1}{T}(p^+_{ij} - p^-_{ij}) \tag{10.36}$$

where

$$p^+_{ij} = \sum_{\alpha,\beta} s_i^{\alpha\beta} s_j^{\alpha\beta} P^+_{\alpha+\beta}$$

$$p^-_{ij} = \sum_{\lambda,\mu} s_i^{\lambda\mu} s_j^{\lambda\mu} P^-_{\lambda+\mu}$$

Here, p^+_{ij} is the expected value of the probability distribution of the input-output data that makes the states of both units i and j 1 when K works by the input and output given from outside and reaches an equilibrium state. Similarly, p^-_{ij} can be interpreted as the expected value of an equilibrium state when there is no input from outside.

(10.36) is the basic expression for obtaining an equilibrium state of the Boltzmann machine K, that is, the state where G takes a local minimum for w_{ij}. A characteristic of this expression is that it uses only information on units i and j to find the steepest descent direction of G for w_{ij} and does not require global information on K. (10.36) can be used for both input-output units and hidden units.

In (10.36), no method for determining the values of p^+_{ij} and p^-_{ij} is given. We will describe such a method below in (b). The p^+_{ij} part, in other words, the part where the link between the neighboring units i and j is reinforced when both units are active, corresponds to the *reinforcement learning mechanism* of the *Hebbian synapse* proposed by Hebb. The p^-_{ij} part, in other words, the part where, in a situation with no input from outside, the link between the neighboring units i and j is weakened when they are both active, plays the role of preventing strange internal representations from being created automatically when K is working freely. That is, in (10.36), p^+_{ij} for making D work according to the input from the outside and p^-_{ij} for preventing K from working automatically according to the input when there is no input from outside resist one another.

(10.36) finds only one local minimum of G, but generally there can be many local minima. But if the state change of K is made stochastically and the size of this stochastic fluctuation is controlled by changing the value of the temperature T, K can move to the global minimum. We will describe this below.

(b) The heuristic method of learning

If the learning rule for a Boltzmann machine K, (10.36), can be computed, a (local) equilibrium state of K can be reached by determining the change of the weight w_{ij} using $\Delta w_{ij} = -\partial G/\partial w_{ij}$. To compute the learning rule (10.36), we need to find p_{ij}^+ and p_{ij}^- and thus the products of the states of the two units, $s_i^{\alpha\beta} s_j^{\alpha\beta}$, $s_i^{\lambda\mu} s_j^{\lambda\mu}$, and the probability distributions of the state vectors, $P_{\alpha+\beta}^+$, $P_{\lambda+\mu}^-$. These probability distributions are unknown and need to be determined statistically from some samples. To determine the changes of the weights, Δw_{ij}, effectively using the Boltzmann machine algorithm, we need to consider the following points:

(1) How large should the value of T be?
(2) How can we determine the values of p_{ij}^+ and p_{ij}^- statistically?

In order to consider these points, we need to define the state transition function for each unit to change its state for a fixed value of T. This can be done by extending the state transition equation (10.23) in the Hopfield network to a stochastic one. For example, the energy gap, s_j, between when the state of unit j takes the energy level 0 and when it takes the energy level 1 for the energy function E of the whole system is given by

$$\Delta E_j = \sum_i w_{ji} s_i(t) + \theta_j \tag{10.37}$$

Then the probability of a new state of unit j taking 1 is given by

$$p_j = \frac{1}{1 + e^{-\Delta E_j/kT}} \tag{10.38}$$

Using (10.38), we can determine a new state of j probabilistically. Here, to determine ΔE_j in (10.38), we need to know the current states of all the units, not just j as in (10.37). To do this in parallel is difficult in a system like a Boltzmann machine, where the state of each unit changes asynchronously; therefore, the value of p_j can be determined only approximately in actual use.

We now consider how to determine the temperature, T. Note that (10.38) is the function illustrated in Figure 10.16 with T as a parameter. In other words, the smaller T is, the smaller the fluctuation of the probability p_j becomes and it comes closer to a linear threshold function. If we set the value of T large in a place far from the global minimum of the energy function, the probability of getting out of a local minimum is large.

In a place near the global minimum, if we make the value of T small, we can obtain the minimum without going far from it. Changing the initially large value of T little by little to a smaller value during the process of energy minimization and state transition based on (10.38) is called *annealing* or simulated annealing.

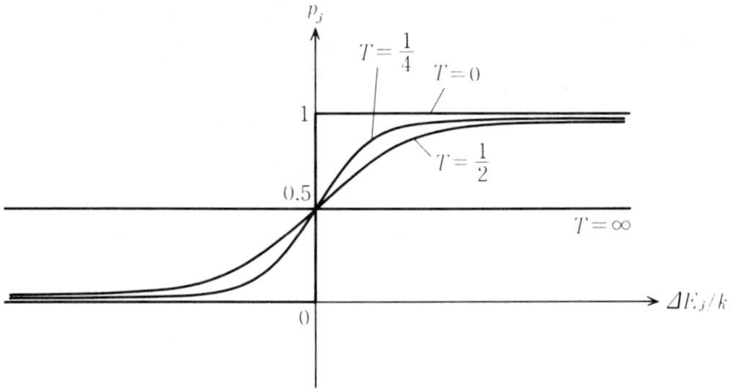

Figure 10.16 Output probability of a Boltzmann machine.

There are many methods of annealing, such as

(i) $T \propto \frac{1}{\xi_1 t+\xi_2}$,

(ii) $T \propto \frac{1}{\log(\xi_1 t+\xi_2)}$,

(iii) decreasing T stepwise in each time interval,

where t is the time or the number of iterations and ξ_1, ξ_2 are constants.

Let us consider how to determine p_{ij}^+ and p_{ij}^-. For p_{ij}^+, we can give the network the same input-output data many times, find the number of times that the states of units i and j are both 1, and assume that p_{ij}^+ is that number. For p_{ij}^-, we do the same thing as for p_{ij}^+, but by fixing the state of each input unit to be 1, and assume that p_{ij}^- is that number. For these T, p_{ij}^+, and p_{ij}^-, we update the weight of each link using

$$\Delta w_{ij} = \frac{1}{T}(p_{ij}^+ - p_{ij}^-) \tag{10.39}$$

$$w_{ij} = w_{ij} + \alpha\Delta w_{ij} \tag{10.40}$$

where α and β are positive constants. The computation is terminated when the value of the energy function becomes smaller than a given criterion. In order to hasten the convergence, we could use heuristic methods rather than (10.39). Note that (10.39) and (10.40) are not the only possible method.

(c) Example of a Boltzmann machine

Unlike Hopfield networks, described in Section 10.4, in a Boltzmann machine it is possible to obtain the global minimum by giving probabilistic fluctuations to state transitions. By efficient annealing that changes the value of the temperature parameter T, it is possible to control the fluctuation effectively and increase the rate of convergence to the global minimum. By making use of this feature, we can use Boltzmann machines for solving optimization problems that include discrete variables. As we saw before, since the algorithm includes many assumptions unsatisfied in the actual computation on a computer, there is no guarantee that the algorithm always is able to attain the global minimum. In the example below, we obtain the minimum value of the energy function by probabilistic state transition and annealing by keeping the link weights fixed rather than learning them as in (10.39) and (10.40).

Let us consider the *n-queen problem* as an example of an optimization problem.

> "Place n queens on an $n \times n$ chessboard so that no queens can capture each other in the vertical, horizontal, or diagonal direction."

Figure 10.17 shows one solution to the eight-queen problem.

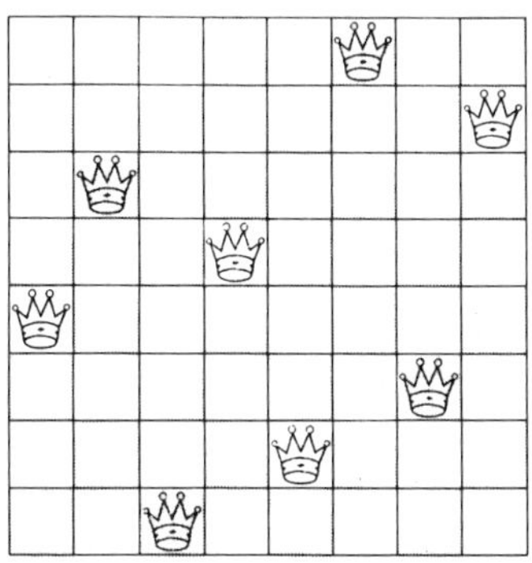

Figure 10.17 A solution to the eight-queen problem.

To solve the n-queen problem, we regard each square on the board as a unit and consider the neural network where all the units are linked to each other. Let (i, j) be the square on the ith row and the jth column. Now, using the variables

$$x_{ij} = \begin{cases} 1 & \text{when a queen is on the box } (i, j) \\ 0 & \text{otherwise} \end{cases}$$

we define the evaluation function of the problem as follows:

$$E = \frac{A}{2}\sum_{i=1}^{n}\left(\sum_{j=1}^{n} x_{ij} - 1\right)^2 + \frac{B}{2}\sum_{j=1}^{n}\left(\sum_{i=1}^{n} x_{ij} - 1\right)^2$$
$$+ \frac{C}{2}\sum_{k=1}^{2n-1}\sum_{i_1+j_1=k}\sum_{\substack{i_2+j_2=k\\ i_2\neq i_1\\ j_2\neq j_1}} x_{i_1j_1}x_{i_2j_2}$$
$$+ \frac{D}{2}\sum_{l=-n+1}^{n-1}\sum_{\substack{i_2-j_2=l\\ i_2\neq i_1\\ j_2\neq j_1}} x_{i_1j_1}x_{i_2j_2} \tag{10.41}$$

The first, second, third, and fourth terms on the right side correspond to the conditions that only one queen exists on each row, column, and diagonal line from the upper right to the lower left or from the upper left to the lower right, respectively.

Then, if we make (10.41) correspond to the energy function (10.28), we have

$$\begin{aligned} w_{i_1j_1,i_2j_2} =& -A\delta_{i1i2}(1-\partial_{j_1j_2}) - B\delta_{j_1j_2}(1-\delta_{i_1j_2}) \\ & - C\delta_{i_1+j_1,i_2+j_2}(1-\delta_{i_1i_2}) \\ & - D\delta_{i1-j_1,j_2-j_2}(1-\delta_{i_1i_2}) \end{aligned} \tag{10.42}$$

$$\theta_{ij} = \frac{A}{2} + \frac{B}{2} \tag{10.43}$$

where $w_{i_1j_1,i_2j_2}$ is the weight of the link from unit (i_2, j_2) to (i_1, j_1), and θ_{ij} is the threshold value of unit (i, j).

Next, using (10.42), (10.43) and (10.37), (10.38), we obtain the probability p_j that the state of unit j moves to 1, where we set $A = B = C = D = 10.0$ and define the schedule of annealing by

$$T = T_0 / \left(\frac{t}{\tau} + 1\right) \tag{10.44}$$

To do the computation, we set $T_0 = 25.0$, $\tau = 4.0$. Then, starting from iteration $t = 0$, we obtain p_j for all the units at each iteration. Every time we obtain p_j n^2 times, we increase t by 1 and then decrease the size of T using (10.44).

In this way, as we probabilistically change the next state to 1 by using p_j obtained at each iteration, we can make the value of the energy function smaller. In the case of (10.41), $E = 0$ at the global minimum.

When we apply this method to the eight-queen problem ($n = 8$), we obtain $E \approx 0$ at $t = 49$ and obtain the result shown in Figure 10.18(a). In

```
+ - - + - - + - - + - - + - - + - - + - - + - - +
|     |     |     |     |     | * * |     |     |
+ - - + - - + - - + - - + - - + - - + - - + - - +
|     |     |     | * * |     |     |     |     |
+ - - + - - + - - + - - + - - + - - + - - + - - +
|     | * * |     |     |     |     |     |     |
+ - - + - - + - - + - - + - - + - - + - - + - - +
|     |     |     |     |     |     |     | * * |
+ - - + - - + - - + - - + - - + - - + - - + - - +
|     |     |     |     | * * |     |     |     |
+ - - + - - + - - + - - + - - + - - + - - + - - +
|     |     |     |     |     |     | * * |     |
+ - - + - - + - - + - - + - - + - - + - - + - - +
| * * |     |     |     |     |     |     |     |
+ - - + - - + - - + - - + - - + - - + - - + - - +
|     |     | * * |     |     |     |     |     |
+ - - + - - + - - + - - + - - + - - + - - + - - +
```

(a) The eight-queen problem

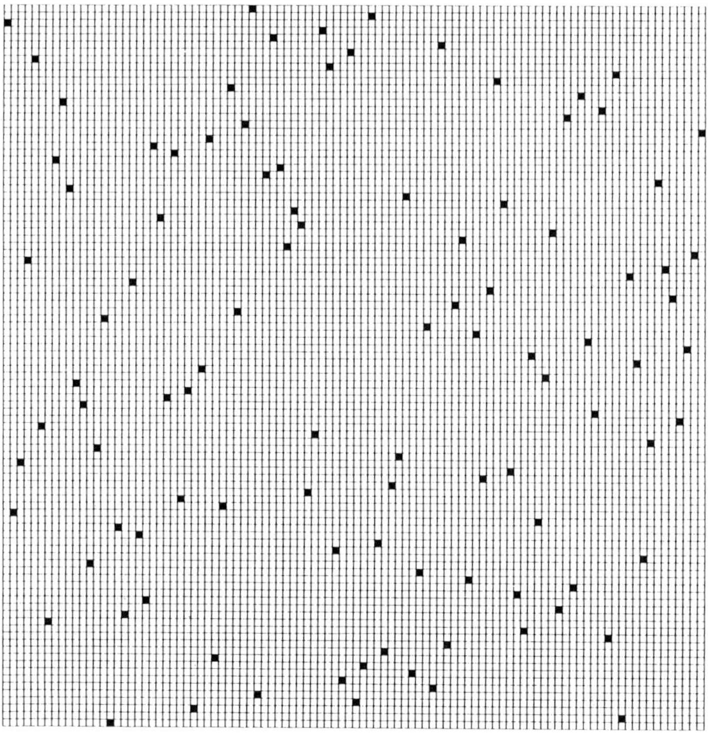

(b) The 100-queen problem

Figure 10.18 A solution to the n-queen problem using the Boltzmann machine.

the 100-queen problem ($n = 100$), $E \approx 0$ is attained at $t = 111$, and we obtain the result shown in Figure 10.18(b).

10.6 Parallel Computation in Recognition and Learning

The Hopfield network and the Boltzmann machine start from an initial value that may not satisfy any constraints and reach a state that satisfies local constraints on the links between the units. This is a *relaxation method.* In the computation of the neural network using the relaxation method, we may not always obtain a solution that perfectly satisfies all the constraints. In other words, the computation of the neural network can be considered a *weak relaxation method.*

The weak relaxation method not only is used in the neural networks described in this chapter but also can be used in models based on other algorithms that use slightly different locally parallel computations. For example, it can be used in a restoration algorithm for a visual pattern based on the concept of a Markov process.

Suppose f is a pattern function that is defined on a set D of a finite number of pattern elements. Assume that the pattern, including noises and defects, appears as a sample from a probabilistic pattern representation. In order to represent this formally, we, for example, assume that a random probability variable X_d corresponds to the element of each pattern $d \in D$ and consider the probability distribution on D as a whole, $X = \{X_d | d \in D\}$.

On the other hand, we assume that the probabilistic value of X_d for some pattern element d is determined not by the whole probability distribution but only by a neighborhood of d. To express this formally, we can do the following: First, assume that the neighborhood of a random $d \in D$, N_d, is defined, where if $d' \in N_d$, then $d \in N_{d'}$. For example, when d is a pixel in a two-dimensional visual pattern, we refer to the set of the pixels that are neighbors of d as N_d. Furthermore, let II be the simultaneous probability distribution function of N_d for all X_d. Using these definitions, we assume the probability of X_d taking the value h is only on $\{X_{d'} | d' \in N_d\}$. In other words, we assume

$$II(X_d = h | X_{d'} = h', d' \neq d) = II(X_d = j | X_{d'} = h', d' \in X_d)$$

When this assumption is true, we say that X is a *Markov process.*

Given a Markov process, under appropriate conditions, we can restore the original pattern function from a sample of the pattern function that includes noise by minimizing some local energy function that can be computed from the simultaneous probability distribution function of each neighbor. Its principle is beyond the scope of this book, so we will not describe it. However, the fact the original pattern can be restored by doing parallel computation on each neighborhood of each pattern element means that we can remove noise by doing many local computations in parallel.

Furthermore, we can use the method of probabilistic state transition to minimize the energy function. Also, while in the Boltzmann machine the equilibrium state is limited to the Maxwell-Boltzmann distribution and expression (10.38) is used for the state transition, recent study begins to show that a weak relaxation method similar to the Boltzmann machine can be used for a wider collection of probability distributions.

What we have described is simply one example to show that a neural network is an example of an algorithm that makes use of *massively parallel computation* that is beginning to be used in pattern information processing. We consider massively parallel computation as a parallel computation using an architecture that closely links many tens of thousands of processors. Due to improvements in hardware technology, we are able to use computation methods like this to process massive data at high speeds, and algorithms for massively parallel computation become important. Also, massively parallel computation is used not only in numeric processing, as in neural networks and algorithms for pattern information processing, but also in inferences based on symbol representation and learning. In this book, we could not cover parallel processing algorithms; however, many algorithms in the area of massively parallel computation will be developed during research on pattern recognition and learning that requires the high-speed processing of massive amounts of data. Such development will play a central role in improving the capability of software that benefits human beings.

Summary

In this chapter, we described methods for learning pattern discrimination, pattern classification, optimization, and so on, using neural networks.

10.1 A neural network is a dynamic network representation that can be defined by giving its nodes (called units), directed edges (called links), the weight of each link, the state transition functions, and the output functions of the units.

10.2 A simple three-layer perceptron is a kind of neural network that can discriminate linearly separable patterns.

10.3 Back propagation error learning is supervised learning in a neural network that is structured as a feedforward graph, and it can be used to obtain a neural network that makes the square sum of the differences between the ideal output values and the actual output values a local minimum.

10.4 Competitive learning is unsupervised learning in a neural network that has clustered units. It can learn to do pattern classification by competition among the units included in each cluster.

10.5 A Hopfield network is an algorithm for a neural network with mutually linked units where the state of each unit takes a continuous value between [0,1] that computes states so that its energy function takes a local minimum.

10.6 A Boltzmann machine is an algorithm for obtaining the global minimum of the energy function by introducing stochastic fluctuation to the state transitions in a Hopfield network.

10.7 Using an annealing method that decreases, based on appropriate rules, the value of the parameter that corresponds to thermodynamic temperature, we can increase the rate of convergence to the global minimum.

10.8 High-speed processing of massive data is necessary for problems concerned with pattern recognition and learning. Algorithms that allow massively parallel computation such as the relaxation method are important for these problems.

Keywords

neural network, parallel distributed processing, linear separability, perceptron, pattern discrimination, pattern classification, back propagation error learning, hidden unit, generalized delta rule, pattern recognition, competitive learning, Hopfield network, optimization problem, traveling salesperson problem, Boltzmann machine, annealing , n-queen problem, relaxation method, Markovian random field, image restoration, parallel computation, massively parallel computation

Exercises

10.1 (i) List the major differences between back propagation error learning and competitive learning.

(ii) List the major differences between a Hopfield network and a Boltzmann machine.

10.2 We assume, in a neural network consisting of an input layer and an output layer, that every input unit has a link to all the output units. We also assume that the output layer consists of units lined up in a two-dimensional array. For this network, let $x_j(t)$ be the input to j at time t and $w_{jh}(t)$ be the weight of the link from input unit j to output unit k. Let us denote the neighborhood of the output unit k at time t as $N(k,t)$ and assume that $N(k,t_1) \subset N(k,t_2)$ holds for any times t_1, t_2 satisfying $t_1 < t_2$ (usually, we use the set of the m^2 units included in an $m \times m$ square whose center is k). Now, let us consider the following:

[1] Set the weight w_{kj} of all the links to a small random value.

[2] Set $t = 0$. Define $N(k,0)$ for all the output units k. ($N(k,0)$ can be, for example, a large square with k as a center.) Let $\alpha(0)$ be a function satisfying $0 < \alpha(0) < 1$.

[3] Stop when there is no datum at time $t+1$. Otherwise, input the datum for time $t+1$.

[4] Compute

$$s_k = \sum_j \{x_j(t) - w_{kj}(t)\}^2$$

for all output units k.

[5] Find $s_{k^*} = \min_k s_k$.

[6] For all output units $k \in N(k^*,t)$, set

$$w_{kj}(t+1) = w_{kj}(t) + \alpha(t)(x_k(t) - w_{kj}(t))$$

for each input unit j.

[7] Define $\alpha(t+1)$ satisfying $\alpha(t+1) < \alpha(t)$. Set $t = t+1$ and go to [4].

Explain what kind of processing this algorithm does. (This algorithm is called a *self-organizing feature map*.)

10.3 List the functions necessary for a neural network description language.

Appendix
Examples of Learning by Neural Networks

Learning errors by back propagation, competitive learning, and the Boltzmann machines explained in Chapter 10 are the most popular learning algorithms using neural networks. In this Appendix we will show sample programs written in C for each of these algorithms. Each program describes only the basic algorithm. Although an interface that shows the execution process and the input-output data of a program using neural networks for learning is important, we have not included the program for such interfaces here. The following programs can easily be executed on a personal computer running MS-DOS.

The examples of back propagation error learning and competitive learning are for the following problem:

Problem 1 (back propagation error learning and competitive learning)

Construct a neural network that learns how to distinguish the four training patterns shown in Figure A.1.

Next, input the eight test patterns shown in Figure A.2 to the resulting neural network and check which test patterns belong to each of the categories of the training patterns.

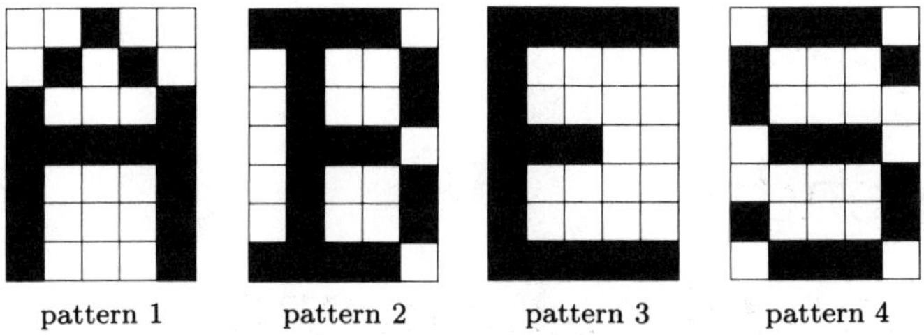

Figure A.1 Four training patterns.

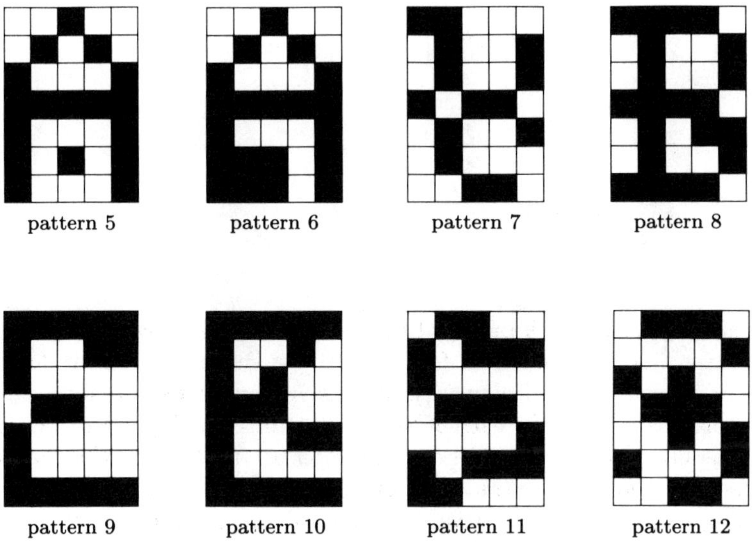

Figure A.2 Eight test patterns.

The results for both programs are

test patterns 5, 6 $\Rightarrow$ training pattern 1
test patterns 7, 8 $\Rightarrow$ training pattern 2
test patterns 9, 10 $\Rightarrow$ training pattern 3
test patterns 11, 12 $\Rightarrow$ training pattern 4

The example of a Boltzmann machine is for the following problem:

Problem 2 (Boltzmann machine)

Suppose we have the neural network shown in Figure A.3. Construct the neural network that outputs (0, 1), (1, 0) for the input (0, 1), (1, 0), respectively. (This problem is called the 2-1-2 symbolization problem.)

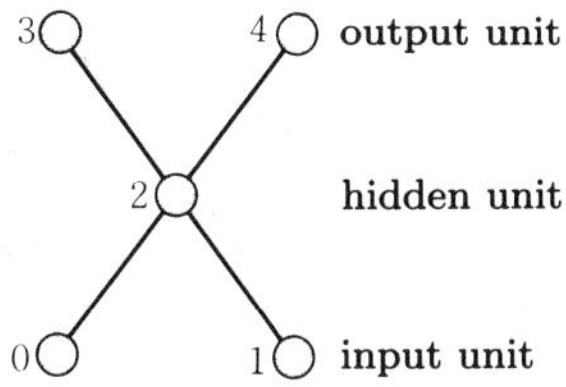

Figure A.3 A neural network.

Program A.1 (Back propagation error learning)

```
#include    <stdio.h>
#include    <math.h>
#include    <string.h>

/* a parameter depending on a network */
#define InputUnitNo   35        /* number of input units    */
#define HiddenUnitNo  16        /* number of hidden units   */
#define OutputUnitNo  4         /* number of output units   */
#define MaxPatternNo  20        /* maximum value of learning pattern  */

#define Eta           0.75      /* learning efficiency                */
#define Alpha         0.8       /* constant on past weighting         */
#define ErrorFunc     0.08      /* error at the end of learning       */
#define Wmin          -0.30     /* minimum value of initial weigting  */
#define Wmax          0.30      /* maximum value of initial weighting */

/* macro */
#define f( x ) (1 / ( 1 + exp( -(x) ) ))     /* Sigmold function */
#define rnd( )  ((double)rand( ) / 0x7fff * (Wmax - Wmain) + Wmin)

/* global function */
double o1[MaxPatternNo][InputUnitNo];       /* output value of input unit */
double o2[HiddenUnitNo];                    /* output value of hidden unit */
double o3[OutputUnitNo];                    /* output value of output unit */
double t[MaxPatternNo][OutputUnitNo];       /* teacher signal pattern      */
double w21[HiddenUnitNo][InputUnitNo];      /* weights
                                               (input unit -> hidden unit) */
double dw21[HiddenUnitNo][InputUnitNo];
double w32[OutputUnitNo][HiddenUnitNo];     /* weights
                                               (hidden unit -> output unit) */
dobule dw32[OutputUnitNo][HiddenUnitNo];
```

```
double bias2[HiddenUnitNo];                /* value of hidden unit */
double dbias2[HiddenUnitNo];
double bias3[OutputUnitNo];                /* value of output unit */
double dbias3[OutputUnitNo];
int    learning_pattern_no;                /* number of learning patterns */
int    test_pattern_no;                    /* number of checked patterns
                                               after learning */

main( argc, argv )
int    argc;
char   *argv[ ];
{
       int    i, j. k;              /* loop counter */
       char   filename[30];         /* data file */
       char   ss[80];               /* working string */
       double errorfunc;            /* variable for confirming the completion
                                           of learning  */
       void   propagation( );
       void   back_propagation( );
       void   state( );
       void   read_file( );
       void   initialize( );

       /* own data file names */
       if( argc <= 1 ){
               printf( "Learning file : " );
               gets( ss );
               sscanf( ss, "%s", filename );
       }
       else
               strcpy( filename, argv[1] );

       /* own initial random number value */
       if( argc <= 2 ){
               printf( "Random : " ):
               gets( ss );
       }
       else
               strcpy( ss, argv[2] );
       srand( atoi( ss ) );
       read_file( filename );              /* read data file */
       initialize( );                      /* initial setting of weights */

       printf( "***** Before Learning *****\n" );
       printf( "\tpattern output1 output2 output3 output4\n" );
       /* execute and display the learning pattern */
       for( errorfunc = 0.0, i = 0; i < learning_pattern_no; i++ ){
               state( i );
               for( j = 0; j < OutputUnitNo; j++ )
                       errorfunc += pow( t[i][j] - o3[j], 2.0 );
       }
       errorfunc /= 2;
       printf( "errorFunc : %.3f\n", errorfunc );

       /***** learning starts *****/
       printf( "\n***** Start to learn *****\n" );
       printf( "counter pattern output1 outpu2 output3 output4\n" );
       for( i = 0; errorfunc > ErrorFunc; ){
```

```
                for( j = 0; j < learning_pattern_no; j++ ){
                        propagation( j );
                        back_propagation( j );
                }
                for( errorfunc = 0.0, j = 0; j < learning_pattern_no; j++ ){
                        printf( "%d", ++i );
                        state( j );
                        for(k = 0; k < OutputUnitNo; k++ )
                                errorfunc += pow( t[j][k] - o3[k], 2.0 );
                }
                errorfunc /= 2;
                printf( "Errorfunc : %.3f\n", errorfunc );
        }
        /***** learning ends *****/

       printf( "\n***** After Learning *****\n" );
       printf( "\tpattern output1 output2 output3 output4Yn" );
       /* execute and display test pattern */
      for( i = 0; i < learning_pattern_no + test_pattern_no; i++ )
              state( i );
}

/* moving data from the input layer to the output layer */
void    propagation( p )
int     p;                  /* learning pattern number */
{
        int     i, j;       /* loop counter */
        double  net;        /* product-sum variable */

        /* output value of a hidden unit */
        for( i = 0; i < HiddenUnitNo; i++ ){
                for( net = 0, j = 0; j < InputUnitNo; j++ )
                        net += w21[i][j] * o1[p][j];
                o2[i] = f( net+ bias2[i] );
        }

        /* output value of an output unit */
        for( i = 0; i < OutputUnitNo; i++ ){
                for( net = 0, j = 0; j < HiddenUnitNo; j++ )
                       net += w32[i][j] * o2[j];
                o3[i] = f( net + bias3[i] );
        }
}
/* correcting the weights */
void    back_propagation( p )
int     p;                          /* learning pattern number */
{
        int    i, j;                /* loop counter */
        double d2[HiddenUnitNo];    /* weights correction value d
                                          (input -> hidden) */
        double d3[OutputUnitNo];    /* weights correction value d
                                          (hidden -> output) */
        double sum;                 /* variable for product-sum computation */

        /* d j= ( o j- y j) f '(i j) */
        for( i = 0; i < OutputUnitNo; i++ )
                d3[i] = ( t[p][i] - o3[i] ) * o3[i] * ( 1 - o3[i] );

        /* Δ w ij = η d jo i */
```

```
        for( i = 0; i < HiddenUnitNo; i++ ){
                for( sum = 0, j = 0; j < OutputUnitNo; j++ ){
                        dw32[j][i] = Eta * d3[j] * o2[i] + Alpha *
                             dw32[j][i];
                        w32[j][i] += dw32[j][i];
                        sum + = de[j] * w32[j][i];
                }
                /* d j= (Σ w ji d i) f '(i j) */
                d2[i] = o2[i] * ( 1 - o2[i] ) * sum;
        }
        for( i = 0; i < OutputUnitNo; i++ ){
                dbias3[i] = Eta * d3[i] + Alpha * dbias3[i];
                bias3[i] += dbias3[i];
        }

        /* Δ w ij= η d jo i */
        for( i = 0; i < InputUnitNo; i++ )
                for( j = 0; j < HiddenUnitNo; j++ ){
                        dw21[j][i] = Eta * d2[j] * o1[p][i]
                                   + Alpha * dw21[j][i];
                        w21[j][i] += dw21[j][i];
                }
        for( i = 0; i < HiddenUnitNo; i++ ){
                dbias2[i] = Eta * d2[i] + Alpha * dbias2[i];
                bias2[i] += dbias2[i];
        }
}

/* state display */
void      state( p )
int       p;
{
          int    i;        /* loop counter */

          printf( "\t%d ->", p+1 );
          propagation( p );
          for( i = 0; i < OutputUnitNo; i++ )
                  printf( "\t%5.3f", o3[i] );
          fputc( '\n', stdout );
}

/* read data from a file */
void      read_file( name )
char      *name;
{
          int     i, j;           /* loop counter */
          FILE    *fp;            /* file pointer */

          /* file open */
         if( (fp = fopen( name, "r" )) == NULL ){
                 fprintf( stderr, "%s : File open error !!\n", name );
                 exit( -1);
         }

         /* read learning data */
         fscanf( fp, "%d", &learning_pattern_no );
         for( i = 0; i < learning_pattern_no; i++ ){
                 for( j = 0; j < InputUnitNo; j++ )
                         fscanf( fp, "%lf", &o1[i][j] );
```

```
                for( j = 0; j < OutputUnitNo; j++ )
                        fscanf( fp, "%lf", &t[i][j] );
        }

        /* read test data */
        fscanf( fp, "%d", &test_pattern_no );
        for( i = learning_pattern_no;
                    i < learning_pattern_no + test_pattern_n
               for( j = 0; j < InputUnitNo; j++ )
                       fscanf( fp, "%lf", &o1[i][j] );

        fclose( fp );
}

/* initializing the weights */
void      initialize( )
int      i, j;                 /* loop counter */

/* initializing the weights (input layer -> hidden layer) */
for( i = 0; i < HiddenUnitNo; i++ )
        for( j = 0; j < InputUnitNo; j++ )
                w21[i][j] = rnd( );

/* initializing the weights (hidden layer -> output layer) */
for( i = 0; i < OutputUnitNo; i++ )
        for( j = 0; j < HiddenUnitNo; j++ )
                w32[i][j] = rnd( );
```

Execution Example A.1

```
***** Before Learning *****
       pattern output1 output2 output3 output4
       1 ->    0.435   0.402   0.446   0.585
       2 ->    0.423   0.360   0.434   0.583
       3 ->    0.450   0.407   0.493   0.585
       4 ->    0.432   0.368   0.450   0.565
ErrorFunc : 1.910

***** learning starts *****
counter pattern output1 output2 output3 output4
1       1 ->    0.225   0.246   0.194   0.088
2       2 ->    0.188   0.242   0.192   0.087
3       3 ->    0.222   0.258   0.260   0.094
4       4 ->    0.205   0.245   0.215   0.092
ErrorFunc : 1.502
5       1 ->    0.132   0.148   0.165   0.039
6       2 ->    0.091   0.169   0.163   0.041
7       3 ->    0.110   0.159   0.264   0.042
8       4 ->    0.101   0.164   0.189   0.044
ErrorFunc : 1.549
9       1 ->    0.219   0.180   0.268   0.049
10      2 ->    0.129   0.242   0.251   0.055
11      3 ->    0.150   0.191   0.472   0.052
12      4 ->    0.137   0.216   0.300   0.057
ErrorFunc : 1.379
13      1 ->    0.326   0.228   0.265   0.087
14      2 ->    0.213   0.380   0.228   0.109
15      3 ->    0.233   0.229   0.608   0.090
```

```
16       4 ->    0.220   0.310   0.311   0.108
ErrorFunc : 1.123
17       1 ->    0.599   0.207   0.175   0.160
18       2 ->    0.180   0.487   0.143   0.226
19       3 ->    0.199   0.190   0.691   0.167
20       4 ->    0.191   0.353   0.240   0.217
ErrorFunc : 0.828
21       1 ->    0.729   0.144   0.126   0.220
22       2 ->    0.113   0.568   0.095   0.362
23       3 ->    0.134   0.119   0.788   0.247
24       4 ->    0.126   0.350   0.201   0.348
ErrorFunc : 0.620
25       1 ->    0.844   0.094   0.097   0.162
26       2 ->    0.091   0.654   0.062   0.344
27       3 ->    0.111   0.071   0.843   0.219
28       4 ->    0.104   0.325   0.165   0.346
ErrorFunc : 0.490
29       1 ->    0.888   0.063   0.077   0.115
30       2 ->    0.079   0.724   0.041   0.294
31       3 ->    0.093   0.043   0.867   0.189
32       4 ->    0.090   0.270   0.138   0.337
ErrorFunc : 0.404
33       1 ->    0.902   0.047   0.064   0.117
34       2 ->    0.069   0.782   0.029   0.301
35       3 ->    0.076   0.028   0.878   0.220
36       4 ->    0.076   0.211   0.119   0.431
ErrorFunc : 0.315
37       1 ->    0.907   0.040   0.056   0.122
38       2 ->    0.064   0.831   0.023   0.282
39       3 ->    0.066   0.020   0.885   0.250
40       4 ->    0.065   0.171   0.102   0.559
ErrorFunc : 0.230
41       1 ->    0.911   0.036   0.051   0.104
42       2 ->    0.063   0.863   0.019   0.216
43       3 ->    0.062   0.016   0.892   0.222
44       4 ->    0.056   0.141   0.090   0.652
ErrorFunc : 0.155
45       1 ->    0.915   0.033   0.049   0.087
46       2 ->    0.061   0.881   0.017   0.170
47       3 ->    0.060   0.014   0.901   0.180
48       4 ->    0.049   0.118   0.083   0.738
ErrorFunc : 0.101
49       1 ->    0.918   0.031   0.048   0.073
50       2 ->    0.058   0.895   0.016   0.139
51       3 ->    0.058   0.013   0.909   0.141
52       4 ->    0.044   0.103   0.078   0.800
ErrorFunc : 0.070

***** After Learning *****
         pattern output1 output2 output3 output4
         1 ->    0.918   0.031   0.048   0.073
         2 ->    0.058   0.895   0.016   0.139
         3 ->    0.058   0.013   0.909   0.141
         4 ->    0.044   0.103   0.078   0.800
         5 ->    0.916   0.036   0.043   0.074
         6 ->    0.858   0.068   0.040   0.076
         7 ->    0.076   0.876   0.018   0.122
```

```
8 ->    0.058   0.889   0.020   0.115
9 ->    0.060   0.016   0.826   0.205
10 ->   0.117   0.013   0.870   0.105
11 ->   0.214   0.058   0.060   0.655
12 ->   0.091   0.129   0.055   0.717
```

Program A.2 (Competitive learning)

```
#include <stdio.h>
#include <math.h>

/* constants */
#define           ON          1    /* ignited     */
#define           OFF         0    /* not ignited */

/* parameters of the network */
#define InputUnitNo   35           /* number of input units */
#define ClusterNo      2           /* number of clusters    */
#define LearnNo       70           /* number of learning    */
#define ExtraLearn    ON           /* apply weak learning rules to losers */
#define MaxPatternNo  22           /* maximum number of learning pattern
                                        + test pattern   */
#define MaxOutputUnitNo 5          /* maximum number of output unit  */
#define G1           1.0           /* learning rate    */
#define G2          0.01           /* special learning rate  */
#define Seed        8936           /* seeds of random numbers  */
int  OutputUnitNo[ ]= {{ 2 },   /* no. of output units (for cluster 1) */
                       { 4 }};  /* no. of output units (for cluster 2) */

/* global variable */
int     s[MaxPatternNo][InputUnitNo];  /* for storing learning patterns */
double  w[ClusterNo][InputUnitNo][MaxOutputUnitNo];   /* weights : w ij */
int     learning_pattern_no;           /* number of learning patterns */
int     test_pattern_no;               /* number of test patterns */

void    main( argc, argv )
int     argc;
char    *argv[ ];
{
        int     i, j, k;          /* loop counter */
        int     winner = OFF;     /* number of the winner unit */
        char    filename[30];     /* file name */
        void    read_file( );
        void    learning_for_winner( );
        void    learning_for_loser( );
        void    pattern_present( );
        void    initialize( );
        int     get_winner( );

        if( argc <= 1 ){
                printf( "usage : comp datafile\n" );
                exit( 0 );
        }
        strcpy( filename, argv[1] );

        initialize( );            /* initialize weighting */

        read_file( filename ); /* read learning + test pattern */
```

```
        printf( "***** Before Learning *****\n" );
        /* execute and display learning pattern */
        for ( i = 0; i < learning_pattern_no; i++ ){
                printf( "Pattern %d\n", i+1 ){
                pattern_present( i );
        }
        /***** learning starts *****/
        for ( i = 0; i < LearnNo; i++ ){
                if ( i%5 == 0 ) fputc( '*', stderr );
                for ( j = 0; j < learning_pattern_no; j++ )
                        for ( k = 0; k < ClusterNo; k++ ){
                                /* decide winner */
                                winner = get_winner( j, k );
                                /* competitive learning for winners */
                                learning_for_winner( winner, j, k );
                                if ( ExtraLearn )
                                        /* competitive learning for losers */
                                        learning_for_loser( winner, j, k );
                        }
        }
        /***** learning ends *****/

        printf( "\n***** After Learning *****\n" );
        /* execute and display test pattern */
        for ( i = 0; i < test_pattern_no; i++ ){
                printf( "Pattern %d\n", i+1 );
                pattern_present( i+learning_pattern_no );
        }
}

/* read data from a file */
void    read_file( name )
char    *name;                  /* file name */
{
        int     i, j;           /* loop counter */
        FILE    *fp;            /* file counter */

        /* file open */
        if( (fp = fopen( name, "r" )) == NULL ){
                fprintf( stderr, "%s : File open error !!\n", name );
                exit( -1 );
        }

        /* read learning data */
        fscanf( fp, "%d", &learning_pattern_no );
        for( i = 0; i < learning_pattern_no; i++ )
                for( j = 0; j < InputUnitNo; j++ )
                        fscanf( fp, "%d", &s[i][j] );

        /* read test data */
        fscanf( fp, "%d", &test_pattern_no );
        for( i = learning_pattern_no; i < learning_pattern_no +
          test_pattern_n
                for( j = 0; j < InputUnitNo; j++ )
                        fscanf( fp, "%d", &s[i][j] );
        fclose( fp );
}

/* competitive learning for winners */
```

```
void    learning_for_winner( winner, patnum, clstnum )
        int     winner;         /* number of the winner unit */
        int     patname;        /* number of the pattern */
        int     clstnum;        /* number of the cluster */
{

        int     i;              /* loop counter */
        double  n_k = 0.0;      /* number of the active units */

        for ( i = 0; i < InputUnitNo; i++ )
                n_k += ( double )s[patnum][i];

        for ( i = 0; i < InputUnitNo; i++ )
                w[clstnum][i][winner]+=
                    G1*(double)s[patnum][i]/n_k-G1*w[clstnum]
}

/* weak competitive learning for losers */
void    learning_for_loser( winner, patnum, clstnum )
        int     winner, patnum, clstnum;
{
        int     i, j;           /* loop counter */
        double  n_k = 0.0;      /* number of active units */

        for ( i = 0; i < InputUnitNo; i++ )
                n_k += (double)s[patnum][i];

        for( j = 0; j < OutputUnitNo[clstnum]; j++ ){

            if ( j != winner )
                    for ( i = 0; i < InputUnitNo; i++ )
                        w[clstnum][i][j]+=
                            G2*(double)s[patnum][i]/n_k-G2*w[clstnum][i][j]
          }
}

/* determine the winner */
int     get_winner( patnum, clstnum )
        int      patnum;            /* pattern number */
        int      clstnum;           /* cluster number */
{
        int      i, j;              /* loop counter */
        int      winner = 0;        /* store the number of the winner unit */
        double   tmp, pre = 0.0;    /* for temperary storage */

        for ( j = 0; j < OutputUnitNo[clstnum]; j++){
                for ( tmp = 0.0, i = 0; i < InputUnitNo; i++ )
                        tmp += w[clstnum][i][j] * (double)s[patnum][i];
                if ( tmp > pre ){
                        winner = j;
                        pre = tmp;
                }
        }
        return( winner );           /* return the number of the winner unit */
}

/* routine for displaying a pattern and a winner */
void    pattern_present( pattern_number )
        int pattern_number;         /* the number of the pattern */
{
```

```
        int      i;                  /* loop counter */
        int      rp = 5;             /* position of a new paragraph for
                                        the pattern display */

        printf( "Input Pattern : " );
        for ( i = 0; i < InputUnitNo; i++ ){
                printf( "%d ", s[pattern_number][i] );
                if ( i%rp == 4 ) printf( "\n                  ");
        }
        /* display the winner for every cluster */
        printf ( "\nWinner : " );
        for ( i = 0; i < ClusterNo; i++ )
                   printf( "      %d ", get_winner( pattern_number, i )+1);
        printf( "\n\n" );
}

/* initialization of the weighting */
void    initialize( )
{
        int     i, j, k;            /* loop counter */
        double  weight_tmp;         /* for temporary storage for normalization */
        srand( Seed );              /* initialize the random number generator */

        for ( k = 0; k < ClusterNo; k++ ){
                for ( weight_tmp = 0.0, j = 0; j < OutputUnitNo[k]; j++ )
                        for ( i = 0; i < InputUnitNo; i++ )
                                weight_tmp += ( w[k][i][j] = rand( ) );
                /* normalization (Σ w ij= 1 ) */
                for ( i = 0; i < InputUnitNo; i++ )
                        for ( j = 0; j < OutputUnitNo[k]; j++ )
                                w[k][i][j] = w[k][i][j] / weight_tmp;
        }
}
```

Execution Example A.2

(The two columns on the right are the numbers of the units that output 1 at the output clusters 1 and 2.)

```
***** Before Learning *****
Pattern 1    Winner :     1   2

Pattern 2    Winner :     1   2

Pattern 3    Winner :     1   3

Pattern 4    Winner :     2   2

***** After Learning *****
Pattern 1    Winner :     2   3

Pattern 2    Winner :     1   2

Pattern 3    Winner :     2   1

Pattern 4    Winner :     2   4

Pattern 5    Winner :     2   3

Pattern 6    Winner :     2   3
```

```
Pattern 7    Winner :   1  2

Pattern 8    Winner :   1  2

Pattern 9    Winner :   2  1

Pattern 10   Winner :   2  1

Pattern 11   Winner :   2  4

Pattern 12   Winner :   2  4
```

Program A.3 (Boltzmann machine)

```
#include <stdio.h>
#incude <math.h>

/* constants */
#define ON          1      /* ignited */
#define OFF         0      /* not ignited */
#define PHASEPLUS   0      /* phase +     */
#define PHASEMINUS  1      /* phase -     */
#define EOC         (-1)   /* End of Connect */
#define INPUTUNIT   1      /* input unit */
#define HIDDENUNIT  2      /* hidden unit */
#define OUTPUTUNIT  3      /* output unit */
#define WIDTH       50     /* the scale width of learning error */

/* macros */
#define attr(n)         /* attributes of the unit */        \
                        ( n < InputUnitNo ? INPUTUNIT :     \
                            ( n >= OutputUnitBegin ?        \
                                OUTPUTUNIT: HIDDENUNIT ) )
#define rnd( )           ( rand( ) / (double)0x8000 )
#define on_off(p)       ( p > rnd( ) ? ON : OFF )
#define prob(dE, T)     ( 1.0/(1.0+exp(-(dE)/(T))) )
#define abs(x)          ( x > 0 ? x : -x )

/* parameters of the network */
#define UnitNo            5      /* the whole unit number */
#define InputUnitNo       2      /* the number of the input units */
#define OutputUnitNo      2      /* the number of the ouput units */
#define OutputUnitBegin   (UnitNo-OutputUnitNo)
#define InputPatternNo    2      /* the number of input patterns */
#define OutputPatternNo   2      /* the number of ouput patterns */
#define RepresentNo       4      /* the number of the input pattern
                                        within one learning cycle */
#define AnnealStep        4      /* the number of the steps in the
                                        annealing schedule  */
#define GetPCycle         3      /* the number of the average unit renewal
                                        at time p */
#define GetPT             10.0   /* the temperature at time p */
#define Epsilon           50.0   /* Δ W ij=Epsilon*(pij+ - pij-) */
#define LearningCycle     100    /* the learning cycle number */
#define TrialNo           100    /* the number of trials for a pattern
                                        at the confirmation of learning */
#define VerifyInterval    5

int     Connect[UnitNo][UnitNo] = { /* the unit data between units */
```

```
                                        { 2,EOC, -1, -1, -1 },
                                        { 2,EOC, -1, -1, -1 },
                                        { 0,  1,  3,  4,EOC },
                                        { 2,  4,EOC, -1, -1 },
                                        { 2,  3,EOC, -1, -1 } };
                                /* input pattern  */
int     InputPattern[InputPatternNO][InputUnitNo]  = {{1,0},{0,1}};
                                /* ouput pattern   */
int     OutputPattern[OuputPatterNo][OutputUnitNo] = {{1,0},{0,1}};
                                /* conditional probability of the output
                                    given the input */
double  OutputFreq[InputPatternNo][OutputPatternNo] = {{1.0,0.0},{0.0,1.0}};
                                /* temperature of annealing schedule  */
double  Th[AnnealStep]          = {20, 15, 12, 10};
                                /* the number of renewal of the average
                                   unit at each temperature  */
int     CycleNo[AnnealStep]     = { 2, 2, 2, 4};

/* global variable */
int     unit[UnitNo];           /* store the state of the unit (ON/OFF) */
double  w[UnitNo][UnitNo];      /* weights : W ij    */
double  bias[UnitNo];           /* bias value        */
int     p[2][UnitNo][UnitNo];
        /* p[0] : pij+ p[1] : pij-
           provided store the one times
           {RepresentNo*InputPatternNo*UnitNo*GetPCycle) */
double epsi = Epsilon/(RepresentNo*IntputPatternNo*UnitNo*GetPCycle);

void    main(argc, argv)
int argc;
char **argv;
{
   int learning;
   int in_pat, out_pat;
   int phase;
   int represent;
   void initialize( ), init_unit( ), one_annealing( ), verify( );
   void init_p( ), get_p( ), change_w( ), display_w( );
   void verify0( );
   int random_pattern( );

   initialize(argc, argv);     /* initialize the weights */

   /***** learning starts *****/
   for(learning = 0; learning < LearningCycle; learning++) {
       init_p( );
       for(phase = 0; phase < 2; phase++) {
          for(in_pat = 0; in_pat < InputPatternNo; in_pat++) {
             for(represent = 0; represent < RepresentNo; represent++) {
                 out_pat = random_pattern(OutputFreq[in_pat], OutputPattern );
                   init_unit(in_pat, out_pat, phase);
                   one_annealing(phase);
                   get_p(phase);
             }
          }
       {
       change_w( );
       if((learning+1)%VerifyInterval == 0)
```

```
            verify(learning);
   }
   /***** learning ends *****/

   /* output results */
   display_w( );
   verify0( );
}

/* initialize the weights */
void initialize(argc, argv)
int argc;
char **argv;
{
   int i, j;           /* loop counter */
   int seed = 123;

   /* initialize the random number generator */
   if(argc > 1)
       seed = atoi(*++argv);
   srand(seed);
   /* 0 clear of the weighting */
   for(i = 0; i < UnitNo; i++)
       for(j = 0; j < UnitNo; j++)
           w[i][j] = 0;

   printf("   |0");
   for(i = 0; i < WIDTH - 1; i++)
       printf(" ");
   printf("%d|\n', InputPatternNo*2);
}

/* initialize the state of the unit */
/*     *PHASE PLUS --> copy the input/output pattern to unit[ ] */
/*     *PHASE MINUS --> copy the input patttern to unit[ ] */
void init_unit(in_pat, out_pat, phase)
int in_pat, out_pat, phase;
{
    int i;           /* loop counter */

    for(i = 0; i < UnitNo; i++) {
        if(attr(i) == INPUTUNIT)
            unit[i] == inputPattern[in_pat][i];
        else if(attr(i) == OUTPUTUNIT) {
            if(phase == PHASEPLUS)
                unit[i] = OutputPattern[out_pat][i-OutputUnitBegin];
            else
                unit[i] = OFF;
        } else
           unit[i] = OFF;
    }
}

/* 0 clear of the arrangement p */
void int_p( )
{
    int i, j, k;       /* loop counter */

    for(i = 0; i < 2; i++)
```

```
        for(j = 0; j < UnitNo; j++)
            for(k = 0; k < UnitNo; k++)
                p[i][j][k] = 0;
}

/* do annealing once */
void one_annealing(phase)
int phase;
{
   int i;
   int annealing;
   int cycle;
   void change_state( );

   for(annealing = 0; annealing < AnnealStep; annealing++)
       for(i = 0; i < CycleNo[annealing]*UnitNo; i++)
           change_state(phase, Th[annealing]);
}

/* renew the state of one unit randomly chosen */
/*     *PHASE PLUS --> renew only the hidden units */
/*     *PHASE MINUS --> renew the hidden/output units */
void change_state(phase, T)
int phase;
double T;
{
   int i;   /* loop counter  */
   int n;   /* the unit number */
   int m;   /* the unit number of the output of the unit */
   double dE;

   dE = 0;
   n=rnd( )*UnitNo;    /* select units randomly */
   if(attr(n) == HIDDENUNIT || (phase == PHASEMINUS && attr(n) == OUTPUTUNIT)
{
       /* compute net-input */
       for(i = 0; (m = Connect[n][i]) != EOC; i++)
           dE += w[n][m] * unit[m];
       dE += bias[n];
       /* revise the state of the unit */
       unit[n] = on_off(prob(dE, T));
    }
}

/* take the statistics of p */
void get_p(phase)
int phase;
{
   int i, j, k;       /* loop counter */
   int n;             /* the unit number on the other side of the unit */

   for(k = 0; k < UnitNo * GetPCycle; k++) {
       change_state(phase, GetPT);
       for(i = 0; i < UnitNo; i++) {
           if(unit[i] == ON) {
               for(j = 0; (n = Connect[i][j])  != EOC; j++) {
                   if(unit[n] == ON)
                        p[phase][i][n]++;
               }
```

```
                p[phase][i][i]++;
            }
        }
    }
}

/* produce the number of the pattern given by the conditional probability */
int random_pattern(head, item_no)
double *head;     /* the head address in the arrangement of the
                     conditional probability */
int item_no;     /* size of the arrangement element    */
{
    int i;       /* loop counter */
    double n;

    n = rnd( );
    for(i = 0; i < item_no; i++, head++) {
        n -= *head;
        if (n < 0)
            return(i);
    }
    return(item_no - 1);
}

/* revise the unit weights */
void change_w( )
{
     int i, j;     /* loop counter  */
     int n;        /* the unit number on the other side of the unit */

     for(i = 0; i < UnitNo; i++) {
         for(j = 0; (n=Connect[i][j]) != EOC; j++)
             w[i][n] += epsi*(p[PHASEPLUS][i][n]-p[PHASEMINUS}[i][n]);
         bias[i] += epsi*(p[PHASEPLUS][i][i]-p[PHASEMINUS][i][i]);
     }
}

/* output the unit weights to standard output */
void display_w( )
{
    int i, j;   /* loop counter */

    printf("\n\n i |");
    for(i = 0; i < UnitNo; i++)
        printf("w[i][%d] ", i);
    printf("|bias[i]\n---+");
    for(i = 0; i < UnitNo; i++)
        printf("-------");
    printf("+-------\n")
    for(i = 0; i < UnitNo; i++) {
        printf("%2d |", i);
        for(j = 0; j < UnitNo; j++)
            if(i != j)
                printf("%7.1f ", w[i][j]) ;
            else
                printf("  ---- ");
        printf("|%7.1\n", bias[i]);
    }
```

```
    printf("\n");
}

/* verify learning */
/* try each input pattern TrialNo times and check its ratio with the output
   patterns */
void verify0( )
{
   int i, j, trial;              /* loop counter */
   int in_pat, out_pat;          /* input/output pattern number */
   int sum[OutputPatternNo+1];   /* how many times each output pattern
                                    appears */
   int which_out( );

   /* display the top two lines of the table */
   printf("   |");
   for(i = 0; i < OutputPatternNo; i++)
       printf(" %7d", i);
   printf("  error\n---+");
   for(i = 0; i <= OutputPatternNo; i++)
       printf("-------");
   printf("\n");
   for(in_pat = 0; in_pat < InputPatterNo; in_pat++) {
       for(i = 0; i <= OutputPatternNo; i++)
           sum[i] = 0;
       for(trial = 0; trial < TrialNo; trial++)
           sum[which_out(in_part)]++;
       printf("%2d |", in_pat);
       for(i = 0; i <= OutputPatterNo; i++)
           printf(" %7.2f", (double)sum[i]/TrialNo);
       printf{"\n");
   }
}

void verify(learning)
int learning;
{
   int i, j, trial;              /* loop counter   */
   int in_pat, out_pat;          /* input/ouput pattern number */
   int sum[OutputPatternNo+1];   /* how many times each output pattern
                                    appears */
   double error = 0.0, temp;
   int which_out( );

   for(in_pat = 0; in_pat < InputPatternNo; in_pat++) {
       for(i = 0; i <= OutputPatternNo; i++)
           sum[i] = 0;

       for(trial = 0; trial < TrialNo; trial++)
           sum[which_out(in_pat)]++;
       for(i = 0; i < OutputPatternNo; i++) {
               temp = ((double)sum[i]/TrialNo-OutputFreq[in_pat][i]);
               error += abs(temp);
       }
       temp = (double)sum[OutputPatternNo]/TrialNo;
       error += abs(temp);
  }
```

```
  printf("%5d|", learning+1);
  for(i = 0; i <= WIDTH; i++) {
      if(i == (int)(error/2/InputPatternNo*WIDTH))
              printf("*");
      else
              printf(" ");
  }
  printf("|%6.3f\n',error);
}

int which_out(in_pat)
int in_pat;
{
    int i, j, out_pat;
    void one_annealing( ), init_unit( );
    init_unit(in_pat, -1, PHASEMINUS);
    one_annealing(PHASEMINUS);
    out_pat = OutputPatternNo;
    for(i = 0; i < OutputPatternNo; i++) {
        for(j = 0; j < OutputUnitNo; j++) {
            if(unit[j+OutputUnitBegin] != OutputPattern[i][j])
                break;
            if(j == OutputUnitNo-1)
                out_pat = i;
        }
        if(out_pat < OutputPatternNo)
            break;
    }
    return(out_pat);
}
```

Execution Example A.3

```
    |0                                           4|
   5|                         *                   | 2.160
  10|                         *                   | 2.120
  15|                *                            | 1.160
  20|             *                               | 0.940
  25|          *                                  | 0.680
  30|       *                                     | 0.540
  35|         *                                   | 0.580
  40|    *                                        | 0.260
  45|  *                                          | 0.080
  50|   *                                         | 0.160
  55|  *                                          | 0.120
  60|   *                                         | 0.240
  65|  *                                          | 0.080
  70|   *                                         | 0.200
  75|*                                            | 0.060
  80|  *                                          | 0.100
  85|  *                                          | 0.100
  90|  *                                          | 0.080
  95|   *                                         | 0.180
 100|  *                                          | 0.080
```

How the sum of the errors in the probability of occurence changes for each pattern (the vertical axis shows the learning cycle; the horizontal axis shows the sum of the errors).

i	w[i][0]	w[i][1]	w[i][2]	w[i][3]	w[i][4]	bias[i]
0	----	0.0	77.1	0.0	0.0	0.0
1	0.0	----	-82.5	0.0	0.0	0.0
2	77.1	-82.5	----	75.0	-61.7	-5.4
3	0.0	0.0	75.0	----	-60.8	-2.9
4	0.0	0.0	-61.7	-60.8	----	60.0

The weights of a unit and the threshold after learning (the rows show the unit number; the columns show the weight of each link and the input bias value (with thresholds in reverse).

	0	1	error
0	0.98	0.01	0.01
1	0.02	0.98	0.00

The probability of the occurence of the output pattern for each input pattern after learning (the rows show the input pattern number; the columns show the output pattern number; error shows the error from the ideal output result).

Answers

Chapter 1: Recognition and Learning by a Computer

1.1 Recognition by a computer means the ability of a computer to recognize the pattern of an object that it already knows, and it can be looked at as a process of transforming the pattern function of an object into a more structured representation of the information. Recognition on a computer is about low-level information processing that can extract the structure of a pattern and high-level information processing that can understand conceptually the structure of a pattern structure using knowledge. On the other hand, in everyday life, the word recognition is used to mean knowing, conceptually understanding, finding true properties of an object, and so on.

1.2 Learning by a computer means that a system automatically generates either new data or a new program from its current state which will change the future output of the system so that some goal is achieved over a certain period of time. Finding the structure of information that is buried in a mass of information within a fixed time frame is also an important aspect of learning on a computer. In everyday life, learning means simply memorizing, understanding, explaining, acting on information, and so on.

1.3 Both recognition and learning by a computer can be looked at as the process of generating a new information that did not exist in the system before and transforming one representation to another. However, while recognition on a computer transforms representations starting from the pattern function representation of an object and, as a result, can generate a representation that is the same as the one that already exists in the system, learning on a computer does not have any constraints on the initial representation and generates a new representation that has not existed in the system before.

1.4 If we change the value of the right side of the expression (a) to -8, only one point satisfies the inequalities (a)–(c) and this point is $x = 4$, $y = 4$.

Chapter 2: Representing Information

2.1 We will show a program written in Pascal and its execution in Answer Figure 2.1.

[Problem 2.1 Program example]

```
program corner(input, output);
label   10;
var data: array[0..21,0..21] of integer;
X, Y: integer;
answerX, answerY: integer;
oldX, oldY: integer;
       procedure search(X,Y :integer; var answerX, answerY :integer);
       { this procedure searches a '1' which is neighborhood
         of (X, Y), and let it in (answerX, answerY).}
       begin
             if data[X+1,Y ]=1 then begin
                     answerX:=X+1; answerY:Y ;
       end
       else if(data[X, Y-1]=1) then begin
               answerX:X ; answerY:=Y-1;
       end
       else if(data[X-1,Y ]=1) then begin
               answerX:=X-1; answerY:=Y ;
       end
       else if(data[X ,Y+1]=1) then begin
               answerX:X ; answerY:=Y+1;
       end
       else if(data[X+1,Y+1]=1) then begin
               answerX:=X+1; answerY:Y+1;
       end
```

```
        else if(data[X+1,Y-1]=1) then begin
                answerX:X+1; answerY:Y-1;
        end
        else if(data[X-1,Y-1]=1) then begin
                answerX:X-1; answerY:=Y-1;
        end
        else if(data[X-1,Y+1]=1) then begin
                answerX:=X-1; answerY:=Y+1;
        end;
    end;

begin
      { reading data }
      for Y:=0 to 21 do begin
         for X:=0 to 21 do begin
              if (X=0) or (X=21) or (Y=0) or (Y=21) then begin
                      data[X,Y] := 0;
              end
              else begin
                      read( data[X,Y] );
              end;
        end;
      end;
      { search a "1" }
      for Y:=1 to 20 do begin
              for X:=1 to 20 do begin
                      if data[X,Y]=1 then goto 10
              end;
      end;
10:
      search( X, Y, answerX, answerY );
      oldX := X;
      oldY := Y;
      X := answerX;
      Y := answerY;

      while data[oldX,oldY]<3 do begin
              if data[2*X-oldX,2*Y-oldY]=0 then begin
                      writeln(' (',X,',',Y,')');
                      search( X, Y, answerX, answerY );
              end
              else begin
                     answerX := 2*X-oldX;
                     answerY := 2*Y-oldY;
              end;

              oldX := X;
              oldY := Y;
```

```
            X := answerX;
            Y := answerY;
            data[oldX,oldY] := data[oldX,oldY]+1;
      end;
end.
```

[Execution Example 1]

```
0 0 0 0 0 0 0 0 0 0 0 0 0 0 0 0 0 0 0 0
0 0 0 0 0 0 0 0 0 0 0 0 0 0 0 0 0 0 0 0
0 0 0 0 0 0 0 0 0 0 0 0 0 0 0 0 0 0 0 0
0 0 0 0 0 0 0 0 0 0 0 0 0 0 0 0 0 0 0 0
0 0 0 0 0 0 0 0 0 0 0 0 0 0 0 0 0 0 0 0
0 0 0 0 0 0 0 0 0 0 0 0 0 0 0 0 0 0 0 0
0 0 0 0 0 0 0 0 0 0 0 0 0 0 0 0 0 0 0 0
0 0 0 0 0 0 0 0 0 0 0 0 0 0 0 0 0 0 0 0
0 0 0 0 0 0 0 0 0 0 0 0 0 0 0 0 0 0 0 0
0 0 0 1 1 1 1 1 1 1 1 1 1 0 0 0 0 0 0 0
0 0 0 1 0 0 0 0 0 0 0 0 1 0 0 0 0 0 0 0
0 0 0 1 0 0 0 0 0 0 0 0 1 0 0 0 0 0 0 0
0 0 0 1 0 0 0 0 0 0 0 0 1 0 0 0 0 0 0 0
0 0 0 1 0 0 0 0 0 0 0 0 1 0 0 0 0 0 0 0
0 0 0 1 0 0 0 0 0 0 0 0 1 0 0 0 0 0 0 0
0 0 0 1 1 1 1 1 1 1 1 1 1 0 0 0 0 0 0 0
0 0 0 0 0 0 0 0 0 0 0 0 0 0 0 0 0 0 0 0
0 0 0 0 0 0 0 0 0 0 0 0 0 0 0 0 0 0 0 0
0 0 0 0 0 0 0 0 0 0 0 0 0 0 0 0 0 0 0 0
0 0 0 0 0 0 0 0 0 0 0 0 0 0 0 0 0 0 0 0

*** answer ***
(13 10) (4 16) (13 10) (4 10)
```

[Execution Example 2]

```
0 0 0 0 0 0 0 0 0 0 1 0 0 0 0 0 0 0 0 0
0 0 0 0 0 0 0 0 0 1 0 1 0 0 0 0 0 0 0 0
0 0 0 0 0 0 0 0 1 0 0 0 1 0 0 0 0 0 0 0
0 0 0 0 0 0 0 1 0 0 0 0 0 1 0 0 0 0 0 0
0 0 0 0 0 0 1 0 0 0 0 0 0 0 1 0 0 0 0 0
0 0 0 0 0 1 0 0 0 0 0 0 0 0 0 1 0 0 0 0
0 0 0 0 1 0 0 0 0 0 0 0 0 0 0 0 1 0 0 0
0 0 0 0 1 0 0 0 0 0 0 0 0 0 0 0 1 0 0 0
0 0 0 0 1 0 0 0 0 0 0 0 0 0 0 0 1 0 0 0
0 0 0 0 1 0 0 0 0 0 0 0 0 0 0 0 1 0 0 0
0 0 0 0 1 0 0 0 0 0 0 0 0 0 0 0 1 0 0 0
0 0 0 0 1 0 0 0 0 0 0 0 0 0 0 0 1 0 0 0
0 0 0 0 1 1 1 1 1 1 1 1 1 1 1 1 1 0 0 0
0 0 0 0 0 0 0 0 0 0 0 0 0 0 0 0 0 0 0 0
0 0 0 0 0 0 0 0 0 0 0 0 0 0 0 0 0 0 0 0
0 0 0 0 0 0 0 0 0 0 0 0 0 0 0 0 0 0 0 0
0 0 0 0 0 0 0 0 0 0 0 0 0 0 0 0 0 0 0 0
0 0 0 0 0 0 0 0 0 0 0 0 0 0 0 0 0 0 0 0
0 0 0 0 0 0 0 0 0 0 0 0 0 0 0 0 0 0 0 0
0 0 0 0 0 0 0 0 0 0 0 0 0 0 0 0 0 0 0 0

*** answer ***
(17 7) (17 13) (5 13) (5 7) (11 1)
```

[Execution Example 3]

```
0 0 0 0 0 0 0 0 0 0 0 0 0 0 0 0 0 0 0 0
1 1 1 1 1 1 1 1 1 1 1 1 1 1 0 0 0 0 0 0
1 0 0 0 0 0 0 0 0 0 0 0 0 1 0 0 0 0 0 0
1 0 0 0 0 0 0 0 0 0 0 0 0 1 0 0 0 0 0 0
1 0 0 0 0 0 0 0 0 0 0 0 0 1 0 0 0 0 0 0
1 1 1 1 0 0 0 0 0 0 0 0 0 1 0 0 0 0 0 0
0 0 0 1 0 0 0 0 0 0 0 0 0 0 1 0 0 0 0 0
0 0 0 1 0 0 0 0 0 0 0 0 0 0 0 1 0 0 0 0
0 0 0 1 0 0 0 0 0 0 0 0 0 0 0 0 1 0 0 0
0 0 0 1 0 0 0 0 0 0 0 0 0 0 0 0 1 0 0 0
0 0 0 1 1 1 1 1 1 0 0 0 0 0 0 0 1 0 0 0
0 0 0 0 0 0 0 0 0 1 1 1 1 1 1 1 1 0 0 0
0 0 0 0 0 0 0 0 0 0 0 0 0 0 0 0 0 0 0 0
0 0 0 0 0 0 0 0 0 0 0 0 0 0 0 0 0 0 0 0
0 0 0 0 0 0 0 0 0 0 0 0 0 0 0 0 0 0 0 0
0 0 0 0 0 0 0 0 0 0 0 0 0 0 0 0 0 0 0 0
0 0 0 0 0 0 0 0 0 0 0 0 0 0 0 0 0 0 0 0
0 0 0 0 0 0 0 0 0 0 0 0 0 0 0 0 0 0 0 0
0 0 0 0 0 0 0 0 0 0 0 0 0 0 0 0 0 0 0 0

*** answer ***
(14 2) (14 6) (17 9) (17 13) (11 13) (9 11) (4 11)
(4 6) (1 6) (1 2)
```

[Execution Example 4]

```
0 0 0 0 0 0 0 0 0 0 0 0 0 0 0 0 0 0 0 0
0 0 1 1 1 1 1 1 1 1 1 1 1 0 0 0 0 0 0 0
0 0 1 0 0 0 0 0 0 0 0 0 1 0 0 0 0 0 0 0
0 0 1 0 0 0 0 0 0 0 0 0 1 0 0 0 0 0 0 0
0 0 1 0 0 0 0 0 0 0 0 0 1 0 0 0 0 0 0 0
0 0 1 0 0 0 0 0 0 0 0 0 1 0 0 0 0 0 0 0
0 1 0 0 0 0 0 0 0 0 0 0 1 0 0 0 0 0 0 0
0 0 1 0 0 0 0 0 0 0 0 0 1 0 0 0 0 0 0 0
1 0 0 0 0 0 0 0 0 0 0 0 1 0 0 0 0 0 0 0
1 0 0 0 0 0 0 0 0 0 0 0 1 0 0 0 0 0 0 0
1 0 0 0 0 0 0 0 0 0 0 0 1 0 0 0 0 0 0 0
1 0 0 0 0 0 0 0 0 0 0 0 1 0 0 0 0 0 0 0
1 1 1 1 1 0 0 0 0 0 0 0 1 0 0 0 0 0 0 0
0 0 0 0 1 0 0 0 0 0 0 0 1 0 0 0 0 0 0 0
0 0 0 0 1 0 0 0 0 0 0 0 1 0 0 0 0 0 0 0
0 0 0 0 1 0 0 0 0 0 0 0 0 1 0 0 0 0 0 0
0 0 0 0 1 0 0 0 0 0 0 0 0 0 1 0 0 0 0 0
0 0 0 0 1 0 0 0 0 0 0 0 0 0 0 1 0 0 0 0
0 0 0 1 0 0 0 0 0 0 0 0 0 0 0 0 1 0 0 0
0 0 1 1 1 1 1 1 1 1 1 1 1 1 1 1 1 1 0 0
0 0 0 0 0 0 0 0 0 0 0 0 0 0 0 0 0 0 0 0

*** answer ***
(13 2) (13 14) (18 19) (3 19) (5 17) (5 12) (1 12)
(1 8) (3 6) (3 2)
```

[Execution Example 5]

```
0 0 0 0 0 0 0 0 0 0 0 0 0 0 0 0 0 0 0 0
0 0 0 0 1 0 0 0 0 0 0 0 1 0 0 0 0 0 0 0
0 0 0 0 1 1 0 0 0 0 0 1 1 0 0 0 0 0 0 0
0 0 0 0 1 0 0 1 0 1 0 0 1 0 0 0 0 0 0 0
0 0 0 0 1 0 0 0 1 0 0 0 1 0 0 0 0 0 0 0
1 1 1 1 1 0 0 0 0 0 0 0 1 1 1 1 1 1 1 0
0 1 0 0 0 0 0 0 0 0 0 0 0 0 0 0 0 1 0 0
0 0 1 0 0 0 0 0 0 0 0 0 0 0 0 0 1 0 0 0
0 0 0 1 0 0 0 0 0 0 0 0 0 0 0 1 0 0 0 0
0 0 0 0 1 0 0 0 0 0 0 0 0 0 1 0 0 0 0 0
0 0 0 1 0 0 0 0 0 0 0 0 0 1 0 0 0 0 0 0
0 0 1 0 0 0 0 0 0 0 0 0 0 0 1 0 0 0 0 0
0 1 1 1 1 0 0 0 0 0 0 0 0 0 0 1 0 0 0 0
0 0 0 0 1 0 0 0 0 0 0 1 1 1 1 1 1 0 0 0
0 0 0 0 1 0 0 1 0 0 0 1 0 0 0 0 0 0 0 0
0 0 0 0 1 0 1 0 1 0 0 1 0 0 0 0 0 0 0 0
0 0 0 0 1 1 0 0 0 1 0 1 0 0 0 0 0 0 0 0
0 0 0 0 1 1 0 0 0 1 0 1 0 0 0 0 0 0 0 0
0 0 0 0 1 0 0 0 0 0 1 1 0 0 0 0 0 0 0 0
0 0 0 0 0 0 0 0 0 0 0 1 0 0 0 0 0 0 0 0

*** answer ***
(5 7) (1 7) (5 11) (2 14) (5 14) (5 19) (8 16) (12 20)
(12 15) (17 15) (14 12) (19 7) (13 7) (13 2) (9 6) (5 2)
```

Answer Figure 2.1

2.2 (We will show an outline of the proof using mathematical induction.) When $|N| = 1$, it is true since $|E| = 0$. Now let us assume that it is true for $|N| - 1(|N| \leq 2)$ and prove that it is true for $|N|$. If $|N| \geq 2$, find a $k \in N$ that has only one branch of the form of (j, k). The graph that is obtained by removing this k from the tree, $G' = (N', E')$ (provided $N' = N - \{k\}$, $E' = E - (j, k)$), is a tree with only $|N| - 1$ nodes. Therefore, by induction, $|E'| = |N'| - 1$ is true for G'. But, $|N'| = |N| - 1$, $|E'| = |E| - 1$, so $|E| = |N| - 1$.

2.3

input: the list of branches $D = (\cdots (n_i n_j) \cdots)$, the initial node n_o, and the final node n_d.

output: the shortest path from n_0 to n_d represented as a list of nodes H, the length of the shortest path (the sum of the weights of the branches; in this problem this is equal to the number of branches) h. If there is no path from n_0 to n_d, output this fact.

[1] Let $h = 0$, *searched* $= \{n_0\}$, $H = (n_0)$, $i = n_0$.
[2] If $n_d \in$ *Searched*, then stop. Output H, h.
[3] If there does not exist a node j where $(i\ j) \in D$ and $j \neq$ *searched*, go to [6].

[4] If $(i\ n_d) \in D$, then stop. Let $h = h+1$ and H be the new list with n_d added as the last element of H. Output H and h.

[5] Pick one node j where $(i\ j) \in D$ and $j \neq Searched$. Let $h = h+1$ and $Searched = Searched \cup \{j\}$. Let H be the list where j is added as the last element of H. Let $i = j$ and go to [3].

[6] Let H be the list H with its last element removed. If $H = \emptyset$, stop. Output the message that a route from n_0 to n_d does not exist. Otherwise, let i be the last element of H and go to [3].

This algorithm is not the logically best algorithm (it is based on the depth-first search method described in Section 3.6). There are many applications for the shortest path search and many algorithms are being studied to make the computation time shorter.

2.4 In Lisp, we can use a function `reverse`. For example,

```
*(reverse '(red green yellow blue))
(blue yellow green red)
```

`reverse` can be defined as follows:

```
(defun reverse (lis)
   (cond ((null lis) nil)
         (t (append (reverse (cdr lis))
                    (list (car lis))))))
```

In Prolog, we can write it as follows:

```
reverse(List,Rlist) :-rev(List,[ ],Rlist).
rev([ ],L,L).
rev([H|T],List,Rlist) :-rev(T,[H|List],Rlist).
```

Then, for example, the result can be obtained as follows:

```
| ?- reverse([red,green,yellow,blue],ReverseList).
ReverseList=[blue,yellow,green,red]
yes
```

Lisp and Prolog are programming languages suited for transforming symbolic representations.

2.5 (b), (d), (e).

2.6

(a) (*weather state raining*) $\Rightarrow$ (*$*$wear raincoat*)(*$*$put-up umbrella*)

(b) (*electric_lightstateoff*)(*electric_switchstateon*)
  ⇒ (∗*check filament*)

(c) (*electric_lightstate off*)(*electric_switchstateon*)
  (*filament state ok*) ⇒ (∗*check fuse*)

In an actual problem we would need to define each condition, the structure of sentences, and the semantic structure of actions. Here we showed examples only of what to write.

2.7 (a) *isa:* network example including multiple inheritance (Answer Figure 2.7.1)

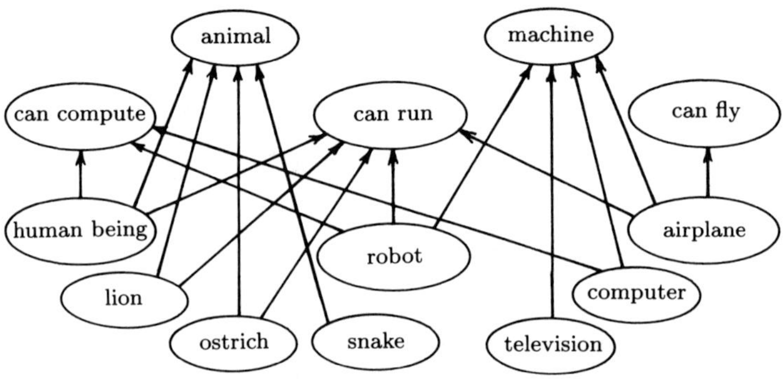

Answer Figure 2.7.1

(b) A network example including both *isa:* and *partof:* (Answer Figure 2.7.2)

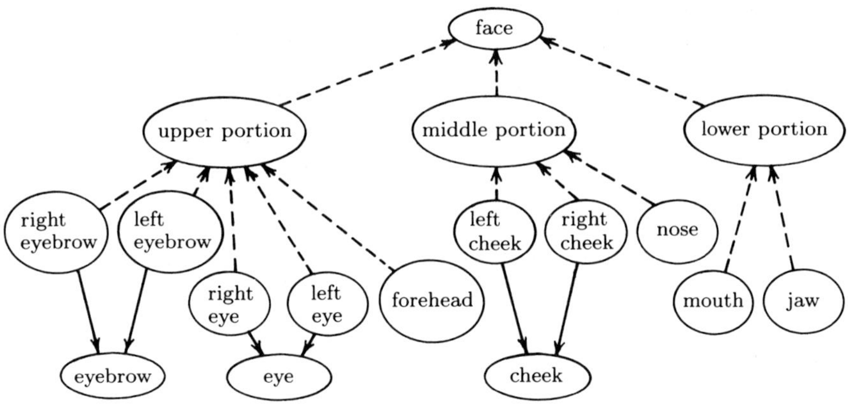

(The label of the branch ⟶ is isa:, the label of the branch - - -➤ is partof:)

Answer Figure 2.7.2

Chapter 3: Generation and Transformation of Representations

3.1 If we let $u = \frac{\omega}{2\pi}$, then $du = \frac{d\omega}{2\pi}$. From this and (3.7), (3.8), and (3.9), we obtain

$$F(u) = \int_{-\infty}^{\infty} f(x)\exp(-2\pi jux)dx$$
$$f(x) = \int_{-\infty}^{\infty} F(u)\exp(2\pi jux)du$$

If we generalize these to two dimensions, we obtain (3.10) and (3.11).

3.2

$$\begin{aligned}\mathcal{F}\left(\frac{\partial f}{\partial x}\right) &= \int_{-\infty}^{\infty}\int_{-\infty}^{\infty} \frac{\partial f(x,y)}{\partial x}\exp(-2\pi j(ux+vy))\ dx\ dy \\ &= \int_{-\infty}^{\infty}\left\{\frac{\partial f(x,y)}{\partial x}\exp(-2\pi j(ux+vy))\Big|_{-\infty}^{\infty}\right. \\ &\quad \left. - 2\pi ju\int_{-\infty}^{\infty} f(x,y)\exp(-2\pi j(ux+vy))\ dx\right\}\ dy \\ &= 2\pi ju\mathcal{F}(f(x,y))\end{aligned}$$

Similarly

$$\mathcal{F}\left(\frac{\partial f}{\partial y}\right) = 2\pi jv\mathcal{F}(f(x,y))$$

Therefore

$$\mathcal{F}\left(\frac{\partial^2 f}{\partial x^2}\right) = (2\pi ju)^2\mathcal{F}(f(x,y))$$
$$\mathcal{F}\left(\frac{\partial^2 f}{\partial y^2}\right) = (2\pi jv)^2\mathcal{F}(f(x,y))$$

and

$$\begin{aligned}\mathcal{F}(\nabla^2 f(x,y)) &= \mathcal{F}\left(\frac{\partial^2 f(x,y)}{\partial x^2} + \frac{\partial^2 f(x,y)}{\partial y^2}\right) \\ &= \mathcal{F}\left(\frac{\partial^2 f}{\partial x^2}\right) + \mathcal{F}\left(\frac{\partial^2 f}{\partial y^2}\right) \\ &= -4\pi^2(u^2+v^2)\mathcal{F}(f(x,y))\end{aligned}$$

3.3 For the Lagrange function

$$L = (x-2)^2/4 + (y-1)^2 + \lambda(x-y+1)$$

the solution to

$$\frac{\partial L}{\partial x} = (x-2)/2 + \lambda = 0$$
$$\frac{\partial L}{\partial y} = 2(y-1) - \lambda = 0$$
$$\frac{\partial L}{\partial \lambda} = x - y + 1 = 0$$

is $(x, y, \lambda) = (\frac{2}{5}, \frac{7}{5}, \frac{4}{5})$. Therefore, $(x, y) = (\frac{2}{5}, \frac{7}{5})$ is a local minimum of the original problem. On the other hand, if the goal function of the original problem is a convex function, then the local minimum becomes the global minimum. So, $(x, y) = (\frac{2}{5}, \frac{7}{5})$ is the global minimum.

3.4

input: The list E of the edges of the weighted directed graph G and the list V of the nodes of G.

output: The list M of the edges of the minimum spanning tree of G.

[1] Generate the list D that sorts all the branches of G in order of increasing weight.
[2] Let $M = \emptyset$.
[3] If $|M| < |V| - 1$, remove the first element of D $(v_i, v_j) \in E$ from D and go to [4]. Otherwise, stop. Output M.
[4] If the subgraph of G that consists of the branches of $M \cup \{(v_i, v_j)\}$ does not include a loop, let $M = M \cup \{(v_i, v_j)\}$ and go to [3].

This is not the fastest algorithm for obtaining the minimum spanning tree, because step [1] can be slow. There are other methods of obtaining the minimum spanning tree faster.

3.5 If we use

$$p(X) \rightarrow q(X) \leftrightarrow {\sim}p(X) \vee q(X)$$

the set of axioms can be written

$$W = \{{\sim}vlsi(X) \vee lsi(X), {\sim}lsi(X) \vee circuit(X, bonyson), \\ {\sim}circuit(X, Y) \vee cpu(X, Y), vlsi(m68386)\}$$

If we use ${\sim}cpu(m68386, Z)$ as a goal, we get $Z = bonyson$ by the refutation process shown in Answer Figure 3.5.

3.6 If we thread the first list in working memory through the root node, *node0* of the discrimination tree, it will go through *node1*, *node2*, *node3*, and

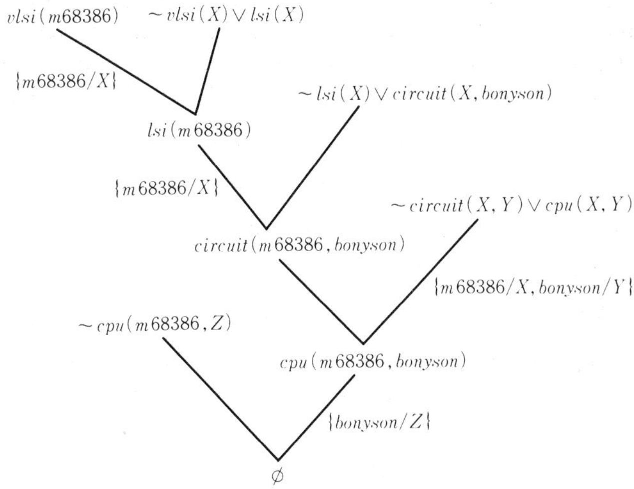

Answer Figure 3.5

finally reach *node*4, where the values of the variables $\$x, \$y$ both become *monkey*. If we thread the second list through *node*0, it goes through *node*5, *node*6, *node*7, and *node*8, and reaches *node*9. In this case, the value of the variable $\$x$ becomes *monkey*. Now, since the assignment of the value to $\$x$ was not contradictory, the thread will extend to *node*10. Therefore, we can see that rule *p*1 is executable. On the other hand, since the list cannot be extended from *node*8 to *node*11, and therefore it cannot reach *node*12, rule *p*2 is not executable. In this case we see that only one rule, *p*1, is executable, and competition among the rules does not occur. If we execute *p*1, the working memory can be rewritten as

$$((context\ grasp\ monkey\ banana)$$
$$(relationlocationmonkeybananacan\_touch))$$

3.7

$$(\forall X)(person(X) \rightarrow working\_method(X, bipedal(X)))$$

where $bipedal(X)$ is thought of as a one variable function. In this way we can represent the simple slot-filler relation of frames using predicate logic. Also, for property inheritance in the frame representation, the properties of the more general frame can be copied into the less general frame beforehand, as long as the property to be inherited does not contain any contradictions. Therefore, inference in the frame representation about simple slot filling is logically equivalent to using a predicate logic representation. However, sometimes it is hard to represent information with heuristic meaning such as possibilities and the relation of cause and effect in predicate logic. For example, we can represent "if you are rich, you can buy a mansion" and "if you are rich, you can buy your own jet" using frames as follows:

$$\begin{aligned} &\textit{rich\_person}\ \textit{can\_buy} : \textit{big\_house} \\ &\qquad\qquad\qquad \textit{can\_buy} : \textit{private\_airplane} \end{aligned} \tag{1}$$

In predicate logic, we can represent them as

$$\begin{aligned} &(\forall X)(\textit{rich\_person}(X) \rightarrow \textit{can\_buy}(X, \textit{big\_house})) \\ &(\forall X)(\textit{rich\_person}(X) \rightarrow \textit{can\_buy}(X, \textit{private\_airplane})) \end{aligned} \tag{2}$$

In this case, we cannot infer "if you are rich, you can buy both a mansion and your own jet" from (1); however, by using the predicate logic inference rule

$$\frac{P \rightarrow Q, P \rightarrow R}{P \rightarrow Q \wedge R}$$

we can infer it from (2). In the first case you can buy either a mansion or your own jet, but it does not mean that you can buy both. This is the only case where we know the meaning of inference using the frame representation when we translate frames into predicate logic.

Chapter 4: Pattern Feature Extraction

4.1 Let $f(x, y)$ be the sampling function at the mn points $x = 0, 1, \ldots$, $m - 1$, $y = 0, 1, \ldots, n - 1$. Then

$$k(x, y) = \sum_{b=0}^{n-1} \sum_{a=0}^{m-1} \frac{(x-a)^2 + (y-b)^2 - 2\sigma^2}{s\pi\sigma^6} e^{-\frac{(x-a)^2+(y-b)^2}{2\sigma^2}} f(a, b)$$

First, computing $2\sigma^2$, $\frac{1}{2\sigma^2}$, $\frac{1}{2\pi\sigma^6}$ requires $6mn$ multiplications and mn exponentiations. (There are two instances of $(x - a)^2 + (y - b)^2$, but they are each computed only once.) Therefore, to obtain $k(x, y)$ for mn points (x, y), we require $6m^2n^2$ multiplications and m^2n^2 exponentiations. Suppose $m = n = 1000$. Then, multiplication will be done 6×10^{12} times and exponentiation will be done 10^{12} times. If, roughly speaking, one exponentiation takes 10 times as long as a multiplication, the computation will take 16×10^{12} the time of one multiplication. If we assume that one multiplication takes a microsecond, it will take more than 185 days to do this computation.

This is a rough estimate, and there are methods for speeding up the computation. However, it should clear from this example that processing patterns requires a very high speed computer.

4.2 For each point of $p_1, \ldots, p_5$,

$$2\cos\theta + 2\sin\theta = r \qquad (1)$$
$$2\cos\theta + 3\sin\theta = r \qquad (2)$$
$$4\cos\theta + 4\sin\theta = r \qquad (3)$$
$$5\cos\theta + 5\sin\theta = r \qquad (4)$$
$$6\cos\theta + 5\sin\theta = r \qquad (5)$$

Using the coordinates (r, θ), we obtain the point of intersection of the above expressions. For example, for (2) and (3), from (3) – (2), the point of intersection is $(r, \theta) = (-4\cos((\tan^{-1}(-2) \pm n\pi) \pm m\pi),\ \tan^{-1}(-2) \pm n\pi)(m, n = 0, \pm 1, \ldots)$. For (1) and (2), from (2) – (1), $\sin\theta = 0$. So, the point of intersection is given by $(\pm\frac{1}{2}, n\pi)(n = 0, \pm 1, \ldots)$. The point X in Answer Figure 4.2 is the point of intersection of (1) and (2). In this case, since the x coordinates of the points p_1 and p_2 are the same, the point of intersection cannot be found by the method described in Section 4.2(c). (1)–(5) can be illustrated as in Answer Figure 4.2. In this figure, A' and B' are the highest points of intersection and they correspond to the straight line through p_1, p_3, and p_4 and the straight line though p_2, p_3, and p_5, respectively, which are shown by the broken lines in Figure 4.7(a).

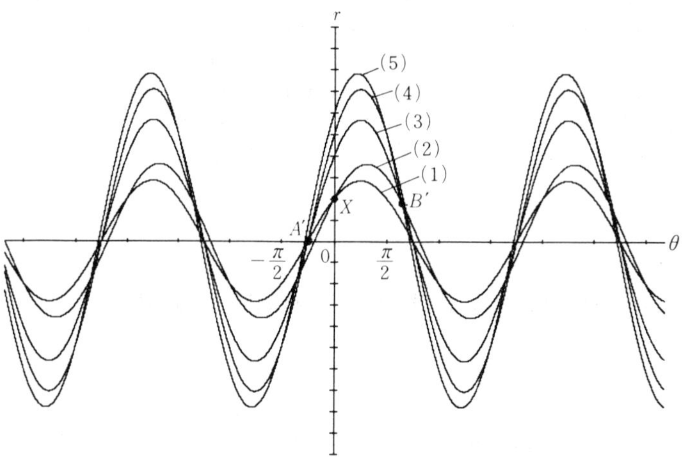

Answer Figure 4.2

4.3

[1] Let S be the given region.

[2] Execute the following steps for all the pattern elements s on the boundary line of S (those whose value is 1).

  [2.1] If none of the pattern elements neighboring s are in the interior of the region (a pattern is in the interior of a region if it is within the region but not on the boundary), leave s as it is.

  [2.2] Otherwise, let the value of s be 0.

[3] Let S be the resulting region and go to [2].

In the above skeletonization algorithm, the skeletal representation of a square, for example, is only the center point. In order to avoid this, when the pattern element s in [2] is the end point of a boundary line, we can leave the value of s to be 1 without doing steps [2.1] and [2.2]. In this way, in the case of the square, the skeletal representation becomes the narrow region along the two diagonal lines of the square.

Another method of skeletonization and linear skeletonization is a method of shaving a pattern using the rule of local linear skeletonization by shifting an $n \times n$ ($n = 3, 5$, and so on) window in a fixed direction.

4.4 The wire frame representation is, as shown in the example of Figure 4.18, a spatial representation using the coordinates of the extreme points of the object, and it can represent solid and plane figures. On the other hand, a representation using the winged-edge model method, as shown in Figure 4.19, consists of the symbolic relation structure that represents the relation among the parts of an object and its features, and it can represent the general structure and features of solids and plane figures. Therefore, if we combine the wire frame representation and the winged-edge method, we can uniformly represent the spatial location, the structural relations, features, etc. of the parts of solids and plane figures.

Chapter 5: Pattern Understanding Methods

5.1 We can extract edges and regions by feature extraction; however, we cannot find out what the object is, what its features are, or what kinds of relations hold among several objects. In order to find this out, we need knowledge about the knowledge. We might need the following kinds of knowledge about an object:

the name of the class it belong to, its spatial structure, its features, the relation between its local features and those of the class it belong to, a procedure for matching patterns with this knowledge, heuristic knowledge for finding features, knowledge about resolving contradictions between extracted features, knowledge for generating plans, inference procedures for using knowledge, and so on.

5.2

input: Two graphs, $G_1(V_1, E_1)$, $G_2 = (V_2, E_2)$ (where $V_1 = V_2 = \{1, \ldots, m\}$).

output: A message stating whether they are graph isomorphic or not.

[1] Let $P = \emptyset$, $Q = \emptyset$, $j = 1$.

[2] Execute the following procedure *graphisomorph*(P, j).

[2.1] If $P = V_2$, output that the subgraph corresponding to Q is a graph isomorphism and stop.

[2.2] for all $v \in V_2 - P$ do the following substeps:

[2.2.1] If, for all $i < j$, $\{i, j\} \in E_{1j}$ and $\{g(i), v\} \in E_2$, let $g(j) = v$. Where E_{1j} is the set of branches of G_1's subgraph and $g(i)$ is the element of V_2 that corresponds to $i \in V_1$. Let $Q = Q \cup \{v\}$.

[2.2.2] Execute *graphisomorph*$(P \cup \{v\}, j + 1)$.

5.3 In order to decide if an object (for example, a car) appears somewhere in a photograph (for example, a photograph of a road), we should divide the pattern into several subpatterns and try pattern understanding on each subpattern. Here the problem reduces to establishing a simple OR goal, and if a system can execute many pattern understanding routines in parallel, high execution speed is possible. For algorithms that generate plans including both OR goals and AND goals, please see *Knowledge and Inference* (Nagao (1990)).

Chapter 6: Learning Concepts

6.1 As we said in Section 6.2(a), we need to decide on what learning algorithm to use, how to use background information, the set of instances and a method of inputting them, and the representation of both instances and concepts. These are strongly related. For example, if we use predicate logic as the method of representation, then we can use the deductive transformations. If we use list representation, we would use algorithms for pattern matching. Also, if the set of instances includes noise, in other words, when it is possible that a positive (negative) example is interpreted as a negative (positive) example, we cannot usually make use of the methods described in this chapter. We will describe a method for dealing with noise in Chapter 9.

6.2

$$p''\eta'' = size(X_1, large) \wedge position(X_1, W_1) \wedge size(X_2, V_2) \\ \wedge\, position(X_2, upper)$$

Suppose

$$\theta_1'' = \{a/X_1, b/X_2, lower/W_1, small/V_2\}$$
$$\theta_2'' = \{c/X_1, d/X_2, lower/W_1, small/V_2\}$$

If we consider the conjunction to be the same as the set, $p''\eta''\theta_1'' \subseteq p\theta_1$, $p''\eta''\theta_2'' \subseteq p\theta_2$, then, by Definition 5, $p\theta_1, p\theta_2$ is a positive example of $p''\eta''$. Also, there is no substitution ξ_1'' for replacing the variable symbols of $p''\eta''$ with constant symbols that satisfies $p''\eta''\xi_1'' \subseteq p\xi_1$. Therefore, by Definition 5, $p\xi_1$ is a negative example of $p''\eta''$.

6.3 For

$$\theta_1 = \{C/burma, X/low\}$$
$$\theta_2 = \{C/japan, X/medium\}$$

the following is a generalization of p_1 and p_2:

$$p = p_1\theta_1 = p_2\theta_2$$
$$= \{temperature(C, high),\ humidity(C, high), mechanization(C, X)\}$$

and there are no generalization p' and substitution ξ_1, ρ_i $(i = 1, 2)$ that make $p \subseteq p_i\xi_i\rho_i$, $p' \subseteq p_i\xi_i$, $p \subseteq p'\rho_i$ $(i = 1, 2)$. So, by Definition 10, p is the MSC generalization of $\{p_1, p_2\}$. The following is the generalization that is not the MSC generalization:

$$q = \{temperature(C, Y), humidity(C, Y), mechanization(C, X)\}$$

with $q = p_1\theta_1 = p_2\eta_2$, where

$$\eta_1 = \{C/burma, X/low, Y/high\}$$
$$\eta_2 = \{C/japan, X/medium, Y/high\}$$

In this case, for the p given above, the substitutions θ_1 and θ_2, and

$$\varsigma_1 = \{Y/high\}$$
$$\varsigma_2 = \{Y/high,\}$$

$q =\subseteq p_i\theta_i\varsigma_i$, $p \subseteq p\varsigma_1$ $(i = 1, 2)$, so q is not the MSC generalization of p_1 and p_2.

Also, in the MSC generalization p, the constant symbols *low* and *medium* are replaced by the generalized variable symbol X, if we assume $X \in \{low, medium, high\}$, then p becomes an overgeneralization. In order to prevent this, we should, for example, consider a representation that uses the disjunction $medium \vee low$ as the generalization. Unfortunately, if we allow this kind of representation, everything becomes very complicated.

6.4 Depending on the form of the functions u and v, integration by parts

$$\int u\ dv = uv - \int v\ du$$

can be easy to apply or hard to apply. For example, $\int 3x \cos x\ dx$ can be reduced to $3(x \in x + \cos x) + c$ (c is a constant) by integration by parts if we let $u = 3x$ and $dv = \cos x\ dx$. Now, suppose that the positive example (where integration by parts can be applied easily)

$$\text{solve} \int 3x \cos x\ dx \Rightarrow \int u\ dv = uv - \int v\ du$$

$$(\text{where } u = 3x,\ dv = \cos x\ dx)$$

is a maximal example, and the integration by parts for the general function

$$\text{solve} \int f_1(x) f_2(x)\ dx \Rightarrow \int u\ dv = uv - \int v\ du$$

$$(\text{where } u = f_1(x),\ dv = f_2(x)\ dx)$$

is a minimal example. Consider the version space shown in Answer Figure 6.4 and search the problem space where integration by parts can be applied easily in this space. For example, suppose

$$\text{solve} \int 3x \sin x\ dx \Rightarrow \int u\ dv = uv - \int v\ du$$

$$(\text{where } u = 3x,\ dv = \sin x\ dx)$$

is presented as a positive example and

$$\text{solve} \int 3x \sin x\ dx \Rightarrow \int u\ dv = uv - \int v\ du$$

$$(\text{where } u = \sin x,\ dv = 3x\ dx)$$

is presented as a negative example. By the former, the part of Answer Figure 6.4 including and below the circled node is left in the version space. By the latter, the part including and below the boxed nodes is removed from the version space. By repeating this operation, we can narrow down the problems that are easy to do by integration by parts. In order to find

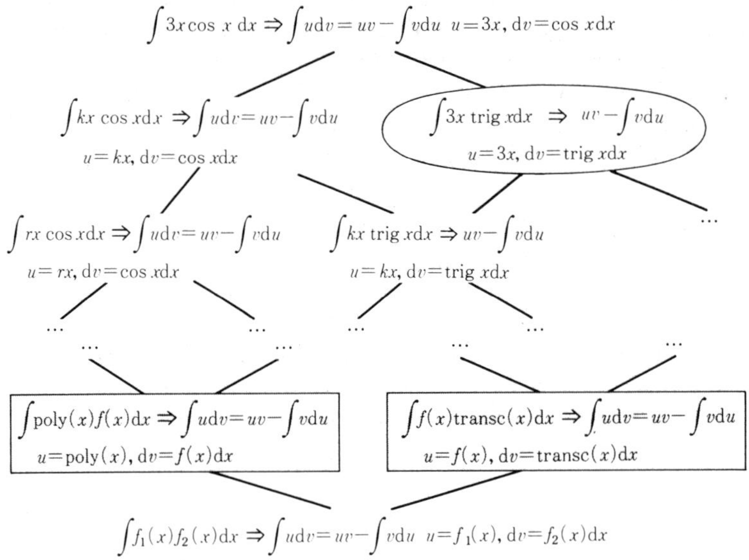

Answer Figure 6.4 Version space for integration by parts (Mitchell *et al.*, 1983).

the circled nodes and the boxed nodes, we make use of the background knowledge that $\sin x$ and $\cos x$ are examples of trigonometric functions.

The above example is from Mitchell *et al.* (1983).

Chapter 7: Learning Procedures

7.1 In the original problem, we would start from the initial state s_0 of Section 7.1(a) (Figure 7.1); however, to simplify we consider here the goal state reached by solving the problem of Section 7.1(a) as the initial.

initial state s_0: *in*(*robot*1, *room*1)
in(*box*1, *room*1)
connect(*door*1, *room*1, *room*2)
connect(*door*1, *room*2, *room*1)
robot(*robot*1)
box(*box*1)
door(*door*1)
room(*room*1)
room(*room*2)

goal state s_d: $in(robot1, room2)$
$in(box1, room1)$
$connect(D, X, Y)$
$connect(D, Y, X)$
$robot(robot1)$
$box(box1)$
$door(door1)$
$room(room1)$
$room(room2)$

Now if we let $g = \{in(robot1, room2)\}$, we have $g = a_1\theta$ for the add list of *walkto* a_1 and the substitution $\theta = \{robot1R, room2/Y\}$. So we rewrite

$$g = p_1\theta = \{in(robot1, X), connect(W, X, room2), robot(robot1)\}$$

From this we prove $s_o \vdash g$ and the substitution we get during the refutation process is $\xi = \{room1/X, door1/W\}$. Therefore, s_0 can be changed to s_d by the operator

$$walkto(robot1, door1, room1, room2)$$

7.2 In the original problem we should start from the initial state s_0 of Section 7.1(a) (Figure 7.1); however, to simplify, we generalize only the part of the problem dealt with in Problem 7.1. First, the triangular table for the answer to Exercise 7.1 is as shown in Answer Figure 7.2.1.

predicates that are used as preconditions in the initial state	
in(*robot*1, *room*1) *connect*(*door*1, *room*1, *room*2) *robot*(*robot*1)	operator 3 *walkto*(*robot*1, *door*1, *room*1, *room*2)
	predicates that are added by the operator 3 *in*(*robot*1, *room*2)

Answer Figure 7.2.1

The above triangular table can be generalized as shown in Answer Figure 7.2.2.

Using the above triangular table, we do the proof again. In other words, prove B using the precondition A and the precondition for the operator 3. The proof process is shown in Answer Figure 7.2.3.

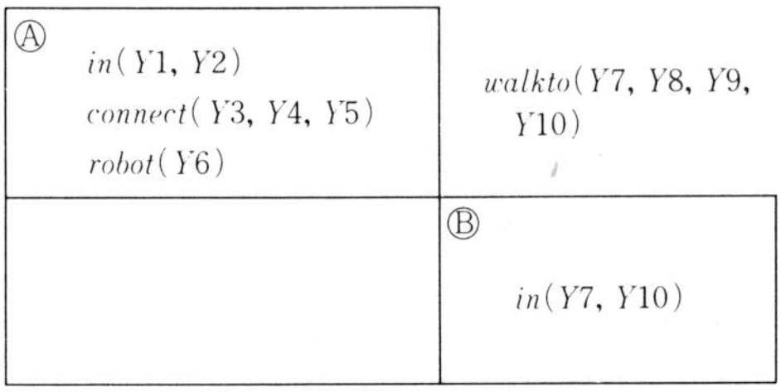

Answer Figure 7.2.2

If we do the substitution obtained from the triangular table, we obtain the generalized operator

$$walkto(Y6, Y3, Y2, Y5)$$

This represents that "the robot $Y6$ moves by walking from room $Y2$ to $Y5$ through the door $Y3$."

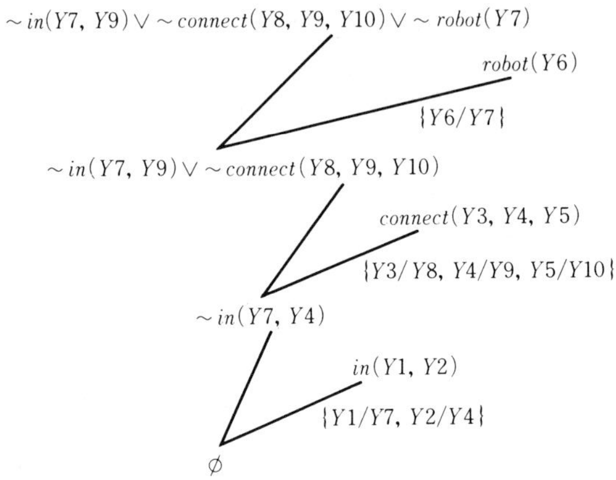

Answer Figure 7.2.3

7.3 The sample program written in Lisp is shown in Answer Figure 7.3. To run this program, we `setq` the list of rules to the atom `productions` and the list containing the working memories to the atom `wms`, and evaluate the function `start`. The rule for generating and adding a new rule to the set of rules,

```
(rg (cond $x)(action $y) => (*build (*gensym)))
```

should be placed in front of the initial set of the rules. If there is no function in the head of the action, we omit `*deposit` (adding the value of the argument to the head of the working memory). Also, the lists maintained in working memory that are candidates for conditions or actions should be in the form `(cond <condition>)` and `(action <action>)`, respectively. For a function with `@` instead of `*` in the head of an `<action>`, `@` is changed to `*` when such a function is entered into the working memory. For example, if `(action (@deposit (a b c)))` is executed as the action of a rule, `(action (*deposit (a b c)))` is added to the front of the working memory. In this program, if at least one list with **cond** and **action** as its head exists in working memory, the program executes the rule **rg**, it generates a new rule (within working memory) consisting of all the lists whose head is **cond** or **action**, and it adds such a rule to the front of the set of rules. Then it deletes the used lists from working memory. By the way, the atoms with * as their head on the action side are all evaluated as functions. In particular, to stop the execution of the rule, we can let the action side execute the a rule including **(*halt)** which evaluates the function **halt**.

```
(defun start nil
       (prog (env)
             (setq haltflag nil)
             cycle (cond (haltflag (return ***halt))
                         ((execute productions) (go cycle))
                         (t (return '***no_production_fired)))))

(defun execute (prods)
       (cond ((null prods) nil)
             ((all_satisfied (extract_conditions (cadr prods)) nil)
              (terpri)
              (prin1 '***fired)
              (prin1 (caar prods))
              (terpri)
              (execute_actions (extract_actions (car prods)))
              (terpri)
              (print wms)
              (terpri)
              t)
             (t (execute (cdr prods)))))

(defun build (name)
       (setq productions
             (cons (cons name
                         (append (sublis 'cond wms)
                                 (cons '=> (sublis 'action wms))))
                   productions)))
```

```
(defun sublis (exp memory)
       (cond ((null memory) nil)
             ((eq (caar memory) exp)
              (cons (cadar memory)
                    (sublis exp (cdr memory))))))

(defun halt nil
       (setq haltflag t))

(defun extract_conditions (lis)
       (cond ((null is) nil)
             ((eq '=> (car lis)) nil)
             (t (cons (car lis) (extract_conditions (cdr lis))))))

(defun all_satisfied (conds bindlist)
       (cond ((null conds)
              (setq env bindlist)
              t)
             ((iffunc (caar conds))
              (predicates_satisfied (car conds) bindlist))
             (t (patterns_satisfied (car conds) wms bindlist))))

(defun patterns_satisfied (pattern wmelements binds)
       (cond ((null wmelements) nil)
             ((and (match pattern (car wmelements))
                   (all_satisfied (cdr conds) binds))
              t)
             (t (patterns_satisfied pattern
                                    (cdr wmelements)
                                    bindlist))))

(defun predicates_satisfied (predicate binds)
       (cond ((eval (evaluable predicate) binds)
              (all_satisfied (cdr conds) binds))
             (t nil)))

(defun match (pattern1 pattern2)
       (cond ((null pattern1) (null pattern2))
             ((atom pattern1)
              (cond ((eq pattern1 pattern2) t)
                    ((ifvar pattern1)
                     (consistent (cons pattern1 pattern2)))
                    (t nil)))
             ((atom pattern2) nil)
             (t (and (match (car pattern1) (car pattern2))
                     (match (cdr pattern1) (cdr pattern2))))))
```

```
(defun consistent (pair)
       (cond ((member pair binds) t)
             ((assoc (car pair) binds) nil)
             (t (setq binds (cons pair binds)))))

(defun evaluable (exp)
       (cond ((null exp) nil)
             ((atom (car exp))
              (cond ((iffunc (car exp))
                     (cons (atomcdr (car exp))
                           (evaluable (cdr exp))))
                    ((ifvar (car exp))
                     (cons (car exp) (evaluable (cdr exp))))
                    (t (cons (list 'quote (car exp))
                             (evaluable (cdr exp))))))
              (t (cons (cond ((iffunc (caar exp))
                              (evaluable (car exp)))
                             (t (cons 'list (evaluable (car exp)))))
                       (evaluable (cdr exp))))))

(defun iffunc (exp)
       (and (atom exp)
            (eq (car (unpack exp)) '*)))

(defun ifvar (exp)
       (and (atom exp)
            (eq (car (unpack exp)) '$)))

(defun atomcdr (exp)
       (maknam (cdr (unpack exp))))

(defun extract_actions (lis)
       (cond ((eq '=> (car lis))
              (extract_actions2 (cdr lis)))
             (t (extract_actions (cdr lis)))))

(defun extract_actions2 (lis)
       (cond ((null lis) nil)
             ((iffunc (caar lis))
              (cons (car lis)
                    (extract_action2 (cdr lis))))
              (t (cons (cons '*deposit (car lis))
                       extract_actions2 (cdr lis))))))

(defun execute_actions (acts)
       (map acts (function (lambda (act)
                             (eval (evaluable (car act)) env)))))
```

```
(defun deposit (pattern)
       (setq pattern (substsym '* '@ pattern))
       (setq wms (cons pattern (remove pattern wms))))

(defun substsym (x y exp)
       (cond ((null exp) nil)
             ((atom exp)
              (cond ((eq y (car (unpack exp)))
                     (maknam (cons x (cdr (unpack exp)))))
                    (t exp)))
             (t (cons (substsym x y (car exp))
                      (substsym x y (cdr exp))))))

(define delete (pattern)
        (setq wms (remove pattern wms)))

(defun remove (list from)
       (cond ((null from) nil)
             ((equal (car from) lis)
              (cdr from))
             (t (cons (car from)
                      (remove lis (cdr from))))))
```

Answer Figure 7.3

7.4 In the course of problem solving described in Exercise 7.3, `(clear a)` caused a loop on the state. For this reason we might put this subgoal at the beginning and change the order of subgoals in the original goal. As a result, we can solve the problem as follows:

subgoal : (*clear a*)
  subgoal : (*move c table*)
  attained
attained
subgoal : (*on bc*)
attained
subgoal : (*on a b*)
attained

This is an example of a case where we can solve a problem by changing the order of the subgoals in different classes or the subgoals in the same class.

Unfortunately, it is not so easy to introduce this operation into procedural learning as described in Section 7.3 and to build a system for learning how to change the structure of a subgoal.

Chapter 8: Learning Based on Logic

8.1

```
| ?- explain(love(hanako,hanako), love(A,B), ProofTree,
GeneralizedProofTree).                                    ... goal
A=_4
B=_5
ProofTree=[[love(hanako,hanako),
[sympathetic(hanako,hanako),
[attractive(good_proportion),[good_point(good_proportion)]],
[have(hanako,good_proportion),[get(hanako,good_proportion)]]]]]
                                                  ... proof tree (i)
GeneralizedProofTree=
[[love(_4,_5),
[sympathetic(_4,_5),
[attractive(_36),[good_point(_36)]],
[have(_4,_36),[get(_4,_36)]]]]]                  ... proof tree (ii)
                                          (generalized proof tree)
```

The following Horn clause is a sufficient condition:

```
love(_4,_5) :-
sympathetic(_4,_5), good_point(_36), get(_4,_36)
```

The above well-formed formula can be interpreted as "a person who has good points and who is sympathetic to other people loves other people." This is an overgeneralization of the positive example

```
sympathetic(hanako,hanako).
```

This is due to the fact that the background information is too general.

8.2

(i) $m = (\{triangle(X), ontable(X), ontable(Y)\},$
$\quad\langle\{b/X, a/Y\}, \{f/X, e/Y\}\rangle)$

(ii) $\{triangle(Z)\} \Rightarrow \{square(Z)\}$

(iii) $\tau_1' = \{circle(Y), triangle(X), ontable(Y), ontable(X)\}$

(iv) $\tau_2 = \{circle(Y), square(X), ontable(Y), ontable)(X)\}$

8.3 The knowledge that a swallow, a sparrow, a robin, and a hawk are birds can be represented by the following well-formed formula:

$$(\forall X)(swallow(X) \vee sparrow(X) \vee robin(X) \vee hawk(X) \to bird(X)) \quad \text{(i)}$$

To say that only swallows, sparrows, robins, and hawks are birds, we use the following well-formed formula:

$$(\forall X)(bird(X) \to swallow(X) \vee sparrow(X) \vee robin(X) \vee hawk(X)) \quad \text{(ii)}$$

Consider the inference rule

$$(\forall X)(p(X) \to q(X)) \to (\forall X)(q(X) \to p(X) \quad \text{(iii)}$$

(where $p(X), q(X)$ correspond to (i) and (ii), respectively). Next, to generalize (iii), consider the following inference rule for an arbitrary well-formed formula $r(X)$ and an arbitrary predicate $w(X)$:

$$P(r) \wedge (\forall X)(r(X) \to w(X)) \to (\forall Y)(w(Y) \to r(Y)) \quad \text{(iv)}$$

where P is a well-formed formula that can be proved from $P(w)$. Since (iv) includes $P(r)$, it is an inference rule of second-order predicate logic and the basic inference rule in circumscription. In this problem, we can assume, for example, the following:

$P(r)$: $(\forall X)(r(X) \to canfly(X)$
$r(X)$: $swallow(X) \vee sparrow(X) \vee robin(X) \vee hawk(X)$
$w(X)$: $bird(X)$

(where $P(w)$, in other words, $(\forall X)(bird(X) \to canfly(X))$ is true). From this we can conclude that if Y is a bird, then Y must be either a swallow, a sparrow, a robin, or a hawk.

Chapter 9: Learning by Classification and Discovery

9.1 One example of a discrimination tree is shown in Answer Figure 9.1. (It does not include the classification of +−.)

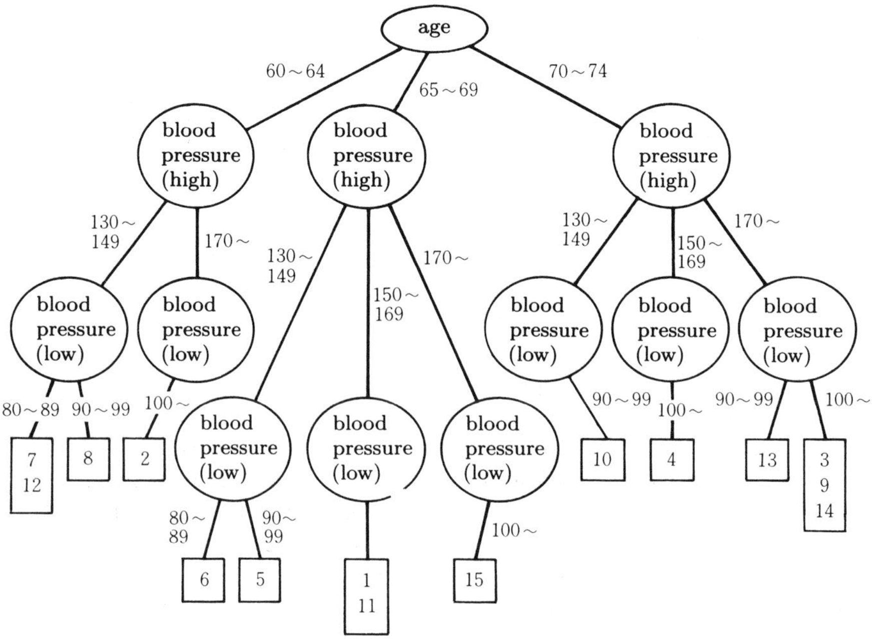

Answer Figure 9.1

9.2 Similar to the answer to Exercise 9.1, we look at the value of each attribute classified as follows (the symbols are those of Section 9.3):

$$t_1 = \text{“age”} \cdots v_{11} = 60 \sim 64$$
$$v_{12} = 65 \sim 69$$
$$v_{13} = 70 \sim 74$$
$$t_2 = \text{“blood pressure (high)”} \cdots v_{21} = 130 \sim 149$$
$$v_{22} = 150 \sim 169$$
$$v_{23} = 170 \sim$$
$$t_2 = \text{“blood pressure (low)”} \cdots v_{21} = 80 \sim 89$$
$$v_{32} = 90 \sim 99$$
$$v_{33} = 100 \sim$$

If we call the number of data points classified as $+, -$, d^1 and d^2, respectively, we have $d^1 = 6$, $d^2 = 9$. Also,

$$\begin{array}{lll} D_{11} = \{2,7,8,12\} & D_{21} = \{5,6,7,8,10,12\} & D_{31} = \{6,7,12\} \\ D_{12} = \{1,5,6,11,15\} & D_{22} = \{1,4,11\} & D_{32} = \{1,5,8,10,11,13\} \\ D_{13} = \{3,4,9,10,13,14\} & D_{23} = \{2,3,9,13,14,15\} & D_{33} = \{2,3,4,9,14,15\} \end{array}$$

Furthermore,

$$\begin{array}{lll} d_{11}^1 = 1, d_{11}^2 = 3 & d_{21}^1 = 0, d_{21}^2 = 6 & d_{31}^1 = 0, d_{31}^2 = 3 \\ d_{12}^1 = 1, d_{12}^2 = 4 & d_{22}^1 = 0, d_{22}^2 = 3 & d_{32}^1 = 1, d_{32}^2 = 5 \\ d_{13}^1 = 4, d_{13}^2 = 2 & d_{23}^1 = 6, d_{23}^2 = 0 & d_{33}^1 = 5, d_{33}^2 = 1 \end{array}$$

Clearly,

$$E'(t_2) = 0 < E'(t_1), E'(t_3)$$

Therefore,

$$G(t_2) = E(d^1, d^2) - E'(t_2) > G(t_1), G(t_3)$$

and $\max_j G(t_j)$ can be obtained by $t_2 =$ "blood pressure(high)." Now, if we choose "blood pressure(high)" as a test in the root node of the discrimination tree, we can maximize the amount of information. Actually, in this example, since E'(blood pressure(high)) $= 0$, the amount of information in the discrimination tree as a whole and the amount of information when we chose "blood pressure (high)" as the first test are the same. This means that the test of "blood pressure(high)" alone can classify the data into two classes of $+, -$.

9.3 For the data vector

$$\begin{aligned} m &= (5.0, 10.0, 15.0, 20.0, 12.0, 8.0) \\ v &= (4.0, 3.0, 8.0, 8.0, 10.0, 5.0) \\ E &= (40.0, 45.0, 480.0, 640.0, 600.0, 100.0) \end{aligned}$$

we let $X_0 = \{m, v, E\}$. If we set the initial state to X_0 and do breadth-first search using the operators $\circ, /$ that are defined in Definition 2 in Section 9.5(a), we obtain the constant vector $m \circ v \circ v/E = (2,2,2,2,2,2)$. (If we generalize this, we can obtain $E = \frac{1}{2}mv^2$, in other words, the expressions of the relation between the speed of an object and energy in Newtonian dynamics.) Answer Figure 9.3 shows part of the search tree.

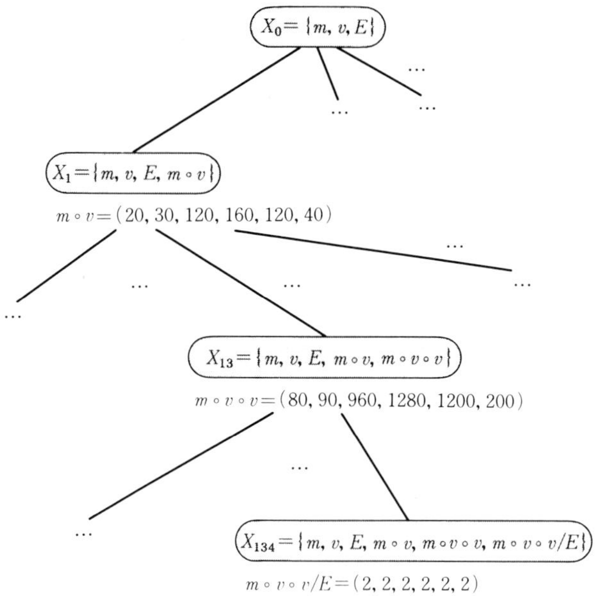

Answer Figure 9.3

Chapter 10: Learning by Neural Networks

10.1

(i)

	back propagation error learning	competitive learning
structure of the neural network	feedforward network	feedforward cluster
learning method	supervised learning	unsupervised learning
learning rule for net weight	generalization delta rule	intensification based on conflict

(ii)

	Hopfield network	Boltzmann machine
behavior of corollary	deterministic	probabilistic
value the state can take	[0, 1]	$\{0, 1\}$
state transition	deterministic	probabilistic

10.2 [4], [5], [6] show that an output unit and the units in its neighborhood where the corresponding input vector is closest to the unit's weight are selected and the weights of the links that combine such units are reactivated. By repeating this operation, the unit weight that represents the distribution of the input vector in some sense is created in several output units. In other words, we can divide the set of the input vector into several clusters by vector quantization.

10.3 The following is a partial list of the necessary functions:

(1) macro commands for simply defining many units and links.
(2) a template for modulizing the computation at each layer and cluster.
(3) commands for making simple definitions of output functions, state transition functions, and so on.
(4) functions for uniform random numbers, probabilistic distribution functions, and so on.
(5) input functions for reading masses of input data and for managing data bases.
(6) descriptions of functions that change the values of the energy function, the unit weights, the states, and so on.
(7) human/machine interface for showing clearly the structure of the network, and so on.

Bibliography

I. Bibliographies

Clowes, M. B.: On seeing things, *Artificial Intelligence*, Vol. 2, pp. 79–116, 1971.

Connell, J. H. and Brady, M.: Generating and generalizing models of visual objects, *Artificial Intelligence*, Vol. 3, pp. 159–183, 1987.

Guzman, A.: Decomposition of a visual scene into three-dimensional bodies, *AFIPS Proceedings of Fall Joint Computer Conference*, Vol. 33, pp. 291–304, 1968.

Huffman, D. A.: Impossible objects as nonsense sentences, in B. Meltzer and D. Michie (eds.), *Machine Intelligence*, Vol. 6, Edinburgh University Press, pp. 295–324, 1971.

Kanade, T.: A theory of origami world, *Artificial Intelligence*, Vol. 13, pp. 279–311, 1980.

Lenat, D. B.: The ubiquity of discovery, *Artificial Intelligence*, Vol. 9, pp. 257–285, 1977.

Marr, D. and Nishihara, H. K.: Representation and recognition of the spatial organization of three-dimensional structure, *Proceedings of Royal Society of London*, Vol. B200, pp. 269–294, 1978.

Matsuyama, K. and Nagao, M.: Structural analysis of aerial pictures, *Information Processing*, Vol. 21, pp. 468–480, 1980 (in Japanese).

Mitchell, T. M., Utgoff, P. E. and Benerji, R.: Learning by experimentation: Acquiring and refining problem-solving heuristics, in I. R. S. Michalski, J. G. Carbonell and T. M. Mitchell (eds.), *Machine Learning: An Artificial Intelligence Approach*, Tioga/Springer-Verlag, pp. 163–190, 1983.

Ohta, Y.: Knowledge-based interpretation of outdoor natural color scenes, *Research Notes in Artificial Intelligence*, Vol. 4, Pitman, 1985.

Poggio, T., Torre, V. and Koch, C.: Computational vision and regularization theory, *Nature*, Vol. 317, 26 September, pp. 314–319, 1985.

Shirai, Y.: Analyzing intensity arrays using knowledge about scenes, in P. H. Winston (ed.), *The Psychology of Computer Vision*, McGraw-Hill, 1975.

Waltz, D. L.: Understanding line drawings of scenes with shadows, in P. H. Winston (ed.), *The Psychology of Computer Vision*, McGraw-Hill, 1975.

II. Reference books for advanced Japanese readers

We only list books written in Japanese or translated into Japanese.

Chapters 1–3

Aho, A. V., Hopcroft, J. E. and Ullman, J. D.: *The Design and Analysis of Computer Algorithms*, Addison-Wesley, 1976.

This is a standard textbook for learning data structure and algorithms.

Bobrow, D. G. and Collins, A. (eds.): *Representation and Understanding: Studies in Cognitive Science*, Academic Press, 1975.

This is a collection of classic theses on knowledge representation.

Goto, S.: *Symbolic Processing Programming* (Iwanami Software Series 8), Iwanami-Shoten, 1988 (in Japanese).

This is for learning Lisp and Prolog.

Iri, M., Shirakawa, I., Kajiya, Y., Shinoda, S., et. al.: *Practice Graph*

Theory–Basics and Applications, Koronasha, 1983 (in Japanese).

This describes in detail the basics of the graphs and networks and their algorithms.

Marr, D.: *Vision: A Computational Investigation into the Human Representation and Processing of Visual Information*, W.H. Freeman, 1982.

This is a must-read book for readers who learn computational theory in visual information processing by Marr.

Nagao, M.: *Knowledge and Inference*, Academic Press, 1990.

This is a suitable book for learning basics of the method of using knowledge bases in the artificial intelligence system and the inference method.

Nagao, M. and Fuchi, K.: *Theory and Meaning* (Iwanami Information Science Series 7), Iwanami-Shoten, 1983 (in Japanese).

This is suitable for learning the basics of predicate logic and model semantics.

Nilsson, N. J.: *Problem Solving Methods in Artificial Intelligence*, McGraw-Hill, 1971.

This is a classic book on the algorithm mainly of searches and problem solving.

Rich, E.: *Artificial Intelligence*, McGraw-Hill, 1983.

One of the standard textbooks for learning basics of artificial intelligence.

Shirai, Y. and Tsujii, J.: *Artificial Intelligence* (Iwanani Information Science Series 22), Iwanami-Shoten, 1982 (in Japanese).

One of the standard textbooks for learning basic methods in artificial intelligence.

Tsujii, J.: *Knowledge Representation and Usage*, Shokodo, 1987 (in Japanese).

This is a good book for learning knowledge representation and inference including the recent research.

Ueno, H. and Ishizuka, M. (eds.): *Knowledge Representation and Usage*,

(Knowledge Engineering Series 2), Omusha, 1987 (in Japanese).

This covers recent research on knowledge representation and methods of inference.

Winston, P. H. (ed.): *The Psychology of Computer Vision*, McGraw-Hill, 1975.

This is a collection of theses on pioneering research at MIT on pattern understanding.

Wylie, C. R.: *Advanced Engineering Mathematics*, McGraw-Hill, 1960.

This is a good textbook for learning, from the engineering standpoint, analytical methods such as Fourier analysis, convolution integrals, and so on.

Chapters 4 and 5

Ballard, D. H. and Brown, C. M.: *Computer Vision*, Prentice-Hall, 1982.

This explains various methods for pattern understanding over a wide range including its relationship to knowledge representation.

Furui, T.: *Digital Voice Processing*, Tokai University Press, 1985 (in Japanese).

We did not talk about voice recognition in this book, but this is a good book for learning voice recognition/synthesis.

Hiratsuka, K., Kitabashi, T. and Ogawa, H.: *Digital Screen Processing*, Nikkan Kogyo News Paper, 1985 (in Japanese).

This surveys methods for feature extractions.

Marr. D.: *Vision: A Computational Investigation into the Human Representation and Processing of Visual Information*, W.H. Freeman, 1982.

This includes a detailed explanation of the zero-crossing method and its significance.

Mori, S. and Sakakura, T.: *Basics of Screen Recognition [O] —Preprocessing Feature Extraction for Shape*, Omusha, 1986 (in Japanese).

This explains in detail the theory of feature extraction and its algorithm.

Nagao, M.: *Screen Recognition Theory*, Koronasha, 1983 (in Japanese).

This is suitable for learning basics of various methods of feature extraction.

Nagao, M.: *Pattern Information Processing*, Koronasha, 1983 (in Japanese).

This is suitable for learning information processing methods for pattern understanding.

Rosenfeld, A. and Kak, A. C.: *Digital Picture Processing I, II*, Academic Press (second edition), 1982.

This is known as a standard textbook on the methods of screen pattern recognition.

Shirai, Y.: *Computer Vision*, Shokodo, 1980 (in Japanese).

This is suitable for learning methods of screen pattern recognition on a computer.

Shirai, Y. (ed.): *Pattern Understanding*, Omusha, 1987 (in Japanese).

This explains various methods of feature extraction and pattern understanding including recent research and applications.

Tamura, H. (supervisor): *Introduction to Computer Screen Processing*, Soken Publishers, 1985 (in Japanese).

This not only explains methods for screen pattern recognition but also includes reference books on screen pattern recognition.

Chapters 6–9

Cohen, P. R. and Feigenbaum, E. A. (eds.): *The Handbook of Artificial Intelligence*, Vol. III, Pitman, 1982.

This book outlines learning algorithms up to the early 1980s.

Furukawa, K. and Mizoguchi, F. (eds.): *Learning Mechanism of Knowledge*, Kyoritsu Publishers, 1986 (in Japanese).

This summarizes research on learning on logic.

Michalski, R. S., Carbonell, J. G. and Mitchell, T. M. (eds.): *Machine Learning: An Artificial Intelligence Approach*, Tioga/Springer-Verlag, 1983.

This outlines research on learning theory and algorithms until the early 1980s.

Michalski, R. S., Carbonell, J. G. and Mitchell, T. M. (eds.): *Machine Learning II: An Artificial Intelligence Approach*, Morgan Kaufmann, 1986.

This is a sequel to Michalski *et al.*, 1983.

Nilsson, N. J.: *Principles of Artificial Intelligence*, McGraw-Hill, 1983.

This is suitable for learning problem solving methods based on logical inference.

Shimura, M.: *Machine Knowledge Theory*, Shokodo, 1983.

This is suitable for learning basic methods of artificial intelligence.

Chapter 10

Aihara, K.: *Neural Computer*, Tokyo Denki University Press, 1988 (in Japanese).

This covers from learning on neural networks to Chaos, especially about neural information processing models.

Amari, S.: *Doctrine of Neural Network*, Sangyo Tosho, 1978 (in Japanese).

This is known as a book summarizing theories of neural network learning.

Aso, H.: *Neural Network Information Processing*, Sangyo Tosho, 1988 (in Japanese).

This book discusses learning in neural networks, especially summaries of models of recognition information processing.

III. Books directly related to the content of this book

Some theses are already listed in I and II.

Chapters 1–3

Anzai, Y.: Production systems and artificial intelligence research—for knowledge acquisition problems, *Computer Software*, Vol. 1, no. 3, pp. 2–12, 1984 (in Japanese).

de Boor, C.: *A Practical Guide to Splines*, Springer-Verlag, 1978.

Connell, J. H. and Brady, M.: Generating and generalizing models of visual objects, *Artificial Intelligence*, Vol. 31, pp. 159–183, 1987.

Feigenbaum, E. A.: The simulation of verbal learning behavior, *Proceedings of the Western Joint Computer Conference*, pp. 121–32, 1961.

Forgy, C. L.: Rege: A fast algorithm for the many pattern/many objects pattern match problem, *Artificial Intelligence*, Vol. 19, pp. 17–37, 1982.

Hayes, P. J.: The logic of frames, in D. Metzing (ed.), *Frame Conceptions and Text Understanding*, Walter de Gruyter, pp. 46–61, 1979.

Horn, B. K. P.: *Robot Vision*, The MIT Press, 1986.

Kowalski, R. A.: *Logic for Problem Solving*, North-Holland, 1979,

Lloyd, J. W.: *Foundations of Logic Programming*, Springer-Verlag, 1984.

Minsky, M.: A framework for representing knowledge, in P. H. Winston (ed.), *The Psychology of Computer Vision*, McGraw-Hill, 1975.

Robinson, J. A.: A machine-oriented logic based on the resolution principle, *Journal of ACM*, Vol. 12, pp. 23–41, 1965.

Winograd, T.: Frame representations and the declarative/procedural controversy, in D.G. Bobrow and A.M. Collins (eds.), *Representation and Understanding: Studies in Cognitive Science*, Academic Press, pp. 185–210, 1975.

Chapter 4

Ballard, D. H.: Generalization of the Hough transform to detect arbitrary shapes, *Pattern Recognition*, Vol. 13, pp. 111–122, 1981.

Chow, C. K. and Kaneko, T.: Automatic boundary detection of the left ventricle from cineangiograms, *Computers and Biomedical Research*, Vol. 5, pp. 388–410, 1972.

Clocksin, W. F.: Computer prediction of visual thresholds for surface slant and edge detection from optical flow fields, *Ph.D. dissertation*, University of Edinburgh, 1980.

Duda, R. O. and Hart, P. E.: *Pattern Recognition and Scene Analysis*, Wiley, 1973.

Duda, R. O. and Hart, P. E.: Use of Hough transformation to detect lines and curves in pictures, *Communications of ACM*, Vol. 15, pp. 11–15, 1972.

Freeman, H.: Computer processing of line drawing images, *Computing Surveys*, Vol. 6, pp. 57–98, 1974.

Fu, K. S.: *Syntactic Methods in Pattern Recognition*, Academic Press, 1974.

Hildreth, E. C.: The detection of intensity changes by computer and biological vision systems, *Computer Vision, Graphics and Image Processing*, Vol. 22, pp. 1–27, 1983.

Horn, B. K. P. and Schunck, B. G.: Determining optical flow, *Artificial Intelligence*, Vol. 17, pp. 185–203, 1981.

Marr, D. and Nishihara, H. K.: Representation and recognition of the spatial organization of three-dimensional structure, *Proceedings of Royal Society of London*, Vol. B200, pp. 269–294, 1978.

Martelli, A.: An application of heuristic search methods to edge and contour detection, *Communications of ACM*, Vol. 19, pp. 73–83, 1976.

Poggio, T., Torre, V. and Koch, C.: Computational vision and regularization theory, *Nature*, Vol. 317, 26 September, pp. 314–319, 1985.

Samet, H.: Region representation: Quadtrees from boundary codes, *Communications of ACM*, Vol. 23, pp. 163–170, 1980.

Voelcker, H. B. and Requicha, A. A. G.: Geometric modeling of mechanical parts and processes, *Computer*, Vol. 10, pp. 48–57, 1977.

Chapter 5

Agin, G. J. and Binford, T. O.: Computer description of curved objects, *Proceedings of the Third International Joint Conference on Artificial Intelligence*, pp. 629–640, 1973.

Ambler, A. P., Barrow, H. G., Brown, C. M., Burstall, R. M. and Poppleston, R. J.: A versatile computer-controlled assembly system, *Artificial Intelligence*, Vol. 6, pp. 129–156, 1975.

Ballard, D. H.: *Hierarchic Recognition of Tumors in Chest Radiographs*, Birkhauser-Verlag, 1976.

Barrow, H. G. and Tenenbaum, J. M.: MSYS: A system for reasoning about scenes, Technical Note Vol. 121, Artificial Intelligence Center, SRI International, March 1976.

Brooks, R. A.: Symbolic reasoning among 3-D models and 2-D images, *Artificial Intelligence*, Vol. 17, pp. 285–348, 1981.

Brooks, R. A., Greiner, R. and Binford, T. O.: Progress report on a model-based vision system, in L.S. Baumann (ed.), *Proceedings of the Image Understanding Workshop*, pp. 145–151, 1978.

Clowes, M. B.: On seeing things, *Artificial Intelligence*, Vol. 2, pp. 79–116, 1971.

Guzman, A.: Decomposition of a visual scene into three-dimensional bodies, *AFIPS Proceedings of Fall Joint Computer Conference*, Vol. 33, pp. 291–304, 1968.

Huffman, D. A.: Impossible objects as nonsense sentences, in B. Meltzer and D. Michie (eds.), *Machine Intelligence*, Vol. 6, Edinburgh University Press, pp. 295–324, 1971.

Kanade, T.: A theory of origami world, *Artificial Intelligence*, Vol. 13, pp. 279–311, 1980.

Matsuyama, K. and Hang, V.: Screen Understanding System SIGMA— integrating the bottom-up and the top-down analysis, *Journal of Information Processing Society*, Vol. 26, pp. 877–889, 1985 (in Japanese).

Matsuyama, K. and Nagao, M.: Structural analysis of aerial pictures, *Information Processing*, Vol. 21, pp. 468–480, 1980 (in Japanese).

Nagao, M.: Control strategies in pattern analysis, *Pattern Recognition*, Vol. 17, pp. 45–56, 1984.

Ohta, Y.: Knowledge-based interpretation of outdoor natural color scenes, *Research Notes in Artificial Intelligence*, Vol. 4, Pitman, 1985 .

Rosenfeld, A., Hummel, R. A. and Zucker, S. W.: Scene labeling by relaxation operations, *IEEE Transactions on Systems, Man and Cybernetics*, Vol. SMC-6, pp. 420–433, 1976.

Shirai, Y.: Analyzing intensity arrays using knowledge about scenes, in P. H. Winston (ed.), *The Psychology of Computer Vision*, McGraw-Hill, 1975.

Waltz, D. L.: Understanding line drawings of scenes with shadows, in P. H. Winston (ed.), *The Psychology of Computer Vision*, McGraw-Hill, 1975.

Chapter 6

Michalski, R. S.: A theory and methodology of inductive learning, *Artificial Intelligence*, Vol. 20, pp. 111–162, 1983.

Michalski, R. S. and Stepp, R. E.: Learning from observation: Conceptual clustering, in R. S. Michalski, J. G. Carbonell and T. M. Mitchell (eds.), *Machine Learning: An Artificial Intelligence Approach*, Tioga/Springer-Verlag, pp. 331–363, 1983.

Mitchell, T. M.: Generalization as search, *Artificial Intelligence*, Vol. 18, pp. 203–226, 1982.

Mitchell, T. M.: Version spaces: A candidate elimination approach to rule learning, *Proceedings of the Fifth International Joint Conference on Artificial Intelligence*, pp. 305–310, 1977.

Mitchell, T. M., Utgoff, P. E. and Banerji, R.: Learning by experimentation: Acquiring and refining problem-solving heuristics, in R. S. Michalski, J. G. Carbonell and T. M. Mitchell (eds.), *Machine Learning: An Artificial Intelligence Approach*, Tioga/Springer-Verlag, pp. 163–190, 1983.

Winston, P. H.: Learning structural descriptions from examples, in P. H. Winston (ed.), *The Psychology of Computer Vision*, McGraw-Hill, 1975.

Chapter 7

Anzai, Y.: Learning/adaptation function model by production systems,

Measuring and Control, Vol. 18, no. 4, pp. 306–311, 1979 (in Japanese).

Anzai, Y. and Simon, H. A.: The theory of learning by doing, *Psychological Review*, Vol. 86, pp. 124–140, 1979.

Anzai, Y.: Cognitive control of real-time event-driven systems, *Cognitive Science*, Vol. 8, pp. 221–254, 1984.

Buchanan, B. G. and Feigenbaum, E. A.: DENDRAL and Meta-DENDRAL; their applications dimension, *Artificial Intelligence*, Vol. 11, pp. 5–24, 1978.

Fikes, R. E. and Nilsson, N. J.: STRIPS: A new approach to the application of theorem proving to problem solving, *Artificial Intelligence*, Vol. 2, pp. 189–208, 1971.

Fikes, R. E., Hart, P. E. and Nilsson, N. J.: Learning and executing generalized robot plans, *Artificial Intelligence*, Vol. 3, pp. 251–288, 1972.

Sussman, G. J.: *A Computer Model of Skill Acquisition*, American Elsevier, 1975.

Vere, S. A.: Inductive learning of relational productions, in D. A. Waterman and F. Hayes-Roth (eds.), *Pattern-Directed Inference Systems*, Academic Press, 1978.

Vere, S. A.: Induction of relational productions in the presence of background information, *Proceedings of the Fifth International Joint Conference on Artificial Intelligence*, pp. 340–355, 1977.

Waterman, D. A.: Adaptive production systems, *Proceedings of the Fourth International Joint Conference on Artificial Intelligence*, pp. 296–303, 1975.

Chapter 8

Arikawa, S.: Inductive inference and analogy—theory and application, in K. Furukawa and F. Mizoguchi (eds.), *Learning Mechanism of Knowledge*, Kyoritsu Publishers, pp. 23–51, 1986 (in Japanese).

DeJong, J. and Mooney, R.: Explanation-based learning: An alternative view, *Machine Learning*, Vol. 1, pp. 145–176, 1986.

Doyle, J.: A truth maintenance system, *Artificial Intelligence*, Vol. 12, pp. 231–272, 1979.

Doyle, J.: The ins and outs of reason maintenance, *Proceedings of the Eighth International Joint Conference on Artificial Intelligence*, pp. 349–351, 1983.

Haguchi, M.: Mechanization of analogy, in K. Furukawa and F. Mizoguchi (eds.), *Learning Mechanism of Knowledge*, Kyoritsu Publishers, pp. 125–154, 1986 (in Japanese).

Kedar-Cabelli, S. T. and McCarty, L. T.: Explanation-based generalization as resolution theorem proving, *Proceedings of the Fourth International Workshop on Machine Learning*, pp. 383–389, 1987.

de Kleer, J.: An assumption-based TMS, *Artificial Intelligence*, Vol. 28, pp. 127–162, 1986.

McCarthy, J.: Circumscription: A form of non-monotonic reasoning, *Artificial Intelligence*, Vol. 13, pp. 41–72, 1980.

McCarthy, J.: Application of circumscription to formalize commonsense knowledge, *Artificial Intelligence*, Vol. 28, pp. 89–116, 1986.

Mitchell, T. M., Keller, R. M. and Kedar-Cabelli, S. T.: Explanation-based generalization: A unifying view, *Machine Learning*, Vol. 1, pp. 47–80, 1986.

Reiter, R.: A logic for default reasoning, *Artificial Intelligence*, Vol. 13, pp. 81–132, 1980.

Chapter 9

Falkenhainer, B. C. and Michalski, R. S.: Integrating quantitative and qualitative discovery: The ABACUS system, *Machine Learning*, Vol. 1, pp. 367–401, 1986.

Langley, P. W.: Data-driven discovery of physical laws, *Cognitive Science*, Vol. 5, pp. 31–54, 1981.

Langley, P. W., Simon, H. A., Bradshow, G. L. and Zytkow, J. M.: *Scientific Discovery: Computational Explorations of the Creative Processes*, The MIT Press, 1987.

Lenat, D. B.: Automated theory formation in mathematics, *Proceedings of the Fifth International Joint Conference on Artificial Intelligence*, pp. 833–842, 1977.

Lenat, D. B.: The ubiquity of discovery, *Artificial Intelligence*, Vol. 9, pp. 257–285, 1977.

Quinlan, J. R.: Induction of decision trees, *Machine Learning*, Vol. 1, pp. 81–106, 1986.

Schlimmer, J. C. and Granger, R.H., Jr.: Incremental learning from noisy data, *Machine Learning*, Vol. 1, pp. 317–354, 1986.

Chapter 10

Ackley, D. H., Hinton, G. D. and Sejnowski, T. J.: A learning algorithm for Boltzmann machines, *Cognitive Science*, Vol. 9, pp. 147–169, 1985.

Amari, S.: A theory of adaptive pattern classifiers, *IEEE Transactions on Electronic Computers*, Vol. EC-16, pp. 299–307, 1967.

Fukushima, K.: Neocognition: A self-organizing neural network model for a mechanism of pattern recognition unaffected by shift in position, *Biological Cybernetics*, Vol. 36, pp. 193–202, 1980.

Geman, S. and Geman, D.: Stochastic relaxation, Gibbs distributions, and the Bayesian restoration of images, *IEEE Transactions on Pattern Analysis and Machine Intelligence*, Vol. PAMI-6, pp. 721–741, 1984.

Hinton, G. D. and Sejnowski, T. J.: Learning and relearning in Boltzmann machines, in D. E. Rumelhart, J.L. McClelland and the PDP Research Group: *Parallel Distributed Processing, Vol. 1: Foundations*, The MIT Press, pp. 282–318, 1986.

Hopfield, J. J.: Neural networks and physical systems with emergent collective computational abilities, *Proceedings of National Academy of Sciences U.S.A.*, Vol. 79, pp. 2554–2558, 1982.

Hopfield, J. J. and Tank, D. W.: Neural computation of decisions in optimization problems, *Biological Cybernetics*, Vol. 52, pp. 141–152, 1985.

Kohonen, T.: *Self-Organization and Associative Memory*, Springer-Verlag, 1984.

Minsky, M. and Papert, S.: *Perceptrons* (expanded edition), The MIT Press, 1988.

Rosenblatt, R.: *Principles of Neurodynamics*, New York, Spartan Books, 1959.

Rumelhart, D. E., Hinton, G. E. and Williams, R. J.: Learning internal representations by error propagation, in J. L. McClelland, D. E. Rumelhart and the PDP Research Group: *Parallel Distributed Processing, Vol. 2: Psychological and Biological Models*, The MIT Press, pp. 318–362, 1986.

Rumelhart, D. E. and Zipser, D.: Feature discovery by competitive learning, *Cognitive Science*, Vol. 9, pp. 75–112, 1985.

von der Malsburg, C.: Self-organization of orientation sensitive cells in the striate cortex, *Cybernetik*, Vol. 14, pp. 85–100, 1973.

IV. Journals, collections of essays, and so on

Most of the books listed in I–III are classics. Here we list popular academic journals, research papers, and collections of essays that include not only classical but also recent research papers.

Journals/research papers

Journal, collections of essays (D), proceedings of annual convention, spcial Interest Group papers, Institute of Electronics, Information, and Communication Engineers of Japan.

Journal, proceedings of annual conventio, special interest group papers, Japanese Society for Artificial Intelligence.

Journal (Information Processing), collections of essays, proceedings of annual convention, special interest group papers, Information Processing Society of Japan.

Journal, collections of essays, proceedings of annual convention, special interest group papers, Society of Instrument and Control Engineers.

Journal, Robotic Society of Japan.

Journal (Computer SoftwareJournal), proceedings of annual convention, Japan Society for Software Science & Technology.

Artificial Intelligence.

Communications of ACM (Association for Computing Machinery)

Computer Vision, Graphics and Image Processing

IEEE Transactions on Computers

IEEE Transactions on Pattern Analysis and Machine Intelligence

IEEE Transactions on Systems, Man and Cybernetics

Machine Learning

Neural Networks

Pattern Recognition

Proceedings of IEEE Conference on Neural Networks

Proceedings of National Conference of Artificial Intelligence, American Association for Artificial Intelligence

Proceedings of the International Workshop on Machine Learning

Proceedings of the International Joint Conference on Artificial Intelligence

Proceedings of the International Conference on Pattern Recognition

Collections of essays

Brachman, R. J. and Levesque, H. J. (eds.): *Readings in Knowledge Representation*, Morgan Kaufmann, 1985.

Fischer, M. A. and Firschein, O. (eds.): *Readings in Computer Vision*, Morgan Kaufmann, 1987.

Ginsberg, M. (ed.): *Readings in Non-Monotonic Reasoning*, Morgan Kaufmann, 1987.

Webber, B. L. and Nilsson, N. J. (eds.): *Readings in Artificial Intelligence*, Morgan Kaufmann, 1981.

Index